THE SCOTTISH COMMANDER

PETER REESE

THE SCOTTISH COMMANDER

*Scotland's Greatest Military Leaders
from Wallace to World War II*

CANONGATE

First published in Great Britain in
1999 by Canongate Books Ltd,
14 High Street, Edinburgh EH1 1TE

10 9 8 7 6 5 4 3 2 1

ISBN 0 86241 833 X

British Library Cataloguing-in-publication Data
A catalogue record for this book is available
on request from the British Library

Typeset by Palimpsest Book Production Limited,
Polmont, Stirlingshire
Printed and bound by Biddles Ltd, Guilford and King's Lynn

For Sylvia, my daughter

CONTENTS

LIST OF ILLUSTRATIONS

LIST OF BATTLE PLANS

ACKNOWLEDGEMENTS

THIS BOOK OWES ITS existence to William Wallace and Robert Bruce, the heroes of Scotland's early wars of independence. The leadership qualities they displayed and their awesome achievements on the field of battle, led me to start considering the exploits of Scotland's other senior soldiers and to ask whether, in fact, there could be a distinguishable Scottish brand of military leadership.

In a book covering so long a period and featuring so many major figures, limits had to be placed on the original material consulted and I therefore pay sincere tribute to the biographers on whose shoulders I have leaned so heavily, men and women who faced the mass of original documents and from them teased out the stories of their champions' lives. This is not to say I have agreed unreservedly with their interpretations of events or with the opinions of later commentators.

Many others have given quite invaluable assistance. I refer to the staff of the National Library of Scotland, the British Library, the Edinburgh Central Library, Edinburgh University Library, the Inverness Public Library, Dingwall Public Library, the Scottish National Portrait Gallery, the National Portrait Gallery, the Scottish National Map Centre, Dingwall Museum and above all the Prince Consort's Library, Aldershot, where most of the text was written and whose military collection supplied so many ready answers.

With regard to individuals, Dawyck, Earl Haig, talked at length about his father and was a most generous host; Mr Paul Vickers, historian and writer, discussed the choice of commanders and much more besides. He also produced the excellent battle maps. Not for the first time Dr Leslie Wayper has given me the benefit of his encyclopaedic knowledge and incomparable analytic mind, while Colonel Mike Wellings lent me well-loved books and 'reacted' as before.

As for preparing the text for submission, Mrs Jennifer Prophet read and 'improved' the whole thing and with her son Charles produced a fine index. Mrs Christine Batten used her computer to transform rough handwritten pages into a presentable form. She was helped in the early stages by my daughter, Sylvia, in spite of the latter's responsibilities with a new generation.

In the case of the professionals whose contribution is vital I am greatly indebted to Hugh Andrew and Neville Moir of Canongate Books for agreeing to the proposal in the first place and for being ever supportive. The script has benefited immensely from the highly skilled treatment throughout of Donald Reid, Canongate's appointed editor.

On a personal note, I would hardly think of embarking on any book without the support of Barbara, my wife.

Notwithstanding I am, of course, entirely responsible for any mistakes or deficiencies.

Peter Reese
Aldershot
March 1999

INTRODUCTION

'Am I no a bonny fighter?'

Alan Breck in *Kidnapped* by Robert Louis Stevenson

A S ITS TITLE SUGGESTS this book is primarily concerned with the remarkable actions and achievements of Scottish commanders over some 650 years, but before readers are caught up by the men themselves they might pause to consider briefly what it takes to become a successful military leader.

What is it, in fact, that makes someone a noted commander and causes generations of military pundits to place certain leaders, time after time, within their pantheon of the world's greatest generals? What, for instance, determines the high ranking of such men as Alexander the Great, Julius Caesar, John Churchill (Duke of Marlborough), Gustavus Adolphus and possibly Ulysses Grant, on any such list? What can a Macedonian, a Roman, an Englishman, a Swede and an American commander possibly have in common across a time span of over 2200 years? The answer, of course, is their success on the battlefield. Equally important, in their case such victories proved of lasting historical significance. Alexander used his outstanding skills to conquer the known world from Mount Olympus to the Himalayas and in doing so broke down the previous barriers between Greek civilisation and the Middle and Far East; Caesar's victories over the Gallic tribes brought western and central Europe under the influence of Mediterranean culture; John Churchill's mastery succeeded in checking the expansion of power by France, Europe's premier military nation; Gustavus Adolphus, the founder of modern warfare, gained a string of victories to save Protestant Europe from the counter reformation, and by his defeat of Robert E. Lee and his army of Western Virginia Grant brought about the unification of the United States.

Such men were fortunate: they were not only formidable commanders but they enjoyed both military and political power. Alexander the Great and Gustavus Adolphus were king commanders with the widest ranging authority; Julius Caesar made himself the most powerful figure in Rome; at the time of his famous victories John Churchill dominated both his Queen and her parliament; and following a number of disappointing earlier commanders President Abraham Lincoln gave Grant his fullest confidence and support.

Even with such outstanding commanders they required adequate resources. However devoted and well-trained their followers they needed the sinews of war. As the Greek philosopher Socrates wrote four centuries before Christ, apart from any strategic and tactical skills, 'The General must know how to get his men their rations and every other kind of stores needed for war.'

Here again the 'famous five' had clear advantages. Alexander inherited a fine army from his father, together with a state geared for war; Caesar had both the training and logistic support of the incomparable Roman army; Churchill was given ample funds with which to create the magazines vital for his army to march across Europe; Gustavus Adolphus came from a fighting line of kings who gave their armies financial priority and he was allowed precious time in which to reshape his forces; while Ulysses Grant enjoyed the economic support of the Northern states with their seemingly inexhaustible supplies of superior weaponry and equipment over their Southern opponents.

Conversely, resources do not always lead to success; bad commanders can fail to use them properly, like the American General Westmoreland who lacked a war-winning strategy during the Vietnam war, or the Frenchman General Nivelle during World War One when he squandered French lives in a most ill-judged offensive against strong German defences.

With the five 'headline stars', along with their undoubted skills and strong political and economic support, the timing of their campaigns seemed fortuitous and they also enjoyed what might best be described as good luck. Many commanders have been far less fortunate in their timing.

Traditionally it has never been a good thing to be a senior commander on the British establishment at the beginning of a major war. Whatever their ultimate leadership potential, during the early stages of both World Wars, British commanders such as Sir John French and Lord Gort struggled against inevitable setbacks and were relatively soon replaced. As for luck, in 1759 when just thirty-two, one of Britain's most promising commanders, General James Wolfe, was killed at Quebec at the hour of his success. His victory ensured that Britain, and not France, would rule Canada. Had he not been killed, it was likely that Wolfe would have taken a leading role against the rebellious American colonists. In view of his past record he would have done much better than the British commanders who served there and, if some of Wolfe's wise measures for government over Canada had been extended to America, the settlers' grievances would probably have been removed as well.

Whatever the fascination of such 'might have beens' it is the solid achievements of victorious commanders and their degree of historical influence that provide the benchmarks against which to compare others. Whatever their seeming advantages – often far less obvious at the time, particularly when they faced superior numbers – their battlefield successes have also been put down to outstanding personal qualities. There will always be discussion about these but they can possibly best be summarised under the three main headings of character, charisma and energy.

With regard to character, Field Marshal Bernard Montgomery described it as 'knowing what you want to do and having the determination to do it'. Together with such determination he identified the equally important 'capacity and will to rally men and women to a common purpose and the character to inspire confidence'. In the case of Western commanders Montgomery went further, expecting them to have a consistent standpoint according to Christian principles of behaviour. With Montgomery the image of a leader was only too likely to be an idealised picture of himself, but having an overall objective and sticking to it appears to be an essential for any military commander. For instance, as a child the Carthaginian leader Hannibal swore eternal hatred to Rome and pledged himself to its destruction. During his fifteen years of ceaseless campaigning in Italy (218–203 BC) his every action was directed towards this end.

Along with such concentration on one's strategic objective, the successful commander needs to take his opponent's skills and weaknesses into account. In this context Napoleon wrote 'to guess at the intentions of the enemy, to divine his opinions of yourself; to hide from him both your own intentions and opinion; to mislead him by feigned manoeuvres; to invoke ruse, as well as digested schemes, so as to fight under the best conditions – this is, and always was, the art of war.' This urge to gauge the reactions of one's opponent was demonstrated by Montgomery when, in 1942, he had a photograph of his German adversary, Erwin Rommel, placed in a prominent position within his caravan. A good example of the ruse, together with speed of thought and action, was seen at the second Battle of Manassas during the American Civil War when, on 28 August 1862, Robert E. Lee and his trusted lieutenant, Thomas (Stonewall) Jackson, hatched a plot for Jackson to move away and confuse the Federal General John Pope. Jackson did so and by the time Pope regained contact and attacked him he was first halted by Jackson's defensive fire, then found his flank driven in by another Confederate force under Longstreet whom Lee had positioned for the purpose. The result was a decisive Confederate victory.

However strong their determination and subtle their minds the ranks of the greatest commanders are barred to those who lack charisma. In recent years the term has been over-worked, but in this context it represents the leader's dynamic presence, some degree of heroic quality that wins his soldiers' hearts and minds and persuades them that with him great things are possible. This power was apparent, for instance, with the Roman general, Scipio Africanus, conqueror of the famed Hannibal. Scipio was not only a master of tactical deception but his self-confidence was such that his soldiers genuinely came to believe he was divinely inspired.

Implicit with such charisma is the commander's refusal to be pessimistic and his instinctive 'feel' for a battlefield. The latter is summed up by the French phrase 'coup d'oeil' and the German expression 'Fingerspitzengefühl' – the animal response to manoeuvre. Wellington showed it at Salamanca on 22 July 1812. After much movement and counter-movement between his army and that of his French opponent, Marshal Marmont, Wellington realised that as the French advanced along a ridge before him they were no longer in supporting distance of each other. Wellington shouted out in his excitement, 'By God, that'll do', and went on to gain a rapid and convincing victory.

As if these were not enough, it is virtually inconceivable for men to become great commanders without rare energy and powers of endurance. Whenever Julius Caesar suffered from ill luck or a military setback his activity grew markedly. He had the gift of reversing things when they were going badly, as he did when he faced the fiery Gallic chieftain Vercingetorix in 52 BC. After suffering a reverse Caesar besieged Vercingetorix in his stronghold of Alesia. Vercingetorix had 80,000 men for its garrison and a quarter of a million tribesmen were coming to relieve him. In spite of the odds Caesar's 60,000 Romans, with Caesar omnipresent, defeated them all and Vercingetorix surrendered. For energy it is difficult to surpass the figure of Jeb Stuart, the Confederate cavalry leader who, as the eyes and ears of his chief Robert E. Lee, appeared at different and widely spaced points of the battlefield. On one occasion in 1862 he rode clear round General McLellan and his Union army.

While we can list the virtues of good leadership it is well to remember that no commander, however distinguished and however lucky, can be sure of excelling in them all and certainly not all the time. Fortunately, for that matter, nor can their opponents. All commanders have to gain experience – and make mistakes – and they are very likely to suffer an 'off day', like Lee at Gettysburg when he was suffering from prolonged diarrhoea. Even the invincible Alexander was repulsed by the Indians at Massaga in 327 BC, before going on to his inevitable victory.

Possibly the greatest fascination about good military leadership is that it is essentially a struggle against adversity when your opponent is actively seeking to destroy you. In fact the waging of war has always been a bloody, exhausting and unpredictable process conducted by leaders, whether of Scottish birth or not, in different states of misinformation.

In its treatment of Scottish commanders the book starts in the 13th century with those who were concerned in the early Wars of Independence against England. It continues with commanders involved with the subsequent battles between the two countries until the union of the crowns in 1603, before moving to the continent with the Scottish mercenary commanders there. A proportion of these returned to Scotland to join others for the struggle between Jacobites and Covenanters. From the 18th century until 1945 senior commanders of Scottish origin fought on the British establishment. During the late 18th century and through the 19th century four men have been chosen, two who fought against Revolutionary France and two who were involved in Britain's wars of Empire. Finally, one commander was selected from each of the two World Wars. Field Marshal Douglas Haig was an obvious choice for World War One, while the unorthodox but inspirational David Stirling, the founder of the SAS, was the chosen representative for World War Two.

It has rightly been said that the Scottish soldier's environment, his ancestry and his very nature combine to make him one of the finest fighting soldiers in history. If so, one would expect Scotland's senior soldiers, her commanders, to be equally successful. Yet however inspirational and skilled, like other commanders they have been required to practise their skills within definite political and economic constraints. In fact, it is arguable whether any Scottish commander has ever enjoyed the freedom of action given to the 'famous five' or other headline commanders of all time. For instance, while Robert Bruce was a king commander it took him years before he gained full control over his country and despite his high military skills he always faced a determined enemy with far greater resources. James Graham, Marquis of Montrose, was an outstanding leader but he fought on behalf of a Stuart king, Charles I, who had already lost the confidence of both his Scottish and English followers. Douglas Haig, commander-in-chief of the British forces in France during World War One, suffered from the handicap of a Prime Minister who, in the later stages of the war, prevented Haig's casualties being made good and actively tried to replace him.

On the other hand it will be seen that Scottish commanders have scored highly in single-minded determination, cool daring and boundless energy while probably no other commander, however famous, showed more charisma than Montrose during his campaigns over the Scottish Highlands, or Colin Campbell at that moment when he and his Highlanders faced superior Russian cavalry on the heights of Balaclava.

The qualities and achievements of such men are for the following pages to reveal and for the reader to gauge. At the book's conclusion some suggestions will be made about whether Scottish commanders, while sharing the qualities of all successful military leaders, are distinguishable as a group.

≈

CHAPTER ONE

THE STRUGGLE
FOR INDEPENDENCE –
WALLACE AND BRUCE

'It is not for glory, nor riches, nor honours that we are
fighting, but for freedom alone, which no honest man
gives up but with life itself'

The Declaration of Arbroath, 1320

IN SCOTLAND, AS IN other feudal countries of 13th century Europe,
it was the monarch's privilege to take command of his country's
armed forces. If the king was absent or if he was a minor, the
responsibility could be undertaken by an appointee or even, as in
Scotland's case, by a number of eminent men acting jointly in the
capacity of Guardians.

With Scotland, such military skills had not been necessary for a
considerable period of time. Until the sudden and unexpected death of
King Alexander III in 1286, over 250 years had passed since Scottish
kings had been required to lead their armies on military campaigns
against England. Military activity over this period had been restricted
to meeting local uprisings from within the country, orchestrated for
the greater part by Highland chiefs living in the semi-autonomous
regions of the far north, and to opposing the King of Norway who
ruled over Orkney and Shetland until his control there was broken
in 1263.

With Alexander III's death and the appointment of Edward I of
England as adjudicator over his would-be successors, the situation
was bound to change. Apart from a large number of contenders for
the vacant crown and the long drawn-out process of deciding upon a
lawful successor, there was also the growing ambition of an English

king who had recently succeeded in subduing Wales. The result was that, after two and a half centuries of relative peace between Scotland and England, from 1296 until 1328 Scotland had to fight for its very existence.

While their feudal training for knighthood and the skills acquired in the jousting ring might have made Scotland's kings and nobles well versed in the practical arts of war, their battlefield experience was extremely limited. In England's case regular military campaigning, both in France and elsewhere, gave its supreme and subordinate commanders precious knowledge of large-scale combat. From the late 13th century onwards such engagements had enabled the English to appreciate the great virtues of some of the weapons used against them – particularly the Welsh longbow – and they had already come to employ a proportion of professional soldiers, including the famed Welsh archers and Gascon mercenaries with their deadly accurate crossbows. In this period a country could count itself blessed if its monarch, along with his other accomplishments, had made himself a master of the battlefield. Conversely, if he did not it could be disastrous.

During the troubled centuries before the accession of James VI of Scotland to the English throne as James I in 1603, Scottish commanders faced a common problem. With its greater size and wealth, and with a population five times greater, England had the capacity to raise, and keep on raising, more formidable armies against them. In some respects the situation can be likened to the problems faced by the Confederates during the American Civil War against the more populous and far wealthier northern states. The imbalance needed some countervailing force which, from the time of William Wallace in the late 13th century, the Scots attempted to redress by seeking help from France, England's traditional enemy. In practice the extent of military assistance coming through the 'auld alliance' usually proved disappointing for Scotland. Like the Confederate general, Robert E. Lee, the finest Scottish commanders understood that their best means of success lay in superior leadership, which meant among other things ensuring they took full advantage of their country's natural features. As in Roman times, Scotland's very remoteness and its lines of natural barriers formed both by rivers and the chains of hills stretching from east to west strongly favoured defence. Yet defensive tactics were often at direct odds with other powerful factors in the Scottish psyche: their commanders' feudal concept of leadership, a high sense of national pride, and the legendary impatience of the Scots, seen in both commanders and men.

After Alexander III's death, Edward I's bullying of John Balliol, his preferred candidate for the Scottish throne, and his treatment of Scotland as part of his feudal property, made a clash between the two countries inevitable. When it came the result was scarcely in the Scots favour. After the English had sacked the great Scottish trading centre of Berwick in 1296, they moved further north, meeting the main Scots army at Dunbar. Here Edward's senior soldier, John Warenne, Earl of Surrey, swept them off the field with contemptuous ease. The Scots showed fatal over-confidence when from their position on Spottsmuir Hill they awaited the English attack across a steep valley to their front with the Spott Burn at its base. As the English made their way across the burn they broke formation and the Scots presumed they were withdrawing. They rushed down from the hilltop in pursuit. In the valley they met the superior English cavalry and were themselves put to flight, leaving their unfortunate infantry at the mercy of marauding horsemen.

The importance of Surrey's victory at this time cannot be over-estimated. It enabled the English king to proceed with his plans to subdue the whole of Scotland by carrying off the country's sacred relics and compelling all Scottish nobles to declare their fealty to him by the 'Ragman Roll', so called because of the numerous ribbons hanging from official seals which were surrendered. After placing his own officials in key positions throughout Scotland, Edward I set out for France in September 1296 to deal with his military problems there.

The year 1296 marked what was probably the lowest point in Scottish history. Notwithstanding its earlier defiance of the Romans, the rugged country with its proud, fiercely independent people had been conquered more easily than Wales. Its king had been humiliated and was imprisoned in England while many of his powerful 'Comyn' faction of nobles were kept under Edward's hands to ensure their continued compliance. Meanwhile that other traditional family of Scottish leaders, the Bruces, seemingly sought friendship with the English king.

William Wallace (c. 1274–1305)

It was of course unthinkable that Scotland should submit so tamely and by the end of the year disturbances were reported in various parts of the country. During the spring of 1297 they increased as two young leaders, Andrew Moray, the younger son of a foremost Highland family, and William Wallace, a modest squire from Elderslie, near Paisley, spearheaded opposition to the English.

They were given much-needed assistance by two men who had stood as Guardians during the interregnum, Robert Wishart, who as Bishop of Glasgow was a senior member of a strongly nationalist church, and the baron, James the Stewart, Wallace's feudal superior. With Moray's base on the Black Isle, near Inverness, and Wallace's lair so many miles further south they were able to keep the defending garrisons off balance.

Initially, both Wallace and Moray used guerrilla tactics, ambushing convoys, picking off castles and, in Wallace's case, spreading terror through his assassination of officials appointed by the English. Wallace was unyielding, and harboured the fiercest hatred for the English invaders and their representatives. His most famous biographer, Henry the Minstrel, believed that Wallace's military apprenticeship was limited to his experience as an outlaw. Limited or not, Wallace used 'his country's native woods and defiles in a masterly fashion and fully understood the importance of timing and speed of movement and deception'.[1] Andrew Moray was similarly skilled in the art of guerrilla fighting, but as he came from a leading family he was also familiar with the traditional arts of warfare. Together the two young men succeeded in halting, and then breaking, the English supremacy by dominating large tracts of the country and retaking a number of castle strongholds. Wallace used the great wood of Ettrick as a secure base while Moray reduced the advantages of mailed horsemen by ambushing them in the narrow passes of the north. However, both men knew that sooner or later the English would bring up much superior forces in order to destroy them. To have any chance of success they would need to unite and devise some way of offsetting the twin means of English battlefield superiority: their mailed cavalry (the main battle tanks of the day), against whom the Scots had no reply, and their bowmen.

It was Wallace's move to attack Dundee in June 1297, that induced a strong English army to set out from Berwick in order to destroy him. Both Wallace and Moray knew the importance of the river crossing near Stirling for any army moving north. They therefore decided their best chances of success against such fearful odds lay in joining forces and meeting the English there. Moray unselfishly acknowledged Wallace as overall commander, probably because of his utter self confidence.

Wallace's methods of preventing his opponent from utilising his full strength and particularly of compressing his forces were reminiscent of tactics used by the great Carthaginian general, Hannibal, against the Romans at Cannae in 216BC. Whereas Hannibal used men to squeeze the Roman flanks, Wallace trapped them within the bend of a major river. Fortunately for Wallace, during 1297 Edward I, whose vast military experience would have made him a formidable opponent, was on the continent subduing a rising in Gascony. In his absence the English forces were led by John Warenne, Earl of Surrey, who had won such a sweeping victory over the Scots at Dunbar. Surrey was older than the combined ages of both young Scottish commanders and not as physically robust as once he had been, but he was a proven soldier. In such circumstances it was not surprising he should underestimate the fighting qualities of what he considered a combination of ill-armed peasants and outlaws led by a modest squire utterly unversed in formal warfare. What was more he had 30,000 infantry to the rebels' 10,000 at most, and among his ranks were redoubtable Welsh bowmen. Most important of all was his striking force of 2000 armoured cavalry that was reckoned to be virtually invincible.

With understandable confidence Surrey decided to seek the Scots out and as he approached the River Forth at Stirling he learned that they had taken up a strong position on Abbey Craig, the volcanic hillock that overlooked Stirling's river bridge. Initially two of Wallace's senior cavalry commanders approached Surrey and offered to negotiate on his behalf with Wallace. Nothing positive came of this but Surrey followed on by sending two Dominican Friars demanding Wallace's surrender. Wallace left them in no doubt of his intentions, saying, 'Tell your people that we have not come here to gain peace, but are prepared for battle to avenge and deliver our country.' Perhaps it was their commander's willingness to negotiate together with the obvious strength of the Scottish position that led

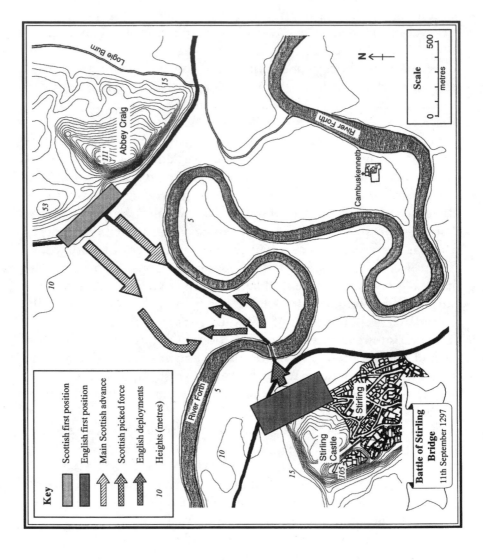

Key

Scottish first position

English first position

Main Scottish advance

Scottish picked force

English deployments

Heights (metres)

10

Battle of Stirling Bridge
11th September 1297

certain of Surrey's staff officers to experience some doubts about a direct attack and to suggest using a nearby ford as an alternative crossing place. But their advice was not taken for, exasperated by the delays, Surrey's arrogant vanguard commander, Cressingham, began lecturing his chief about wasting time. Surrey thereupon gave the order for the attack to go ahead. If the rebels dared to stand and fight his magnificent army would sweep away their disparate ranks.

Most significantly for Surrey, the river bridge at Stirling was long and narrow, allowing no more than two horsemen to cross it riding abreast. He not only determined on a frontal attack, but decided to conduct it in full sight of the Scots standing on their hill nearby. Surrey could hardly have been unaware of the priceless opportunity this gave his opponents to time their counter-attack if, of course, they were even capable of mounting one. Apart from the folly of such English overconfidence, the battle of Stirling Bridge was notable for Wallace's perfect control of his troops. None of them moved from the high ground until Wallace was sure the time was right – an amazing feat with irregular troops, some of whom were declared outlaws.

He kept his men immobile until about a third of the English had crossed over, a force small enough for him to beat but large enough for their defeat to demoralise the rest of the English army. Wallace also knew two other important facts. With the wet and uneven carse land on his side of the river the English could not use their cavalry to advantage, while the speed with which his lightly armed foot soldiers could cross the grassy hummocks and join with the English in combat would prevent their longbowmen being used to full effect. Once Wallace had blunted his opponent's two most telling weapons and sealed the southern end of the bridge, the battle would be reduced to a static contest of savage hand-to-hand fighting where horses and the heavy armour of their riders would be changed from a priceless assct to a heavy liability.

Wallace's iron control of his forces was crucial. As they watched the great English warhorses picking their way across the narrow bridge and forming up on the other side one can imagine the feelings of his soldiers. In all probability they would mark some of the enemy out for targets. But they would scarcely have been human if their nerves had not jangled as the colourful and menacing force below them grew steadily in size. They must have directed many uneasy looks towards their inscrutable leader sitting astride his horse to their left. When would he signal the attack? Surely he couldn't leave it any longer! At last the signal came, described by Blind Harry as a single blast on Wallace's horn ('In all the host suld no man blaw but he'). With that his men bounded downwards, their charge marking one of the great moments of Scottish history and Wallace's high noon of leadership.

Andrew Moray was in the thick of the fighting while Wallace had to curb his own fighting instincts to read the progress of the battle and confine the English vanguard within the small area of land enclosed by the loop of the river. He succeeded, for whether the bridge was fully destroyed or not, the bulk of the English did not recross it to safety. Within the deadly bridgehead, dirks ripped open the bellies of warhorses and after their riders were sent crashing to the ground they too became easy prey. How much Andrew Moray contributed to the victory will never be known for he was to die of his wounds soon afterwards. But it was not just the English vanguard that suffered there. As the army's main body watched the slaughter they became disheartened and restless. Then came the realisation that the Scots were likely to infiltrate their position by crossing the river fords to their flanks. The result was panic turning into headlong flight. Foremost in retreat went their commander, the Earl of Surrey.

Wallace, the guerrilla commander, had only decided to meet the English in open battle when his use of ground could tilt the odds firmly in his direction. The nature of his defensive position at Stirling was all-important. If Surrey had used other crossing places Wallace still had the means to extricate his army by moving northwards. Wallace's conduct at Stirling resembled that of a master commander rather than a young man whose experience was confined to leading irregular forces. His victory was to play a fundamental role in preserving Scotland as a separate kingdom and in encouraging her assorted inhabitants to develop a sense of national identity.

After Stirling the Scots could be in no doubt the English would return and next time they would not allow Wallace such a free hand in choosing the site of the battle. As the fearsome English king sailed back across the Channel he and his knights vowed to take their revenge upon the man who, after humiliating their army in battle had flayed the skin from Surrey's dead vanguard commander and sent samples of it across Scotland. Wallace himself, now appointed sole Guardian of Scotland, had no illusions; he spent time assembling an army which he hoped would stand a chance of meeting the full might of the English forces. To this end he created formations which he called schiltrons; these were based on the phalanxes of massed spearmen used in classical times that were oval-shaped and equipped with 15-foot spears. Wallace's schiltrons were four in number made up of 2000 men each equipped with 14-foot pikes. They varied from their classical forebears in that Wallace made them circular. This was to make sure they could still defend themselves if cavalry got behind them. The men of the human porcupines were in two ranks, one directly behind the other, while within the circle there was a reserve of men ready to rush forward and fill any gaps that might appear. He recruited shortbowmen (the only ones available) to cover the intervals between his schiltrons. His success at Stirling also enabled him to attract a few more cavalry to his colours, but they remained heavily outnumbered by the English.

Across the 700-year divide it is impossible to know the full circumstances of Wallace's military conduct during 1298. He faced an English army led by its King which had a numerical advantage in infantry of some thirty per cent and a preponderance in cavalry of some six to one. Unlike his forces many of their foot soldiers were veterans of earlier campaigns and over fifty per cent of the English cavalry was full time.

Initially, however, Wallace was very successful. As the English moved into Scotland he gave way using scorched earth tactics to deny them provisions. By the time the English reached the Forth at Kirkliston, near Queensferry, they were close to starving. Then a new problem beset the invading force; after a convoy reached it carrying more wine than food its Welsh archers became both drunk and abusive and had to be driven out of the main camp. With one of his best weapons blunted, Edward let it be known he would fall back on Edinburgh for food, and at this point Wallace decided – quite soundly – to harass the English rearguard in order to hasten the army's disorganisation.

Unbeknown to him, an important event occurred at this time. Up to now Edward had been hamstrung by a shortage of information. In a bitterly hostile country no civilian would give him any help. But on 21 July 1298 a spy brought him the priceless news that the Scottish forces were just eighteen miles away.

Due to the deteriorating condition of his army and the fact that it was late July and the grass needed for his horses had already been cut Edward realised this was his one and only chance to destroy his quarry. He set off on a forced march towards the Scots' position. Wallace, whose intelligence was good, would have known of this approach and by his own rules of war he might well have continued to move away, destroying crops and livestock as he went and harrying the English while they were on the march. It is quite possible he did not because his scouts, who had kept him fully informed throughout the campaign, might have over-emphasised the poor state of the English. Alternatively he might have given way to nobles among the ranks of his cavalry who felt it unchivalrous not to offer battle. There was a third possibility, that he might have accepted battle because he realised he could never keep his present army in being for a further year's campaign. Whatever the reasons, Wallace drew up his army on a small, insignificant hill near Falkirk. When the English cavalry had crossed some moderately wet ground and a small stream that covered part of the Scottish position, they started their charge. Close behind them were the Welsh archers restored to the King's control. Wallace allowed his relatively untried and less well equipped forces to face the fury of the English led by their formidable royal commander. He may have done so reluctantly, for in contrast to his defiant pre-battle address sent to Surrey the year before, he made do with the wry words to his soldiers, 'I have brought you to the ring: dance the best you can.'2

Those who had been with Wallace at Stirling found things very different at Falkirk. Far from being able to watch the English before deciding to make their own charge, they were forced to keep station as the enemy cavalry, with deadly momentum, swirled round them ready to smash into any gap appearing in their spear walls. In any case, the circular-shaped schiltrons were unlikely to have been suitable for offensive moves and, after Wallace's own cavalry, facing such over-whelming odds, fled the field during the battle's early stages, the English were able to threaten their rear.

Wallace's other covering force, his archers from Ettrick forest, were cut down where they stood and his beleaguered schiltrons became completely surrounded. Once the English archers, by now quite unopposed, thinned the outer ranks of the circles, the cavalry were able to break in and the slaughter began. Although Edward had little opportunity for further campaigning in 1298, after Wallace's defeat Scotland faced a period of great suffering and national humiliation. If Wallace had refused battle at Falkirk and had continued to move away before an English army close to disintegration he would have rightfully taken his place as one of Scotland's finest commanders as well as its supreme patriot. As it was Wallace was relieved of his post as Guardian and was reduced to comparatively minor roles during the seven-year period that was to end in his savage execution. However, his contribution to his native country did not end there. The terrible manner of his death helped to inflame the strong level of hostility felt for England and ensured the desire for national independence would not end with him.

Robert Bruce (1274–1329)

At Wallace's capture prior to his execution in August 1305 a number of letters were found on him from other Scottish nobles. Among them was likely to have been one or more from Robert Bruce, the grandson of Bruce the Competitor, John Balliol's chief rival for the Scottish crown. Whether these fully compromised Bruce or not, from this time Edward I planned to arrest him for treason, although Bruce was alerted to the King's new-grown enmity by his friend the Earl of Gloucester and fled north. Bruce set the revival of the Scottish crown as his goal and if crowned himself he would never rest until Scotland was free again. During the previous year Bruce had entered into a secret compact with John Comyn, senior member of Bruce's rivals for the crown of Scotland and married to Eleanor, John Balliol's sister. The agreement was for John Comyn to support Bruce's attempt at regaining the Scottish throne in return for Bruce's vast estates. On his flight north Bruce apparently intercepted a messenger from John Comyn to King Edward carrying the bond made between Bruce and himself.

On entering Scotland, an incandescent Bruce requested a meeting with John Comyn in Greyfriars Church, Dumfries. This was accepted and they met there on 10 February 1300. Not surprisingly, angry words were exchanged and after Robert Bruce had wounded him, John Comyn was stabbed to death before the High Altar by Roger Kirkpatrick, one of Bruce's followers.

In the early 14th century such a murder in a sanctified place was guaranteed to arouse deep shock and anger. Notwithstanding, Bishop Wishart of Glasgow – an unceasing champion of Scottish nationalism – granted Bruce absolution and on 25 March 1306 in the Abbey of Scone he crowned Robert Bruce King of Scots.

It was as well for Robert Bruce that he enjoyed the support of the Scottish church for he did not lack for enemies. Edward I was furious at his escape and particularly for his crowning at Scone. He undertook to avenge the death of Comyn and the sacrilege to the church by a fresh invasion of Scotland. This was to be spearheaded by the Prince of Wales with the old king following at a more leisurely pace due to his physical disabilities. Bruce also had to contend with the wrath of the Pope who excommunicated him at Edward's request and refused to recognise him as king. In Scotland Bruce faced the enmity of the Comyn family who barred much of the country to him and were determined to hunt him down.

Things could hardly have begun worse for the newly crowned king. He had but a hundred barded Knights in support when he was surprised near Methven by the English led by Aymer Valence, Earl of Pembroke, Edward's cousin and brother-in-law of the murdered Comyn. Many of his most devoted followers were captured and executed like common outlaws. Bruce himself was made a fugitive and at this time his brother Nigel, Bruce's wife Queen Elizabeth, his daughter Marjorie, his sisters Christian and Mary, along with the Countess of Buchan (who had assisted in his coronation) were captured. Nigel was hanged and beheaded and the women were confined, Mary Bruce and the Countess of Buchan being suspended in wooden cages jutting from castle battlements.

Within six months Robert Bruce, King of Scots, was reduced to hiding on the little island of Rathlin off the coast of Ireland. There he remained for five months until in early 1307 with fresh supporters he attempted a return to the mainland. He split his forces and landed himself on the Isle of Arran before crossing to Carrick. The other detachment under his younger brothers Thomas and Alexander set sail for Galloway. There they were captured and at Edward's command hanged and beheaded.

This was Bruce's darkest hour and hiding in a cave somewhere in the wild hill country of Carrick and Galloway he was reputed to have seen a spider make seven attempts to anchor its thread before starting a web. He vowed to be no less resolute and to use guerrilla tactics until he could revive his strength. Bruce's sixty followers somehow survived and grew to some 300, who then put to flight 1500 English knights who entered the deep valley of Glen Trool. This success was repeated at Loudon Hill near Kilmarnock where Bruce defeated a much superior force by choosing ground where it could not manoeuvre. Other local successes followed and in May a Scottish lord on the English side wrote that:

> Sir Robert de Brus never had the good will of his own followers or of the people at large or even half of them so much with him as now; and it now for the first time appears that he has the right and that God is openly for him, for he has destroyed all King Edward's power both among the English and the Scots and the English force is in retreat to its own country not to return.[3]

Such reports of Bruce's success helped to bring Edward I north to spur his commanders on. Edward was a sick man and the physical effort was too much, for he died at Burgh-on-Sands five miles north of Carlisle on 11 July 1307. On Edward's death, the English attacks lost momentum and after moving no further into Scotland than Cumnock on 25 August, Edward II retired to England. Robert Bruce had the breathing space he required to make his kingship a reality.

Like Wallace and Moray before him, due to the limitations of his forces, Bruce's political ambitions depended on him using his speed, surprise and mobility by capturing, then razing, castle strongholds – some held by his Scottish rivals, others by English garrisons – before he could take control of his native country. Only when he was in control would he have the option of meeting the English in battle and, through victory, force them to come to terms, but this risked all his success so far and it was certainly not one favoured by Bruce. Consequently when, after an interval of three years, Edward invaded Scotland in 1310, Bruce withdrew his main army and sent flying columns of horsemen to harass and weaken the English forces. Moving northwards from Berwick the English found themselves in a country where the grain had been harvested, the cattle driven to the hills and humble dwellings destroyed. In pursuit of his strategy Bruce, like Wallace, was willing to scorch and scar his own country. As a result Edward II, despite wintering at Berwick and expending considerable resources in rebuilding his castles in Lothian and Galloway, found Scotland unsubdued. Before he could mount a new campaign in the spring of the next year Edward had to break off and meet with his rebellious barons in London.

Taking advantage of the king's absence Bruce collected his army and on 12 August 1311 made a limited invasion of England into

Tynedale. After much burning and killing he recrossed the border, bearing with him cattle and other booty. He followed this by an even larger raid into the Tyne valleys. Such attacks not only weakened the English but gave Bruce money and supplies and kept his army in fighting shape.

The conflict between the English king and his barons continued so that in the following year, 1312, Bruce was able to undertake a larger-scale invasion, forcing the English northern countries to pay him protection money (Durham, for instance, gave £2000 in return for a ten-month truce). Over a period of three years Bruce received more than £40,000 in such tributes. The disadvantage of such a strategy, one few other Scottish leaders would have attempted, lay in its protracted nature. Before the age of artillery Scottish castles were difficult to take and Bruce had to adopt elaborate deceptions in order to surprise their garrisons. At Edinburgh, for instance, while a decoy raid was made on the main gate, experienced climbers utilised a route dismissed by the garrison as impossible, and were thus able to penetrate its defences.

Successes accumulated steadily but in midsummer 1313 Robert's brother, Edward Bruce, as headstrong as Robert was calculating, pledged the Scottish king to something which hazarded everything. Edward Bruce was besieging Stirling Castle, and although he had sealed it off and would have starved out its defenders in time, he found it a tedious process. In his impatience he accepted the offer made by its English commander that 'if by midsummer a year thence he was not rescued by battle, he would yield the castle freely'. Edward Bruce had not consulted his brother, who was understandably appalled, not least by the full year given the English to raise forces. He shouted out in his anger: 'We are so few against so many. God may deal us our destiny right well but we are set in jeopardy to lose or win all at one throw.'[4]

From now on Bruce felt he had no option but to prepare his troops for the inevitable battle. On the other hand Edward II regarded Edward Bruce's acceptance as a golden opportunity to confront the elusive Scots with his far superior forces. By 10 June 1314, the English had assembled a most impressive army. Within its ranks were 2500 heavy cavalry, 3000 Welsh longbowmen and 15,000 foot soldiers, all well armed and protected. Against them the Scots had but 5000 to 6000 in all, including 500 light horse and a company of shortbow archers from Ettrick forest. Because his army would have to fight on foot, Bruce based his tactics on the schiltron, although he took pains to train the four units – now probably in oblong rather than Wallace's circular formation – to move onto the attack.

While small, Bruce's army represented all Scotland. Its vanguard was commanded by Bruce's nephew, Thomas Randolph, Earl of Moray, with its members coming from the far north, from Ross-shire and the coastal strip stretching east from Inverness to Forres. The second division, led by Edward Bruce, drew upon men from middle Scotland, Buchan, Strathearn and Lennox, while the third division, officially under Walter Stewart, but commanded by James Douglas, had men from Lanark, Renfrew and the Borders. The fourth and last division, with a double strength of 2000, was commanded by the king. This contained many Highlanders from the west, men from the Western Isles and others from Bruce's own estates at Carrick, Kyle and Cunningham. In addition there were the 'small folk', grooms and camp-followers, poorly armed but stiffened by soldiers who arrived too late for enrolment. These Bruce decided to conceal in a valley behind his wagon train.

He had subjected his men to a rigorous training schedule and tactically developed the schiltron. Now he had to choose the ground where he could first constrict and then baffle the English. Bruce selected a point along the road from Falkirk to Stirling, following the main axis of the anticipated English advance. As the English army approached Stirling he reckoned they would have to pass through the area of New Park, where grassland was flanked by almost impenetrable woods, while higher ground lay before them; moving into New Park one English flank would be impeded by a series of woods and water-filled ditches, while on the other and to the rear there was a dangerous river with wet, broken country beyond. On both sides of the road Bruce 'improved' the selected position by digging 'pots' a foot across and to the depth of a man's knee. If the English accepted battle and started to move westwards they had to cross the Bannock Burn, a stream which was both deep and muddy, before coming upon the open ground where Bruce had placed his men close to the woods. (See battle map.)

In spite of the carefully chosen site, their considerable fighting experience and Bruce's leadership, the Scots were grievously outnumbered, utterly outclassed in cavalry and seriously lacking

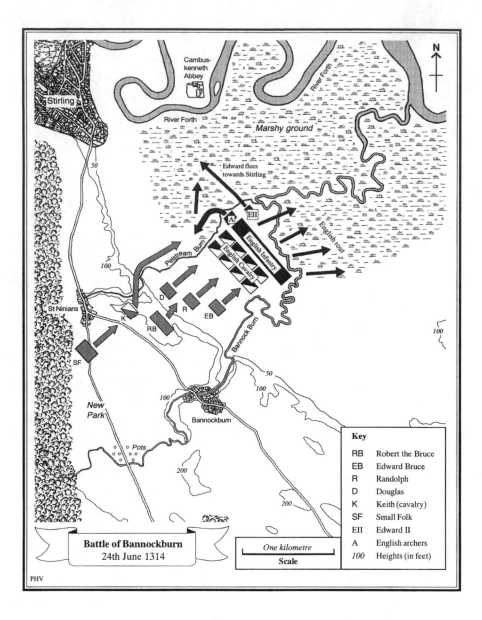

Battle of Bannockburn
24th June 1314

One kilometre
Scale

Key

RB	Robert the Bruce
EB	Edward Bruce
R	Randolph
D	Douglas
K	Keith (cavalry)
SF	Small Folk
EII	Edward II
A	English archers
100	Heights (in feet)

in longbowmen. This was underlined on 22 June, as Bruce was strengthening his position near the Bannock Burn, when he sent out two of his senior commanders, James Douglas and Sir Robert Keith, to bring back information on the English army. They returned with the bleak message that 'the whole landscape was covered by mounted men with many banners, columns of foot soldiers and archers and lines of wagons stretching into the distance.'[5] Mindful of the need to preserve his army's good morale, Bruce told them to put it about that the English 'were advancing in great disorder'.[6] But nothing could alter the great disparity in numbers; furthermore the English, split into ten divisions, were 'followed by a massive wagon train which one observer judged would have exceeded twenty miles in length'.[7]

The extended formation which Bruce's patrol had seen was far from deliberate. On 21 June the English army was still in Edinburgh, giving the king dangerously little time to meet the terms of the challenge, namely to relieve Stirling by 24 June. To satisfy the time scale Edward II ordered his men to undertake a forced march of some twenty-two miles within a single, hot summer's day, after which marathon the English would only have the final ten miles to cover before reaching Stirling. Edward II's hastening of such a massive force was hardly an ideal preliminary for a major battle, especially as Bruce had been unhurried and thorough in his own preparations. He began to assemble his army in April and all his troops knew their leaders and what was required of them. As Barbour recounted: 'The King made himself available and even as he met them, he greeted them cheerfully, speaking an encouraging word to one or another and they, seeing their king welcome them in so forthright a manner were greatly heartened and were ready to fight and die to uphold his honour.'[8]

At sunrise on 23 June, the Scots had risen and heard mass together. As it was the vigil of St John the Baptist they took only bread and water. Then, while they stood to in their agreed positions, the king issued a challenge to each division that 'if any were of faint heart let him depart at once',[9] producing, as intended, a great shout and a promise from the troops that they would conquer or die.

As the English advanced over the last leg of their journey to Stirling they encountered Sir Philip Mowbray, commander of Stirling Castle, who had taken a diversion round the Scots position to meet them. He reminded Edward that as their army had now come within three miles of the castle it was officially relieved by the terms of the challenge. In reply the king told Sir Philip that they had not come so far to take advantage of a technicality, but to destroy the enemy. The governor, however, from his vantage point upon the high walls of the castle, had watched the care of the Scots' preparations and he urged Edward II to be cautious. Despite his warnings the English vanguard continued on its frontal approach, although a body of some 800 cavalry commanded by two senior knights, Clifford and de Beaumont, was to be placed between the Scots and the castle 'to cut off their escape and help complete the victory'. The Scots would effectively be corralled in a shallow river valley.

The early attacks by the English vanguard started inauspiciously. As Bruce continued to adjust the positions of his forward units an English knight, Sir Henry de Bohun, fully armed and ready for action, saw an opportunity he thought too good to miss and charged towards the Scottish king. Bruce was mounted only on a small pony, but he countered his attacker by swerving to one side and bringing down his battle axe (which he always carried) to cleave de Bohun's head almost in two. At this Bruce's division moved forward against the English who were in some difficulty trying to negotiate Bruce's 'pots'. After they had repulsed the English cavalry Bruce recalled them to their original battle lines. Meanwhile the English knights, Clifford and de Beaumont, together with their body of horse, taking advantage of some dead ground had moved stealthily round the Scots brigade commanded by Randolph. Bruce, however, noticed the movement and, pointing to the English horsemen, reprimanded Randolph's poor observation saying, 'A rose has fallen from your chaplet,' at which Randolph straight away put his men into a schiltron formation and charged at the English.

For infantry to attack cavalry on open ground was an unheard of venture but the schiltron was so well-formed that the English riders, unsupported as they were by archers, could make little impression on it. As the battle raged Douglas asked Bruce whether he could give additional help but the king delayed him, for he was anxious to let Randolph have his due credit. Sure enough, after the initial clash Randolph started pushing on and threatened to cut the English squadron in two until it took off. The Scots were triumphant and, although the exchanges were yet relatively minor, Barbour leaves us in no doubt that Bruce realised their significance to English morale:

> Fra the hert be discumfite
> The body is nicht worth a myt[10]

Bruce deliberately continued to profess himself cautious and give his men the option to withdraw but, as he expected, they opted unanimously to fight. By now the performance of Randolph's schiltron against English cavalry and the cavalry's discomfort when they encountered Bruce's 'pots' had gone far to persuade the Scottish king that he could beat his formidable enemy. His mind must surely have been made up when a Scots knight in the English service, Sir Alexander Seton, disgusted with the lack of leadership on the English side, came over to him. Seton told the king that now, if ever, was his time to win the country, for the English were in deep discouragement, they were in mortal dread of a sudden, open attack, and he pledged himself to be drawn, hanged, beheaded and quartered – the traitor's sentence – if by attacking them next morning Bruce did not win with little loss.[11] Bruce must therefore have been delighted when he saw how the enemy were moving into positions bounded by the Pelstream Burn and the Bannock Burn which were both tidal and would be impassable at the start of the next day.

When the English camp learned that an experienced cavalryman like Sir Robert Clifford had been driven from the field by foot soldiers there was general dismay. Edward II felt obliged to send heralds throughout the army to raise their morale by explaining that these were just skirmishes; in the major battle of the next day victory would be certain.

The main battle took place on midsummer's day, 24 June 1314. Dawn was at 3.45 a.m. and from the early hours the Scots had been astir. First they attended mass and, after all had taken some light food, Bruce knighted certain individuals on the field, including James Douglas. He went on to give a general address to those assembled before him, telling them 'We have right on our side. Our enemies are moved only by desire for dominance, but we are fighting for our lives, our children, our wives and the freedom of our country.'[12] While he was by no means the first commander to speak in such terms, he had already achieved such success with many of these men that the words had great effect. After the address he went along the ranks of each schiltron exchanging words with individuals, then as the sky lightened fully, the Scots army began to move forward.

The English host had slept for an even shorter time than their opponents, cramped together on whatever dry patches they could find in the marshes. Although some of his advisers counselled delay to set things into better order, Edward was determined to commence his attacks, but before he had given out his orders he was amazed to see the Scottish spearmen coming forward in a move pre-empting his own. 'What! Will yon Scots fight?' he cried out. Then when he observed the Scots halting and kneeling for a moment in prayer he asked, 'They kneel to ask mercy?' Sir Ingram de Umfraville, the Anglo-Scot who had given his allegiance to the English, knew better and replied, 'For mercy, yes, but not from you; from God for their sins. These men will win all or die.' 'So be it,' said the king and ordered the trumpets to sound the assembly.[13]

The English vanguard went forward, crashing against the Scottish right commanded by Edward Bruce. It had no more success than on the previous day; many knights died trying to penetrate the Scottish spear wall, including the Earl of Gloucester, Sir Robert Clifford and Sir John Comyn. When Randolph's men joined those of Edward Bruce they pushed the whole of the English vanguard onto their main body before it had been able to form up.

Douglas now joined Edward Bruce and Randolph so that three Scottish divisions blocked the mouth of land enclosed by the Pelstream Burn and the Bannock Burn. The Scots moved forward, the rear ranks pushing on those in front, until they compressed the English, as Wallace had done at Stirling, with the result that the English archers dared not fire for the risk of hitting their own men. Sensibly they moved to the right flank where they started pouring their deadly missiles into Douglas' division, but Robert Bruce was equal to the crisis; he ordered up Sir Robert Keith with his 500 Scottish light horse and the archers were swept off the field. The battle was desperate but Bruce, sensing the English were about to waver, committed his reserve under Angus Macdonald and as the English started to waver the triumphant cry was taken up and repeated in the Scottish ranks, 'Press on. Press on. They fail.' The whole English army began to give way even though its masses still heavily outnumbered the Scots. An extra element seemed to be needed to clinch victory, and it came with Robert Bruce's camp followers. They began appearing over the brow of Gillies Hill carrying makeshift banners and crying out, 'Slay. Slay.' There must have been frantic activity below the hill as the proportion of regular soldiers among them tried to organise such untrained recruits, and others, into some semblance of military formation. Fortunately the beleagured English were in no position to be discriminating. As they struggled to hold their ground it seemed as if a strong force of fresh troops was reinforcing the Scots. At this point the 500 knights of Edward II's bodyguard insisted on leading the king away to Stirling Castle. There the governor refused him entry on the grounds that if he was forced to surrender the castle the king would be made a prisoner. The king and his escort made for Dunbar, harried all the way by Sir James Douglas initially with about sixty Scottish horse then reinforced by a further eighty.

On the battlefield itself in the growing crush panic spread among the now leaderless English, and many men and horses were lost trying to cross the Bannock Burn. While the Earl of Pembroke succeeded in getting most of his Welsh levies away the English casualties – including large numbers who surrendered in front of Stirling Castle – were immense. From the battlefield alone 200 spurs of knighthood were taken off the dead. Besides the knights at least 500 men of rank, noble knights and squires, were captured and held to ransom.[14] The plunder taken amounted to £200,000, including the whole English baggage train. With the exception of the Welsh, the foot were dispersed and, quite apart from those who took refuge around Stirling Castle, and were captured, most never succeeded in reaching the border. By comparison Scots losses were very small and 'the victory was as complete as could be'.[15]

Bannockburn was Scotland's greatest military success, for with Bruce still king, the victory made it possible for Scotland to be reaccepted as a sovercign, independent country. While detracting nothing from Wallace's earlier achievements at Stirling Bridge in a battle that was crucial to Scotland's survival, that great victory only earned his country a remission. Bannockburn was a triumph for the military leadership of Bruce, although it did depend on much support from others: his veteran soldiers and their own fine commanders; his followers' preparedness to meet superior forces not only with equanimity but confidence; and their willing acceptance of the demanding training instituted by their leader.

Without his earlier years of fighting Bruce could never have developed the unique relationship he enjoyed with his men, founded on shared sufferings, and on overcoming serious early reverses, but like other notable leaders Bruce's appreciation for fighting men extended to both sides, as he demonstrated by his humane treatment of the defeated English after the battle.

Whatever Bruce achieved at Bannockburn, it represented an abandonment of his long-term strategy of using guerrilla tactics to strike at soft targets while steadily harvesting enemy castles, and avoiding staking everything against the English main army. He was confident that such warfare would tire the English first, since for his own people to give up would entail their willing surrender of all they loved and believed in. Yet when challenged by his brother's actions, Robert Bruce put all his military skills into fashioning an army that could beat the English. Still relatively weak in cavalry he had no choice but to revive the schiltron, although he extended its role. He also followed Wallace in bringing together whatever archers he could, for if his cavalry could disperse the English archers or even defend his own he knew they might make a significant contribution.

In numbers Bruce's army was less impressive than Wallace's at Falkirk, but Bruce had far longer to assemble and prepare it. Over long years of fighting he realised that to be outnumbered was not necessarily disastrous. The quality of military skills and high morale were worth more than the quantity of actual troops. It was as well he did, for despite his best efforts he could only put together a third of the English strength and had to accept a greater disparity still in the cavalry. And despite his own powers of leadership, abetted by the experience and spirit of his men, Bruce still had to find other means to equalise the odds – namely the use of natural features in a carefully selected defensive position. While Bannockburn had no prominent hill, there were water courses and wet ground, which he further strengthened by his man-made barriers to impede the English cavalry. Above all he knew the ground intimately and was confident of the English using certain lines of approach on their move towards Stirling. After the clash of the vanguards on the first day he placed his men in positions that led the English to occupy marshy and broken ground, enclosed on three sides by rivers that in the early morning were swollen by flood waters.

This not only restricted the English opportunities for manoeuvre but hampered, if not negated altogether, their cavalry. Once the English were on his chosen killing ground he gave his soldiers belief in their success, never forgetting to treat them as men to whom he presently owed his life and on whom he had built his past successes.

At Bannockburn Bruce was the classic leader, ever confident, observant and in full control. After his personal encounter with the knight De Bohun he still had the presence of mind to alert Moray's division to an English flanking move. When, having formed their schiltron-like formation, they charged the opposing cavalry and became locked in a swaying, uncertain contest, it was Bruce who detected the early signs of the enemy's discouragement and held off superfluous reinforcements. On the day of the main battle Edward II was justly amazed when he saw the Scots footsoldiers coming towards him over open ground – ground seemingly made for cavalry – but Bruce knew the schiltrons also needed good ground to keep formation and build up their own momentum, while the flanking ground contained his hidden snares. During the battle his timing was immaculate; the Scots cavalry scattered the English archers just when they were doing most damage and he called up his unorthodox 'reserve' at the critical moment when the English, while still formidable, were experiencing serious self-doubt.

Bruce's victory at Bannockburn not only marked a personal triumph for him as an outstanding king commander, it marked a new age in warfare. His spearmen had shown that the long day of feudal cavalry was over, a fact re-emphasised by the defeat of the Austrian knights by Swiss infantry shortly afterwards.[16] The English certainly understood its significance and they were to use their knowledge to devastating effect against the French at Crecy. But in spite of his success at Bannockburn the Scottish king, lacking Welsh bowmen, never lost his respect for guerrilla warfare nor the power of defence. Indeed as late as 1327 when the English – led by their new sovereign Edward III – challenged the Scottish army in Durham, Bruce's lieutenant, Douglas, refused to abandon his strong defensive position, although he mounted a devastating night attack and almost captured the young English king.

Such caution paid off, for during the next year as Bruce threatened another major raid against the border counties, the English finally agreed to his life's aim, an aim helped immensely by his triumph at Bannockburn, that the realm of Scotland should be 'free quit and entire; without any kind of feudal subjection, for himself and his heirs forever'.

≈

CHAPTER TWO

THE LEGACY OF BRUCE

'God grant that they who are come of his offspring, shall uphold the land, and keep the people in all safety'

John Barbour, *The Bruce*

DESPITE THE PEACE TREATY of Northampton, signed by England and Scotland during 1328, the bitter conflict had caused such a degree of mutual dislike that further fighting between the two countries was inevitable. There was, too, Scotland's faithfulness to the 'auld alliance' with France that England saw as a serious threat to its national security. In 1332, just three years after Robert Bruce's death, the Second War of Independence began. This has been given far less attention than the first, not just because it lacked the successes of Wallace and Bruce, but after Bannockburn and the ringing Declaration of Arbroath sent to the Pope in 1320 reaffirming Scotland's determination 'as long as one hundred of us remain alive, never will we on any conditions be brought under English rule', there was a feeling that things could never be as bad as for Wallace before Stirling Bridge or when Bruce was a hunted fugitive. It was as well there was somewhat greater confidence, for after Bruce's death Scotland lacked commanders like him and Wallace. During the Second War of Independence and in later years the country was far too frequently in the hands of minority kings which meant placing it under men who inevitably lacked the unique authority of kingship. Unhappily when the soldiers were led by their kings the results were no better.

Despite reverses that would have crushed other nations, at no time did the Scots lose their fighting spirit nor for that matter did their leaders lose their antipathy towards the English, their natural enemies. If only their ambitions had sometimes been less, the military outcome might well have been happier for Scotland.

The triumph of Bannockburn proved a disastrous precedent when others tried to apply its tactics in quite different circumstances with armies lacking the equivalent battlefield experience or discipline, and when the science of war had moved on. Worse still, there were times when, although possessing equal or greater numbers and occupying strong geographic positions, they were nevertheless tempted to quit them and thus became a prey to the enduringly effective weapon of the English, the longbow – to be followed by its natural successor, artillery, which, despite the Scots' technical acumen, the English often handled better. In the years between Bannockburn and the union of the two crowns in 1603 Scottish bowmen and artillery were never a match for their English equivalents. As for that unique Scottish formation, the schiltron, it could in certain circumstances still foil heavy cavalry but it was always vulnerable to deadly showers of arrows and, in later days, to cannon playing on its massed ranks.

Regents and Military Reverses

The Second War of Independence arose directly from Edward III's determination to avenge both Bannockburn and his own battlefield humiliation at the hands of Robert Bruce in 1327. His eyes were set on recovering the mercantile centre of Berwick, thereby reasserting his grandfather's dominance over Scotland. The English parliament was reluctant to support yet another costly expedition to the north and Edward therefore determined to exploit Scotland's internal divisions. Whereas Bruce's seven-year-old son, David, had been crowned and anointed at Scone during November 1331, his succession was not without challenge. Edward Balliol, son of the Scottish monarch who had been humiliated and deposed by Edward I, headed an insurgency of Comyn nobles disinherited by the crowning of Robert Bruce and whose claims were still unsettled. Edward gave them ships in which to sail north in return for Balliol's declaration of fealty to him.

Edward's moderate investment was not in vain for during 1332 at Dupplin Moor, near Dunfermline, Edward Balliol and Henry, Earl of Beaumont, defeated a much superior, if disorderly, force under

Scotland's newly elected guardian Donald, Earl of Mar. Mar himself was suspected of having some sympathy with Balliol, and from their strong hillside position the Scots were only too aware how much they outnumbered the invaders.[1] With fatal over-confidence they caroused most of the night away so that Balliol's army was able to draw near to their position. With their opponents so close the Scottish attack the following day lacked co-ordination. Archers took a heavy toll of their massed ranks for they wore little protective clothing and in the confusion more Scots died of suffocation than battle wounds, among them the ill-starred guardian, Mar. It was fortunate for the Scots that they had another field army commanded by Patrick of Dunbar and although Balliol was set on the Scottish throne he enjoyed little support and the Bruce faction retaliated by driving him out of the kingdom to seek refuge in Carlisle.

During the next year, 1333, Scotland faced a renewed challenge from the English when Edward III, again supported by his puppet, Edward Balliol, brought another powerful army northwards and beseiged Berwick. The Scots now found themselves in a position analagous to that of the English before Bannockburn in that they had little time. With this threat to their premier trading centre, they had to act quickly. Under a new regent, Archibald Douglas, who as a commander was no more than a shadow of Bruce's lieutenant Sir James Douglas, the Scots hastily put together a relief army.

The English deployed in three divisions on Halidon Hill, a strong defensive feature dominating the approaches to Berwick. The right-hand was commanded by Thomas, Earl of Norfolk, the centre by the king while Balliol commanded the left. On the flanks of each division and slightly forward of them the English placed a detachment of archers. It was a formation that would be used again with terrifying success against the French at Crecy.

Unless the English could be dislodged, the Scots knew they would lose the town. Again they had a clear numerical advantage. Their army was divided into three great schiltrons of spearman totalling 13,000 or more and they had assembled no less than 1200 knights with their men-at-arms. For once they were not deficient in cavalry: one brigade was commanded by John, Earl of Moray, the second was under the boy king (but in reality headed by Sir James Stewart), a third was led by the Guardian, Douglas, and the last by Hugh, Earl of Ross.

On ground unsuitable for both cavalry and their schiltrons the Scots moved into the attack. They descended the rough slopes facing Halidon Hill but experienced unexpected difficulties in the wet ground at its base, and were barely able to sort themselves out before they faced Halidon's steeper flanks where the English forces occupied the crests. The muddy ground forced the Scots to dismount and as they struggled upwards in dense masses they presented a magnificent target for the English bowmen. As many arrows found their mark the momentum slowed. Edward bided his time until their faltering push almost stopped, then he signalled his knights to charge. At this the Scots broke and ran.

For the Scots to vacate a defensive feature, dismount, then allow English heavy cavalry to come thundering downhill upon them was the greatest folly. To pit a boy king, whatever the quality of his advisers, against the pugnacious and doughty Edward III represented a fatal miscalculation.

Just twenty years after Bannockburn, Scottish commanders paid a high price for their over-confidence and by ignoring Bruce's lessons on the importance of defence. In the melée the Guardian, Douglas, was killed together with the earls of Ross, Sutherland and Carrick, Berwick fell and the young King David was forced to flee to France.

Edward III looked for the knockout blow and in 1335 prepared a large invasion force. The Bruce faction continued to resist the English but under Sir Andrew Moray, son of Wallace's co-leader at Stirling Bridge, they sensibly reverted to the traditional practice of scorched earth tactics and gained a decisive local success at Culbean Forest. Although Scottish resistance was by no means universal across the country, Edward spent three further years trying to pacify the country until he came to the conclusion that, without another set battle, subduing Scotland would be a long and expensive process. He therefore diverted his attention to France, where his tactical flair would grant him fresh victories.

King David II (1324–71)

In 1341 with the threat from the English king temporarily withdrawn and most of the home country back in Scottish hands, King David II, now seventeen years of age, returned from France to claim his kingdom. However, in 1346, after five years on the throne and with Edward III preparing for a major expedition to France, the Scottish king made the fatal step of attempting to take advantage of what he believed was English weakness by offering military support to his French ally. In any case from a strategic point of view his decision to aid the French came too late, for only two months before, at Crecy, English bowmen had inflicted a great defeat on the French and had destroyed the cream of their nobility. Notwithstanding, under their king a formidable Scots army moved down into the northern counties of England. The English anticipated the move by assembling an army of their own under two northern lords, Henry Percy and Ralph Neville, who were joined by William de la Zouche, Archbishop of York. The Scots king contemptuously dismissed the English force as 'miserable monks and pig drivers',[2] but unbeknown to him they had advanced close to the Scots camp at Bearpark, outside Durham, near the hamlet of Neville's Cross. The English were about 15,000 strong to the Scottish 20,000 and they occupied a ridge some 200 feet above the Scots camp.[3] They were drawn up in three divisions with massed archers to the front. Percy commanded on the right, Neville as senior commander was in the centre and Sir Thomas Rokeby on the left. Neville concealed his reserve under John Balliol in a fold of the ground.

King David also had his army in three divisions. John Randolph commanded the right, David himself was in the centre and Robert Stewart on the left. With memories of Halidon Hill still fast in their minds the Scots were reluctant to leave their defensive position, but the English moved their bowmen forward and the Scots' inability to counter the regular flights of English arrows loosed at short range and their growing numbers of casualties finally persuaded King David to advance. The decision was seemingly taken without an adequate knowledge of the ground between the two armies, which was not only broken but split by high dykes. A defile forced Randolph to change his line of march in a leftward direction, virtually uniting his own men with those of the king's division. Labouring over the rough ground the great masses of spearmen lost formation and, as before, such squadrons of close-packed, stumbling men made a perfect target for the English bowmen. However, on the left under Robert Stewart it seemed as if sheer numbers would prevail: they scattered the forward screen of archers and were about to come to terms with the English foot soldiers when Edward Balliol unleashed the English reserve against the flank of Stewart's division. This unexpected development drove the Scots back. To their disgrace the Stewart and the Earl of March fled, along with their troops, an inconceivable event in the days of Wallace and Bruce. The English now concentrated their fire on the Scottish centre and the day was lost. The Scots king might be a poor commander but he was undoubtedly brave and after being wounded in the face by an arrow, he was captured as he hid under a bridge.

Despite the recent example of Crecy and the superiority there of the longbow the Scots had once more allowed the English to occupy ground of their choice and had been compelled to attack English forces screened by archers. William Wallace had never trusted his schiltrons to move onto the offensive in this way and when Bruce's highly trained formations did so, it was over good ground supported by horsemen – horsemen who could sweep the opposing archers away.

At both Halidon Hill and Neville's Cross with unfavourable conditions underfoot the advancing schiltrons were seriously weakened before they could come to blows with their opponents. The valour of such spearmen was unquestionable; not so the performance of their leaders. At Halidon Hill Scottish leadership was found wanting and at Neville's Cross the courage shown by their seventeen-year-old monarch was by no means equalled by others, namely the Stewart and his division. On the English side Edward Balliol was unquestionably a good soldier, and his intervention when given the signal by Neville was all-important in deciding the outcome.

Following Neville's Cross things would have been far worse for Scotland if the English had not been particularly weakened by the scourge of the Black Death. Directly after the battle Scottish affairs were over-shadowed by the capture and prolonged captivity of their king, for while in English hands he was always liable to be used to extract major political concessions. Fortunately for Scotland, following Edward III's major success against France, notably his son's victory at Pottiers in 1356, the English king showed himself willing to resolve things with Scotland. He demanded a high price but at the Treaty of Berwick in October 1357 Edward agreed to King David II's release for a huge ransom of 100,000 merks (£67,000) to be paid in instalments over the next decade and for a truce to be signed between the two countries. Twenty-eight years after the Treaty of Northampton that recognised Scotland's renewed independence and forty-three years after Robert Bruce's victory at Bannockburn that opened the way for the treaty, the Wars of Independence were at an end. After Bannockburn subsequent English victories at Halidon Hill and Neville's Cross had not crushed the northern Kingdom and following the Treaty of Berwick the English would never again try to replace a Scottish King.[4]

This did not, of course, rule out further full-scale battles between the two countries, nor prevent their outcome from being of the utmost consequence, although after Neville's Cross more than 150 years would pass before the next national duel took place on Flodden Field in 1513.

In the interim relations were hardly warm between the two countries. A number of military clashes took place and on occasions the Scots were supported by French troops but in the main the fighting was confined to, or close to, the border regions. It was prevented from developing into full scale wars by political convulsions in both countries and because of the heavy demands upon English resources by its campaigns in France. However, Scottish military activity was not confined to its home country. After 1418, in response to French pleas for help, volunteer companies of Scottish soldiers crossed over to the continent and under their own commanders fought against the English there. In the second half of the 15th century England's dynastic problems during the Wars of the Roses were mirrored by Scotland's own political problems. Much of the reigns of James II (1437–60) and James III (1460–88) were spent in attempts to outwit their contesting barons, particularly the powerful Douglases. These were often encouraged by the English and in 1482 a coup led by Scottish nobles against James III prevented him from attacking English troops occupying Berwick which never returned to Scottish hands. In 1488 James III was killed by a group of rebels among whom were the leading Border families, Hepburn and Hume, along with his own son, the future James IV. It was under James IV that the Scottish crown would reassert its traditional authority and the next national duel between the two countries would take place.

King James IV (1473–1513)

With the accession of the sixteen-year-old James IV Scotland gained the strong king for whom it had long yearned. A true Renaissance prince, he was probably the most affectionately regarded of all the Stuarts: pleasure-loving like others of the line, with a string of beautiful mistresses, he showed he had a conscience by wearing an iron chain round his waist to help atone for his part in the rebellion against his father. James IV defies an easy description. John Prebble writes of him as being 'intelligent and curious, colourful and high-spirited, raven-headed and gay, generous and extravagant'.[5] The scholar Erasmus was also complimentary, calling him a man who 'had a wonderful intellectual power, an astonishing knowledge of everything, an unconquerable magnanimity, and the most abundant generosity'. On the other hand James IV was wilful and proud, obstinate and extravagant. The confidence he needed as a good king inclined him to arrogance and, most dangerous of all, he was liable to be over-confident. While avoiding the internal dissensions of the recent past, under him the monarchy moved close to absolutism and his will became largely unchallenged. James enjoyed physical combat and was always at the forefront of the jousting tournaments held at his court. Looking beyond such mock combats he pledged himself to have Berwick returned to Scotland and after he had tasted real conflict in 1494 during a major, if abortive, raid across the border, and more of the same in 1497, he showed disturbing signs of developing an unrealistic conceit about his skills as a military commander. Despite his undoubtful shrewdness, under such a monarch war with England became much more likely. The Spanish ambassador to Scotland, Don Pedro de Ayala, reported in 1498 that James 'loves war so much that I fear . . . the peace will not last long.'[6] Nevertheless, Scotland prospered under its vigorous king. He was keenly interested in technological advances, particularly ones related to war, sponsoring the new printing press in Edinburgh, experimenting with the manufacture of artillery and instituting the building of ships. To England's alarm, in order to counter his country's vulnerability to seaborne attacks, James IV created the first Scottish fleet including 'The Great Michael', which was reported to be the largest ship afloat at the time and was said to have cost £30,000 alone.[7] It was larger even than the 'Great Harry', launched during the next year (1512) by the English. In his passion for artillery he 'himself supervised the moulding of guns that could throw shot weighing almost 60lbs.'[8]

In the early years of the 16th century relations between England and Scotland were mixed but as long as the cautious Henry VII was on the English throne, there seemed little possibility of outright war between the two countries. In the final years of Henry VII's reign things improved to such an extent that in 1503 James IV and Henry's eldest daughter, Margaret Tudor, were married at Holyrood Abbey to seal the Treaty of so-called Perpetual Peace between the two nations concluded the year before. The treaty, however, was only made possible by the good relations then existing between England and France.

The situation between the two countries was bound to change when in 1509 James IV met his match as a restive and pugnacious Henry VIII succeeded to the English throne; raids into northern England and any support for pretenders to the English throne like Perkin Warbeck were now likely to meet with a very different reaction. Predictably the break came over France. In 1512 Henry VIII joined a coalition against France and, in response to an appeal from that country, James IV sent a threatening message to the English king (already in France) to cease his aggression. At the same time he sent a fleet of nine vessels to combine with the French fleet, with the promise that if Henry VIII did not stop his warmaking the Scots would advance into England. On receiving no reply, during 1513 the Scottish king led an impressive army southwards, estimated at some 30,000 men, accompanied by a formidable artillery train of 17 heavy guns requiring no less than 400 oxen to draw them.

Just across the border James brought his artillery to bear on the great castle of Norham. Two hundred years before it had defied its Scottish beseigers for a full year; within six days he had breached its outer walls and it soon submitted. Elsewhere, however, the Scots' military affairs were less successful. Prior to the movement of their main army an advance guard of 5000 mounted troops entered Northumberland in what became known as the 'Ill Raid' where they were ambushed by 1000 English foot, including archers. By the time they extricated themselves they had suffered several hundred casualties.

From the leisurely pace of his army's move southwards, it seems highly unlikely that James had a major invasion in mind. In all probability he intended to confine himself to a show of military strength on behalf of his ally, the French king. Contemporary observers were probably correct when they reckoned him canny enough not to provoke the out and out enmity of Henry VIII, but unfortunately, they did not appear to realise how dangerously inflated James' estimate of his powers as a commander had become. In any case Henry VIII had already anticipated a full-scale Scottish invasion and before setting off for France had ordered a levying of the northern counties under their commander Thomas Howard, Earl of Surrey. Surrey was a septuagenarian, even older than the Surrey who in earlier years faced William Wallace and Andrew Moray at Stirling Bridge, but old as he was he remained vigorous and shrewd. Surrey's forces, some 26,000 strong, moved close to the border at Newcastle upon Tyne, and when they reached Alnwick they were joined by his youngest son, Thomas Howard, a newly appointed admiral who had sailed over from France with 1200 or so regular marines.

In accordance with conventions of the time, prior to any major conflict, diplomatic exchanges were undertaken between the two sides. Surrey had far less room for manoeuvre than the Scots, for like virtually every English army before him, he was short of supplies and therefore favoured an immediate battle. He knew the Scots had the choice of moving back into Scotland and if they did so he would then have to disperse his own forces through want of supplies, whereupon James IV could move south again at his leisure and devastate the English border counties. The Scottish king not only possessed far more options, but could reasonably consider the need to fight had passed since Henry VIII had already defeated the French during a confused engagement called the Battle of the Spurs and the war was virtually over.

Surrey was disappointed to have missed the French campaign and he decided to lure the Scots into fighting by a daily exchange of

insults through his herald Rouge-Croix. While many of the Scottish
nobles would have been only too glad to withdraw, their king seized
the bait. He detained Rouge-Croix and, against the advice of his
senior councillor, Bishop Elphinstone, sent his own herald, Islay,
to tell Surrey he would wait to give him battle. Surrey responded
by agreeing to fight by the Friday next – 9 September. With such a
chivalrous opponent Surrey might have expected to meet the Scots
on a relatively flat site, one that did not unduly favour either side.
To his surprise and anger he discovered James had occupied a
very strong defensive position on Flodden Hill where the obvious
approach from the south was guarded by his formidable guns. Surrey
was not prepared to commit military suicide and he attempted to
change things by writing to James challenging him to descend to
the plain. Unsurprisingly the Scottish king refused to agree, saying,
'that it was not for a mere earl to dictate to a King' and that he
would 'take and keep his ground and field at his own pleasure'.[9]
The wily Surrey then left his camp at Wooler on 8 September and
marched his army north, thus threatening to cut off James' line of
retreat to Scotland.

In heavy rain Surrey re-encamped near Barmoor Wood, some four
miles to the north-east of Flodden Hill. As James still showed no signs
of leaving his own position, Surrey held a council of war, during
which the fiery Admiral Howard proposed attacking the Scots from
the rear and the 'most part of the army thereto agreed'.[10]

On the following morning, 8 September 1513, the English split
their forces into two: Howard's division was in the forefront
together with the guns, followed by Surrey at the head of the
main body. They crossed the River Twizel and, after experiencing
great difficulties in the muddy ground, formed up north of and
below Branxton Hill on the northern flank of the Flodden massif.
A more cunning or experienced commander than James might have
attacked the English vanguard before they were properly organised,
but when his scouts reported them firmly in position there was a
feeling among the Scottish leaders, including the king, that they
had been outwitted. Some of the king's advisers, notably the old
earl of Angus, urged him to block any possible English invasion
of Scotland by withdrawing northwards, but pride combined with
James' anger at what he saw as English trickery, and he decided to
give battle.

At mid-day on the 9th he about-faced his army and marched it towards Branxton Hill which he occupied by about 2 p.m.[11] This seemed a reasonable decision for it was a formidable feature that rose to 500 feet and was almost as strong as the one he had just left. But if James intended to attack the English he would have to come off the hill. According to custom the Scots, before they set out, set fire to their refuse – mainly straw used for bedding – but contrary to the theories of many commentators, the smoke was unlikely to have obscured their advance. Both sides, therefore, were jockeying for new positions with the English expending much greater effort so doing. After a laborious march of almost eight miles in continuous and heavy rain it was afternoon before they struggled to form a battleline on ground sloping upwards to the Branxton ridge a mere quarter of a mile away. Once again the Scots king surprisingly made no attempt to harass them.

Whether he was influenced by this seeming passiveness or had been fired by the ardour of his admiral son is not clear, but Surrey decided to move immediately against the enemy and at 4 p.m. opened the battle in conventional fashion, with artillery fire. The Scots responded in kind. The English artillery was of a lighter calibre and, due to the muddy ground, they had only been able to move their smaller guns to the base of the hill. While the Scots artillery was unquestionably heavier and made a much greater noise, it was less effective and its heavy gunstones flew harmlessly over the English. Before beginning his campaign the Scottish king had sent his most senior gunners to France. Those remaining proved inadequate so that the English artillery gained the advantage, raking the Scottish divisions and their artillery placed on the skyline and killing James' master gunner, Robert Borthwick. However, due to the continuing rain and gusting wind, that other formidable weapon of past years, the English archers, were able to play little part. To escape from the artillery fire the Scots could have withdrawn to the reverse side of the ridge and waited there until the English closed, before returning and falling on them as they toiled up the slippery slopes. But this was not James IV's way and in any case to move backwards might have caused a panic. Although it was entirely understandable that they should not hide themselves, it was followed by what proved to be a far more serious blunder: impatient with the galling fire of the English artillery the king gave

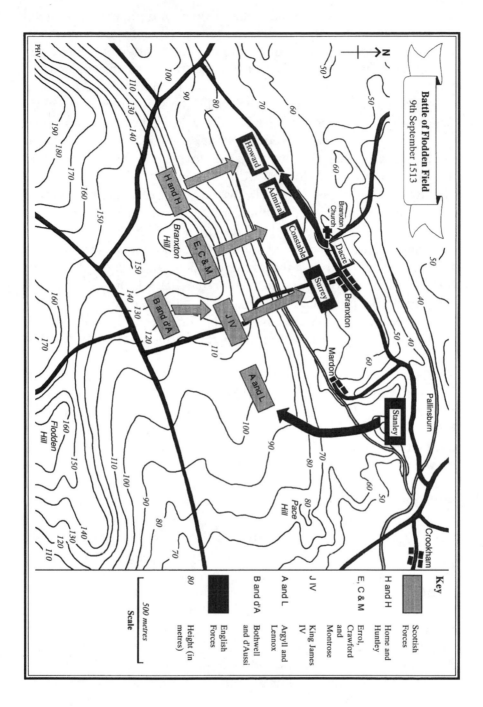

Battle of Flodden Field
9th September 1513

Key

	Scottish Forces
H and H	Home and Huntley
E, C & M	Errol, Crawford and Montrose
J IV	King James IV
A and L	Argyll and Lennox
B and d'A	Bothwell and d'Aussi
	English Forces
80	Height (in metres)

Scale
500 metres

his army the command to move downwards and impetuously joined the front ranks. 'Keeping no order among his men from a position in which he could be attacked only with difficulty and danger he rushed down upon the enemy.'[12] In fact, the Scottish left flank under Lord Hume seemed to have anticipated the royal command and by doing so might have forced the king's hand. The slope there was more regular than the others and the Scots' levelled pikes crashed against the English right commanded by Surrey's second son, Edward, at which his raw levies gave way. By the time the victorious Scots had decided to turn upon Howard's division some of their number had already resorted to plunder. The weakened thrust lost momentum and the English succeeded in intercepting it with a contingent under Lord Dacre stationed just behind the main line for the very purpose of giving succour 'when need should seem to appear'. Dacre drove the Scots back and a stand-off developed. Amazingly these two bodies stood inactive for the rest of the battle. One explanation was that both contained men from the border counties, none of whom seemed anxious to shed blood unnecessarily 'for, among other things, the dread of incurring the unquenchable vendetta of the blood-feud'.[13]

When the Scots' central two divisions started their descent fronted by their 18-foot lances of continental pattern, they had probably already sensed Hume's success. However, their hopes of emulating it wavered as they found themselves struggling to keep their footing on the wet grass. Worse still they came upon a shallow valley which they had to enter, and climb out of, before the next downward slope towards the English position some 200 yards away.

This clash between the two Scottish divisions, commanded by the king and the Earl of Crawford, and the two English ones under Surrey and Howard, was bloody and fierce. To the Scots' surprise, while their heavy wooden shields and armour had protected them well against English arrow shafts, they came up against the bill, a combination of axe blade and curving hook mounted upon an eight foot staff. Some considered bills obsolete but the majority of Surrey's soldiers used them to great effect, first lopping the heads off the unwieldy Scottish spears and then killing their owners.[14] While the central divisions were locked in fierce combat and men struggled for a footing on the sloping ground, on Branxton Hill above and to the right of them the Islesmen and Highlanders under the earls of Argyll and Lennox stood watching the murderous battle below. As they were on the point of coming down to assist the king they were attacked themselves by the English reserve under Earl Stanley, who had led his men up the east slope of the hill without being seen. He commenced his attack from the front, where his archers poured a barrage of arrows into the Scottish position, and, as the Scots' ranks loosened fell on their flanks and rear.[15] More seriously still, Stanley's troops went on to attack the king's division from the rear.

With the Scottish left inactive, its right surprised and broken and the left centre, under the earls of Crawford and Montrose, badly cut about by Howard's and Surrey's bill hooks, the fate of the king's division seemed forlorn. Unlike Stanley's forces, the Scottish reserve under the Earl of Bothwell failed to make an impact on the general course of the battle for Bothwell had been killed, probably at an early point in the contest.[16] By 6 p.m. as darkness began to fall the battle was over.

Contemporary commentators described how at one stage the Scottish king launched a desperate charge against the English commander and came within a spear's length of him. If Surrey was in the rear directing his men, this meant that 'James very nearly penetrated the entire depth of the English line'.[17] He fell with his body suffixed by arrows, one hand hanging useless and his neck gashed from a bill. In his chronicle of 1548 Edward Hall wrote, 'O what a noble and triumphant courage was this for a king to fight in a battle as a mean soldier'. Magnificent it might have been, but cool and skilled leadership was definitely lacking. It was vital for the Scots to keep to their ground on Branxton Hill despite the English cannon fire or at least to move a short distance backwards onto the reverse slope. After they had moved forwards and their veteran Borderers broke the inexperienced English on the left flank, nothing seemed to succeed, for clear leadership was wanting. Lord Hume's division was allowed to stand immobile for far too long, keeping to the high ground they had seized, until they finally slipped away to Scotland at dawn. The reserve and right centre did not become involved until the issue had virtually been decided, while on the right flank the Highlanders were surprised and defeated. Despite being the overall commander the king allowed his appreciation of the battle to be confined within his own battle division and then hazarded everything on a desperate charge from there. The knowledgeable Spanish ambassador, Don Pedro de Ayala, wrote critically of the king's leadership:

> He is courageous, even more so than a king should be. I have seen him often undertake most dangerous things in the last wars. I sometimes clung to his skirts and succeeded in keeping him back . . . He is not a good captain, because he begins to fight before he has given his orders . . . he does not think it right to begin any warlike undertaking without being the first in danger.

At Flodden the Scots again paid a fearful price for supporting France. Apart from their king, nine earls and fourteen barons fell along with 10,000 soldiers. The effects were felt across the whole nation. Like other towns Selkirk contributed a company of spearmen; after the battle just one man returned home.

It is all too easy to criticise a defeated leader but at Flodden James IV allowed himself to be worsted by Surrey, a cunning, immensely experienced English commander. After the Scots' first successful charge the initiative moved across to the English and, quite apart from the mayhem caused by the English billhooks on spearmen that had lost cohesion, much of the credit must go to their command organisation. With so much to lose, James IV not only chose open battle but failed to make sure geographic factors were in his favour. To charge down from Branxton Hill was utterly at odds with his initial decision to stay on Flodden Hill. He allowed his passions free rein, a black sin in a commander, bringing to nothing his seeming advantages while his massed artillery train utterly failed to gain the distinction expected of it.

The Scots not only lost their king at Flodden, a disaster when his son was little more than a baby, but also the cream of their aristocracy and a large number of soldiers. Quite as serious as the material losses was the blow to national pride. It has been said that as a result of Flodden 'the purpose, drive and unanimity which James IV had instilled in the political community were shattered, and Scottish national self-confidence was lost for the remainder of the century'.[18] Even so there was no comparison with the deadly danger to Scotland as a free country experienced during the earlier Wars of Independence.

*   *   *

Thirty-four years after Flodden the last major battle was fought on behalf of Scottish monarchs against the English at Pinkie Cleuch, near Edinburgh. The interval saw a grim continuity in the rival attempts by England and France to bring Scotland under their control. Along with such continuity came remarkable changes; most importantly the Reformation in Northern Europe had broken the Catholic church's long-held sovereignty over religious matters. In Scotland, it was only in the last five years before Pinkie that the move to Protestantism began to be felt strongly in the south of the country, although by that time half of Germany and the whole of Scandinavia were Protestant and England had cut itself off from Rome. These challenges to orthodox beliefs and the sanctions against them brought widespread conflict which among other things led to technological changes in the conduct of war. Once more within Scotland such developments were only felt later.

Religious considerations added a new dimension to Anglo/Scottish relations prior to Pinkie by fuelling Henry VIII's xenophobia towards the northern kingdom and its possible use against him as the spearhead of Catholic Europe. It was the marriage of the Scottish king, James V, to the French noblewoman, Mary of Guise-Lorraine, that decided Henry VIII on an invasion of Scotland in 1542. After early reverses the English army trapped the Scots at Solway Moss. It was hardly a battle for in their panic at finding themselves on marshy broken ground the Scots forces disintegrated. His despair on hearing the news killed James V and the country was left in the hands of a baby girl, Mary, only a few days old. Henry's aim was now to unite the two countries by a marriage between the infant Queen and his own son, Edward. In 1543 a peace and marriage treaty was concluded between the two countries but religious currents through the revival of the Scots Catholic party under Cardinal Beaton, Archbishop of St Andrews, intervened. The Scots decided to renew their ties with France and refused to send the infant Mary to England for the agreed wedding before her tenth birthday.

Henry again resorted to war. He sent the Earl of Hertford with powerful forces, including mercenaries, to force the Scots to accept the royal marriage proposals. While brutal and destructive the 'rough wooing' proved disappointing and Scotland once more showed its stubbornness and resilience.

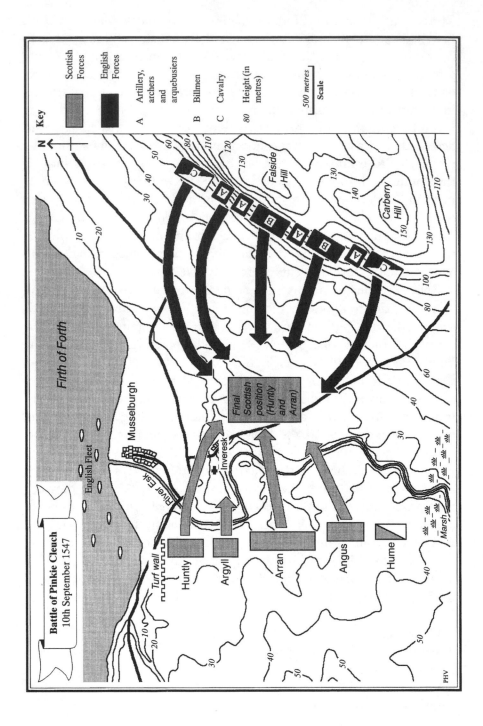

Battle of Pinkie Cleuch
10th September 1547

Key

Scottish Forces

English Forces

A   Artillery, archers and arquebusiers

B   Billmen

C   Cavalry

80 Height (in metres)

500 metres
Scale

N

Falside Hill

Carberry Hill

Firth of Forth

Musselburgh

English Fleet

River Esk

Inveresk

Final Scottish position (Huntly and Arran)

Turf wall

Marsh

Huntly

Argyll

Arran

Angus

Hume

PHV

Henry VIII died in 1547 but Hertford, now Duke of Somerset and styled Protector of England, was still determined to force the Scots into accepting the marriage of their child queen and the new English boy king, Edward VI. He sought a major victory to be followed by a permanent English presence in the country.

With child monarchs in both England and Scotland, Somerset was opposed by the Scottish Governor, James Hamilton, Second Earl of Arran. He was a wily diplomat but not a good commander and his deficiencies had already been exposed during the border clashes of 1544.

On 1 September 1547 the English approached the border with some 17,000 men well supported by artillery, comprising 15 heavy guns and 60 lighter pieces. The soldiers included 4000 heavy cavalry, the first time since Edward II that they were intended to be used as cavalry and not to dismount and fight on foot. Among their number was a unit of Spanish harquebusiers, carrying firearms. In addition to his orthodox artillery Somerset could also call upon the English fleet which was shadowing the coast and carrying his army's provisions. On 8 September Somerset deployed his forces on two hills near Prestonpans, from where he could keep watch on the Scottish army to the north. Opposing him behind the River Esk was the Earl of Arran with 25,000 men, a force numerically superior although, like Scottish commanders before him, his cavalry was made up of light border horse, and he, of course, lacked the supporting fire of the English fleet. Added to this he could not be certain about the full loyalty of all his subordinate commanders with their religious differences exacerbating things further.

The Scots were in four divisions. Their extreme left wing was commanded by the Earl of Huntly; next came 3000 Highlanders under the Earl of Argyll; in accordance with tradition Arran himself commanded the centre; and on his right were more footsoldiers under the Earl of Angus. The Scottish cavalry occupying the right flank was commanded by the Earl of Hume. Arran's army held a strong geographic position: the Firth of Forth was to their left, the small River Esk across their front and a marsh protected their right flank. On the left they had erected a turf wall to help give extra cover from the cannon of the English fleet.

Despite his superior firepower Somerset dismissed the option of a frontal attack against an enemy force one and a half times larger than his own, that occupied such a redoubtable position. Like

Surrey at Flodden, he needed to move the odds in his direction and providentially, on the morning of 9 September, his opponents played into his hands. In a show of scorn for the invaders the Scots allowed their cavalry, mounted on small but surefooted garrons, to cross the Esk and parade in front of the English, daring their cavalry to come out and fight. Initially Somerset refused to release them but at length he gave way to Lord Grey, his cavalry commander, who dashed forward with his heavy horse and, catching the Scottish detachments off balance, rode them down. Lord Hume was badly injured in the exchange and his cavalry were no longer fit to take any worthwhile part in the battle.

As Somerset was undertaking a detailed reconnaissance of the ground between the two armies he was met by a Scots herald from Arran, who offered the English peace terms and safe conduct to withdraw across the border but encouraged by the Scots' apparent reluctance to fight and the good performance of his own cavalry, Somerset decided to decline. He also refused out of hand Arran's naive offer to have the matter settled in personal combat between Huntly and Somerset, supported by twenty men apiece. He replied, 'We have been a good season in this country and am here now but with a sober company and they a great number: and if they would meet us in the field, they shall be satisfied with fighting enough.'[19]

Another version of events was that Somerset offered to withdraw if Arran would agree to the terms of the marriage between Mary and Edward Tudor. Whatever the preliminaries, despite his fewer numbers Somerset came to believe he had a good chance of success and at 8 a.m. the next morning, Saturday 10 September, he started moving forward to occupy Inveresk Hill, which was to the front and right of the Scottish position. If he could place his fifteen pieces of heavy artillery on it he would be able to dominate the field. The move exposed his own left flank, but as the Scots were without cavalry he reasoned they could not exploit his move. If nothing else, the feint might persuade them to move off their defensive position. To his surprise and delight he observed his opponents starting to abandon their positions and cross the river towards him.

It is not clear why they did so. They could have thought the English were about to retreat or it could have been that Arran realised that once English artillery played on him from Inveresk Hill his defensive position would be largely untenable. Alternatively the Scots were likely to have advanced in anger and pride when they saw an English army with the temerity to manoeuvre across their front. Whatever the reason it was a grievous blunder, as Arran was outmatched in both cavalry and artillery. When Argyll's Highlanders on the left of the Scottish line left the protection of their earth wall and started crossing the Esk they came under artillery fire from the warships and, because of their traditional fear of the guns, fled from the field. On the same flank the Earl of Huntly's division showed more resolution, continuing to move forwards although the artillery fire made them veer right towards Arran's centre divisions. These had already moved some way in front of Angus' division on the right flank that had shown initial reluctance to move forward. Huntly's and Arran's double division, subsequently joined by Angus, assumed schiltron formation and continued to advance. This serried mass of pikemen trotting forward shoulder to shoulder, shouting in unison to give themselves courage, must have presented an awesome spectacle to the waiting English. Somerset knew, however, that with the Scottish infantry now in the open the day must be his. He ordered his guns to be dragged round to face the schiltrons where from short range they could loose their shot deep into the massed ranks. Each round was sure to claim multiple casualties. First he must slow or halt the spearmen, and to do this he ordered up his cavalry. Two charges were made against the spear walls. Both failed to break in but at considerable cost they achieved his purpose. With spiked and dying horses obstructing their front the pikemen were slowed to a halt. The land-based cannon firing at a range of just 200 yards were joined by the fleet's guns, while from the flank and rear 200 Spanish arqubusiers galloped up and fired point blank into the ranks. Somerset waited until what he believed was the decisive moment before ordering his infantry to move forward. At this, their bowmen sent a cloud of hissing arrows to join the assorted missiles ravaging the Scottish ranks. After a further cavalry charge the Scots broke. From his position behind the forward squadrons Angus succeeded in getting most of his men off the field, but from Huntly's and Arran's broken schiltrons soldiers had to try to escape as best they could. They left a grim sight. 'Some (soldiers) with their legs off; some but hought (ham strung) and left lying half dead; others, with the arms cut off; divers, their necks half asunder; many, their heads cloven; of sundry, the brains pasht (smashed) out; some others again,

45

their heads quite off; with a thousand other kinds of killing.'[20] The English followed up vigorously and about 10,000 Scots died, along with many of their nobles, while the English casualties were put at about 500, the majority among their heavy cavalry.

The Scots had once again been persuaded to leave a strong defensive position with only too predictable results. By 1547 the schiltron formation adopted by William Wallace 250 years before not only had to face bowmen but the longer range and greater destructive power of artillery. It required better commanders than the vacillating Arran to recover the fame of Scottish arms and Scottish leadership, in open battle.

He was hardly alone here, for, after the superlative triumph of Robert Bruce at Bannockburn, the Scots appeared unable to beat the English. The reasons are not hard to detect. In spite of isolated instances like the Highlanders' flight in face of artillery at Pinkie or the 'canny' Borderers under Dacre holding back at Flodden, such defeats did not come about through reluctance to fight or cowardice on the part of the ordinary soldiers. In fact, the bravery of the spearmen who filled the schiltrons and performed so valiantly for Wallace and Bruce was repeated at Neville's Cross and at Flodden where, even when their spears were headless, they obstinately stood their ground to be hacked down. The performance of the Scottish cavalry is probably the one instance where valour was sometimes found to be wanting, but it must be said that they were usually far outmatched by the English both in the size of their mounts and in sheer numbers. At Falkirk, for instance, the performance of the cavalry was at best undistinguished but its full allegiance to the squire Wallace was always in doubt. Under Bruce the small number of cavalry at Bannockburn performed magnificently and at Pinkie Cleuch, in spite of their first foolhardy gestures, it is hard to see how the Scottish cavalry on their ponies could stand up to heavily armed English knights astride formidable shire horses.

Responsibility for the Scots lack of battlefield success between Bannockburn and Pinkie Cleuch must fall on deficiencies in leadership. In no encounter between the Scots and English after Bannockburn was there the disparity in numbers suffered by Bruce. Admittedly, the Scottish commanders faced superior weapons, there were always English archers and cannon to be dealt with, but the truth is that in the great set battles between the two countries they were outmanoeuvred into fighting on ground that was unsuitable and, worse still, about which they were ignorant.

In their eagerness to close with the enemy they chose to ignore the pattern of Wallace's campaigns before he accepted battle at Stirling Bridge or Bruce's years of campaigning before he met the English at Bannockburn. One can appreciate the difficulties of a regent or a guardian unexpectedly pressed into service and the massive problems faced by the teenage David II at Neville's Cross but, at Flodden, King James IV allowed himself to be outmanoeuvred by Surrey to accept battle and, once he had done so, fought like a private soldier or, at best, a junior commander, ignorant of what was happening and what decision should be made elsewhere on the field. Compared with the chivalrous and fiery king, Surrey fought a cunning and 'dirty' war although one that proved far more effective.

For almost two and a half centuries following Bruce's triumph at Bannockburn Scotland's national armies were led by men who were neither patient when it was needed nor original in their tactics, nor had they established the complete control over their soldiers that distinguishes the most notable commanders. Fortunately for Scotland, after their senior commanders had been defeated, others routinely reverted to the guerrilla tactics for which their country was so well suited. Following his victory at Pinkie Somerset was no more successful than other invaders in bringing Scotland under his full control and his attempts at garrisoning the country were a failure.

After Pinkie until the union of the countries' two crowns in 1603, religious issues were paramount and although violence continued along the Border areas there was no desire for a full scale war. With James VI of Scotland becoming James I of England the dangers of an English invasion northwards seemed over and with James' successful campaign against the robber clans on both sides of the border this cause of friction ended too.

Few could foresee that by the 1640s religious and constitutional disorders on both sides of the border would bring about a civil war involving the whole British Isles. With war, opportunities would arise for good military leadership and Scots would provide their proportion of military commanders, including James Graham, 1st

Marquis of Montrose, who rightly deserves to be considered along with other great commanders of history.

Before turning to the Civil War another group of Scottish military leaders deserves attention. These are the 'Soldiers of Fortune' who gave their allegiance to European monarchs. The tradition was an enduring one: one of the most distinguished Scottish mercenary leaders served during the 15th century and possibly the most successful of all served his monarch, Frederick the Great, during the 18th century. As mercenaries they were never likely to be given that independence of decision-making that marks outstanding leaders but their soldierly qualities rightly earned them high reputations.

≈

CHAPTER THREE

THE SCOTTISH WILD GEESE – D'AUBIGNY, HEPBURN, GORDON AND KEITH

'The contempt of commerce ... the poverty of the country of Scotland, the normal disposition to wandering and adventure, all conduced to lead the Scots abroad into the military service of countries that were at war with each other.'

Sir Walter Scott, *Quentin Durward and the Legend of Montrose.*

THE RESTLESS SPIRIT OF many Scots and their traditional search for military action led them to become regular soldiers of fortune. There are references to Scots serving in the armies of Charlemagne as early as the 8th century and by the early 15th century considerable numbers of Scottish troops were assisting their traditional ally, France, against the English during the later stages of the Hundred Years' War. It has been estimated that between 1419 and 1429 alone over 15,000 Scots were serving in Europe, some three per cent of the total population of the country at that time, and it became a regular practice for Scottish soldiers to fight in whole regiments not only for France but also in the armies of Sweden, Holland and Poland. They were not always popular in the host countries. In the 15th century some Frenchmen were speaking in derogatory terms about their northern allies: 'Rats, lice and Scotsmen: you find them the world over' – although the comment referred partly to merchants and scholars this was principally thought to be a jibe at soldiers.[1] No doubt motives which lead men to accept the regimen of military life will not always be the noblest ones. Then, as now, some pledged themselves because of the employment offered when they had none in civilian life; some because it gave them a chance to escape temporary crises at home, like falling into debt or clashing with the law; some because they had been ordered by their clan chief to do so – like the Hamiltons sent into Swedish service in 1631 by James, Marquis of Hamilton; some because they wanted to see more of the world or fight for a particular cause; and some because they were determined to make the military their professional career. In any case, during conflicts like the Thirty Years' War from 1618–1648, the numbers of volunteers from the participating countries would prove inadequate and soldiers of fortune performed a valuable role, while the best of their officers became outstanding servants for their adopted masters. In the 300 years from the mid-15th century to the mid-18th century four Scottish leaders, in particular, stand out.

Bernard Stuart of Aubigny (1447–1508)

First in chronological order and the most shadowy of the great mercenaries was Berault or Bernard Stuart, Seigneur d'Aubigny, likened somewhat extravagantly by one commentator 'for his battlefield skills to Robert Bruce'.[2] Bernard Stuart was a Franco-Scot whose family had branches both at Aubigny-sur-Neve and at Darnley in Renfrewshire. The Stuarts enjoyed a special relationship with the French and they might well have been among those who helped make up the bodyguards for the French kings from the 9th century onwards. Whether they did or not, in 1419 when the Dauphin, later Charles VII, requested a Scottish expeditionary force to help him gain the crown he specifically asked for Stuart of Darnley to accompany it. In 1421 this force beat an English army at the battle of Baugé and for his part there Stuart of Darnley received the lands of Concressault and later those of Aubigny-sur-Neve.[3]

From 1425 a full Scottish company certainly existed within the French royal bodyguard that accompanied the sovereign on all his campaigns in both France and Spain. Sir John Stuart of Darnley served continuously with them until 1445, during which year the French army was put on a permanent footing and the Scots company guarding the king with its 100 lances became officially known as 'Les Gendarmes Ecossais' and later the 1st Company of the Gendarmes. In fact the 100 lances represented a formidable force of 600 armed men. Each mounted knight was supported by a further five soldiers: his page and valet along with three archers, also mounted. All the knights were men of noble birth. The unit continued to be made up of Scots and remained the continuous responsibility of the Stuart family for an amazing 243 years. For all that time it remained unfailingly loyal to its French sovereigns, in spite of changing political relations between France and Scotland. Due to its constancy 'Les Gendarmes Ecossais', strikingly dressed in their white surcoats richly embroidered with gold and silver, came to take precedence over the fifteen companies of French men-at-arms – also nobly born – who had similar responsibilities to safeguard the monarch.[4]

The 1st Company enjoyed another privilege, that of providing a smaller detachment responsible for the actual person of the king. This was twenty-four in number with its commander (the first gentleman at arms of France) also selected from 'Les Gendarmes Ecossais'.

Bernard Stuart, Sir John's grandson, followed the family tradition by serving as a man-at-arms in the Scots Guards to the French sovereigns until he succeeded John Cunningham as its captain in 1483. Ten years later he succeeded Cunningham as Captain of the Scots bodyguard and held both posts until his death in 1508.[5]

A true mercenary, Bernard d'Aubigny spent all his military service outside Scotland, fighting in Spain, England and Italy, and through his leadership skills his family was to achieve its highest military glory.[6] As a young man and in a junior capacity he served with distinction under the Spanish monarch, Ferdinand of Arragon, against the Moors but during the next twenty years or so Stuart was to lead his devoted Scottish men-at-arms on behalf of two French sovereigns, Charles VIII and Louis XII, as they embarked on successive military campaigns within Italy. Charles VIII was the first king of all France and after his accession in 1483 Stuart was given the honour of representing him at the Scottish court of King James III when the two countries renewed their traditional alliance. Charles VIII also sent Stuart as his ambassador to the Pope to submit the French claim to the crown of the two Sicilies. In 1485 it was back to soldiering and Stuart accompanied a Franco-Scottish contingent to England in support of Henry Tudor. At the battle of Bosworth Field it contributed to the victory that led to Henry Tudor becoming Henry VII of England. In his poem 'Bosworth Field' the sycophantic courtier, Sir John Beaumont, paid high tribute to Stuart's contribution there.

> Whom Charles, for Henry's succour, did provide
> A lord of Scotland, Bernard was their guide,
> A blossom of the Steuart's happy line
> Which is on England's throne ordained to shine . . .

> Saw not a braver leader in that age
> And Bosworth Field must be the glorious stage
> In which this northern eagle learns to fly
> And tries those wings which after raise him high
> When he beyond that snowy Alps renowned
> Shall plant French lillies on Italian ground.

The accounts of the battle are far less specific as far as Stuart is concerned. We know that Henry Tudor's division under the overall command of John de Vere, Earl of Oxford, had Philbert de Chandée and Bernard Stuart as captains for the Franco-Scottish mercenaries along with the Welshman, Rhys ap Thomas, over the Welsh archers. Oxford's division spearheaded the rebel forces and certainly adopted a defensive formation that threw back an attack by the much superior forces of Richard III. Michael Bennet concludes that Oxford doubtless banked 'on the professionalism of his French and Scottish brigades' to sustain the raw levies amongst his troops.[7] Conjecture aside, we know that Oxford's success provoked Richard III into making his gallant but vain attack on Henry Tudor's bodyguard, which resulted in the king's death and absolute success for the rebel cause.[8]

Stuart's French sovereign, the hunchbacked Charles VIII, was reputedly not the easiest of monarchs to serve but he clearly appreciated both Stuart's military and diplomatic gifts. The diplomatic ones were again in evidence in 1488 after the Scottish king, James III, was murdered, when Stuart headed an embassy to Scotland in order to meet the new young sovereign, James IV, and reconfirm the alliance between Scotland and France.

Stuart's promise as a senior commander became evident when he accompanied the French forces that invaded Italy in 1494 to free it from Spanish control. After high early hopes the campaign turned into a protracted and mutually damaging contest that dragged on for over thirty years, although Stuart's contribution was restricted to its first half.

Charles VIII's invading army was, by the standards of the day, massive, with over 18,000 horsemen and, once in Italy, he had plans to raise its infantry strength to about 22,000. Unlike the earlier Italian wars involving the mercenary princes, the Condottieri, Charles VIII came seeking military adventure through battle rather than spending the greater part of his time in wars of manoeuvre. He even hoped to go on from Italy to crusade in the Holy Land. His army's strength, however, was soon reduced by having to place a string of garrisons in the cities it conquered. The highly rated Stuart was given an independent role and led 1000 horse across the Alps through the St Bernard and Simplon passes into Romagna, from where he joined the main French army. After crossing the Alps and advancing southwards into Florentine territory the French enjoyed a number of successes. Following the taking of Pisa on 15 November 1494 the king made a state entry into Florence with Stuart and his Scots guards accompanying him. Among a shower of awards that followed, Stuart was made a Knight of the Order of St Michael and promoted to general rank. From Florence the French forces moved downwards to Rome and Stuart obviously had independent command again for he was reported as bringing his men across the Appenine hills into Tuscany. In the event Rome did not resist and Charles VIII made a bloodless entry into the city.

During the following year Stuart saw renewed action as Charles VIII faced a fresh coalition of the Italian states masterminded by Spain. In June 1495 at Seminara, near the toe of Italy, Stuart gained a notable battlefield success over Ferdinand, King of Naples, and his redoubtable Spanish commander, Gonsalvo de Cordoba, who would become influential in the eventual eviction of the French from Italy. On this occasion Ferdinand made the fatal mistake of distributing much of his army within fortresses and was thus outnumbered. However, while he was at Naples Stuart contracted a lingering malarial fever which was to plague him for the rest of his life and the Italian chronicler, Francesco Guicciardini, was certainly of the opinion that the prosperous state of the French affairs began to decline on account of Stuart's long sickness. In fact, in July 1495 after a hand-fought battle at Fornovo in northern Italy where both sides claimed victory, both the northern and southern Italian provinces rose against the French and Stuart, who was operating in Calabria in the extreme south, experienced extreme difficulties against Gonsalvo de Cordoba. The French faced expulsion from Italy when Montpensier, the commander of the main French army, was compelled to surrender in July 1496 and this was confirmed when Stuart's own forces capitulated soon afterwards, although he was allowed to do so on honourable terms.

At the end of 1497 Charles VIII was collecting forces for a new invasion when he died in an accident. His plans for conquest were taken up wholeheartedly by his successor, Louis XII, and in 1499 the French expeditionary forces re-entered Italy. Initially their fortunes were mixed: they occupied the Duchy of Milan, only to lose it before re-occupying it in 1500. However, Louis XII's main aim was Naples. After making a secret compact with Spain not to oppose him there, he was confident the 1000 lances (of his men-at-arms), together with 4000 Swiss and 6000 French infantry, would be sufficient to overcome the defenders. Command of the forces was divided between Stuart, the Count of Caiazzo and the Duke of Valentinois. By skilful use of their artillery the French breached the walls and succeeded in occupying the city. Following this Louis XII appointed the Duke de Nemours as its Viceroy at which Stuart, who earlier had been governor of Calabria and could be prickly and jealous where his personal reputation was concerned, considered himself unfairly superseded and requested a return to France. This was refused; his battle skills were too valuable in Italy.

On Christmas Day 1502, Stuart confirmed such opinions by winning an engagement with the Spaniards with what he was convinced were inadequate forces. After further successive victories Louis XII gave him the honorary title of Duc di Terina. Elsewhere it was a different story and on 21 April 1503 Stuart was compelled to relieve the pressure on other French forces by attacking the Spanish at Seminara in Calabria. He was seriously deficient in artillery and pikemen, with his force largely made up from half-armed peasants. As a result he was heavily defeated.

To Stuart's despair, casualties among his Scottish veterans were high – no less than 300 Scottish men-at-arms and 60 archers were killed in the battle – and a French battlefield observer, Jean d'Autun, reported that the 'Seigneur d'Aubigny almost bereft of reason seeing his men all dead and prisoners ran here and there trying to rally his scattered soldiers.' He was about to return and make a lone attack on the Spaniards when his followers persuaded him to retire.

Eighteen days later he had plainly calmed down, for it was said he approached his Spanish conquerors apparelled in rich brocade and 'with a composed undismayed countenace, yielded himself upon condition that every one of his company should be set at liberty and himself only kept in free custody'. Stuart was imprisoned in the great tower of the Castel Nuovo until he was set free by the truce of 11 November 1503.

At sixty years of age Stuart accompanied King Louis XII on his successful seige of Genoa, but not as the senior commander. In spite of being much reduced physically he was not allowed to rest. Although he was granted his long-felt wish to visit St Ninian's shrine in his native country, he was at the same time required to consult with James IV of Scotland about a proposed marriage of the king's daughter, the Princess Claude, with the Duc d'Angoulême. Passing through England in 1508 the soldier who had fought at Bosworth Field more than twenty years before was lavishly entertained by Henry VII at Greenwich and on reaching Scotland was received by James IV, who graciously called him the 'Father of War', appointing him judge of the jousts and tournaments organised in his honour. However the long journey followed by continuing social duties proved too much for a weakened constitution. As he travelled from Stirling to Edinburgh he was taken ill and died.

Stuart was a chivalrous and accomplished leader of men-at-arms who remained unfailingly loyal to his French monarchs, but while the battlefields of Italy have been described as 'a vast melting pot of change', those in which Stuart fought were closer to the medieval world than the vastly different conditions seen towards the end of the Italian wars or those of northern Europe a century later.[9] In addition to his military skills Stuart proved himself as a diplomat and a man of culture. When acting as a military governor, he not only ruled with a notably light touch and involved local people in his administration but acquired a reputation for encouraging learning and the arts in the principalities that came under his control.

His treatise entitled 'The Duty of a Prince or General towards a Conquered Country'[10] advocated an even-handed and revenge-free approach that was centuries ahead of its time. On his death the Scottish court poet William Dunbar wrote a well-deserved eulogy to this remarkable soldier/diplomat, in which he addressed him as:

> Prince of freedom and flour of gentilness,
> Sweryd of Knyghtheid, and choise of chevalry[11]

Bernard Stuart d'Aubigny set a high standard for subsequent mercenary captains.

Sir John Hepburn (1598–1636)

Nine years after Stuart d'Aubigny's death came Martin Luther's challenge to the universal religion of north-west Europe. Along with the questioning of past values, including those relating to the rights of individual conscience and the self-determination of states, came a quickened scientific curiosity. The religious disputes brought a fresh approach to warfare and the Thirty Years' War, which ended with the Treaty of Westphalia in 1648, was fought with new weapons and amended tactics, even if some of the armies involved displayed a savagery more akin to the Dark Ages and reduced much of prosperous Europe into a desert region.

In the first part of the 17th century Scotland offered comparatively few opportunities for military adventurers and a remarkably large number of Scots sought action in Europe by joining the protracted struggles between Protestant and Catholic states there.

One of these was John Hepburn, a tall and powerful man who has been described by his biographer as someone 'who from his earliest childhood was remarkable for his high spirit, quick courage and invincible resolution'.[12] Whatever his physical activities, however, as a second son he could not expect to inherit the family estate. In 1620 when Sir Andrew Craig came to Monkrig, near the Hepburn home, seeking recruits for Frederick V, the Elector Palatine of Bohemia, to fight against Ferdinand II of Austria, the 1500 men who pledged themselves included John Hepburn. Frederick V's cause attracted popular support in Scotland because he was married to Elizabeth, daughter of James VI. Such considerations were likely to have helped to persuade Hepburn, a Catholic, to fight for a Protestant prince. Hepburn must have made a good impression for he was soon given command of a company of pikemen entrusted with guarding the Elector.

In November 1620 the Bohemian forces met those of Austria at the battle of the White Hill a few miles outside Prague. The Austrians quickly got the better of things and the Elector, a timid and inexperienced leader, fled, leaving his army to its fate. Despite taking some casualties the Scots companies succeeded in escaping and after a number of dangerous adventures offered their services to Sweden's Gustavus Adolphus, the so-called Lion of the North and arch defender of Protestantism. It proved a sound decision, for the Swedish king was not only a magnificent fighting soldier but Europe's leading military progressive. His reforms were both widespread and fundamental. He streamlined the cumbersome medieval divisions of foot into regiments of 1000 men each (the strength of what would become the classic British battalion), reduced the numbers of their ranks in battle to six – later to three – and split his infantry into two main groups, musketeers (carrying better-designed muskets with paper cartridges for their shot) and pikemen. Both were given improved equipment, including pouches to hold their ammunition which made them less dependent on re-supply. In support he introduced lighter and more portable field artillery. As for cavalry, he wanted it to resume its true offensive role: the practice of cavalry approaching the enemy, discharging their weapons and galloping away was ended, and henceforth after firing cavalry were to charge home with bared swords. Above all he insisted on his infantry, cavalry and artillery working closely together in a combined arms team. The Swedish king went on to improve the conditions of military life. He regularised punishments by making all ranks subject to general and regimental courts-martial and provided each of his regiments with four surgeons and two official chaplains. Each morning, prayers would be read to the troops who would be drawn up around their evangelical chaplains, although other religions were fully respected. The ribaldry and licence of other armies was strictly forbidden and in such an egalitarian, if highly disciplined army, the wearing of gaudy uniforms by officers was strongly discouraged.[13] The latter was not to Hepburn's liking. He apparently looked most impressive when dressed in the decorated half armour of the period and was by no means lacking in conceit.

Whatever his reforms, Gustavus still held resolve and aggression in battle as the most prized of military virtues. Here Hepburn's dash and ardour must have quickly caught the king's eye for by 1625 Gustavus had appointed him as commander of the Scottish regiment from which the First or Royal Scots of the British line evolved.

Since 1617 Gustavus had been warring against Poland in an effort to extend Sweden's control of the Baltic and its adjoining coastlines, and during 1625 Hepburn took part in the series of battlefield actions that marked him out as one of Gustavus' leading mercenary captains. At the relief of Mitau, near Riga, 3500 men, including Hepburn and his regiment, climbed a steep hill overlooking the town where they fell with incredible fury on the Polish soldiers who were in the process of entrenching themselves.[14] Afterwards they were compelled to hold off the whole Polish army numbering some 30,000 men, while Gustavus carried out the relief of Mitau itself. Hepburn took post on a rock around which fierce horsemen, both Cossacks and Heyducks, surged. They apparently taunted the Scots, shouting 'The Scottish arms cannot abide the bite of the Polish wolves'.[15] They were proved wrong for Hepburn and his men successfully defended themselves for two entire days against overwhelming odds. By the time of their relief it was estimated that each had killed at least one of the enemy, yet lost only a seventh of their own number.[16]

From this time it became customary for Hepburn to volunteer for any desperate duties that presented themselves. Hepburn's regiment accompanied Gustavus Adolphus when he invaded Prussia in 1627 and enjoyed a string of victories there. During the next year the Swedish king was joined by more Scottish and English veterans, together with some German mercenaries. From Scotland came remnants of its 'auld' standing army cast adrift by the Union of the Scottish and English crowns. The year 1628 was another successful one for Gustavus for, after failing to capture the fortress of Danzig, he led his army into Livonia and captured town after town before approaching the gates of Warsaw, the Polish capital. In August 1629, following a mutually costly battle at Stumm near the Polish city of Marienburg, Sweden and Poland agreed on peace terms.

This gave Gustavus Adolphus his opportunity to prepare for a great offensive campaign against Ferdinand II of Austria. In his battle-hardened formations there were now 1000 Scottish officers with 12,000 Scottish soldiers in whom it was said 'he always principally confided, conferring on them the glory of every critical and trying adventure'.[17] Among them Hepburn's regiment held a notable position for on many occasions its members were said to have proved themselves, 'patient of fatigue and privation, frugal, obedient and sober soldiers'.[18] Such conduct warranted promotion and from this time all references to their leader in the contemporary Swedish Intelligencer referred to him as Colonel Sir John Hepburn. So pleased in fact was the king with the battlefield performance of his Scots that he gave orders to raise yet another 8000 soldiers.

During June 1630 the offensive opened. Gustavus crossed the Baltic into Pomerania at the head of a small, but elite, army of veterans, including Hepburn's regiment which, along with three other Scottish regiments, was made into a brigade. Hepburn was put in overall command and his brigade was granted pride of place on the right of the line. Thereafter it came to be called Hepburn's Scots Brigade or the Green Brigade; by his thirty-first year John Hepburn could justly boast he had the privilege of heading the four best regiments of the Swedish army.

To bring the German Protestant princes over to him Gustavus needed battlefield successes and, in March 1631, the Swedish king suddenly left his winter quarters and moved further into Pomerania to clear it from Imperial control. His objective was the important fortress of Frankfurt-on-Oder which he intended to capture without the usual prolonged bombardment. For this Gustavus used Hepburn's brigade and one other. Under heavy supporting fire they crossed the fortress's fosse, waded the moat and having set their ladders against the outer wall were over it before the defenders rallied. Rushing to the nearest gate they used a petard to blow it in and poured into the town. The raiding party was headed by Colonels Lumsdell and Munro (Hepburn's lifelong friend), for although the brigade commander was up with the front ranks who reached the gate, he had been wounded in the knee. In fact he was only the second senior officer to suffer in this way during the year-long campaign. In typical fashion, as soon as his injured knee had been dressed Hepburn resumed command. The Scots earned much praise, for to take a fortified and strongly defended town by surprise and escalade was an unprecedented feat at the time.

The campaign continued and, in September 1631, Gustavus gained a major victory against the renowned Imperialist general, John of Tilly, at Breitenfeld in Saxony. This enabled him to dominate north Germany. At Breitenfeld Gustavus' experienced soldiers demonstrated high mobility, remarkable firepower and good co-ordination. For their particular contribution to the victory Gustavus publicly praised the Scots Brigade, 'being led and conducted by an expert and fortunate cavalier, the valiant Hepburn'.[19] It was, in fact, the brigade's charge that decided the battle.

So highly did Gustavus rate the Scots that he became reluctant to undertake any expedition of importance without the assistance of Hepburn and his veteran troops. In 1632 Gustavus was to meet Tilly again near Donauworth. Tilly held an immensely strong position barring the route to the Austrian heartland, but Gustavus attacked it and beat him once more. After this battle Hepburn's brigade were again given public thanks for their contribution. Following Tilly's death from wounds shortly after Donauworth, Gustavus clashed with the Imperialist's other legendary commander, Albrecht von Wallenstein. This was at Nuremberg where, in July 1632, the Swedish king had the worst of a drawn contest.

In June, prior to this battle, the strain of constant campaigning began to tell on both Gustavus Adolphus and John Hepburn: both had been wounded, Gustavus on three occasions, the latest of which still troubled him. He had become extremely irritable and the two men clashed when Hepburn felt himself slighted by being passed over in favour of a younger officer, Sir John Hamilton, for a dangerous assignment. The blood ran high between them and at one point a furious Gustavus not only upbraided the Scotsman for the richness of his apparel – one of the king's favourite themes – but reproved Hepburn for his religion. As Hepburn was a Catholic fighting for a Protestant prince this was intolerable. Hepburn's own fiery temper made him incapable of taking sharp words even from a king and he immediately resigned his commission and haughtily withdrew.[20] Gustavus was fully conscious of his own irritability – he had apologised earlier for it during one of his war councils – and tried to make amends, but Hepburn proved immovable. Although he undertook a further dangerous reconnaissance prior to the battle, on completing it he turned to the king and said: 'And now sire never more shall this sword be drawn in your service; this is the last time I will ever serve so ungrateful a prince!'[21]

As Hepburn prepared to leave, all the Scottish officers serving in the Swedish army accompanied him along the first mile of his road, and Colonel Munro, his especial friend, said the separation was like that which death makes betwixt friends and the soul of man. In November of the same year the Swedish king was killed during the battle of Lutzen when he and a small group had become detached from their accompanying cavalry. Coincidentally, this was the first occasion on which he had engaged the enemy without the direct support of his Scottish troops who, under their new commander Sir John Henderson, were in reserve.

For Hepburn there was a brief interval in his fighting career before, early in 1633, he offered his sword to Louis XIII, the French king, who eagerly accepted him into the French service. In March 1633 Hepburn left France for Scotland to raise 2000 men. By August he was back with his full quota, whom he described as good men, mostly gentlemen. The remnant of the Scots Archery Guard to the French kings was incorporated into his regiment and on the strength of this Hepburn's troops claimed to be the oldest regiment in France, a claim resented by the Picardy regiment, raised in 1562, who, in scorn, nicknamed Hepburn's men 'Pontius Pilate's Guards'.

Hepburn took part in the French conquest of Lorraine and in September was appointed Marechal-de-camp (brigadier-general). Under the more relaxed regime of the French army Hepburn could freely indulge his love of rich dress and he succeeded in becoming friendly with France's noted soldier, the Duke of Vallette, along with the Duke of Richelieu, who was apparently amused by his blunt manner and foreign accent.

Hepburn's regiment was long remembered in France for its haughty and spirited soldiers of fortune and 'proud as a Scotsman' became a well-known saying among the French. In spite of Gustavus' death, the Thirty Years' War continued and, in 1635, Hepburn and his troops were engaged when the French armies, who had now intervened on the Protestant side, gained a succession of victories over the Imperial forces. While he was with the French rearguard Hepburn was captured by the Imperialists, but he pretended to be a German and gave orders in the language 'with so much assurance that they felt it quite an honour to let him go'.[22] About the same time Duke Bernard of Weimar joined forces with the French and the remnant of the Scots brigade that accompanied him was incorporated into Hepburn's regiment, which thus became 8300 strong. At the ceremony of amalgamation it was reported 'that the last solitary piper of Mackay's Highlanders blew a prolonged and loud welcome on the great war pipe of the north'.[23] During 1635 the brigade was frequently engaged and as its strength had been increased to twenty companies, Hepburn asked that it take precedence over any other. In addition he requested that an Austrian named Meternie who had been captured, be considered his own prisoner 'as the 4000 crowns ransom would be of service to him'. He even hinted that if his requests were refused his dignity would not allow him to stay in the French army.

Both wishes were granted although he had not received the ransom when, in the following year, the regiment led an assault against the Imperialists at Saverne in Alsace. Typically, Hepburn volunteered to examine the principal breach, but while doing so he was shot in the neck and died two hours later. While he was sinking he expressed the characteristic regret of so many Scottish wanderers that he would not be buried in his native kirkyard along with the bones of his forefathers.

Immediately before his death, as a recognition of Hepburn's fighting qualities, Louis XIII had ordered the diploma of a Marshal of France to be sent 'to Le Chevalier d'Hebron under the Royal Seal'. Sadly he died before the baton and diploma could be placed in his hands. He was buried in the southern transept of Toulon cathedral and the French gave him the proudest of epitaphs, namely:

'The best soldier in Christendom, and consequently in the world'

Nor did they forget their financial obligation: Hepburn's nephew was page to Richelieu and Meternie's ransom was assigned to him.

John Hepburn was the 'beau sabreau' among Scottish soldiers of fortune rather than a senior commander of the first rank. He was more impetuous and less thoughtful than D'Aubigny, fiercely proud, always liable to take affront but unfailingly loyal to whatever sovereign he served. And along with his greatest master, Gustavus Adolphus, Hepburn never lost his eagerness to shoulder the greatest risks on the battlefield.

General Patrick Gordon (1635–1699)

Patrick Gordon was a soldier of the late 17th century. Unlike D'Aubigny and Hepburn, his allegiance was to Muscovy, the vast country bestraddling Europe and Asia, and to two of its Tzars in particular, Alexis Mikhailovitch and Peter the Great.

Gordon was born at Auchleuchies in the parish of Cruden, Aberdeenshire. His father, John Gordon, was of modest standing, being a guidman (a yeoman), and the family lands of Auchleuchies came from his wife. John Gordon was also a staunch Catholic and a supporter of the Stuart monarchs. Patrick grew up in turbulent times marked in Scotland by the military clashes between Montrose, fighting on behalf of his Stuart King, Charles I, and Archibald Campbell, 1st Marquis of Argyll, leader of the Covenanting forces. With nine sons, money was understandably short in the Gordon family and they suffered other disadvantages, the most notable of which was that as Catholics the Gordon boys were banned from attending a Scottish university. Patrick was therefore sent to the Continent to complete his education. After two years spent in a Jesuit college at Braniewo near Koenigsburg, where he showed no inclination whatever for the clerical life, running away and at age nineteen enlisting as a soldier in the army of Charles X, King of Sweden.

In 1655 Sweden declared war against Poland and in June of 1656 Charles X marched against Warsaw with its garrison of 50,000 men. During the seige Gordon was wounded and taken prisoner by the Poles who freed him on condition he joined them. After the Swedes re-took the city he was welcomed back into their army. At this time he acted in the dangerous capacity as a marauder who collected much-needed food and supplies. While acting in this role he was caught by the Poles and accused of robbing a church for which he was sentenced to death, only to be saved by the intervention of an old Franciscan monk.

When in 1661 Sweden concluded peace with Russia, having already come to terms with Poland and Denmark, their army was run down and Gordon's services were no longer required. After being rejected by the Austrians he approached the Russians and, by imaginatively recounting his military experiences so far, drove an unquestionably good bargain, being offered service in Tzar Alexis' army with the rank of major. Under Tzar Alexis veteran soldiers were much sought after and in 1663 there were 60,000 foreign troops in the Russian service, including a Scottish legion.[24] Gordon's first military task was to deal with civilian rioters at Moscow. He put the disturbances down in an unsqueamish and efficient manner, for which service he was promoted lieutenant colonel. His biographer, Baroness Buxhoeveden, talks of Gordon's character as a strange combination of the highest Christian thought with a practical, hard and calculating mind.[25] If she is correct it is perhaps not surprising to find him calculating, for he could hardly be expected to forget his family's treatment in Scotland for supporting the wrong dynasty. It was vitally important, therefore, for a foreign soldier serving in Muscovy, where there was a well-known hostility to strangers, to act according to contemporary precepts. Any undue leniency with the rioters, for instance, would not have been appropriate in Russia at that time, nor in his best interests.

Gordon became accepted by the elite of the Scottish residents in Moscow and, in January 1665, he married Catherine Von Bockhoven, a strong Catholic whose father had served in Charles I's foreign legion. The Tzar, conscious of Russia's political isolation at this time, gave Gordon his own mark of approval by choosing him as his envoy to England where Gordon was to assure Charles II about the continuing privileges offered to British merchants in Moscovy. Alexis was in the habit of using foreigners for such tasks rather than his own nobles who too often made hapless ambassadors, but it still represented a signal honour. In England in 1667 Gordon was graciously received by the king who gave him a present of £200. Five years afterwards Gordon was again sent as the Tzar's envoy to Scotland.

During the 1660s Gordon became known in Moscow for his enthusiastic study of warfare, particularly the art of fortification and ballistics. He realised only too well that he and his fellow Scots would always be a potential target for jealous Muscovites and that his best response lay in displaying the highest professionalism. Gordon's wife died quite early in their marriage and when he married for a second time he chose Elizabeth Roonuer, a lady of Dutch extraction. It proved a canny decision, for with someone of her nationality he avoided becoming involved in the contesting Muscovite factions and they proved most happy together.

During 1677 Gordon distinguished himself in Russia's short war with the Turks over contested Russian lands on the right bank of the

Dnieper. Now reckoned to be the leading foreign soldier in the tzar's army, honours were heaped upon him. As the army's chief engineer, he was promoted to major general and appointed commander of Kiev garrison, at the time a key port in the defence of the Ukraine from renewed Turkish or Polish attacks. The Ukraine suited Gordon who was able to enjoy a more relaxed social life in Kiev than in Moscow and to suffer less discrimination for his Scottish nationality and Catholicism. It was here that his lifelong habit of keeping a diary began.[26]

With the unexpected death of Tzar Alexis in 1676 and that of his ailing successor Theodore in 1682, the Tzarina Sophia became regent as her brother Peter, the future tzar, was too young to assume control. The reactionary policies of the new administration did not find favour with Gordon and he showed it by requesting to go home. Initially Sophia refused, but permission was eventually granted for him to visit England as a Russian envoy and in that capacity he was treated warmly at the court of James II.

On his return to Russia, Gordon, a lifelong supporter of the Stuarts, bore a request from James to release him from his Muscovite service. Sophia would not consider the possibility of losing such a capable soldier, and she compelled him to sign an agreement to stay in Russia. Having given his word, Patrick Gordon realised from then on he had to accept that 'Russia had claimed him definitely'.[27]

In 1687 Gordon took part in Russia's Crimean campaign against the Turks with Sophia's favourite, Galitzen, appointed as its Field Marshal and commander-in-chief. The army was 100,000 strong along with 50,000 Cossack horsemen, but Galitzen was a poor commander and they suffered a series of defeats, losing between 40,000 and 50,000 men. This did not stop rewards being heaped on both Galitzen and other commanders, including Gordon, at the end of the campaign. Gordon's responsibilities had included the command of the Foreign legion as well as the Streltsy regiment, a hereditary national guard of Russian officers and soldiers originally founded by Ivan the Terrible. To his surprise Gordon found himself promoted to full general, but he had no illusions about the need for military reforms or of the hatred between Galitzen and tzar Peter's supporters. From now onwards he vowed to keep in personal contact with Peter, although he continued to be loyal to his military superior, Galitzen. It must have been both a difficult and dangerous path to tread. Gordon went with Galitzen to the Crimea for a second inconclusive campaign, where the Russians interpreted their retreat as a success. The field commanders were again rewarded but so unimpressed was Peter by their military achievements that he refused to meet them and Gordon freely acknowledged the justice of his reaction.

A break between the supporters of Sophia and Peter became inevitable when she began to make overtures with members of the Streltsy opposed to Peter. At this point a message was sent to the foreign officers warning them about a conspiracy against Peter and ordering them to report to him. Although Gordon communicated this to Galitzen he had already decided to declare his loyalty to Peter. It was obviously the right decision for at Peter's coming to power Galitzen was sent into exile and Sophia confined in a convent. As the new tzar took up the reins of government he made Gordon his chief military adviser and they became very close due to Peter's love of military manoeuvres and his frequent discussions with Gordon about necessary reforms to the Russian military establishment. The autocratic monarch even broke custom by visiting Gordon at his home, the first time a tzar had ever called on a foreigner, following which he made many further visits to Gordon's and other houses in the German suburb. Gordon had a great affection for 'the Great', as he started to call Peter long before the adjective came into general use. Yet, despite Gordon's impressive progress in the Russian service, Scotland remained in his thoughts; he was still ready to sacrifice all he had achieved in Russia to lay his sword at the feet of his hero, King James II.[28] On 15 November 1690 after William of Orange's accession to the English throne, Gordon gave his reactions to a leading supporter of the Jacobite cause, the Catholic Duke of Gordon: 'The sad revolution in our country . . . has occasioned inexpressible grief to me, which brought me in a sicknesse and even almost to death's doore . . . If there were any likelihood of doing any good and that I had a commission I am ready still to hazard lyfe and all I have in his Majesties service and for the maintaining of his just right and that in any place where His Majestie shall command in whatsoever quality I may be thought capable of . . .'[29]

Six months later Gordon had hopes that France and Russia would take joint action to help the Stuarts return to Britain but these were not realised and Gordon was compelled to watch as, at a dinner, Tzar Peter heartily toasted the new Protestant King of England. Gordon had the courage to remain seated and solemnly drink the good health of King James. To his credit Peter was not angry at such dissent, for Gordon had already proved his loyalty in Peter's own case. In 1694 Gordon, who was still the army's chief engineer, was given the additional rank of rear admiral when he and the tzar sailed together off Archangel. In fact, Gordon spent a great deal of time with Peter discussing the creation of a Russian navy, while at the same time pushing forward with innovations for the country's land engineers. Shortly afterwards Gordon's short temper (like that of D'Aubigny and Hepburn before him) led to a falling out with the tzar's Swiss general, Lefort, a staunch Calvinist and Peter's long-time favourite. Lefort was much younger than Gordon, recklessly brave but far less of a strategist. In the short term Lefort was preferred, being appointed to command a regiment of 16,000 men while Gordon's numbered just 3000.

In 1695 Tzar Peter embarked upon his first military campaign, against the Turks in the Crimea. Its object was the fortress town of Azof-on-Don which blocked Russian access to the Black Sea. Things were not well planned and there was no supreme commander although the last word rested with Tzar Peter who had insisted on limiting himself to the lowly rank of a bombardier sergeant. Gordon proposed digging entrenchments close to the town but he was overruled by both Lefort and the tzar. Gordon watched as the Russian attack on Azof failed at the cost of many casualties.

Peter was determined to succeed the next year. He had a number of barges and galleys built to help him seize command of the river and with them he cut off Turkish assistance for Azof. This time Gordon erected forts round the town and supervised the building of a massive mound of earth from which to dominate it, but before the work was complete Azof surrendered on 28 July 1696. The Russians had gained their long-awaited victory, and in their triumphal parade through Moscow Gordon placed himself last of the senior commanders, for he insisted on leading his Foreign legion, but he was upstaged by Peter who was still further back, heading his bombardiers. The exchange apparently delighted both men.

In 1698 Tzar Peter went abroad to learn about ship building and in his absence Gordon was made joint commander of the Moscow garrison. Once more he was to help save Peter's throne when, taking advantage of Peter's absence, an army of Streltsys loyal to the Tzarina Sophia marched on the capital. Gordon's regular soldiers routed it and selected prisoners were put to the torture. On their own evidence twenty-four were condemned to death by beheading; following this the rebels were decimated and further conspirators hanged. However, on his return the tzar considered Gordon had, if anything, been far too lenient and hundreds more were condemned to be axed or hanged.

This was to be Gordon's last military initiative, although Peter continued to call on him for advice. With the full knowledge of the Tzar, Gordon came to champion Catholics living in Russia openly. During Gordon's last short illness Peter came to see him five times, the last two visits on the night he died. When a Jesuit appeared with the patient's last sacraments the tzar asked him to perform his offices despite his own presence. At the end Peter turned to the Jesuit and said, 'He is indeed dead, Father', and the hard, twitchy face of the great tzar was bathed in tears.[30] The tzar walked at the head of Gordon's funeral cortege and a monument was raised to him in the centre of the old Catholic church in Moscow. Peter the Great plainly loved this agreeable foreigner with his high intelligence, good common sense and practicality who, in later years, acted as a father figure to the lonely autocrat. Gordon's continuing loyalty to his Stuart king and his Catholic religion only served to remind Peter of his constancy.

Patrick Gordon was certainly no military genius nor, as a soldier of fortune in Russia, was he given full independent battlefield command. In his early days he had to dissimulate and adapt as conditions demanded, but when Peter the Great came to power he was able to play a significant part in helping the tzar modernise Russia's unwieldy and hitherto backward military establishment.

James Keith (1696–1759)

A military adventurer of the 18th century, James Keith's highest success came while serving the Prussian Royal House and its 'enlightened' monarch, Frederick the Great, although by the time he joined Frederick he had already spent twenty-one years serving other European sovereigns. By no means a typical mercenary officer, Keith came from one of Scotland's leading families which, for 700 years, had provided the country with its hereditary marshals. However, as a younger son, he had no such expectations. Born at the castle of Inverugie, near Peterhead, he attended the local school before being educated privately by his kinsman Robert Keith, Bishop of Fife, and then by William Meston, the Jacobite poet. This was followed by a period at Aberdeen University where, as a member of Marischal college founded by his great grandfather, Keith could not fail to be aware of his family's prominence. He went from there to read law at Edinburgh, but he was determined to join the military and in 1715 he was on his way to London to seek a commission when he met his brother George, the 10th Earl of Marischal, who was hurrying north to take part in the ill-fated insurrection led by the Earl of Mar on behalf of James Francis Stuart, the 'Old Pretender'. Both brothers fought bravely at the Battle of Sheriffmuir on the flank where the Jacobites drove their opponents before them, although the younger Keith was wounded in the action. Elsewhere the Earl of Mar's disastrous leadership, together with the resoluteness of his opponent, the Duke of Argyll, ensured all would be lost.

With the flight of the Pretender to the continent, Keith and his elder brother were themselves forced to leave Scotland. Nevertheless, even after such an unsatisfactory experience Keith was sure he had found his vocation as a soldier. He justified his decision with the observation: 'Command true gentlemen to stand before the mouth of a cannon for a few minutes, this either makes a man in an instant or he dies gloriously in the field of honour.'[31] It was a test he had passed himself at Sherrifmuir.

Whatever enthusiasm Keith might have had for military life, Europe at that time must have seemed an unpromising place for a young adventurer who favoured the Stuarts' return to the English throne. The great powers were either at peace or on friendly relations with the Hanoverian king of England. Keith occupied his time with more study, this time at Paris University, where he read mathematics, although he continued to make applications to serve in the armies of both Sweden and Russia. He was unsuccessful in both cases.

James Keith's frustrating inactivity ended when Spain declared war against England over England's opposition to Spain's designs in the Mediterranean, and invited Scots, including the brothers Keith, to serve in a Spanish army intended to support a Stuart restoration. In 1719 the Spanish fleet with 6000 soldiers on board (mostly Irish) sailed for Scotland but it was scattered by a storm off Cape Finestere. However, a tiny force of 307 Spanish infantrymen, under the joint command of the Earl of Marischal and the Earl of Tullibardine, did manage to land off Loch Alsh below Eilean Donan Castle. They were accompanied by James Keith and a small group of Jacobite exiles from France. Supplies and ammunition were short and this unrealistic attempt to arouse Scotland ended with the Battle of Glenshiel where the invaders, together with the relatively few clansmen who joined them, were routed. Keith was once more on the run and after three months of hiding he sailed for Holland. Meanwhile, the Spanish Cardinal Guilio Alberoni, who had favoured war with England, fell from power and in 1720 peace was agreed between the two countries. The swashbuckling Keiths must have impressed for, although Europe was once more at peace, Philip V of Spain offered them permanent commissions in his army. James rose to the rank of colonel and took part in the Spaniards' unsuccessful siege of Gibraltar during 1726–7, but because of his Protestant beliefs he thought it unlikely he would rise much further, and so in 1728 he asked for leave to go to Russia. This was granted, if reluctantly, and before he left Madrid he was given the rank of temporary major general. Despite this no one could say that Keith's career as a soldier of fortune had, as yet, been a marked success.

In 1729 the young tzar, Peter II, offered him a lieutenant colonel's commission in his new regiment of guards appointed to protect the monarch; Keith acquitted himself so well here that he was shortly put in command. On the death of Peter II in 1730, the new Empress Anne Ivanowna confirmed Keith's appointment. When a change of monarchy in Poland brought war between the two countries, the Russian forces, including Keith, forced the Poles to abandon Warsaw after a siege that cost the attackers 8000 men. Keith so distinguished himself by his energy and fearlessness under heavy artillery fire that in 1734 he was made a major general.

War between Russia and Prussia followed soon afterwards and the Empress sent 14,000 men under Field Marshal Lascy to assist her allies, with Keith as his second-in-command. After an involved campaign Keith found himself responsible for all Russian troops in the Ukraine. There he enforced strict water discipline to counter a serious attack of dysentery and had entrenchments dug to block attempted incursions by the Turks and Tartars which promised to delay the Russian campaign for the following year. When this opened in 1737 Keith served with Marshal Munnich. During the Russian seige of Otchakoff, defended as it was by 20,000 crack Turkish troops, the Russians were embarrassed by the non-arrival of their field artillery, but the gallant conduct of Keith, who exposed himself perpetually and was seriously wounded, helped to bring about the unexpected capture of the fortress.[32] For his outstanding conduct the Empress sent him a present of 10,000 roubles and raised him to the rank of lieutenant general. His disregard for danger had led him to be wounded on two previous occasions, but this time a ball lodged in the interior of his thigh, preventing him from taking any further part in the campaign, which ended with the Russians surrendering their conquests. His wound went septic and amputation was recommended but his brother arrived and took him to Paris where some fragments of cloth were successfully extracted from the wound.

At Otchakoff Keith had earnestly recommended the sparing of lives and helped save a six-year-old child, even taking the trouble to send her to the Keiths' family home in Scotland where she received a liberal education and eventually took charge of the Earl Marischal's household.

Three years later the Russians appointed Keith as an envoy to England where, on 15 February 1740, he was presented to George II who received him as a successful soldier and the representative of a great power. At this time the Jacobite cause seemed hopeless and in London Keith abandoned his former Jacobite activities, formally acknowledging George II as his lawful sovereign, and recognising the House of Hanover as legitimate successors to the British throne. Peace, meanwhile, was concluded between Russia and Turkey and all the leading soldiers in the campaign were rewarded, Keith receiving a gold-plated sword and, far more importantly, being made governor of the Ukraine. From London he went directly to his new command.

In October 1740 the Empress Anne died, to be succeeded by an oligarchy. In the Ukraine Keith decided not to acknowledge them. Although he was stripped of his office this proved a sound decision, as the regime ruled for just twenty-two days until they were supplanted by the Empress' mother who rapidly re-confirmed Keith as governor of the Ukraine. There he proved a great success, quickly showing himself both incorruptible and even-handed.

With the Russians' renewal of war against Sweden in August, 1741, Keith returned to active soldiering under the command of Field Marshal Lascy. At Vilmanstrand during a successful attack on the Swedish vanguard Keith showed 'many instances of extraordinary courage and conduct'.[33] Meanwhile in November 1741, when another change occurred in the head of state, and Elizabeth, daughter of Peter the Great, mounted the throne, Keith had no hesitation in acknowledging her as the legitimate heir and his position had never seemed more assured. However, between her accession and the customary celebrations that followed a Muscovite campaign, Keith threatened to leave the Russian service as he considered his honour had been questioned. With his personal reputation at stake he showed no hesitation in hazarding all his impressive positions and privileges.

The Empress proved so determined to keep him that she awarded him the revered order of St Andrew, an honour normally restricted to Russian nationals, at which he agreed to stay on. When war resumed against Sweden, Keith shared in the Russian battlefield successes whereby the whole of Finland was conquered before Sweden accepted a Russian candidate for its king. After Denmark began to threaten Sweden, the Russians sent 10,000 men to support their new ally where Keith acted as commander-in-chief of the Russian forces and minister plenipotentiary to the Swedish court. He appeared equally successful in managing the conduct of the war and the negotiations for peace. His high reputation in the Ukraine must have undoubtedly helped for it was said of him that 'The least amount of disingenuity always disgusted him heartily; and he spoke out very plainly . . . when he met with usage of this kind'.[34]

In 1745 Keith was again made commander-in-chief of the Russian forces, this time for service against the Prussians, although peace was concluded before the forces clashed. With peace came a rising animosity towards foreigners serving on the Russian establishment and Keith found himself stripped of all his commands, except for two militia regiments. At such treatment he requested permission to leave; this was granted and, after consulting his brother, the Earl Marischal, he travelled to Berlin.

There the King of Prussia was only too anxious to enlist such an able soldier into his army and at the same time deprive the Russians of his further service. Frederick was prepared to pay a high price; in September 1747 James Keith was made a Prussian field marshal along with being appointed governor of Berlin. The Berlin Royal Military Academy gladly admitted him and whilst he was there he established a system of war-gaming, whereby strategy and tactics for large bodies of troops could be practised in miniature. He used to 'play' with the Prussian king and Frederick had cast about 20,000 small statues of men in armour. 'These he would set on a table opposite to each other and range in Battallia in the same manner as he was drawing up an army.'[35]

With Prussia, a state that depended for its continued existence on its army, theory soon gave way to practice. In 1756 when Frederick the Great determined to increase Prussian power by invading Saxony, Keith commanded the forces that entered nearby Bohemia. On this campaign Christopher Duffy has no doubt that Keith was not only prized by Frederick for his experience but for his courage and his resourcefulness in action.[36] Frederick certainly needed good supporting generals for he faced the formidable alliance of Austria, Russia, France and Sweden, together with other German states. During the campaign's early stages Keith was at the battle of Lobositz against the Austrians, where he rivalled the king in disregarding danger and where, at the battle's turning point, he gave orders for the Prussian infantry to advance.

During the next year Keith commanded a 32,000 man corps at the successful battle of Prague. The operations that followed were far less favourable but Frederick showed his continuing trust in Keith by giving him the difficult task of withdrawing the royal army from Bohemia. On 5 November 1757 Keith shared in the Prussian victory at Rossbach where 21,000 Prussian troops gained the upper hand over about 60,000 opponents, of whom over 30,000 were French. Keith's skilful use of his own battalions had a powerful influence on the successful outcome.

In 1758 Frederick again faced much superior numbers as he attempted to cut the Austrian lines of communication. Near the town of Hochkirch the Prussian right wing, including Keith, was in a dispersed formation. Keith had already warned Frederick about the probability of a surprise attack when, at 5 a.m. on 14 October 1758, in heavy mist, he was set upon by overwhelming numbers of Austrians. Keith's message to the king said: 'I shall hold out here to the last man and give the army a chance to assemble. We are in the hands of God, and I doubt whether we shall see each other again.'[37]

In the close combat the Austrians caught the sounds of Keith's voice attempting to rally his men and they concentrated their cannon on him. He received two serious wounds, the first when the fleshy part of his left arm was torn off, at which he still refused to leave the field, and the second when a musket ball hit him in the stomach and plucked him dead from his horse. His body was returned to the Prussians, who buried him with great pomp and solemnity, with Frederick himself acting as a chief mourner.

All Keith's possessions went to his mistress, Eva Merthens, whom he had met during his Russian campaigns and who survived him for a remarkable fifty-three years.

As a soldier Keith was by far the greatest of the four remarkable Scottish mercenaries. He commanded at a more senior level than the other three and was the inventor of 'Kriegspiel', the playing out of future battles, which is seen today in the virtual reality of computer technology. Like the others he was a man of fine manners and cosmopolitan culture but only too liable to take offence at anyone who questioned his honour. Like lesser soldiers of fortune the famous four, in their different ways, provided the professionalism and the steel core for armies that would always include a number of partly trained and unbloodied men, and gave their adopted masters a loyalty of service seldom equalled by their own nationals.

During the late 1630s with civil war in Britain virtually inevitable it was no wonder the continent was scoured for such veterans and strong inducements were offered to persuade them to come home. This applied not only to Scottish but to English and Irish veterans as well. To their surprise those who returned would discover they did not long have the field to themselves and other men would excel who, at least in the war's early stages, had no knowledge of military command. Among these would come a middle-aged English squire and a young idealistic Scottish nobleman.

CHAPTER FOUR

COVENANT AND CIVIL WAR – MONTROSE, LEVEN AND LESLIE

'Fight for Freedom and Truth'

Ibsen, *An Enemy of the People*

A MONG THE SOLDIERS OF fortune who returned from the continent in 1638 to save their country from probable attacks by the English were Alexander Leslie (soon to be Lord Leven), a senior soldier with the Swedish army commanded by King Gustavus Adolphus, and David Leslie, an energetic and fearless cavalryman also in the service of the Swedish king. Both returned to support Scottish Presbyterianism – the system of church government with a democracy of laymen who elected their parish ministers and were represented at all stages leading up to the kirk's controlling 'body', its General Assembly, which replaced the traditional hierarchical system working upwards from parish priests to bishops.

At the General Assembly ministers of religion sat side by side with lairds and members of the nobility to decide on matters of both church and state. Leven and Leslie were firm supporters of the so-called 'National Covenant with God' signed in 1638 by representatives from every parish through Scotland. The Covenant declared Episcopacy (the rule by bishops) abolished despite moves in its favour by Charles I, and restored the full Presbyterian government of the church. Although the Covenanters superscribed their document with the words 'For God and the King', the Covenant could be taken to mean that support for their king was only valid if he upheld Presbyterianism.[1] This was the Leslies' interpretation and it was to lead them into the swiftly eddying currents of the Civil War where they gave their support at different times to their monarch Charles I, to the English Parliamentarians who opposed Charles I, to the extreme Covenanter party in Scotland led by the Duke of Argyll and finally to Charles II after he had come to an accommodation with Argyll. As far as their loyalty went, things had been far simpler when they served Gustavus Adolphus.

Prominent as both men were in the military affairs of Scotland, their leadership did not go unchallenged, for in 1643 when the main Scottish army under Leven, with Leslie as its cavalry commander, was supporting the English Parliamentarians against King Charles I, another commander appeared in the shape of James Graham, Marquis of Montrose. Although in the initial stages Montrose had been one of the most enthusiastic supporters of the Covenant, he would embark on a campaign for his king, Charles I, against the Scottish Covenanters that would mark him out as one of the most colourful figures of Scottish military history. A poet and intellectual, chivalrous and daring, he was to develop from a brilliant leader of irregular troops into a commander far in advance of most of his contemporaries in his mastery of the battlefield.

James Graham, Marquis of Montrose (1612–50)

Whereas Robert Bruce had fought to establish his dynasty as kings of all Scotland and to regain Scottish independence from the English crown, Montrose fought against the majority of his fellow Scots for a king who was ruler of both nations. Montrose's Stuart king, by his tactlessness, duplicity and belief in divine kingship, had already aroused a clear majority of formidable opposition both north and south of the border.

Montrose's own road prior to 1643 had hardly been a straight one. He first took up arms under the overall command of Leven in an attempt to force the king to recognise the Covenant; but this in no way affected his belief in the monarchy as an institution, and he was firmly against giving licence to his own country's over-weaning aristocracy.[2] Montrose particularly distrusted Archibald Campbell, Duke (later Marquis) of Argyll, the powerful leader of the Covenanting movement whom Montrose considered opposed the king for the worst reasons, because as Montrose put it, 'he had ambitions to be dictator of all Scotland after the Roman fashion'.[3]

Montrose had thought deeply on the issue of sovereignty and

accepted the necessity of some power over the people above which power there was no greater on earth. But it had to be far from absolute, 'limited by the laws of God and nature, the law of nations and what Montrose called the law fundamental to the country'.[4] Whether Montrose was ever as steadfast in his convictions as his admiring biographer John Buchan would have us believe, or was in fact 'a man racked by doubts and uncertainties, desperately trying to come to terms with a situation created by history',[5] as Edward Cowan concludes, he undoubtedly followed his own interpretation of events, even if this was at variance with the majority of his countrymen, including many of his noble friends. In the 17th century someone who was consciously out of step and found himself on the losing side was only too likely to lose his head or worse. Montrose fully understood this and put his philosophy into heroic verse:

> He either fears his fate too much
> Or his desert are small
> Who dares not put it to the touch
> To win, or lose it all.

By the autumn of 1643 when the Covenanters signed an agreement with the English whereby the Scottish army would support the Parliamentarians against the king if the English would accept Scottish Presbyterianism, Montrose concluded it could only lead to anarchy and the tyranny of Argyll. The only hope for his country lay with the success of Charles I, whom he believed had by that time accepted all the demands of the National Covenant. He therefore offered his sword and his life to Charles. It was Montrose's tragedy, and for that matter the tragedy of other Jacobite generals, that the Stuart sovereigns were not the great, good and just men their followers expected them to be, nor were their causes always worthy of such whole-hearted devotion.

In fact in January 1644 when the Scottish army commanded by Leven crossed into England to support the Parliamentarians the Civil War seemed finely balanced. But following the victory of the combined forces of the Scots and English Parliamentarians at Marston Moor in July 1644 the tide was turning strongly against the king, particularly in the north. By the time Charles I agreed to accept Montrose's help Scotland was firmly in the hands of the Covenanters 'and the greater part of the nobles had joined their standard'.[6] Montrose's task was to threaten Scotland in the hope of drawing back the bulk of the Scottish army that had invaded England. The king offered him the title Captain General of the royal forces in Scotland, but Montrose declared himself content to be called the lieutenant general. The forces allocated for his great task were distinctly modest, although the King had agreed that Ranald MacDonald, the Catholic Earl of Antrim, should raise men in both Ireland and the Isles and land them on the west of Scotland to keep Argyll occupied. Additionally, Montrose was to be given a party of horse from the Marquis of Newcastle's forces in the north of England and hopefully some German cavalry from the King of Denmark. In fact Newcastle was unwilling to part with any forces while the Scottish army was close to him and Montrose crossed the border with no army at all, just two companions. As he moved northwards he heard by chance that Alastair MacColla MacDonald, together with his Irish brigade, had landed at Kintyre on the west coast of Scotland and had moved into Lochaber, accompanied by their women and children. Montrose ordered MacDonald to a rendezvous at Blair in Atholl country. On receiving Montrose's message MacDonald promptly seized Blair castle, not only to the anger of the local clans but to the jeopardy of the whole enterprise. Montrose donned Highland dress for the meeting and, after a twenty-mile walk, he was greeted enthusiastically by both the Irish, now reduced to about 1100 soldiers following clashes with their legendary enemies the Campbells, and by 800 Athollmen under Donald Robertson, tutor of Struan. The next morning Montrose formally raised the royal standard on a small mound near Blair castle. It was as well for Montrose that he met MacDonald when he did for at Atholl the Stuarts and Robertsons had put out the fiery cross to raise the clans against the Irishman and his wild followers. Without Montrose's authority as the King's Lieutenant and the belief of the western clansmen that he alone could challenge Argyll, who attracted their mutual hatred, the movement would never have developed.

It would be wrong, however, not to acknowledge from the outset the crucial role played in Montrose's exploits by Alastair MacDonald and his Irish brigade. MacDonald himself was already a veteran of many military clashes in Ireland. The son of a Colonsay chief known as Colla Crotach (Coll who can fight with either hand) his name became shortened to Colkitto. Like William Wallace before him,

Colkitto was a man of great stature: 'As a boy he had wrestled Highland bulls in Colonsay and full-grown he was accounted the greatest warrior among his father's people. He was sullen-tempered, proud as Achilles, and he drank "strong-waters" – sometimes too deep.'[7] The story went that when he demanded command of the expedition to Scotland, he did so on the grounds that 'My sword is wielded by the best hand in Ireland'. When another Irish captain challenged him as to who was second best he reputedly tossed his sword from his right to his left hand and replied 'It is there'. When Alexander Leslie went as commander-in-chief to Ireland he noticed the huge Colkitto and, rightly marking him as a dangerous enemy, had tried to recruit him by persuading Argyll to release his father, whom he kept fast in one of his remote dungeons because the old chieftain had disputed MacCallein Mhor's claim to the family's land. Argyll refused and consequently Colkitto was to form a remarkable partnership with Montrose, who invariably placed him and his veterans in positions of responsibility on the battlefield. But while Colkitto was a tower of strength in a fight and had a fine eye for ground, he did not share Montrose's sense of strategy. The Irishman's impetuosity tended to lead him into trouble, and too much should not be claimed for him at the expense of Montrose. Only Montrose could have persuaded the clans to accept Colkitto and his savage followers, and Montrose was able to succeed in battle when Colkitto and the bulk of his men were absent. In fact, the Irish who were such a great asset to Montrose on the battlefield tended to be a serious liability off it.

Nevertheless, Montrose and Colkitto enjoyed a year of amazing battlefield successes, stretching from Tippermuir on 1 September 1644 until the day of savage reckoning at Philiphaugh on 13 September of the following year. While Montrose's final campaign of 1650, which ended with his capture and execution, added to his romantic image and confirmed his bravery, his reputation as a military commander rests upon the *annus mirabilis* of 1644–5.

During that year of immense activity James Graham, a slim and still young man of thirty-two, quietly spoken, with a degree of wistfulness about his grey eyes, showed a nerve and capacity for daring, characteristic of history's great commanders. By his deeds he was to earn the near adoration of his followers and the high respect of his enemies. From the beginning he claimed no privileges over his soldiers; Wishart reported that during winter in the inhospitable Highlands he lived 'for the most part in the open air without quarters, without even tents. He endured all war's hardships with nothing to appease his thirst and hunger but icy water or melted snow, without bread and salt, and with only a scanty supply of lean and starveling cattle'.[8]

This was no romantic exaggeration for Montrose's eldest son, a boy of fifteen, died from his exertions in the harsh conditions. Such behaviour as Montrose's was important for any successful leader of irregular troops, particularly Highlanders, but it was essential for someone who was to require such immense physical efforts in his use of forced marches. Montrose needed this speed of movement to evade and outwit his opponents who, although they might not have vastly superior manpower at the point of conflict, could rely on unlimited reinforcements. After such manoeuvring in at least three of his battles – Auldearn, Alford and Kilsyth – he was to show that his leadership was in another class to that of his opponents. Meanwhile beneath its royal banner Montrose had a force far smaller than the 10,000 men Antrim had promised him, although his 1100 Irish and 800 Athollmen had an unexpected supplement from 400 bowman commanded by Lord Kilpont, the eldest son of William Graham, Earl of Airth and Monteith. The Covenanters had sent them to repel a band of Irish raiders but finding that Montrose carried the king's commission they agreed to join him. Despite their name the bowmen almost certainly brought with them some muskets and pikes.

Completely untried, Montrose's small Highland army was short of arms and ammunition and lacking in horse and cannon. It was also ringed with enemy forces and therefore had no choice but to attempt to break out. With this in mind Montrose led his ragged men into the rich valley of Strathearn where the Covenanter commander Lord Elcho waited with his Lowland levies, augmented by 800 troopers led by the local gentry.

The battle at Tippermuir on 1 September 1644 was in some ways a preview of those to come. Finding himself outnumbered and with no horse to match those of his opponents, Montrose thinned his lines to three.[9] Colkitto took the centre with his Irishmen, while Lord Kilpont and his bowmen were on the left together with a company of men from Lochaber. Montrose himself took the right with the Athollmen, both Robertsons and Stuarts.

Before the battle Montrose sent out an envoy, the master of Madertie, under a flag of truce to postpone the battle from the Sabbath to the next day. The request was refused and despite the flag, Madertie was seized and subsequently hanged.

While the parley was in progress two troops of Covenanters' horse moved forward to take advantage of a slight realignment taking place in Montrose's line. They were observed and Irish skirmishers met them, driving them back in disorder to their own lines. At this Montrose ordered a general advance and, after overrunning the enemy's cannon, the Highlanders approached the main position so quickly that Lord Elcho's musketeers only fired a single volley. In the centre, Colkitto's Irish stopped immediately before the opposing centre and loosed off one murderous volley with their three ranks firing simultaneously, the front kneeling, the second stooping and the third standing, a tactic given them by Montrose. It was fortunate that it quickly proved effective, for no man carried more than a single round on him. The Highland charge, supported by volleys of stones from the otherwise unarmed clansmen, proved too much for levies used to more orthodox means: they broke and the pursuit began. Accounts vary about the Covenanters' casualties but it is probable that 1500 were killed and 1000 taken prisoner, a total equivalent to the Royalist's complete force. Montrose's own casualties were light but certainly higher than the two deaths he acknowledged. That evening he entered Perth, but sensibly kept the Irishmen from joining him in the city.

Tippermuir was a victory won not merely by boldness but by a leader who recognised the talent of his forces: the fighting qualities of the Irish; the need to involve his whole force even if they were reduced to using the stones at their feet as missiles; the superiority of the Highlanders in attack; and probably most of all, his ability to detect the tell-tale signs of his opponents losing heart. Despite the importance of this first success it came after Charles I's northern army had been destroyed and there seemed little chance of large contingents, either from the Highlands or beyond, joining Montrose unless he himself could transform the military balance and, by extension, the political position as well.

In the meantime in order to survive he would have to continue the strategy of catching and then defeating individual armies before they could unite and crush him with far superior numbers.

Montrose's next engagement occurred near Aberdeen. Here he had
1500 foot made up from 800–900 Irish, possibly 600 Athollmen
and some Gordons with about 70 horse, to the Covenanter Lord
Burleigh's 2500 foot and 500 cavalry supported by stronger artillery.
The Covenanting clans of the Forbes and Frasers provided about
1500 infantry while the rest came from nearby garrisons and through
a proclamation to all the townsfolk of Aberdeen between sixteen and
sixty years of age. The Covenanters occupied a strong position on
the crest of a hill. Their foot was in three divisions with 250 horse
on either flank. Their cannon which was positioned in front of the
main battle line could direct accurate fire against Montrose's men
below them. In the case of the Royalists, Montrose was in the
centre of his line of battle with the Irish brigade. During the initial
artillery and cavalry exchanges, the Covenanter artillery had much
the best of it, although Montrose's two small cavalry detachments of
some forty riders each did extraordinarily well against far superior
numbers. The Covenanters next tried to work round Montrose's
left flank. As he had no reserve he countered this by moving some
troops across from his right wing. The Covenanters now directed
a troop of horse against the Irish. As it rushed towards them at a
full gallop the veteran Irish allowed the heavy horses to thunder
through their ranks and kept them going by hacking at their flanks
with axes while those with ammunition discharging a volley at
their backs. The Covenanters had tried all their options without
success although they resumed their damaging cannonade. Montrose,
sensing the danger to his outnumbered force from such long range
action, ordered a general advance. His men tore up the hill and
crashed against the Covenanters' formations, which recoiled and
broke. The Covenanters lost about 700 men while the Royalists
admitted to seven deaths, almost certainly an underestimate! During
the preliminaries before the battle the drummer boy whom Montrose
had appointed to beat the parley was treacherously shot down and in
his anger Montrose ordered 'No quarter', and at least one of his Irish
regiments spent up to four days in Aberdeen. Over 100 townsfolk
were killed and many outraged. It was hardly a massacre but it
was contrary to Montrose's character and did not help in bringing
unattached recruits to his cause. Henceforth he was to keep a tight
hold on his men and no other comparable incident occurred under
his leadership.

There was little time to enjoy his victory since Argyll was close behind with some 4000 men, both horse and foot.[10] Montrose had sent Colkitto recruiting and was much reduced in numbers as other clansmen took their booty home, so he had no option but to lead Argyll a dance amidst the desolate areas of Badenoch before returning to Blair to await Colkitto and his expected reinforcements. Although at times Montrose was pressed hard, after several indeterminate clashes Argyll admitted himself outwitted and decided to end the campaign. He returned to Edinburgh where he surrendered his commission as general-in-chief to William Baillie of Letham, one of Alexander Leslie's best generals who had served under Gustavus Adolphus. From now onwards Montrose would have a formidable adversary.

Meanwhile Montrose had been heartened by the long-expected return of Colkitto who brought with him 800 fighting men from the western clans in addition to his Irish regiments.[11] They were spoiling for action, so Montrose took his army on a sweep into Campbell country. From Atholl they went to Loch Tay and then into Strath Dochart and Glen Fillan burning as they went, until they came to the head of Loch Awe and to Inverary. The castle's defences were too strong for them but they sacked the town and pillaged Campbell lands for miles around. While brilliantly successful the raid brought Montrose further problems, for according to custom many clansmen again left him to take their loot home. As a result Montrose found himself caught in the Great Glen with not many more than 1500 men when about 5000 Seaforths were mustering before him at Inverness, while to his rear 3000 Campbells were thirsting for revenge and yet another army was forming further south. Montrose's response was to take the offensive, and on 31 January he made the momentous decision to turn about, cross the inhospitable Highland passes and fall on the Campbell's positions round Inverlochy castle in Lochaber.

Strategically it was sound. Despite his successes the rising had still attracted limited support in the Highlands and none in the Lowlands. A blow against Argyll's homeland would be to the heart of the Covenant. But its execution was infinitely more difficult. How could he be confident that his 1500 men would defeat twice their number of Lowland levies and tough Campbell clansmen? To move them into the battle zone was another seemingly insuperable problem involving crossing the high passes over ice-laced rocks in the face of fearsome, scouring winds. Taking with them only the minimum of food, would they be in any condition to fight when they arrived? Would their precious troop of horse even survive such a hazardous journey? In the event the weather favoured them and despite a numbing east wind there was no blizzard. They had to take a circuitous route in order not to alert Argyll's scouts. They climbed out of the Great Glen onto the high plateau stretching towards the Pass of Corrieyarack and moved to Kilcummin, their furthest point north. From there they turned south over the moors and struggled over the shoulder of Carn Dearg (2500 ft) by Turret Bridge into Glen Roy. Due to enemy raiding parties they kept to the high ground along the Altan loin to the skirts of Ben Nevis. At five o'clock on the evening of Saturday 1 February they halted on the lower slopes of Meall-an-t'suidhe where through the gloom they could see the Campbell watch fires and the darker outline of Inverlochy Castle. In two days and a night they had covered over thirty miles of inhospitable country plodding through knee-deep snow and having to wade rivers up to their thighs. Before them was an army twice their size. At dawn Montrose unleashed his shivering and half-starved army down upon the Campbell encampment. The Irish holed the Campbells' flanks and then Montrose smashed the centre. Argyll made his escape by boat but their field commander, Sir Duncan Campbell, was killed, together with some 1500 others. On a smaller scale this march by Montrose over the high mountain passes to recapture the strategic advantage had parallels with Hannibal's arduous crossing of the Alps sixteen centuries earlier.

Montrose marched his victorious army up the Great Glen to Elgin where he sent proclamations throughout Moray for recruits to join the king's banner but the results were disappointing and when he moved to attack Dundee Montrose's army was in the greatest danger from superior Covenanting forces. By April 1645 it seemed as if his victory at Inverlochy had achieved little; he still had few men to match Covenanter forces in Scotland.

While recognising Montrose's qualities as a great commander John Sadler criticises him for his political naïveté. He writes 'He could win Scotland by his sword but he could not hold it ... The Year of Miracles was an impossible adventure sustained by a heady tide of success; failure brought reality and reality meant defeat'.[11]

However it was military reality not political naïveté that led to Montrose's undoing. There is, in any case, evidence that Montrose was far from naïve: unfailingly optimistic maybe, but acutely aware of the greater significance of his successes. There were, for instance, his letters to the king; on 20 April 1645 he wrote deploring the fact that 500 English cavalry had been promised but never sent to him.

> That had I but for one month the use of those 500 horse, I should have seene you with twenty thousand of the best this Kingdome can afford; though I may justly say I have continued things this halfe yeare bygone without the assistance of either Men, Armes, Ammunition, or that which is the nerffes of warre and I cannot chuse but think it strange that this unhappy Country which had beene the bane and cause of all your woes, being in so faire a way of reducing, that not only the ordinary but easy means should have been neglected.[12]

He went on to point out the interaction of his fighting with the king's other campaigns, namely that Parliament had sent regiments of foot from England to oppose him. In the event Montrose's messenger, James Small, was captured by the Covenanters and executed, so that Charles did not receive this letter. If he had, and in deciding to reinforce success had succeeded in marching north, the power of the Covenant could well have been broken in the northern areas and the lowland royalist sympathisers may well have given him their support. In such circumstances Montrose's 'impossible adventure' would have looked far different. But Charles' failure to receive Montrose's letter and his indecision about moving north enabled the Covenanters to block him with their army in England. And following the outright defeat of the king at the Battle of Naseby by Cromwell and his New Model Army all such hopes ended. It is difficult to see what more Montrose could have done from a political point of view and he certainly could not have done more militarily with the numbers at his disposal. In Scotland, although some of the northern Catholics came over to him, their support was often lukewarm and the Covenanters still kept a firm control over the middle and southern regions.

It was only a matter of time before Montrose faced a challenge from another Covenanting army, this time commanded by Baillie and Hurry. While Baillie was undoubtedly able, Hurry was the better strategist, energetic and confident, hell-bent on outperforming others and defeating the obstinate rebels. In early May he succeeded in luring Montrose along the north coast from Forres and Elgin towards Nairn where there were no royalist supporters. Then after receiving reinforcements from Inverness Hurry doubled back hoping to surprise his adversary. Montrose's army lay near the village of Auldearn close to Nairn and Hurry might have succeeded if it had not been for the sound of shots from some of his approaching infantry as they cleared their muskets of damp powder. Montrose was in a perilous position as he was outnumbered by at least two to one in a region unfamiliar to him. Retreat might have seemed his best option until he learned that General Baillie was moving northwards; if he did not fight Hurry he would be confronted by the two armies acting in conjunction. Montrose hardly had time to draw up his lines but nonetheless he did so with skill and rare cunning. He put 500 men of the Irish brigade to the north of the village in view of the enemy and placed the remainder, about 1750, together with his 250 cavalry, to its south, where they were hidden on reverse slopes. If Hurry marched into the trap and attacked Colkitto Montrose could fall on his flanks. To hinge the trap Montrose limited his centre to a few sharp shooters positioned in Auldearn's cottages. To Montrose's delight Hurry moved his 3500 foot and 400 cavalry headlong into the snare, but the plan was almost ruined by Colkitto who, after blocking the superior numbers of enemy, straightaway attacked those below and in front of him.

Inevitably, with odds of eight to one, the Irish were badly mauled and to relieve the pressure they attempted to regain the high ground. A mounted courier reported to Montrose that the Irish were done for; from his viewpoint Montrose could see the enemy milling round the Irish and saw the Covenanters' cavalry turning their back upon him. Seizing the opportunity he turned with incredible coolness to Lord Gordon and his cavalry and with a sang froid worthy of William Wallace at Stirling Bridge cried out: 'Why are we lingering here my dear Lord when our friend MacDonald is driving the enemy before him? Shall all the glory of the day be his?'[13] Emerging from concealment Gordon's cavalry charged, swords in hand, and their impetus scattered the Covenanters' cavalry under Major Drummond, entangling them with their own infantry. Simultaneously Gordon's brother, Viscount Aboyne, charged the enemy's left and Montrose brought the infantry against the centre. Hurry's army, including four front-line regular regiments, was destroyed with roughly 2000 casualties, while the royalists lost only approximately 200 men.

Stuart Reid, no uncritical supporter of Montrose, while emphasising the disorganised nature of the battle's early stages, acknowledged that despite the early alarms Montrose's forces were saved, not just by the tenacity of the rebels holding Auldearn itself, but by his decisive leadership and by his perfectly timed counter attack.[14] Montrose showed himself immeasurably superior to that of an experienced and determined opponent who commanded a force twice the size of his own. Hurry vented his anger on Major Drummond, his cavalry commander, who was immediately court-martialled and executed by firing squad 'standing on his feet but not at one post'.[15]

Hurry's army might be destroyed but after Auldearn the Gordons were recalled by their clan leader and with them went Montrose's cavalry. Lord Gordon and Colkitto were therefore sent off to recruit, for in his weakened state Montrose was in no position to offer battle. Despite his success he had gained precious little breathing space since General Baillie and Lord Lindsay of the Byres were still in the field. Indeed Baillie's forces crossed the Grampians on the very day of Auldearn and on 2 July 1645 he caught up with Montrose at the foot of the Correen hills, roughly 25 miles west of Aberdeen. Montrose drew up his army on Gallowhill ridge overlooking a ford over the River Don near the tiny township of Alford. For once Montrose had superiority of numbers as far as the foot were concerned, about 2000 men to Baillie's 1800, although this was more than offset by Baillie's superiority in cavalry of almost fifty per cent. However, to Montrose's delight Lord George Gordon had returned.

Montrose's formations were set out in his customary manner with his horse on both wings, 100 horse under Lord George Gordon supported by light skirmishers under Nathaniel Gordon on the right, with Aboyne supported by a small force of Irish on the left. His centre was mainly made up of Gordon foot together with the depleted Irish who, in the absence of Colkitto were commanded by Eneas MacDonald of Glengarry. His reserve under Archibald, master of Napier, was concealed by a slight depression. As before Montrose had much of his force on the reverse slopes both for their own protection and in order to confuse his enemy.

Baillie probably approached the Royalist position not from below Alford itself but at Mountgarrie, where there was a better river crossing and he could 'form up in relative security'.[16] Whatever his line of approach Baillie was under the impression the Royalists were continuing to withdraw, although Montrose was then swivelling his own troops round almost thirty degrees to face him. Baillie moved forward, with his much superior cavalry under Alexander Lindsay of Balcarres in the lead. Opposite Balcarres stood Lord George Gordon with his own cavalry. At this point the Gordons were apparently infuriated to see a herd of cattle with the Covenanting forces that had been stolen from them, and charged at Balcarres. A fierce fight occurred with Balcarres' superior numbers seeming most likely to succeed until Irish skirmishers placed on the right by Montrose joined in and caused much confusion by hamstringing their opponents' horses. Meanwhile on the other flank a charge by Aboyne's horse put the Covenanters under Colonel Robert Hackett to flight. With both their flanks exposed, the fate of Baillie's footsoldiers was now serious. They had been 'contesting every foot of ground at push of pike, but now, assailed on both flanks and in the rear, they simply gave way.'[17] When Montrose ordered his reserve forward a rout became inevitable. In the pursuit little quarter was given, for Montrose was distraught at the death in action of his greatest friend, Lord George Gordon, who was not only a brilliant cavalry commander but for Montrose 'the ornament of the Scottish nobility, the stoutest champion of royal authority in the north.'[18] He was the best of the Gordons, and Montrose's hold over those brilliant but fickle fighters was much diminished as a result of his death.

Once again the battle had started in an unexpected way, this time with Gordon's charge against the superior forces of Balcarres, but Montrose's tactical skills, including the initial positioning of his men, and more importantly the timing of Aboyne's cavalry charges and the commitment of his reserve carried the day. On this occasion he had not enjoyed the support of Colkitto, although the much-reduced Irish contingent once more fought with distinction.

Baillie's army was destroyed and Argyll who accompanied him narrowly escaped, having had two horses killed under him[19] – Montrose's own casualties were light in comparison but with his strictly limited support from the Scottish nobility any losses were important, particularly if they occurred among his leading lieutenants. At Aberdeen he lost Donald Farquarson, one of his leading commanders of foot soldiers, and now his outstanding cavalry commander, Lord George Gordon. As a measure of their loss the grieving royalists raised a monolith to Gordon on the battlefield that became known as the Gordon Stone.

Shortly afterwards Colkitto returned with 1500 men, in addition to his Irishmen, loyal clansmen came from Argyllshire, other parts of the west coast and the Western Isles. Although Montrose's cavalry was very weak he now had enough men to confront the Covenanter General Baillie. This had to be done quickly for an Act had been passed to levy a new Covenanter army of 10,000 foot and 500 horse. More important still 1000 foot and 500 horse were even then marching to join Baillie. For such reasons on 15 August 1645, less than six weeks after Alford, Montrose again faced the Covenanters in battle. Many battle wounds would scarcely have healed but in England the Royalist defeat at Naseby made it imperative for Montrose to intervene on behalf of the king by marching south to bring middle Scotland over and provide support for any Royalist force that might still consider moving north. If he won, the Covenanters might lose heart; if he lost he faced the real danger of extinction. At Kilsyth Montrose had the largest numbers under his command so far, although the actual strength of the two forces is still in dispute. Seymour put Montrose's strength at around 4400 infantry and 500 cavalry, with the Covenanters having 6000 infantry and 800 cavalry, although he acknowledges that among the former the Fife levies were raw and ill-disciplined.[20] John Buchan also favoured these general figures, although unsurprisingly Baillie's narrative makes them far more equal, and Stuart Reid follows this source to assess the Covenanter forces at some 3500 infantry and possibly 300 cavalry.[21]

Whatever the actual figures involved it was the contrasting patterns of leadership that were to prove significant. Montrose enjoyed the trust of men who under his command had never been beaten. Baillie was far less fortunate, since he was harried unmercifully by his Parliamentary committee under Argyll and had not only been defeated but had resigned his command more than once, only to be ordered to serve out his term until a successor arrived.

The dispositions of the two armies were important. Montrose drew his men up in a basin of low-lying fields just north-east of Kilsyth and waited for Baillie to reveal his intentions. However, he did not neglect to raise his men's spirits by asking them – as Bruce had at Bannockburn – whether they were fighting or withdrawing, to which they roared out the expected reply. In anticipation of the coming fight he indicated it would be hot work in the blazing sun in their coarse saffron shirts, but to avoid any confusion between his and the enemy's horse he ordered his cavalry to wear saffron shirts over their jerkins so they would be easily recognisable.

Baillie positioned his army on the eastward rim of the basin where he had a steep and rough slope between himself and Montrose. It was undoubtedly a strong position although theoretically there was nothing to stop the Royalists scaling the northernmost part of the rim. However, Baillie's Parliamentary committee headed by Argyll ruled that the army should move across the face of the rebels' army (for the most part concealed from them) to prevent Montrose making for the north and safety. Baillie set about the move with considerable skill, but things began to go seriously awry after Montrose ordered Ewen MacLean of Treshnish with about 100 men to occupy a number of buildings and enclosures on the lower slopes of the hills between him and the Covenanters. According to the account of Clan MacLean, Ewan was in no doubt that Montrose was placing him as a potential hostage to impede the Covenanters.[22]

The success of this manoeuvre became apparent when Major John Haldane, commanding Baillie's vanguard, left his line of march along the ridge and started downwards to attack Ewan MacLean. This brought the headstrong Colkitto and the rest of the western clans into the battle and a dog-fight occurred between the Highlanders and the strongest of Baillie's regiments effectively cutting the Covenanters' army in two and separating the Fife regiments from their forward and central units.

As Montrose watched the battle unfold he saw his Highlanders becoming outnumbered as the bulk of Baillie's army joined against them. He also noted that part of Baillie's vanguard had almost reached the heights to his left where they might outflank him. Although he was unable to judge their exact strength he nevertheless sent 200 or so of the Gordon's footsoldiers to block it, but they were almost immediately surrounded at which Aboyne led his own small detachment of horse to assist them. This in turn was soon surrounded and Montrose then ordered a counter attack by his cavalry's main body. Looking up the hill they baulked at the prospect but Montrose turned to the Ogilvies under Airlie, their old commander, and in an appeal that could not be refused he cried, 'All eyes and hearts are

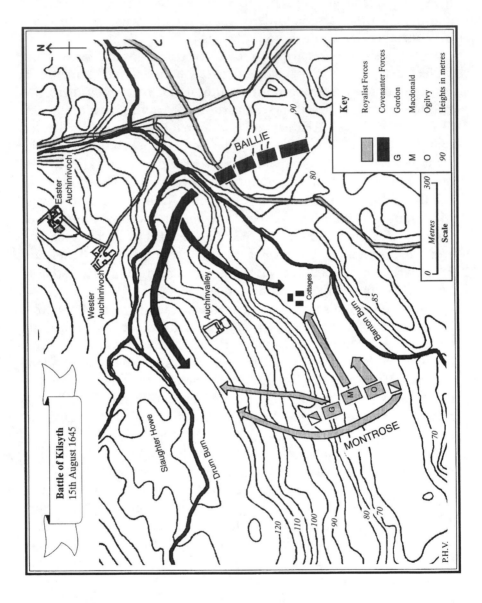

Battle of Kilsyth
15th August 1645

Key

Royalist Forces
Covenanter Forces
Gordon
Macdonald
Ogilvy
Heights in metres

G
M
O
90

Scale
Metres
0   300

BAILLIE

Easter
Auchinrivoch

Wester
Auchinrivoch

Auchinvalley

Cottages

Barnon Burn

90

80

85

Slaughter Howe

Drum Burn

MONTROSE

G M O

70

80

70

90

100

110

120

P.H.V.

on your Lordship, as the only man fit for the honour of beating back the enemy to save our comrades, and repairing by cool veteran courage the error of headstrong youth.'[23] The earl drove at a full gallop into Balcarres' horsemen and scattered them, followed by the rest of Montrose's cavalry charging up the slope. In the centre the Highlanders had been regrouping behind stone dykes and now they too charged upwards. Baillie responded by calling on his reserve but, to his disgust, he found the Fife levies were already quitting the field.

Montrose sounded the general advance and the remainder of the Royalist army burst up the hill. Another Covenanting army was beaten, and most decisively at that. Seymour wrote that 'of the 6000 infantrymen who saw the sun rise that August day, scarcely 100 were alive to see its going down'[24] but later commentators, including Reid, while acknowledging the army's destruction as a disciplined body, rightly disputed the subsequent massacre.

For a few days Montrose was the master of Scotland but, as in the pattern of other Highland victories his troops tended to melt away with their spoils while most of the Irish under Colkitto went off to plunder the Campbell regions. Less than two weeks after the battle David Leslie was riding north to seek out the rebels, while Montrose, lacking any assistance from the king, knew that if he was to have any chance of conquering Scotland as a whole he would have to venture into the Lowlands, a region still almost universally opposed to him. At Philiphaugh, near Selkirk, his small force was surprised and destroyed by Leslie's much superior one. At the beginning of the battle 'Montrose's detachments were so scattered he had only 200 infantry and no more than 100 cavalry with which to fight off the 4000 government troops'.[25] But it was not merely numbers that told against him. Leslie brought a level of determination and self-confidence that had hitherto been lacking in previous government commanders.

Rallying 150 horsemen around him, Montrose fought desperately and would have died on the field had his friends not begged him to escape, 'implored him with tears, wrung from them with deep affection, by the memory of his past achievement, for the sake of his friends, his house, his sweet wife and children, for the king, country, and church, to have a care for his life. Next to God he was their only hope. . . .'[26] Unfairly or not, with this reverse

Montrose suffered a terrible blow to his reputation and his efforts to raise a further army met with far less success than he could have hoped. However, the brilliant commander who had beaten one Covenanter army after another to offer his king a precious, if temporary, opportunity to regain the initiative, was to have no further opportunity to demonstrate his ability on the field of battle.

The King ordered him to disband his forces after which he was forced to cross over to the continent as an exile. After Charles I's execution, Charles II followed his example by appointing Montrose as Captain General for Scotland, but he gave him less than his full support for a fresh invasion. When Montrose landed in Orkney on 26 March 1650 and assembled an army of 1500 men, 1000 of whom were locally recruited Orcadians with virtually no cavalry support, he received two letters from the king's messenger. One (which was personal) assured him of the king's support, while the official letter told him negotiations were in hand between the king and the Scottish commissioners, and the latter could only deflect would-be supporters from Montrose's banner. Charles was playing a dangerous double game and when on 8 May 1650 he signed a public letter to the Scottish estates telling them he had ordered Montrose to stop fighting and withdraw from Scotland, Montrose's ramshackle forces had already been defeated and their wounded leader had been betrayed and brought down to Edinburgh to face his inevitable execution.

In attempting to assess Montrose as a military commander it is necessary to tread a careful path between the unashamed adulation and rolling oratory of his great biographer, John Buchan, on the one hand and the intricate accounts of his battlefield performances by Stuart Reid on the other. There are, of course, other commentators but these two occupy the farthest poles of opinion.

To Buchan, Montrose was the foremost Scottish man of action, with illimitable potential, someone fully worthy to be spoken of in the company of other great commanders, but more than this, a romantic figure who 'must always haunt those who travel the rough roads of Scottish history' and whom he saw as striding into battle with 'a flush on his cheek, a youthful ardour in his eye, but his mouth set in iron'. Away from the battlefield he was a man who stood 'among his friends conquering all hearts with wit and grace' and by reason of his courage 'a guardian of the human spirit, the proof of what one mortal frailty can achieve'.[27] With Reid, although he is perfectly willing to accept that Montrose had leadership ability and enjoyed good luck he could never see him conquering Scotland with 'an undisciplined rabble of poorly armed Highlanders'.

According to Reid, Montrose also had a serious fault as a commander. Despite his tactical brilliance, his inability to grasp the importance of thorough reconnaissance led him to lurch 'from one near calamity to another and to be finished at last'.[28] But in this condemnation of Montrose for not being able to turn his rebellion into a civil war, Reid minimises the disastrous role of Charles I and the minimal resources that the king gave to his ablest general.

Like any commander, Montrose had to make the most of the military qualities of the troops available to him. 'Colkitto' MacDonald was already fighting in the western Highlands when Montrose arrived and Montrose's first test was to have the wild Scoto-Irishmen accepted by the other proud Scottish clansmen, and for them all to acknowledge Montrose as their leader. Inevitably the nature of discipline that Montrose imposed upon the Highland chiefs and their men was far different from that exercised by Covenanter or English commanders over their Lowland levies. Clan leaders and their men came and went as they pleased – discipline was by agreement, not by means of the lash. The leader of such men had to teach by example and this Montrose certainly did. He experienced all the physical hardships of campaigning and demonstrated the same physical bravery as some of the most fanatical of his fellows, while all the time maintaining the aura of the king's commander and never wavering in his belief for a near hopeless cause.

Yet, with the exception of Aberdeen where some of his Irish were given permission to sack the town, Montrose kept his men under a remarkably tight rein; booty was their accepted reward of war but meaningless terrorising and assaulting the civilian population was not recognised as permissible.

Like the great English soldier, John Churchill, Duke of Marlborough, sixty years later, Montrose required his followers to exert themselves mightily in the hazardous enterprises undertaken by their cool and daring commander. Montrose appreciated his Celtic troops' love of fighting and called on the chivalric spirit of such men at arms. In battle he aimed to bring all his detachments into action as soon as possible, although he tended to use his best troops in the early stages so that the enemy must be given evidence of their worth. But as success beckoned all had to take part in the final charge.

While criticising Montrose's poor system of reconnaissance and less than perfect use of patrols for gathering intelligence, Reid seems unwilling to acknowledge that even in the Highlands, where only a proportion of the clans opted for the king, Montrose was often operating in hostile territory where accurate information was difficult to obtain; with enemies all about him he succeeded in eluding them time after time. He knew well enough that the Covenanters would assemble new armies to replace those he defeated, and with the exception of Philiphaugh he was not negligent nor careless of any possible threats.

As for his battlefield conduct, Montrose was always governed by the principle that he could not afford heavy casualties nor a crushing defeat. Although the Royalist communiques after a battle undoubtedly minimised their casualties, his brilliant use of ground, together with his sense of timing, were invaluable. Montrose also showed himself as a natural commander of cavalry, using their shock tactics not only to secure his own flanks but to expose those of his opponents, before crashing his main body against a wavering enemy. What cavalryman could resist the challenge he gave to their Gordon leader at Auldearn or, for that matter, to old Aislie at Kilsyth?

Montrose had a swashbuckling quality, an unmistakable style about all he did. At Kilsyth when he ordered the Highlanders to strip down to their saffron shirts, he not only indicated they would be in for fierce fighting but before most armies wore distinctive uniforms he showed them the need to be recognisable as his elite band of fighting brothers. He demonstrated, too, the arrogance of a commander confident in his powers. This was also seen at Kilsyth in his decision to occupy a basin between hills, knowing that when he asked his troops to attack uphill they would do so successfully. On this occasion it is true that he passed the initiative to the enemy, but he was quick to bring forward spoiling elements to help wreck their plans.

If important qualities for a commander are personal example, energy and ability to deploy or redeploy his troops on the battlefield then Montrose had them all. In the end it was lack of information about a fast-approaching enemy in a region strongly hostile to him that brought about a defeat which proved disastrous. Before that he had succeeded in playing hide and seek with a succession of armies assembled by the vengeful Argyll. Contrary to Reid, Cowan describes Montrose's scouts being on every hill watching for enemy fires and listening for the clink of metal on the still night air,[29] while Ronald Williams even goes as far as to say that at Philiphaugh it was the first time in the whole campaign that he neglected to set the watch or brief the scouts in person.[30] Before Philiphaugh Reid draws attention to one of Montrose's standing patrols that was carousing rather than keeping a good watch. This was inexcusable behaviour but probably not that uncommon, and raises again the question of the character of Montrose's troops. What Highland detachment would be free of its hard-drinking members? The occasional carousal and its cost had to be accepted as part of their other fighting qualities. What was lacking at Philiphaugh were more standing patrols, but with Montrose's great weaknesses in manpower these would have been difficult to mount. In the end it is, of course, the commander who is responsible and Montrose having correctly read and exploited the weaknesses of those he faced earlier appears to have underestimated his new opponent, David Leslie, whom he had known as a colleague but never as an adversary. After a year of constant fighting Montrose was tired, possibly overconfident and, however talented he was as a commander, with such adverse odds the law of averages could not be denied for ever.

Nothing, however, certainly not his final humiliation and death, can take away the solid reality of Montrose's battlefield achievements over a period of twelve months. They earned him a fulsome tribute, not this time from John Buchan but from that cool English observer of military performance, Sir John Fortesque, who said that he was 'perhaps the most brilliant natural genius disclosed by the civil war' and one that 'put Cromwell's powers as a tactician in the shade'.[31] As such he deserves to rank alongside his great exemplar of 300 years before, Robert Bruce.

Alexander Leslie, 1st Lord Leven (1582–1661)

> 'No-one who had spent his days at home in England or Scotland could have a chance against him in the field, or compete with him for the command of an army'
>
> John H. H. Burton, *The History of Scotland*, Vol. 6

Alexander Leslie's career followed a very different pattern from that of Montrose. Prior to his return to Scotland in 1638 at the request of the Covenanters, Leslie had enjoyed much success on the Continent starting when, as a young man of twenty-three, he was promoted captain in a Dutch regiment of Scottish volunteers. After three years, together with many others of his countrymen, he transferred to the service of Sweden and by 1628 had risen to the rank of colonel under the redoubtable Gustavus Adolphus. In the same year Leslie distinguished himself during the siege of Stralsund, the Hanseatic town that defied all assaults by the renowned general Wallenstein acting on behalf of the Austrian Emperor. Afterwards Gustavus Adolphus appointed him military governor of Stralsund and other Baltic cities, and so efficiently did he carry out these duties that in April 1631 he was acting joint commander of the Swedish forces along with the king himself. Four years after Gustavus's death Leslie attained the Swedish army's highest possible rank, that of field marshal.

For many men Leslie's successes with the Swedish army would have been quite enough but at sixty – almost twice Montrose's age – when most of his contemporaries had retired or were at the very least considering the prospect of greater ease, his ambition seemed undiminished. When his cousin, the Earl of Rothes, asked for his help to defend those Scots who in 1638 had signed the National Covenant opposing King Charles I's attempts to introduce a new church liturgy into Scotland and to recover church lands that had recently been allocated to members of the Scottish nobility, Leslie agreed to return home. There he set about raising and afterwards commanding an army on behalf of those who supported the Covenant. Leslie looked for recruits with some experience who were like-minded believers; on revisiting the Continent he took along with him a copy of the Covenant as he sought volunteers among the Scottish mercenaries there.[32]

In appearance Alexander Leslie was not only squat but rather inelegant. His homely, if strong features, were in marked contrast to those of the sensitive, good-looking Montrose, his junior co-commander during the Covenanters' army's first campaign. Although by no means as prominent as the Grahams, Leslie's family dated back to the 12th century with lands in the Garrioch area of Aberdeenshire. Leslie himself suffered from the disadvantage of being illegitimate. His father was a competent soldier, sometime captain of Blair Castle in Atholl, while his mother, 'a wench in Rannock', was possibly the daughter of the laird of Ballechin. After the death of his father's first wife his parents married to give their son the family name; although, despite their strong allegiance to the boy, by then Leslie had received nothing more than a rudimentary education. Lord Hailes referred to him as illiterate, but Leslie's army reports were coherent enough, if never elegant and when circumstances required he was capable of 'adopting' a certain courtly language. A distinguished, if uncritical, commentator on the Leslies has described him fulsomely as 'a very striking example of a man with a neglected education possessing a great military genius and raising himself in the profession of arms.'[33]

Despite this singular tribute from Sir William Fraser and notwith-standing the exploits of the 19th-century commanders Abercromby and Clyde, who also achieved their foremost battlefield successes while in their sixties, it would have seemed reasonable to think that when he returned to Scotland in 1638 Leslie's outstanding battlefield feats were probably behind him, although his experience of war was unparalleled amongst his Scottish contemporaries.

However, from the time he returned to Scotland Leslie showed his Covenanter masters, particularly the most senior, Archibald Campbell, Duke of Argyll, that he had an immediate and vital role to play, namely as the mature and skilled head under whose direction they could assemble and train military forces capable of withstanding those raised by Charles I. In this context a contemporary observer, the Reverend Robert Baillie, wrote of Leslie, 'We were feared that emulation among our Nobles might have done harm when they should be met in the field; but such was the wisdom of that old, little, crooked soldier, that all with an incredible submission from the beginning to the end, gave over themselves to be guided by him as if he had been the Great Solyman'.[34]

Baillie's delight in Leslie embraced more than the general's military skills, for the clergyman recognised in him a strong Protestant heart and a champion of the Covenant.[35] As a pupil of Gustavus Adolphus Leslie could hardly fail to see the military advantages of disciplined Puritanism. Gustavus, however, used religion as a powerful support and adjunct to his army's efficiency but never allowed it to become a divisive force. His prayer sessions in the morning and at sunset were not just to bolster his soldiers' self confidence but to encourage their self-discipline, for along with their prayers the padres preached vehemently against the licence given the opposing imperial troops by such commanders as Wallenstein. As Leslie set out his training programme for the Scottish levies of his Covenanter army he was confident their religious beliefs would help him demand the high level of discipline that was particularly important for a war likely to be within their native country.

In 1639, as the military preparations progressed against the expected invasion by Charles I, Leslie was given the chance of displaying his practical military skills. He personally took charge of an attack on the immensely strong castle of Edinburgh with its garrison of Royalist troops. He approached in full sight of the defenders and demanded its surrender. When this was understandably refused he made as if to retire but, instead, placed a petard on the castle's outer gate. The resultant explosion destroyed the gate, and in the confusion the Covenanters were able to scale the castle's walls and capture it without suffering a single casualty. Apart from this success the royal castles of Dumbarton, Dalkeith and Tantallon were also taken by surprise leaving only Caerlaverock in Charles' hands.

Likened by Baillie to a kind of military Odysseus, the ex-field marshall was considered by some as the most powerful man in Scotland, '. . . the real head and guiding spirit of the Scottish movement, a member of the Privy council and a member of important commissions and committees'.[36] In joint letters of intent his signature came before those of the other nobility but unlike them, his reputation depended solely on his military ability. As Charles I drew near to the border with his army of 12,000 men and 2000 horse, Leslie was able to face him with an army of 20,000 that was better armed, better trained and paid more regularly than that of the Royalists. At this stage neither side wanted outright war and Charles proposed a truce but when this broke down Leslie was empowered to pursue active war against the king.

By the beginning of July 1640 the Covenanters were concentrating their army on the borders. While among the subordinate commanders a young Montrose might dress his own men in blue bonnets and blue ribbons, the army's organisation was fashioned on the pattern dictated by Leslie. In August Leslie crossed the River Tweed with the object of seizing Newcastle, together with its adjacent coal fields that provided the main fuel supply for London. In a flanking movement he forded the River Tyne at Newburn where the Royalists had only weak defensive forces and went on to occupy the city and reduce the surrounding countryside. Not only were the tactics sound enough, but at the same time Leslie showed he understood the importance of an army as a political as well as a military instrument. It was kept under strict control and his summary execution of a small number of men whom he discovered pillaging was entirely appropriate in a situation where neither side wanted an all-out war. Negotiations which were opened between the two sides at Ripon and were concluded at London on 7 August 1641 resulted in a virtually bloodless victory for the Covenanters and fuelled their confidence to demand the adoption of Presbyterianism south of the border. At this point the stock of Leslie, the architect and senior commander of their forces, stood very high indeed.

After the conclusion of this so-called Second Bishop's War, King Charles visited Scotland and as he passed through Newcastle he was greeted with loyal demonstrations by the Covenanting army. Leslie prostrated himself before the king who gave him his hand to kiss, commanding him to remount and accompany him on an inspection of the troops. The inspection was followed by a magnificent dinner supplied by Leslie, after which the king apparently discussed the offer of an earldom for him. The royalist commentator Clarendon, no friend of the Covenanters, was quite clear about the circumstances: 'and Lesley, the general whom he made Earl of Leven with precedence of all earls for his life, had told him voluntarily and with an oath that he would not only never serve against him, but would do him any service he should command, right or wrong.'[37] The king's efforts to bring Leslie over to his side were well judged for at this time it seemed to some observers that 'the old soldier stood in rather the same (dominant) situation to the king in Scotland as Cromwell stood in England after the founding of the New Model Army.'[38]

The Reverend Baillie, true Covenanter that he was, put quite another gloss on the meeting between Leslie and the king where 'with the bluntness of the soldier (Leslie) was careful to explain that in accepting honours from Charles he by no means renounced the principles which he had fought for throughout his active life'.[39] Whatever the truth (and both Baillie and Clarendon were strongly biased sources), on 6 November 1641 in an elaborate ceremony Alexander Leslie was created Earl of Leven and Lord Balgonie. At this Leven resigned as Lord General of Scotland but staying on as commander of the country's standing forces. In 1642 a rising in Ulster by the native Irish led to the king appointing Leven to command the troops appointed to suppress it; the Scots army crossed to Ireland during the spring but Leven himself took little part in the campaign. He disliked heartily the conduct of war against insurgents, and in any case important political events were unfolding in England that were of much greater concern to him.

A full scale civil war was developing between the King and his English parliament and in the following year, after the English parliamentarians had somewhat reluctantly agreed to adopt the Scottish Solemn League and Covenant, the Scottish convention agreed to provide an army to fight against the king. As their outstanding soldier Leven was appointed its commander on 26 August 1643.

Nothing can conceal the fact that less than two years after Charles I had made Leslie Lord Leven he accepted command of a Scottish army pledged to support the English parliamentarians against the king. Predictably, Baillie strongly defended Leven's actions. But Baillie's defence this time seemed to contradict his earlier support. 'It is true he past manie promises to the king that he would no more fight in his contrare; but (as he declares) it was with the expresse and necessar condition that Religion and Country's rights were not in hazard; as all indifferent men thinks now they are in a verie evident one.'[40] Not surprisingly Clarendon criticised Leven's decision in equally strong terms calling him one 'who had so solemnly promised the king not only never to bear arms against [the king] but to serve him, let the cause be what it would without any hesitation undertook the command of it.'[41]

Plainly Leven could not satisfy both sides. He already had evidence of Charles' renewed dislike for the Covenant but, as a Scot, he might well have suspected the new-found enthusiasm for it on the part of the English parliament could not possibly survive long under the pressure of events. His first hand experience of religious wars on the Continent could have led him to conclude that Scottish Presbyterianism was not exportable and that the English would hardly be prepared to accept a rule by clergy who, 'by means of church discipline, enforced in the most inquisitional manner, (determined) to bring a whole population under the yoke of moral law.'[42]

In an uncertain age Leven appears above all as a pragmatist with a deep concern both for his own country and his private interests. For someone of manifestly high ability whose own childhood had been uncertain and whose education and looks were unimpressive it was fully understandable that above all he should seek to protect himself and his newly ennobled family. There were earlier indications that family concerns had always been important to him. For instance, throughout his life he carefully accumulated wealth and, while acting as a mercenary on the Continent, returned to Scotland to plough some capital back into his family estate. Although personally abstemious (even when commander-in-chief Leven was apparently content to live in a mean lodging in Edinburgh) he knew when to use his money to impress, for when he attended church or was otherwise in the public eye he dressed elegantly, and it was said his clothes could exceed £2000 in value.

Leven was now at the height of his professional success, after his brief service for Charles I he commanded the most professional army in Britain, a force of 18,000 foot and 3000 mounted men together with artillery detachments, committed to clearing the north of England of Royalist formations. He did not move southwards with winged feet, making a leisurely halt before Newcastle until he joined forces with the English parliamentarians under Sir Thomas Fairfax. Together they started besieging York but, when they learned that Prince Rupert was on his way to relieve the city, they moved to Long Marston to bar his approach. Leven's whole stance thus far was to protect the interests of his native country and not to move any further from Scotland than he could avoid. He was determined to preserve his Scottish forces at all costs.

However cautious Leven might be, Rupert was essentially a fighting commander and the opposing forces clashed at Marston Moor on 2 July 1644. The battle was between the two largest bodies of troops yet assembled in the civil war and just conceivably it might have turned out to be Leven's Blenheim. He was given the privilege of drawing up both the Scottish and English Parliamentary formations. He put them into three great bodies each three lines deep after the pattern of Gustavus Adolphus. On the right were the dragoons and horse under Sir Thomas Fairfax, in the centre the Allied foot and on the left an impressive body of horse both English and Scots, under the overall command of Oliver Cromwell. Leven saw that Rupert was seriously outnumbered and favoured an attack as soon as possible. Rupert himself intended to attack on the next day. It was early evening and Rupert was in the rear taking his supper when Leven gave the order to attack and caught the Royalists unprepared as the allies moved swiftly over the intervening space between the two armies. However, in the heat of battle Cromwell would never acknowledge Leven to be his supreme commander as Prince Eugene had with John Churchill. Despite Leven's great experience and his superior numbers of troops the English would always consider themselves the major partner in the alliance. Partly as a result of such shared leadership, Marston Moor turned out to be a most muddled engagement with the allied army strangely intermingled.[43] For instance, in the centre the Scottish infantry was commanded by Leven, along with Manchester and Fairfax commanding their own English brigades, while on the left Cromwell's cavalry was supported by considerable numbers of Scottish horse under their own commander, David Leslie. The battle reflected the lack of overall commanders on both sides: the Royalist horse under Rupert gained a significant advantage but the situation was restored by the Scottish horse and then exploited by Oliver Cromwell. After defeating their opposing cavalry the allied cavalry turned upon the Royalist infantry and were able to win the day.

In the centre the fight was both confused and stubborn. After joining battle the Scots' foot were attacked from the front and the flank by both cavalry and infantry and Leven's attempts to rally them proved unsuccessful. In plaintive despair he cried out, 'Although you run from your enemies yet leave not your General.'[44] Amazingly amidst the noise and chaos of the battle all three allied infantry commanders quit the field. Leven went furthest, scarcely drawing 'rein until he reached Leeds. Lord Fairfax made for his castle at Cawood. Lord Manchester, more courageously, retired only a short distance and soon re-entered the fray to lead his men to ultimate victory'.[45]

No one could call the battle of Marston Moor a great hour for Leven as a force commander. He not only left the field of battle but continued his flight for many miles. It was fortunate for the Scots infantry that his subordinate, Baillie, fought on until the cavalry were able to assist them. His past record had marked Leven as a brave and resolute soldier but at Marston Moor he allowed himself to become entrapped within the swirling and bloody battlelines, and decided that all was lost. He was certainly not the only one to do so but to flee from an ultimate victory was an embarrassing misjudgement.

On discovering things had turned out far differently than he feared, he returned. In his subsequent communique to Scotland recounting the success he complimented himself for drawing up the forces but neglected to give due praise to David Leslie, the cavalry commander who, to many Scots, was the true hero of the hour.

Leven survived the crisis but the continuing task of clearing Royalist forces from the north of England was hampered by the detachment of the Scottish cavalry from his main army sent to block any move northwards by the king. In any case following reports from the Highlands of Montrose's victories on behalf of his king, Leven became even more determined not to move his army far from the Scottish borders. It made little sense to help beat the Royalist forces in England if the army's absence from Scotland led to the home country falling to Montrose. One of his despatches at the time revealed his attempts to placate an angry Fairfax over his relative inaction: 'Your Lordship will be pleased to consider that if we had taken the other way (into England) we should have left our own country altogether naked, but we are confident by God's blessing to recover anything we may seem to lose in this interim.'[46]

Leven continued to drag his feet as far as the Parliamentarians were concerned, but he also strongly opposed Royalist attempts to divide the Scottish Presbyterian army from the English Puritans. In England the king's cause seemed doomed and by now Montrose had been defeated at Philiphaugh and was reduced to hiding in the mountains with a small number of followers. Charles was forced into the desperate expedient of throwing himself on the mercy of the Scottish army as it lay near Newark. The king had legitimate hopes that Leven would attempt to help him but, acting on instructions from the Duke of Argyll, Leven made him a prisoner to keep him safe from the influence of 'all papists and delinquents'. As the king arrived in Leven's camp the Covenanter General was all courtesy but he left Charles in no doubt who was in control. On receiving the king, Leven was said to have tendered his sword 'in token of submission' at which the king retained it as if he would assume command, whereupon the earl suggested that it were better to leave that to him as the older soldier 'especially as he was in command here, though in humble duty to his majesty'.[47]

Leven was wise to be courteous – and cautious – for the alliance with the English Parliamentarians had not proved beneficial to his army which had received no pay for six months and whose men were in rags. At the same time throughout Scotland strong elements of support were developing in favour of the Stuart monarchy and there were continuing hopes that Charles would find some way to recognise the Covenant. Within Leven's camp, negotiations with the king foundered on Charles' continuing devotion to Anglicanism, despite a personal plea from Leven himself. Amid rumours of plots designed to help the king escape, Leven put him under stricter guard until, in January 1646 the army handed him over to the English under certain conditions, namely for Presbyterianism to be established south of the border and for a payment of £200,000, with the promise of another £200,000 to defray the army's expenses during the war. In fact by giving up the king Scotland lost all chance of imposing Presbyterianism in England. Predictably Clarendon was enraged at Leven's conduct. He said that Scots were 'negotiating about what price [the English] should pay for the delivery of his person, whom one side was resolved to have and the other as resolved not to keep, and so they quickly agreed that, upon the payment of £200,000 . . . they would deliver the king up into such hands as the parliament should appoint to receive him.'[48] Implicit in Clarendon's account is the strong influence over Leven by the extreme group of Covenanters under the Marquis of Argyll who had decided they would have no further dealings with the king.

From now onwards Leven appears to lose influence, although acknowledgement of his ability to raise and train armies remained unaffected. He plainly viewed the growing differences between England and Scotland with some alarm. When he brought the Scottish army back to its homeland it was largely disbanded but he was retained – against his wishes – as commander-in-chief of those regiments remaining in service, although his was largely an advisory role. By this time Leven certainly appeared to have the strongest reservations about any initiatives coming from the king. In 1648 he opposed plans drawn up by three of Scotland's senior commissioners led by the Duke of Hamilton (a group hereafter known as the Engagers) for raising a Scottish army to assist the king. This was on the condition – the Engagement – that Presbyterianism be established in both kingdoms for a minimum of three years, something Leven believed the king would not carry out. After refusing to command a Scottish army in a projected plan to invade England and assist the king, Leven was relieved of his military responsibilities. This was confirmed by the Scottish Parliament on 11 May 1648, but it was on 'condition that if further forces needed to be raised for the defence of Scotland he would become their General'.[49]

The Engagers' army moved south and Cromwell met it during August 1648 at Preston where he had little difficulty in defeating a force that, while numerically superior, lacked training, ammunition and comparable leadership. As Scotland was now without an army Argyll commanded Leven to raise new forces and, together with David Leslie, he recruited a force of 8000 foot and horse which was dubbed 'the Whiggamores'. This, of course, backed Argyll's faction in the Scottish parliament but since the Whiggamores were not strong enough to beat Cromwell militarily it was necessary to offer him political sweeteners. At Argyll's bidding Cromwell was invited to Edinburgh where it was agreed that Carlisle and Berwick be returned to the English. As keeper of Edinburgh Castle, on 4 October 1648, Leven gave Cromwell a sumptuous banquet and on his departure saluted him with numerous cannon.

Relations between the two countries again became strained after Charles I's execution, when the Scots defied the English by proclaiming Charles II as their Stuart king. This was bound to bring Cromwell northwards to force them back into line and Leven was given the task of raising yet another national army to meet the Lord Protector. Having no illusions about Cromwell's military talents he tried to excuse himself pleading age and infirmity and actually laying his baton before Parliament, but his resignation was refused on the grounds that, with David Leslie as his active deputy, he would not be asked to do more than he could undertake.

How far Leven influenced Leslie's military decisions at this stage it is impossible to say, but their policy of scorched earth across the border regions south of Edinburgh soon brought Cromwell's invading army, like others before it, to a sorry state. That the policy bore Leven's influence can be gathered when King Charles II proposed an attack upon the English at which Leven threatened to lay down his commission if such a rash decision went ahead. However, when the Scots army occupied the passes north of Dunbar its field commander was David Leslie. As at Preston two years before it enjoyed considerable numerical superiority over Cromwell's force but its discipline was not good and too often rank was conferred solely for religious rather than military qualities and any 'ex-engagers' whether good soldiers or not were purged from its ranks. Leven could not have been happy with such a situation after the example set him by Gustavus Adolphus who always kept his pastors under control, nor in the light of his own emphasis on thorough-going training when he raised his first Scottish army twelve years before. But he was now seventy years of age and his words carried far less weight than in former years.

From his past conduct it is virtually certain that Leven would have opposed the decision at Dunbar when the army came down from their near impregnable position only to be routed by Cromwell, but there is no definite evidence to confirm it. Leven accompanied the army as it withdrew to Stirling and in November he made a petition to the Scottish parliament (presided over by Charles II) in which he admitted responsibility for Dunbar. While it is just possible he might still have been highly influential at Dunbar, it is far more likely that in consequence of such a confession he hoped he would finally be relieved of his duties. Against all the odds he continued to be kept on, and in June of the following year his duties were demanding enough to prevent him being given leave of absence to attend his wife's funeral.

Leven was not, however, to witness the final sad chapter of the war when Cromwell crushed the Scots at Worcester, for on 28 August 1651 he and a large number of other officers were captured by General Monck's dragoons. Leven was placed in the Tower, but at Cromwell's intercession he was allowed the liberty of it with a servant to attend him. Shortly afterwards his son-in-law, Sir Ralph Delavall, was permitted to take him to Northumberland on sureties of £20,000, a clear indication of Leven's considerable wealth. Nor did Queen Christina of Sweden forget her old servant in distress and her petition helped to persuade the authorities to restore his land to him. He was able to return to his estate at Balgonie, where he finally died in 1661 at over eighty years of age.

Unlike many other prominent figures in those troubled times, including Montrose and Leven's chosen political superior, Argyll, Leven kept both his head and his title. He probably did so because while in his younger days he was known for his loyalty to the Swedish king, after he returned to Scotland for the civil war Cromwell acknowledged him as a professional soldier dedicated to serve his native country in the way he thought best.

After his distinguished service as a mercenary Leven was the obvious choice as the Scottish parliament's military commander, highly versed in both the raising and training of armies and in the practice of war, although he was to prove far less enthusiastic for the hazards of the battlefield than in his former days. It was also an immeasurable help towards his selection that he was a strong believer in Presbyterianism and the Covenant, enabling him to remain close to the Marquis of Argyll, the most powerful individual in Scotland at this time.

Whereas on his return from the Continent men deferred to Leven as a Goliath in war with a knowledge that stretched from strategic and tactical considerations to the construction and use of ordnance, after Marston Moor his reputation as a field commander was permanently eclipsed by Cromwell and even David Leslie. Marston Moor had a profound effect upon him and as a result of his terrible fright there caution became his watchword. He reverted to that brand of war-fighting where the preservation of an army became all-important and its safety was the key consideration, especially with an opponent like Oliver Cromwell. This gives credence to the likelihood that it was Leven who suggested the scorched earth policy for the Scottish forces before Dunbar.

Despite his early military achievements overseas Leven can be seen as a Machiavellian figure, military guru and chief of staff rather than an outstanding field commander. By temperament he could never adopt the swashbuckling approach of the Jacobite leaders, although what he lacked in daring he appeared to compensate for by shrewdness and a deep instinct for survival. It is therefore unsurprising that in such turbulent times he inclined towards the premier civilian faction in Scotland whose ideas seemed closest to his own, ideas that he judged would have the best chance of succeeding. After the king's execution he safeguarded his own security with friend and enemy alike by detaching himself from factions and making it clear he returned to his role as a mercenary soldier who loyally carried out the instructions of the civilian authority prevailing at the time.

David Leslie, 1st Baron Newark (1610–1682)

The fortunes of the second Covenant commander were firmly linked with those of both Montrose and Alexander Leslie, Lord Leven. Despite their common name, David Leslie was no relation of Leven. He was nobly born, the fifth son of Sir Patrick Leslie of Pitcairly, Fifeshire, and Lady Jean Stewart, the second daughter of Robert, first Earl of Orkney. David Leslie was a strong Presbyterian and when there appeared little opportunity at home for taking up arms he followed the example of Leven and many other Scots and entered the service of the Swedish king and Protestant champion, Gustavus Adolphus. A vigorous horse soldier, he was soon promoted colonel by Gustavus and, whilst engaged in a daring sally during the summer of 1640, he was badly wounded. By the autumn he was recovered enough to join the many other Scottish officers in Sweden who requested permission to return home to support their Covenanter kinsmen. David Leslie was one of the most capable of those who returned and he was promoted to major general in the Scots army which Leven raised and then led across the River Tweed into England during 1643.

In the following year Leslie was given command of the Scottish cavalry in the joint Scottish/English Parliamentary army at the battle of Marston Moor near York. It was in many ways David Leslie's finest hour when, under the overall command of Oliver Cromwell, he led the cavalry reserve. The battle started late in the day as the light began to fail and when the Parliamentarians opened the attack they caught the Royalists off guard. In typical fashion Prince Rupert responded by hurling himself and his men against the opposing cavalry: the Parliamentarian horse recoiled from the momentum of his assault and Cromwell, who was slightly wounded in the neck, retired to the rear for treatment. With Cromwell absent David Leslie took command and led the allied cavalry in a determined attack against the flank of Rupert's cavalry. This was followed through so well that when Cromwell returned he combined with Leslie to drive the Royalist cavalry off the field. The allied cavalry were now free to enter the battle elsewhere and they moved against the rear of the Royalist infantry where David Leslie's quarry were the white-coated infantry commanded by the Earl of Newcastle. Leslie was assisted by English and Scottish infantry under Fairfax and Baillie, but so well did he press forward with his attacks that the whitecoats were killed to a man. Newcastle's infantry had fought on after their ammunition was exhausted and because of their white coats it was said they 'brought their winding sheets about them into the field'.[50] The final outcome was a heavy defeat for the Royalists and one that marked a serious setback for Prince Rupert's reputation as a commander. Marston Moor was a confused battle, much of which in the later stages was fought in moonlight, and it was Royalist errors, particularly on the part of Rupert, that determined the outcome. It would be wrong, however, to say it was decided purely on errors, since every battle has actively to be won, and the heroes among the English Parliamentarian leaders were Thomas Fairfax and Oliver Cromwell. Within the Scottish army there were two outstanding leaders, General William Baillie, who succeeded in steadying his infantry when they were hard-pressed from many quarters, and David Leslie, who gathered up the allied cavalry at a vital time and furthered his initial success by playing a leading part in the destruction of Newcastle's infantry.

Cromwell, with his ability to grasp the larger strategic picture, made an immense contribution to the allied victory, but in his control of the cavalry David Leslie ranked not far behind his leader. With his quick thinking and rapid action he turned a crisis to his own advantage. Leslie might even have been the undisputed hero of Marston Moor since the historian, Gardiner, maintains that when the Scots first joined forces with their Parliamentarian allies Cromwell, being junior in experience, urged that David Leslie should have command of the united cavalry. Leslie, recognising Cromwell's stature, was said to have agreed to serve under him. With markedly less generosity, Oliver Cromwell chose to throw a veil over Leslie's whole-hearted co-operation at Marston Moor, writing to his brother-in-law, Valentine Walton, 'The left wing which I commanded being our own horse, saving a few Scots in our rear beat all the Prince's horse . . . We charged their regiments of foot with our horse and routed all we charged'.[51] In fact, Leslie and his Scots made up twenty-two troops of the seventy under Cromwell's command.

Among the Scots there was a far better appreciation of Leslie's contribution to the victory. Robert Baillie, for one, was sure that Leslie's performance was much superior to that of his leader, Cromwell.[52] Nothing could change the fact, however, that from then onwards Cromwell was acknowledged as the outstanding military leader among the Parliamentarian soldiers and, with the possible exception of Montrose whose activity and daring so terrified Argyll and his commanders, in the whole of Britain. Cromwell also began to exert a malign influence over Leslie, who by the time of the battle of Worcester in 1651 had become convinced he could never get the better of him.

After Marston Moor Leslie was sent on detached duty from Leven's main Scottish army to help block any northwards movement by the king. He continued to enjoy local successes, initially against Royalist forces in Northumberland and then in besieging and taking Carlisle on 28 June 1645. However these actions were soon to be dwarfed by a far more dramatic mission. It originated with unrest amongst Leslie's men who after Montrose's great victory at Kilsyth on 16 August 1645 refused to continue in England while Scotland lay defenceless.[53] At Newcastle, Leslie met the Scottish Covenant Committee of Estates to discuss his course of action and was given immediate authority to proceed against Montrose.

On 6 September 1645, Leslie crossed into Scotland at the head of 4000 horse and 1000 foot. His original plan had been to meet Montrose near the Forth but, after receiving information that Montrose was at Philiphaugh, near Selkirk, he changed his plans. Montrose at this time had only a small proportion of his former army since after his victory at Kilsyth a good proportion of his followers had dispersed leaving him woefully weak, being down to some 700 foot and 200 mounted men. Yet Leslie should not be denied credit for the military skills he displayed nor for the tactics he adopted at dawn on 13 September. He was not to know how weak Montrose actually was. Leslie showed undoubted courage when he split his forces into two, keeping the main body under his command and sending 2000 dragoons to take up a position in the rear of Montrose's camp. Chance favoured him, for a dense mist helped to cover their approach. Once they were in position just thirty minutes before dawn, David Leslie gave the order to attack and despite Montrose's own frantic efforts, there was little real opposition. Accurate information combined with sound tactics and speed of action gave David Leslie a facile and overwhelming success over a much-feared and brilliant opponent.

However, after his triumph on the battlefield Leslie acted in a way that did little to enhance his subsequent reputation. As a strong Presbyterian he had absolutely no sympathy for papists and absolute contempt for them if they happened to be Irishmen. It must also be acknowledged that after their own victories Montrose's Highlanders and Irish troops had pursued their enemies with bloodthirsty delight – with good reason since it was only by destroying their opponents' forces rather than worsting them that they could reduce the great disparity in numbers facing them. But no extenuating circumstances can change the fact that after Philiphaugh Leslie's 'trained and disciplined soldiers of the Covenant slaughtered not only the male camp followers but 300 Irish women, the wives of their slain or captured enemies, together with their infant children'.[54] The outrages were not confined to the rabble of camp followers or their soldiers' dependants. Fifty soldiers who surrendered to Leslie were abandoned by him near Linlithgow and no respect nor mercy was shown. His soldiers were 'bidden fall on (them) and they did as they were bidden'.[55] Placed in the context of the time, David Leslie's actions were no worse than Oliver Cromwell's in Ireland and not that much worse than Montrose's Irishmen when removed from his tight control. But Montrose's men had acted in hot blood and while they were in pursuit of a defeated enemy; Leslie's was a deliberate act the like of which never occurred in England during the Civil War and one that offended against the more chivalric code practised by Montrose himself and by Lord George Murray a century later. Nevertheless, the Covenant Committee responsible for the conduct of the war rewarded Leslie with 50,000 marks of gold for his success over the feared enemy.

Another outcome of his success at Philiphaugh was that when Leslie returned to the main Scottish army it was as their premier fighting soldier. Charles I now recognised that, if he were to succeed in winning the support of the army without being required to adopt Presbyterianism, it was imperative for him to win Leslie over. Accordingly an offer was made on Charles' behalf to create Leslie Duke of the Orkneys and make him a knight of the Garter and captain of the guard. To his credit Leslie remained true to his belief in Presbyterianism and rejected the proposed honours. This appears to support Gardiner's belief that Leslie was no average Covenanter but a warm partisan of Argyll whose faction of extreme Presbyterians was committed to the establishment of a strictly constitutional monarchy.[56] Having failed in his efforts to bribe Leslie the king was handed over by the Scottish army to the English in January 1647. On its return to Scotland the army was reduced to 6000 men; for all practical purposes this force came under the command of David Leslie, although Leven remained the nominal commander-in-chief.

Leslie continued in active service leading his troops against rebels who were holding out in the far north, particularly the Huntlys, and afterwards driving out Montrose's allies the 'Irish' MacDonalds from Scotland. He remained an implacable enemy, for on one occasion, after the garrison of an obstinate stronghold at Dunaverty had surrendered, he butchered all 260 of them despite a promise of quarter.

Not all Scots were as unyielding Presbyterians as Leslie. In a country where there was more general support for the monarchy than in England, a new agreement was signed with Charles I on 26 December 1647. The Engagement, as it was termed, required the king to accept Presbyterianism for a limited time only but its most important element was the undertaking to raise an army on his behalf that could be used against the English Parliamentarians to help achieve what its supporters hoped would be 'a lasting peace'. Leven refused to be involved in helping to raise such a force and David Leslie, although pressed to command its horse, also rejected the offer. David Leslie, like Leven, could not have been unaware of the probable fate awaiting this half-trained, poorly equipped force if it had to meet Oliver Cromwell in battle and Cromwell's victory over it at Preston fully confirmed their fears.

In fairness Leslie's decision against joining 'the Engagers' was not based on military considerations alone: he was so opposed to the designs of Charles I and the Duke of Hamilton, the king's main ally in Scotland, that after the Engagers' defeat he joined in plans for assembling 'the Whiggamores', a rival force of approximately 8000 armed Covenanters, in support of Argyll who intended treating with Oliver Cromwell. In what became known as 'the Whiggamore Raid' they took Edinburgh, following which on 22 September 1648 Leven and Argyll opened negotiations with Cromwell over the return of

Berwick and Carlisle to England. After the execution of Charles I, which came as a shock to most Scots, and their defiance of Cromwell in recognising his son, Charles II, as their king, the Whiggamores remained guarded in their support of Charles II who had not yet accepted the Covenant. However, when Charles II encouraged Montrose to invade the north of Scotland for a second time, Leslie took with him ample troops to hunt down the Graham.

In his usual fashion Leslie acted quickly to frustrate Montrose's plans to gather additional support. Moving northwards in a succession of forced marches he instructed his forward detachment under a sectarian fanatic, Colonel Strachan, to delay Montrose as far as he could. Strachan did far better; on 27 April 1650 he and his Lowland troopers brought Montrose to battle, surprised him and destroyed his polygot force of a few hundred Danish mercenaries and a thousand Orcadian levies. Montrose managed to escape but he was injured and eventually he was delivered up to Leslie, who had by now reached Tain along the north-east coast. The price of his betrayal was 25 thousand Scots pounds, part of which was paid in oatmeal. Montrose was taken south in an ignominious manner 'upon a little shelty horse without a sude [saddle], but a guilt of raggs and straw, and pieces of roaps for stirrups, his feet fastened under the horse's belly'.[57] When he reached Inverness he was shivering with fever, but Leslie showed no trace of respect for his enemy and along with other indignities caused him for some days 'to be in the same clothes and habit in which he was taken'.[58] Chivalrous behaviour towards someone who had fought for the Stuart kings against the Covenanters was plainly deemed unnecessary. Leslie was in no doubt that Montrose deserved to be executed and this was carried out on 21 May 1650, less than a month after his capture.

The situation changed radically in June 1650 when Charles II signed the Covenant and later in the year acknowledged his father's and mother's misdeeds against the Scottish Kirk. After Charles II had paid the due price for Scottish support they raised an army with Leslie as its de facto commander although officially he again deputised for the now infirm Leven. This acceptance by the Scots of a monarchy that had been expelled by the English led Cromwell to invade Scotland once more. Leslie met him with traditional scorched earth tactics, and placed the Scottish army in a near impregnable position, across a line of hills from Leith on the Firth of Forth to the outskirts of Edinburgh. Cromwell realised that in the circumstances an attack could not succeed and he was compelled to retreat to Dunbar where the English fleet had landed his supplies. As he did so he was shadowed by Leslie who kept to the high ground. In these opening exchanges Leslie had much the best of things and Cromwell's casualties through sickness were high.

On 2 September both armies faced each other. Cromwell's had its back to the sea and its strength was reduced to some 11,000 effectives compared with Leslie's 17,000. Leslie's forces then edged their way from high ground near Doon Hill to its lower slopes. As Leslie manoeuvred Cromwell noted that although Leslie's formations were favourable for an attack, they were close-bunched and not well placed to receive one. The decision to move off the high ground was almost certainly taken against Leslie's instincts since he told the Committee of Estates that by 'lying there [on the hills] all was sure, but that by engaging with gallant and desperate men all might be lost'. He also maintained he did not have 'the absolute command'. By this he was not referring to Leven but to the large number of ministers who accompanied the army and who not only purged it of experienced soldiers, if they happened to be ex-Engagers, but set up their sons as officers and cut across the normal military codes of discipline, urging Leslie to come down from the hills to offer combat.

Whether or not Leslie was in full control he faced a commander who unquestionably was and who, at daybreak on 3 September 1650, ordered his veteran, if outnumbered, army to advance before Leslie had his formations properly drawn up. The result was a crushing defeat, which Leslie finally attributed 'to the failure of his men, after moving down from the hills, to stand to their arms during the night and of the officers to stay by their troops and regiments'.[59]

Characteristically, despite Cromwell's occupation of Edinburgh and the Lowlands, Scotland remained unsubdued. On New Year's day 1651 Charles II was crowned by Argyll at Scone and the Scots began assembling yet another army. Leslie had been exonerated of all blame 'anent to the miscarriage at Dunbar', and Charles II was persuaded to make him 'lieutenant general of the army' due to his very long experience, and a very good name in war, with the Duke of Middleton commanding the horse'.[60]

Following in the footsteps of Robert Bruce, Leslie occupied a strong position at Torwood, near Stirling, but Cromwell, declining battle on such terms, moved past them and placed himself to the north across Leslie's lines of supply from Perth. Leslie was for reopening his lines of supply but Charles II decided to move into England to rouse the Royalist sympathisers there against Cromwell. Sadly for both Charles II and Leslie the move south brought far less support than they had anticipated. Their cause was not helped by a Committee of Members that accompanied the army and had a declaration issued emphasising the king's support for the Covenant which served to alienate many would-be English recruits.

After the army's move from Stirling morale declined and in this regard Clarendon was strongly critical of David Leslie. He relates how the king, having observed David Leslie was sad and melancholy on the march south, 'slow in giving orders and riding by himself . . . [he] rode up to him and asked him with great alacrity how he could be sad when he was in the head of so brave an army . . . To which David Lesley answered him in his ear, being as some distance from any other, that he was melancholic indeed, for he well knew that army, how wellsoever it looked it would not fight'.[61] By any standard it was not the example required from a commander. With the disappointing numbers of new recruits Charles II had to abandon his grandiose plans of marching on London and selected Worcester as a place where his army could refit. Cromwell had forces shadowing the Royalist army and at Worcester tightened a noose round them. As news of his approach came to the Royalists Clarendon reported: 'There was no good understanding between the officers of the army. David Leslie appeared dispirited and confounded and gave and revoked his orders and sometime contradicted them. He did not love Middleton and was very jealous that all the officers loved him too well.'[62] It is likely that Clarendon, as a strong Royalist, with firm opinions of his own, would favour Middleton in preference to David Leslie for no better reason than he could never forgive Leslie for his treatment of Montrose. In fact the battle of Worcester was hard fought and, as Cromwell admitted, for four or five hours as stiff a contest as he had ever seen. Yet if one leader distinguished himself on the Scottish side, it was the king himself and Clarendon maintained that many who fled Worcester were 'so unsatisfied with (Leslie's) whole conduct and behaviour that they did, that is many of them did, believe he was corrupted by Cromwell; and the rest, who did not think so, believed him not to understand his profession in which he had been bred from the cradle'.[63]

Responsibility for appointing Leslie lay with Charles II although according to Clarendon his confidence was never complete: the king always thought Leslie an excellent officer of horse in distributing and executing orders, but considered him in no degree capable as a commander-in-chief. Criticisms of Leslie at Worcester were by no means confined to Clarendon. In the State papers there is a reference to the king (who undoubtedly fought well) deciding on making a sally and seeing Leslie 'riding up and down as one amazed or seeking to fly'.[64] Even in flight there was chaos. Many panicked on the journey towards Scotland and, either from accident or by design, Leslie and Middleton were alone when they were captured. Any question of Leslie being directly disloyal seems unfounded, but clearly the stature of Cromwell dominated his mind after the outcome of their earlier encounters. If Leslie had been disloyal it is probable he would have expected a degree of preferential treatment on being captured but this was not so; with many others he received no favours and underwent all the severities of imprisonment, being confined for a full nine years until 1660.

While Charles II might have thought Leslie lacking as an army commander at Worcester, he could have hardly thought him false since after the Restoration, on 3 August 1661 he created Leslie 1st Lord Newark. Argyll, the Covenanter champion, was to pay with his life for perceived disloyalties and by making Charles II publicly acknowledge his parents' faults, but whatever hostile rumours might continue to swirl around David Leslie, the king must have seen merit in him for in 1667 he sent Leslie a communication assuring him of his continuing royal confidence.

As a battlefield commander David Leslie had undoubted strengths, namely abundant energy and the ability to make rapid decisions, combined with a good sense of timing and tactical awareness. He displayed all these qualities to the full at Marston Moor and Philiphaugh. But he also had his limitations and they too were significant. He altogether lacked the dominance and vision necessary for a successful commander as shown at Dunbar when he allowed rampaging ministers to do untold mischief to his army. Greater commanders such as Gustavus Adolphus and Cromwell led equally religious armies but they never allowed their church representatives such disastrous latitude.

While acknowledging the inherent difficulty for a 17th century Scottish commander to ride roughshod over his army's ministers, another serious situation developed at Dunbar when Leslie acknowledged the battle was lost because both officers and men had left their appointed posts. This they should never have done and it was Leslie's responsibility that they did not. Scottish soldiers had shown no lack of aggression in previous battles but under Leslie at Dunbar all was over after just an hour's fighting.

Finally at Worcester Leslie seems to have been lacking those two essential qualities of any recognised commander, self-belief and enthusiasm. While rightly wary of Cromwell, he failed to make the defences around Worcester as strong as he might have. He should never have risked dissension among his fellow commanders by openly criticising his cavalry leader, Middleton, who was unquestionably popular; he should either have supported him or replaced him. Above all he seems to have broken the cardinal rule of all commanders, that they must radiate confidence to their subordinates.

As a good middle piece commander, David Leslie did not possess the calibre for high independent command. He was also by no means a gracious soldier in his treatment of prisoners and towards his wounded, fever-ridden adversary, Montrose. When one questions why Leven should have been kept on despite his advanced years, it might indeed have been to give David Leslie the benefit of his vast experience and also to help compensate for Leslie's own temperamental shortcomings. While Leven and Leslie returned to Scotland with enhanced reputations and served as senior military figures throughout the Civil War, neither even remotely approached the levels of command reached by Montrose during his 'annus mirabilis' or, for that matter, by that remarkable civilian soldier, Oliver Cromwell.

≈

CHAPTER FIVE

JACOBITE REBELLION – CLAVERHOUSE, MACKAY AND MURRAY

'The Scottish Highlanders are a people totally different in their dress, manners and temperament from the other inhabitants of Britain.'

Austrian Observer in John Laffin's
Scotland the Brave

A FTER THE CIVIL WAR and the restoration of a Stuart king over both Scotland and England, many Scots might well have hoped their country would never again witness the ravages of opposing armies nor act as an arena for opposing military commanders. Such hopes were misplaced for Scotland remained divided, with the clans in the north still organised on military lines and many of their chiefs at odds with southern Scotland over fundamental religious, economic and cultural issues.

Southern Scotland not only diverged from the Highlands but resented its seeming inability to influence decisions made by the king in London. Its strong allegiance to Presbyterianism, and its depth of hatred for Roman Catholicism were, for instance, never fully appreciated by the later Stuarts and on his coronation James II directly antagonised the Scottish hierarchy by refusing to take the oath to defend the Protestant religion and by his appointment of Roman Catholics as his Chancellor and Secretary of State. If this were not enough he followed it by an Act of Parliament ruling that anyone undertaking a Covenant was guilty of treason and the presence of believers at a conventicle or assembly of Covenanters was punishable by death. Although James was subsequently forced to give freedom of worship to dissenters this caused even more problems in Scotland where the previously 'ousted' Presbyterian ministers returned to their parishes and fomented opposition. It was the birth of a Catholic male heir that caused men from both north and south of the border to turn towards James' Protestant son-in-law William of Orange, together with his wife, James' Protestant daughter Mary, as their accepted King and Queen. National figures in England including senior military ones like John Churchill, James' best soldier, betrayed their Stuart king and invited William to be their sovereign. Soon after William's entry into England and James' flight to France, William summoned the Scottish Estates to meet in convention at Edinburgh where they voted that James had ruled unconstitutionally and officially offered the Crown of Scotland to William and Mary.

This decision brought renewed civil war to Scotland. It caused a brigadier serving with James' Scottish forces, Graham of Claverhouse (made Viscount Dundee by James shortly before he sailed) to lead a rebellion on James' behalf against the Scottish Estates and appeal to the Highlands for military assistance. Dundee's opponent was the newly appointed commander-in-chief of the Estates' forces, Hugh MacKay of Scourie. The two men were well known to each other for both had served during the 1670s in the Dutch United Provinces with the Scoto-Dutch Brigade there.

Following Claverhouse's rebellion the Stuart cause continued to receive support from the north-western clans during the risings of 1715 and 1719, although good leadership was lacking on both occasions and the fighting was soon over. It was not until the denouement of Jacobite hopes in 1744–5, when the young Prince Charles Edward attempted to raise the clans once more, that another commander of true ability would appear in the person of his general, Lord George Murray and Scotland would experience major conflict again.

This chapter is concerned with the battlefield performances of the two Jacobite commanders, Graham of Claverhouse, Viscount Dundee and Lord George Murray, together with that of Claverhouse's opponent, Hugh MacKay of Scourie. Murray was in fact the last Scottish rebel commander to fight pitched battles on Scottish soil.

Graham of Claverhouse, Viscount Dundee
(1648–1689)

In a similar way to Montrose and Lord George Murray, Claverhouse possessed an impassioned loyalty for the ill-fated house of Stuart, a loyalty which in his case was all the more remarkable for it being to James II, one of the least lovable of the line. While a conscientious, energetic, if humourless monarch, he was a fervent Catholic when most of Scotland was ardently Protestant. To make things worse, by 1688 the once enthusiastic soldier and brave prince who had served in France under Marshall Turenne and in 1665 commanded the naval force that routed the Dutch off Lowestoft had suffered a broken blood vessel at hearing of his daughter Anne's desertion to William of Orange. In addition to his lack of diplomatic skills and the pernicious habit of breaking his promises – often to his most loyal supporters – he had become muddled and irresolute. But to Claverhouse, who was himself a Protestant, the concept of strong hereditary government was infinitely preferable to the prospect of the endless strife which he was sure would ensue when a group of self-seeking Scottish nobles chose to recognise a king or queen from Holland. As a boy going from his home to Dundee Claverhouse must have seen an arm of his great forebear, Montrose, which after his execution in 1650 was nailed over the town's south gate (in 1661 Charles II ordered the arm and Montrose's other scattered remains to be brought together and given the Christian burial denied him by the Covenanters). Claverhouse could have had few illusions concerning his fate if he should fail. Like Montrose, however, he would make superhuman attempts to support an inadequate Stuart king and his incompetent royal advisers.

From birth Claverhouse was destined for high rank. As a Graham, he came from a family that had been accustomed to playing a prominent part in Scottish history. Sir John de Grahame, for instance, the friend and brother-in-arms of William Wallace, died at the battle of Falkirk in 1298. His brother Sir Patrick de Grahame had fallen at the battle of Dunbar two years earlier and in the succeeding centuries other Grahams fought on behalf of the Scottish kings, in 1346 at Neville's Cross and in 1402 at Halidon Hill. One Graham, Sir Robert of Strathearn, betrayed his king, being involved in the assassination of the highly unpopular monarch James I, but even here Catherine Douglas, who was directly related to Claverhouse, tried to save the king: when she learned the door stanchion to the king's chamber had been removed, she showed amazing courage by thrusting her own arm forward as a bar to delay the king's pursuers.

When young, Claverhouse was of striking appearance with luxuriant black hair, dark complexion and perfect bow-like lips, although his later portraits show a degree of aloofness and proud austerity along with the predominant sensitivity of his earlier years. Montrose was always his hero and when young not only did he listen avidly to Montrose's exploits with the Highland clansmen but even became a determined reader of the Roman poet Lucan, Montrose's own favourite.

During the last months of his life when his own military abilities became fully apparent it was entirely appropriate that one of his followers should liken him to 'a new phoenix risen from the ashes of Montrose'. Claverhouse served his military apprenticeship under Marshal Turenne of France. One of his fellow officers there was John Churchill, although unlike Churchill Claverhouse afterwards served with the Dutch. Claverhouse was in the Prince of Orange's own company of Guards and in 1674 at the battle of Seneffe he distinguished himself by saving the Prince who had lost his horse and was in the greatest danger of being killed or taken prisoner. Claverhouse rode into the thick of the enemy, mounted the Prince on his own horse and carried him safely off. For this he was promoted to captain. As a junior commander he soon gained a reputation for daring and bravery as well as for his quick temper and insistence on speaking his mind. In 1677 when the Prince of Orange came to England to marry his cousin Princess Mary, eldest daughter of the Duke of York (the future James II), he reputedly spoke highly of Claverhouse's military abilities. This led him to be accepted into the Duke's own regiment of horse. It was to prove a mixed blessing for at thirty years of age Claverhouse was given the most difficult posting imaginable for an ambitious soldier. He was sent to his native Scotland as captain of an independent troop of horse, responsible for the militarily unsatisfactory task of suppressing conventicles in Dumfriesshire and Annandale. Some of the preachers held their unlawful meetings in the open and their many followers brought arms with them. They came in such numbers that they were able to form themselves into small armies. Such worshippers thought of regular soldiers as 'spawn of Satan'. If they came upon small groups of soldiers they would hunt them down and kill them. Less than a year after taking up his appointment Claverhouse was serving in a force under the command of the Duke of Monmouth which fought a pitched battle at Bothwell Bridge near Hamilton, against a far superior force of 3000 or so Covenanters who brought a huge gallows on which to hang any soldiers delivered to them by the Lord, while a further 5000 Covenanters gathered nearer Glasgow. At Bothwell Bridge Claverhouse behaved with singular gallantry and with his own hands captured two enemy standards.[1]

After Bothwell Bridge Claverhouse was appointed commander of the military forces in Galloway and in his additional capacity as sheriff of Wigtown, he became responsible for bringing the rebellious region to order. Military operations against terrorists are arguably the most difficult and frustrating of all, especially for forceful commanders like young colonels of horse. Two hundred and fifty years later, following the end of World War One, an equally ambitious soldier, Bernard Montgomery, was posted to Ireland at the time of the Republican troubles there. Unquestionably tough, he ordered that 'any civilian or Republican soldier or policeman who interferes with any officer or soldier is shot at once'.[2] However he was delighted to get away after about 18 months for he observed 'that such a war is thoroughly bad for officers and men; it tends to lower their standards of decency and chivalry'.[3] Claverhouse had to spend the best part of ten years in the south-west of Scotland on such a role exercising both judicial and military powers and pursuing the canticlers.

With a vast area to cover and with relatively few men the excitement of the chase must have often appealed to him. But, as a good soldier, he kept his troopers under iron discipline and adopted a policy of pursuing the ringleaders rather than the rank and file, much to the fury of his peppery commander-in-chief General Dalzell. Claverhouse had the dual responsibility for both ordering and supervising executions against opponents who were set on magnifying any instances of perceived injustice. Inevitably, he was demonised by the Covenanter divines for his successes against them and because of his apparently charmed life in avoiding a succession of ambushes and traps, a 'belief grew among ordinary people that he was under the special protection of the powers of darkness'.[4] Among the credulous a rumour was spread that ordinary shot or steel could not hurt him. It would, they believed take a silver bullet to penetrate his 'magic' coat.

Even in such difficult conditions Claverhouse's ability as a soldier was never doubted by the other commanders of the six troops of horse for which he was responsible. These included distinguished men like the Earl of Drumlanrig, Lord William Douglas and the Earl of Airlie who in his younger days had earned a high reputation in Montrose's wars. In recognition of this, when in 1683 Argyll led a Covenanters' rebellion against James II, Claverhouse was made a joint brigadier of the Royalist horse – but only for the campaign's duration.

Towards the end of his time in south-west Scotland, and in spite of his successes in restoring order, Claverhouse's career could still be seen as one of highest promise remaining unfulfilled. One explanation for this was his ability to make powerful enemies, figures such as James Douglas, the Duke of Queensberry, his long-time rival, who was angered when Claverhouse took the part of soldiers against Colonel James Douglas, Queensberry's brother, for dismissing them arbitrarily and wrongly taking arrears of pay due to them. Lord Moray, the joint Secretary of State for Scotland also plotted against Claverhouse misrepresenting him to James II and having him removed from the King's Privy Council. With Claverhouse's temperament he could never be a dissembler and he fearlessly exercised his own moral judgments regardless of the consequences. With such freedom of spirit came a proud and ironic manner accompanied by a caustic humour. In many respects Claverhouse must have been a difficult subordinate, openly contemptuous of his rivals, especially if they were time-servers with more elastic moral standards than his own. He not only kept himself aloof but physically very fit; he loved horses and the competition of the turf but he had no interest in the mindless carousing and revelry so prevalent at court. Such independence of mind was seen in his marriage to Jean Cochrane, who came from a disaffected and strongly Presbyterian family. It seemed a most unwise choice for a Royalist and Episcopalian, but Claverhouse in love was determined to go forward with a liaison that appeared 'not only to go against his political and religious instincts [but one] which would seriously threaten his career'.[5] The Duke of Queensberry put it about that because he had married into Lord Dundonald's fanatical Presbyterian family it was not safe to commit the king's secrets to Claverhouse, a slander utterly without foundation. But whatever problems he might have with the noble peer Claverhouse's troopers revered him for he was a natural leader, fearless and bold, demanding from them the highest standards and always willing to share their physical privations. They knew too by his clash with Queensberry that he was quite willing to fall out with a powerful superior if he believed his soldiers had suffered any injustice.

The crisis that led to Claverhouse's momentous decision to support James II began in October 1688 when there could no longer be any doubt about the Duke of Orange's coming invasion. To help counter it the king ordered the Scottish army led by lieutenant general Douglas with Claverhouse as its second in command to London, there to unite with his other forces. After William of Orange's landing at Torbay widescale desertions occurred, including that of General Douglas, and against Claverhouse's advice the king ordered the army disbanded, giving out that he would leave the country. Claverhouse, now created Viscount Dundee, was said to have shed tears at the news and prior to James' flight he and his great friend James Lindsay, fourth Earl of Balcarres, demonstrated their continued loyalty by accompanying the king as he was about to take a lone walk down the Mall prior to sailing for the Continent.

Once established in London William of Orange was careful to announce publicly that his sole object was the preservation of the Protestant religion and securing for the whole British nation the free enjoyment of all their laws, rights and liberties under 'a just and legal government'. Only after this did he call for a convention of the Scottish Estates. When they met on 14 March, William Douglas, Duke of Hamilton, was elected as the president, an unpropitious development for Dundee since, despite being related to Dundee's wife, Hamilton and he were natural enemies. Dundee had advised James II to send a conciliatory letter regarding matters of religion and liberty so 'that those who had declared in favour of the Prince of Orange would reconsider their position and return to their duty'.[6] Instead, the letter which was sent had been drafted by the king's inept adviser, the Earl of Melfort, and it adopted an arrogant and threatening tone. The message dealt a fatal blow to James II's cause. By a majority vote an incensed convention decided to turn their backs on their Stuart king and support William and his wife as the new King and Queen of Scotland. This was the trigger that caused Dundee to leave Edinburgh with his forty to fifty troopers and move into the Highlands to seek military support for his Stuart master. Moving up to Dunblane, Dundee met with Locheil of the Clan Cameron; they were already known to each other and had probably met at court where Locheil spent some time before his knighting by the Duke of York some seven years before. At Dunblane, the veteran chief gave Dundee his pledge of loyalty and with it a precious fingerhold with the other western clans.

Meanwhile the Convention's president had not been idle. While Dundee was at his home of Dudhope Castle awaiting the birth of his first child he was visited by the Duke of Hamilton's herald who demanded his immediate return to Edinburgh or else be branded an outlaw. Dundee's response was a proud refusal. He begged the favour 'of a delay till my wife is brought to bed,' and ended ironically, 'Seeing . . . so reasonable things offered, and the Meeting composed of prudent men and men of honour, and your grace presiding over it, I have no reason to fear further trouble.' Following this he was proclaimed a traitor.[7] Dundee's response was to undertake sole responsibility for raising the Royal standard on behalf of King James. Meanwhile the Convention had levied 6000 foot, 12 troops of horse (600 men) and a regiment of 300 dragoons, and appointed Hugh MacKay of Scourie as their commander-in-chief. The new commander-in-chief was eager to hunt down the recusant, but raising such numbers was bound to take time, and MacKay knew he would have to start his pursuit with far fewer men.

In 1689, at forty-one years of age, Dundee's chance had come, although the odds he faced were fearsome. His commitment to James II was absolute and when he prepared to ride out of Edinburgh for the north, the Duke of Gordon whom Claverhouse had persuaded to hold Edinburgh Castle until he saw what the Convention intended to do asked him where he was going. His reply, 'wheresoever the spirit of Montrose shall direct me',[8] showed how conscious he was of his family's proud tradition, yet in his planning he was far less naïve than these words would suggest.

The man who defied his country's political assembly had just a handful of men, no money, no ammunition nor supplies. He knew full well his one hope lay in arousing the Highlanders' traditional fervour and raising an army from the clans strong enough to meet and defeat the Government's forces. By means of such a victory he might persuade his king to send additional forces. The speed and certainty of his actions, and the manner of his approach to such proud and undisciplined men would reveal him as an avid student of Montrose's earlier campaigns.

Meanwhile General Hugh MacKay, Dundee's pursuer, had not been idle. Basing himself in the area of Perth, Dundee and Stirling he energetically beat up for recruits. As yet his forces were relatively small, consisting only of about 1100 men from the three Scots regiment brought back from Holland, instead of their full complement of 3600. But while, as yet, he lacked manpower, he had no shortage of money, and MacKay used it liberally in an attempt to buy the loyalty of the Highland chiefs. He wrote to Lochiel offering him a large bribe, together with the governorship of Inverlochy Castle and command of a regiment.[9] He did not succeed for the magic of the Graham name had already served Dundee well. Lochiel ignored the offer and Glengarry, when similarly approached, passed the communication over to Dundee and asked him to dictate the answer.[10] Apart from offering bribes to the chiefs, Mackay reasoned that if he intercepted Dundee while his followers were so few he could kill the rebellion in its infancy before Dundee 'could ply his personage among the nobility and gentry of the north.'[11]

Dundee succeeded in eluding MacKay, who planned to surprise him at Glen Ogilvy near Glamis, and pressed on northwards at rare speed through rugged hill country until he reached Keith, where nearby at Gordon Castle he received his first recruits, a maximum of fifty Gordon horsemen under Lord Dunfermline. While few in number they became exceedingly important to Dundee. Carrying with him further pledges of Gordon support, Dundee moved swiftly westwards along the northern coast through Elgin and Forres to Inverness. Even with his small band he was convinced he had certain advantages over MacKay; he was confident that he, rather than MacKay, could attract support from the Highland clans. Dundee needed no reminding that, whether the independent, mutually antagonistic and immensely proud Highlanders would stay under his command was dependent upon his powers both as a leader and his skills in battle. They had also to accept his own complete conviction of purpose.

At Inverness Dundee met with his first Highland chief in arms, MacDonald of Keppoch, along with 700 followers whom Lochiel had ordered to greet him. For both men the meeting was something of a surprise. Keppoch had seized the city's most prominent citizens and obliged them to pay a ransom for their release; for good measure he had also plundered adjacent lands belonging to his hereditary foe, MacKintosh of MacKintosh. Dundee knew he must not hesitate. Standing in front of his small group of horsemen, he faced the mass of Highlanders, ordered the clansmen to stand to their arms, and told Keppoch roundly that 'by such behaviour, instead of advancing the king's interest and acquiring the character of a patriot, he would be looked on as a common robber and an enemy of all mankind.'[12] Amazingly he faced down Keppoch who offered excuses although little help, for his men were more interested in returning home with their plunder than staying to support the rising. Dundee set about placating the citizens of Inverness by promising them 4000 marks in compensation – to be paid on the king's return. He also sent out the Fiery Cross, the time-honoured method of gathering the Highland clans together for war, commanding them to meet at Lochaber on 18 May. In the meanwhile Dundee's few horsemen could only flee before MacKay, but later he expected the situation would be very different.

While MacKay had a low opinion of such Highland 'rabble', Dundee fully recognised their loyalty to the Stuart cause, and knew that under Montrose their achievements in battle had been virtually illimitable. Eight days after the meeting with Keppoch he issued a royal letter telling all the faithful clans to be ready by 18 May 'to follow the orders and the camp of the Graham'.[13] In the meantime Dundee did everything he could to strengthen his powers. Basing himself in Badenoch and Lochaber he easily avoided MacKay and, at the head of his small band of horsemen, swooped on Dunkeld and ambushed the government tax collectors there. With no more than seventy followers he followed this by taking the city of Perth, where he appropriated more public funds, but when he arrived at Dundee he met with a reverse in that he failed to bring his old regiment, the Scots Dragoons, over to his banner.

The Lochaber gathering was postponed until 26 May, but when it occurred it included many of the clans that had earlier achieved so much for Montrose. It is difficult to be accurate as far as numbers are concerned but a report by the king's messenger put the total attendance at 1700, from clans right across the north of Scotland. These included 600 with Lochiel and his Camerons, 200 with Keppoch and his MacDonalds (many other MacDonalds were away taking their plunder home), 300 with Glengarry and the MacDonells, 200 with Glencoe and his MacDonalds, 200 with Morer and the Clanranald MacDonalds and 200 with Appin and his Stuarts.[14] This broad representation was as important as the numbers themselves. Their weapons were varied in the extreme; they included old Matchlock muskets, axes, javelins and even clubs. But there was unquestionably a deep pride and fierceness about all present.

At Lochaber Dundee addressed them proudly and confidently, outwardly portraying none of the fears which, as his standard bearer reported, caused him to 'pass a sleepless night pondering the future and the doubtful chances of fortune'.[15] Although he spent a few days drilling the clansmen in basic army formations, he accepted Lochiel's advice that he should acknowledge and maximise the strengths of the Highland method of fighting, in particular the Highland charge.

Over the next two months Dundee did everything he knew to win the clan leaders over to his pattern of leadership. His personality was all important and he was an engaging figure, chivalrous and determined, a man they came increasingly to respect and admire. A daring and accomplished soldier he led them to believe that under him they could expect success instead of the high probability of confiscation, exile, death and disaster which was the normal fate of rebels. Knowing well the clansmen's love of celebration, on 29 May he linked the anniversary of Charles II's restoration with a toast to the return of James to Scotland.

On the following day by taking and burning the Castle of Ruthven, near Kingussie, he prevented MacKay linking up with a powerful reinforcement under Colonel Ramsey, yet when Dundee started stalking MacKay's force he was hampered by the clansmen's unruliness when Keppoch and his Macdonalds independently sacked Dunachton Castle, the property of their clan enemies, the MacIntoshes. A furious Dundee confronted Keppoch and told him that 'if he was thus resolved to do as he pleased, without regarding the king's interest or the public welfare he had better begone with his men'. Despite the MacDonalds forming the larger part of Dundee's small force, Keppoch humbly apologized, probably for the first time in his life, and swore that neither 'he nor any of his men should henceforth start hostilities without Dundee's express command'.[16]

Unfortunately soon afterwards, just as had happened to Montrose at Badenoch, Dundee fell ill, worn out by the ceaseless strain. Not only had he shared the same exertions and short rations as his men but, he had also been required to display constant optimism as well. With Dundee ill, MacKay, with increased forces, was able to assume the offensive. It was a difficult time for Dundee: as he learned about the substantial reinforcements reaching MacKay, there also came a report about auxiliary troops from Ireland destined for him being repulsed with heavy losses. Somewhat recovered in health he returned to Lochaber and, although there was now a high price on his head, he dismissed the greater number of his men – food was increasingly becoming a problem – on condition that they return should the enemy pursue him further.

It was a time for reassessment on both sides. MacKay decided not to enter Lochaber country but to ring it with garrisons at Inverness, Strathbogie and Elgin, while Dundee launched a diplomatic offensive warning clans that were either wavering or had given their allegiance elsewhere that Londonderry was about to surrender and that with it powerful reinforcements would be sent to Scotland. He wrote to the Duke of Melfort, the king's chief adviser, for immediate help, particularly in respect of arms and ammunition. He arranged for a great gathering at Blair Castle for 29 July in the hope that, if the anticipated 5 or 6000 Highlanders arrived, together with a further 5000 Irish promised by the king, he could surely bring back all Scotland for King James. In the event Dundee received not 5000 Irish but a mere 300, mostly raw recruits under their Scottish Lowland officer, Colonel Cannon – nothing like the experienced fighters led by Colkitto who had supported Montrose so well. Regardless of such poor reinforcements, Dundee had already decided to move south once he had learned that MacKay was continuing to amass his troops and others were being gathered against him in the west. In any case Dundee knew that without action his clansmen would melt away.

On 22 July he left Lochaber with a force of approximately 1800 men. After a long march on the usual short rations they succeeded in reaching Blair Castle before MacKay who was fast approaching Dunkeld with two troops of horse and 4000 foot, including his famous Scoto-Dutch brigade. The problem was what to do next. While perfectly capable of making the decision himself, at this important juncture Dundee resolved to hold a council of war and put the different courses of action before it. His professional

Lowland officers, including Colonel Cannon, were for giving their men time to recover from their long march before facing an army of disciplined troops under an experienced leader. In contrast the Highland chiefs were for fighting immediately. Dundee offered the final word to Lochiel, the much-respected, veteran clan leader, assuring the council that Lochiel's judgement would determine his own. With typical Highland courtesy Lochiel said he had not given his opinion so far because Lord Dundee, who understood so well the Highland spirit, needed neither counsel nor enlightenment. But as the general honoured him by asking his advice, he gladly gave it; it was that they should fight immediately. Highlanders were different from other troops. They were in good heart and eager to engage the enemy, whose greater numbers would but serve to give an 'added glory to the victory'.[17]

At this Dundee added his own approval and there was a unanimous agreement to fight. Before the meeting ended Lochiel approached Dundee and entreated him not to take any personal risks because 'On your lordship depends the fate not only of this brave little army, but also of our king and country'.[18] Dundee refused to stay at the rear however, saying that without showing courage himself he could not keep the respect of the clans. The most he would agree to was to change his red tunic for a leather jerkin of a grey or 'sad-colour', but he insisted on retaining his white helmet, the badge of the leader.

Positioned near the small township of Killiecrankie, Dundee rejected the option of inflicting a reverse on MacKay as he toiled through the pass of that name. Nothing less than annihilation would satisfy him. Accordingly MacKay emerged unharmed from the long, narrow pass only to come face to face with some of Dundee's detachments, although more Highlanders coming down the high hill of Creag Eallaich from the right appeared to him to be the main body. MacKay turned his troops to the right, ordering them to climb upwards to find a level space on which to give battle, then dissatisfied with this he marched them up the further hill of Raon Ruariedh only to find that it too was dominated by clansmen on higher ground. It was early afternoon: Dundee had pinned his adversary and battle was virtually inevitable, for a little way behind MacKay lay a steep defile with the fast-flowing River Garry at its base.

As Dundee hoped MacKay responded defensively, and to avoid being outflanked stretched out his battalions in long lines three

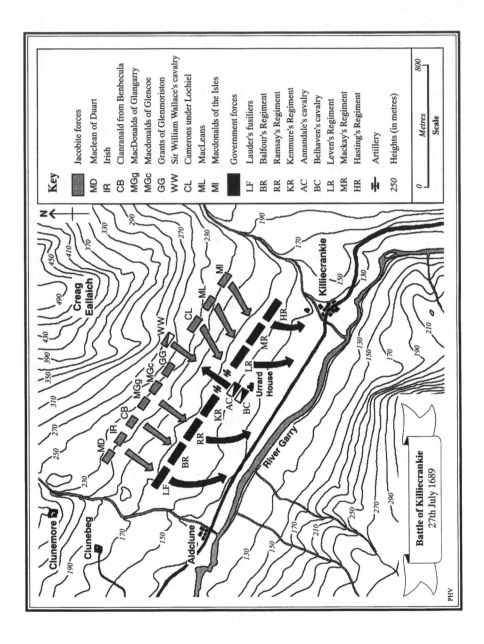

Key

Jacobite forces
MD Maclean of Duart
IR Irish
CB Clanranald from Benbecula
MGg MacDonalds of Glengarry
MGc Macdonalds of Glencoe
GG Grants of Glenmoriston
WW Sir William Wallace's cavalry
CL Camerons under Lochiel
ML MacLeans
MI Macdonalds of the Isles

Government forces
LF Lauder's fusiliers
BR Balfour's Regiment
RR Ramsay's Regiment
KR Kenmure's Regiment
AC Annandale's cavalry
BC Belhaven's cavalry
LR Leven's Regiment
MR Mackay's Regiment
HR Hasting's Regiment

⚔ Artillery

250 Heights (in metres)

0   Metres   800
Scale

Battle of Killiecrankie
27th July 1689

PHV

men deep. Nothing could change the fact that Dundee and his Highlanders faced odds of over two to one and he too adapted the positions of his men in the best way he could. He knew his main chance of victory lay in unleashing his Highlanders in an impetuous charge and cutting through MacKay's extended line at several places, breaking its cohesion. Realising he could not match MacKay's extended lines he kept his units in deeper formations with large gaps between them. On Dundee's right stood Sir John MacLean of Duart with his men, then 300 Irish under Colonel Purcell, then the men of Clanranald from Benbecula, the Macdonells of Glengarry, the MacDonalds of Glencoe and the Grants of Glenmoriston. In the centre was his diminished troop of cavalry, no more than fifty in all, commanded by Sir William Wallace of Craigie, who had been sent over by the king and who therefore superseded Dundee's faithful friend and gifted commander, Lord Dunfermline. Dundee's left wing had the Camerons under Lochiel, the MacDonalds of both the Isles and Kintyre and then the MacLeans.

MacKay's forces were commanded by himself on the right and by his second-in-command Brigadier Balfour, another veteran of the Scoto-Dutch regiment, on the left. Under Balfour's command were three regiments of foot, Balfour's own together with those of Colonel George Ramsay and Viscount Kenmuir with Colonel Lauder and his fusileers on the extreme flank. On the right stood the Earl of Leven's foot alongside MacKay's own regiment and on the extreme flank Colonel Ferdinando Hastings' foot reinforced by a detachment of flintlocks taken from each battalion in the army to decimate the Highlanders with their enfilading fire. In the centre McKay's two troops of horse were behind the foot as he dared not expose them to Dundee's cavalry, less than half their number.

The Highlanders' battle plan was not complicated but all depended on one man, Dundee. Although MacKay was unable to advance uphill Dundee refused to move as long as the slanting sun shone in his men's eyes, and while he waited MacKay played his four light guns upon the Highlanders, supplementing this with long range musket fire. The noise from the guns was considerable, although they caused few casualties. Firing their guns was all MacKay and his men could do as they were obliged to wait amid the lowering hills until Dundee released his Highlanders down on them.

Shortly before giving the long-awaited order to charge, Dundee ranged along the battle lines addressing his followers with a message that was simple but eloquent. He said they had come to fight in the most noble of all causes – for their king, their country and religion, against usurpation and rebellion. He asked them for nothing more than he would do himself. 'Let this be your word, King James and the Church of Scotland, whom God long preserve.'[19] At last, at 8 p.m. on that summer evening when the glare from the sun lessened, Dundee ordered the charge. His Highlanders moved amazingly quickly across the intervening ground and, as soon as they closed with the enemy, their weapons – muskets fired at close range then discarded, followed by claymore and dirk – were markedly superior to MacKay's muskets which could not be fired when their bayonets were attached. However, in the charge the lie of the ground edged the attackers right and they took heavy and well-aimed fire from MacKay's regular regiments with their massed flintlocks on the right of his line. On the left, MacKay's men broke, particularly the old soldiers of Colonel Balfour's regiment, and the Highlanders easily repulsed an attempted cavalry charge by Belhaven's cavalry troop. While MacKay knew he had lost the day he maintained control of his right hand formations and attempted to fall back in some semblance of order, but even so he could not stop the sense of panic that ran through his army. Five hundred of his soldiers subsequently surrendered and were led back in triumph to Blair Castle.

MacKay lost over half his men and his army virtually ceased to exist, but the Highlanders' losses were also heavy, about 600 in all, most of them caused by the enfilade fire that burst on their opening charge. Most important was the wounding of Dundee. The manner of it was entirely in character. As the cavalry approached the enemy's cannon, Sir William Wallace suddenly wheeled to the left, leaving Dundee riding directly towards the guns. Finding himself alone he raised himself in his stirrups and waved his hat for the others to follow, at which Lord Dunfermline immediately responded. But a cloud of smoke then hid their leader and moving through it they found Dundee shot through the side of his breastplate. He probably lingered on for a few hours and a letter purporting to be from Dundee to James contained the words, 'Therefore sir, for God's sake assist us – though it be with such another detachment of your Irish forces as you sent before – especially of Horse and Dragoons ... However, Sir, I beseech your Majesty to believe, whether I live or die, I am sincerely yours.'[20] Whether the letter was authentic or not it accurately reflected Dundee's loyalty for when a soldier caught him as he fell from his horse he asked: 'How goes the day?' 'Well for the king,' replied the soldier, 'but I am sorry for your Lordship.' 'It is the less matter for me' said Dundee, 'seeing that the day goes well for my Master.'[21] One thing was certain: with Dundee's death the rebellion was over and perhaps we can agree with King James when he said the chance shot from a flying and defeated enemy changed the fate of the three kingdoms. The clansmen carried his body to a small secluded kirk near Blair Castle, where the restless and ambitious heart of their leader joined the Atholl clansmen buried there – most of whose lives were far longer than his.

Like Montrose, Dundee never commanded large numbers and his warlike operations were constrained by both the numbers and the characteristics of his followers – proud, combative and above all independently minded Highlanders. It is unlikely that the man so widely known in his own country as the persecutor – Bluidy Claver'se – and attainted traitor will ever be given the recognition his military gifts deserve although later writers have been markedly more impartial towards him.[22] Yet in addition to his skills on the battlefield Dundee had that quality so necessary for a great commander, a constant awareness of political as well as the military significance of all his actions. Two days after Killiecrankie other chiefs and fresh clans that had promised him their support arrived, with many more ready to join them from middle Scotland. It was the culmination of Dundee's work over the previous four months and with their help there were good grounds for believing he would have won back Scotland for King James. But his death destroyed everything. During that same four months he had shown the strength of personality coupled with unceasing energy that could inspirit men in battle. From the outset his confidence affected his followers and enabled him to take the daring initiatives that baffled and checked his enemy. Finally at Killiecrankie Dundee maximised the positive attributes of his men, in particular the Highland charge, pushing his offensive forward with firm determination to win the day. His personal example was all-important for it was a hard fought victory against a well-disciplined enemy with far superior numbers, and over a third of

Dundee's soldiers were killed gaining it. For his military skills during the four month campaign of April–July 1689 ending with his success at Killiecrankie, 'Bonnie Dundee' deserves to join the elite company of Scotland's finest early commanders.[23]

General Hugh MacKay of Scourie (1640–1692)

By birth Hugh MacKay was a Highlander, the third son of Hugh MacKay of Scourie in Sutherlandshire, chief of the clan of that name, and of Anne, daughter of John Corbet of Arkbole, Ross-shire. By far the greater part of his military career was spent abroad, and although Hugh MacKay succeeded to the family estates in 1668 he probably never visited them. Unlike the vast majority of Scots who display a deep affinity for their native land, it was Holland, the birthplace of his wife, that was both his spiritual and domestic home. By religion, temperament and allegiance, therefore, MacKay had little in common with many of the Highland chiefs who supported his adversary, Dundee.

Although Dundee was himself a Lowlander, as a Graham he was able to relate effortlessly with his countrymen from the north. Dundee was probably not that much more familiar with the Highland fastnesses than Hugh MacKay but, through his studies of Montrose's campaigns, he could well appreciate their advantages for a fugitive or for a commander seeking both mobility and surprise. To MacKay the language of the Highland chiefs – even when they spoke English – was for the most part unintelligible and, after the Low Countries, the Uplands themselves were an alien and perplexing region. It was a blank spot in his worthy military career and one that would cost him dear.

From his early years Hugh MacKay was a soldier in the tradition of other leading Scottish mercenaries. By the age of twenty he was an ensign in Dumbarton's regiment, subsequently the Royal Scots, and served with it in France. In 1669 he fought for the Venetian Republic against the Turks and was decorated for his valour. As a captain in the Royal Scots he fought under the great French soldier Turenne against the Dutch United Provinces. In 1673 things changed radically when he married into a pious Dutch family and their influence became all powerful on him. Henceforth religion was the mainspring of his actions, including his military decisions. Bishop Burnet referred to MacKay as 'the piousest man I ever knew in a military way'.[24] With this devout stance it became morally impossible for MacKay to serve in the armies of France when they fought against Protestants and he transferred to the employ of the States General, becoming a captain in their Scoto-Dutch brigade.

In 1677 both he and Claverhouse were in contention for command of one of the Scots regiments, and when Hugh MacKay was preferred for the post Claverhouse quit the Dutch service in disgust.[25] MacKay must have continued to impress his masters for when, in 1680, James II called the Scots brigade over to England to help quell the Monmouth rising, MacKay was promoted to temporary major general. His brigade was not involved in the actual fighting but as a result of the promptness of his response MacKay was appointed a privy councillor of Scotland. He took the appropriate oath in Edinburgh but while there he did not bother to visit his own estates and after the king had reviewed the Scots brigade on Hounslow Heath, MacKay returned immediately to Holland.

Eight years later when James II demanded the recall of the Scots brigade to help meet the expected invasion from the Protestant Prince of Orange, MacKay's response to his king was quite different. With the majority of his fellow officers he elected to remain in Holland and, as a result, James' military forces were considerably weekened. Apart from the ties made during his long service in Holland, MacKay's refusal to support his own king owed most to their divergent religious beliefs. Accordingly he eagerly supported William of Orange in his claim to the English crown and commanded the English and Scots detachments of the invading army which came ashore at Torbay. Once William had established himself in England he gave MacKay his reward, appointing him major general and commander-in-chief of the forces in Scotland.

In spite of his ample experience as a middle rank officer, MacKay had never yet had the privilege of independent command at a senior level but he was well qualified for his promotion: he was a highly conscientious, brave soldier well aware of the part played by sound tactics and adequate logistic support. He possessed other attributes necessary for any good soldier: self-possession – as amply demonstrated in his memoirs – and impressive reserves of energy. Such qualities had served him well up to divisional level; now he had to demonstrate the mark of a successful commander in his ability to take bold initiatives. It was MacKay's fate, like that of

David Leslie and Leven in his declining years, to be opposed by an outstanding adversary. MacKay's biographer, while strongly biased in his subject's favour, acknowledged Dundee's 'lofty bearing and chivalrous spirit' in dealing with the Highlanders, a quality for which MacKay was not himself noted.[26]

Ironically despite his wilful inexperience of the Highland regions, during his campaign against Dundee MacKay did little wrong, wasting no time in pursuing his adversary whom he rightly believed still had only a handful of men. But Dundee's brilliant use of the Highland terrain helped him turn the tables and link up with his own reinforcements, becoming MacKay's pursuer. MacKay reasoned correctly (his ideas were to be implemented later by others) that the only certain way to beat the elusive rebels was to build a chain of fortresses across the northern Highlands which, if strongly garrisoned, could become the springboards for rapid attacks on them. Such a policy needed more time to execute than MacKay was allowed and very much superior forces to carry out, but it resulted in bringing the two sides into open battle.

On 26 July 1689, MacKay decided that Dundee must be denied Blair Castle which the Stuarts of Ballechin were holding on his behalf. Accordingly MacKay hastened from Perth and reached Dunkeld at midnight, only to learn that Dundee had already occupied Blair with some of his forces. However, Dundee appeared unwilling to be bottled up and had retired to the wild mountainous area near Killiecrankie, where he had positioned a guard at the head of the pass. MacKay decided on immediate pursuit; his numbers were superior and reinforcements were coming to join him from Stirling. He rightly saw this as his great opportunity before Dundee's active spirit working on the Highlanders could bring 'a vast accession of force to the enemies of the government'.[27]

MacKay therefore resumed his march towards the pass of Killiecrankie. Despite his numerical superiority of two to one it seemed a rash decision to venture into such a forbidding pass where the road was extremely narrow, confined between a range of craggy precipices on one hand and on the other the river tumbling down from rock to rock on a level for the most part considerably lower than the road.[28] The wily Dundee allowed him unmolested passage. After clearing the pass, no doubt with considerable relief, MacKay halted on a low field near the river for his baggage and reinforcements to arrive. From the time he caught sight of the Highlanders moving down higher ground to his left MacKay lost the initiative. When he responded by moving up to higher ground himself he found his position was still dominated by a further slope leading up to the heights of Creag Eallaich. He had no option but to prepare for battle where he stood. While he was shrewd enough to move 500 yards or so from the River Garry it still presented a considerable barrier for foot soldiers. As Sadler has rightly observed, because of this river, 'If this line was broken any form of orderly withdrawal would be difficult in the extreme.'[29]

Once committed to battle MacKay set about forming his troops into the most advantageous formations possible. However, through fear of being outflanked and cut off from the line of the pass he surrendered part of his numerical advantage by stretching out his battalions in a long line, three men deep, leaving a space in the middle in which he placed his two troops of horse.[30] Going from left to right he first posted Colonel George Lauder's fusileers 'in a little hill wreathed with trees'. Next came Balfour's, Ramsay's and Kenmure's three regiments. The horse under Lord Belhaven 'formed the centre while Leven's regular regiment, together with MacKay's and Hasting', stood on the right where the slope levelled somewhat (see battle plan on p. 134).

In a country which he found alien, positioned at the end of an intimidating pass with his room for manoeuvre strictly limited, MacKay had good reason to feel apprehensive. He could not be certain that Dundee's force was as small as it was said to be, and he so feared Dundee's cavalry (which in the event was only sixty strong) that he dropped his own mounted forces back from their central station in the line and placed his cannon in front to protect them. Nevertheless he adjusted his formations to meet the expected attack in a thoroughly efficient way.

When the attack was delayed as Dundee waited for the sun to set MacKay attempted to hearten his men by rallying them in the traditional manner of a commander before battle. Unfortunately, his address was less than inspiring and considerably longer than he subsequently made out. After commencing by justifying their cause he expanded his arguments in favour of Protestantism to include not only Britain but the whole world. As his men stood there in that most hostile country, with the prospect of a hazardous battle before them, they were lectured on the country's need to maintain law and order as well as the vital necessity for them not to betray 'a criminal faintheartedness'. Nor were the reasons he gave for holding their ground calculated to raise their spirits, since they were told if they happened to give way they would scarcely be able to escape their hated pursuers who were 'speedier of foot than they'![31]

As MacKay and his men stood immobile, the demons of fear began to plague them further. MacKay became worried that the order to attack might come as it was getting dark, for the fright and disorder that the attackers could produce in such conditions were incalculable. As John Mack wrote, 'It was not without the most intense anxiety that MacKay beheld the sun sinking towards the horizon and just as this feeling was wound up to its highest pitch about half an hour before sunset, he perceived the Highlanders moving slowly down the hill, bare-footed and stript to their shirts.'[32] The plain fact was (and MacKay knew it) that he had no answer to the Highland charge if it were pushed forward relentlessly against him. Despite the inevitable casualties as the clansmen attempted to close upon his superior forces, once they were near enough to throw away their muskets and draw their broad swords they would in all probability prevail.

In his account of the battle, Hugh MacKay's biographer felt bound to acknowledge the 'extraordinary achievements of Highlanders on the field of battle as exemplified on this occasion'.[33] Hugh MacKay was understandably less fulsome, and stressed the severe casualties suffered by the Highlanders as they rushed down the hill towards his position: 'The enemy lost on the field six to our one, the fire to our right being continued and brisk, whereby not only Dundee with several gentlemen of quality of the countys of Angus and Perth, but also many of the best gentlemen among the Highlanders, particularly of the MacDonald of Isles and Glengarie were killed coming down the hill.' MacKay, who in his account always quaintly referred to himself as the general, then went on to point out that his regiment on the right together with Leven's regulars made the best fire and all the execution. No such justification, however, could change the fact that the charge succeeded and that after gathering what men he could, MacKay fled for some sixty hours before he reached Stirling.

To his credit when MacKay learned that his formidable enemy was dead he acted like a man reborn. Two days after the battle the clans flocked to the Stuart standard until they numbered around 5000. But instead of Dundee the command fell upon an officer,

Colonel Alexander Cannon, who was no equal of MacKay. With 2000 men MacKay hastened to save Perth from the clans and near the city surprised and defeated 300 men of Clan Robertson, whereupon a nervous Cannon withdrew towards Aberdeen. MacKay pursued him vigorously and Cannon moved west to Atholl, where he discovered Dunkeld was being held by a single regiment of Cameronians, commanded by the same fanatical William Cleland who ten years before had fought with the Covenanters against Claverhouse at Drumclog. Cannon, whose Highlanders were now reduced to 3000 men, no doubt felt it would present a relatively easy target and give his men a victory that would put heart into them. The result was far different: the narrow streets of Dunkeld gave little scope for the Highland charge and, against their zealot defenders, the Highlanders suffered heavy casualties before pulling back. The clans showed their contempt for Cannon by deserting in large numbers: they needed someone who would give them success, and anyway there were harvests to be taken in. Maintaining his own furious pace MacKay moved northwards to Blair Castle where he received its surrender. He had recouped his position to what it had been before Killiecrankie, but with the added advantage that now his great rival was dead.

For MacKay the fighting in Scotland was largely over and he could pursue his fortress policy with the building of a great fort at Inverlochy which he named Fort William in honour of his king. During the next year his dragoons, under Sir Thomas Livingstone, had no difficulty in putting down another rising under Cannon's successor, Major General Buchan, and with the northern threat extinguished, MacKay was able to accompany the king to the Hague and spend the winter with his family in Holland. He left Scotland with absolutely no regrets. As he wrote, 'All these considerations made the General look upon Scotsmen of those times in general as void of zeal for their religion and natural affection. Seeing all men hunt after their particular advantages . . . gave him a real distaste of the country and service resolving from that time forward to disengage himself out of it as soon as possible he could get it done and that the service could allow of.'[34]

Yet MacKay who heartily disliked both his country and fellow Scots went on to demonstrate his continuing powers of leadership in other fields. During 1691 he served in Ireland as second in command to General Ginkel, the veteran Dutch soldier fighting on behalf of William III. There he led 1500 grenadiers on a brilliant assault of Irishtown after fording the River Shannon at a perilous place. One month later, at the battle of Aughrim, he led his cavalry across a hitherto impassable bog using a pathway of hurdles, and it was MacKay's initiative that was chiefly responsible for the resulting victory. In October 1691 MacKay returned to Holland with the British forces fighting alongside the Dutch and Germans for the Protestant Grand Alliance against the French. In the following year he was appointed general in command of 16,000 Dutch and British troops. He distinguished himself in the vanguard of the allied attackers at the battle of Steenkirk but was then commanded to hold an exposed position without the reinforcements he considered were necessary. Upon hearing his request for reinforcements had been refused by the Dutch general Hendrik Solms he appeared resigned at the likely outcome, shouting 'The will of the Lord be done'. In the battle that followed he and the greater part of his division were slain.

Compared with the other Covenanting generals who fought the Jacobites, Hugh MacKay was by far the most pious. Bishop Burnet was convinced this did not make him a better commander, since in the final analysis he saw everything as being the will of God. 'His piety made him too apt to mistrust his own sense and to be too tender or rather fearful in anything where there might be a needless effusion of blood.'[35]

He had another quality that did not work in his favour: if his opinion was overruled by a Council of War, even if he was not convinced, he would not persist in his own ideas, but rather go on to justify the majority verdict 'as if his own opinion had prevailed'.[36]

Notwithstanding a fundamental lack of confidence when in sole command, his almost unworldly piety and his strong need for self justification, Hugh MacKay was a good soldier who gained a deserved reputation in Holland and who later distinguished himself both in Scotland and Ireland. Yet, like David Leslie, he seemed most happy when working under a supreme commander and, almost alone among Scottish military leaders, he had a poor regard of both his native country and many of his fellow Scots. The Highlands were a foreign country to him and the fertile mind of Dundee, with his ability to fire what MacKay saw as 'Highland rabble' to selfless and heroic deeds, was quite beyond MacKay's imagining. In fairness it would have required a far greater commander than MacKay to withstand Dundee and the north-western clans at Killiecrankie.

Lord George Murray (1694–1760)

Like Montrose and Dundee Lord George Murray fought for the House of Stuart to liberate Scotland from what he saw as foreign domination and like them he was destined to fail. In his case he was never formally acknowledged as the true leader of the army he was appointed to command, and had to endure constant criticism from among its ranks as he struggled to make it into an efficient military machine.

While unquestionably the Jacobites' outstanding commander during the '45 campaign his royal leader only made him joint lieutenant-general together with the thirty-two-year-old Duke of Perth. In fact the duke, in spite of having no military training, was granted his lieutenant-general's commission first and thus technically outranked Lord George. Such a situation was bound to cause serious problems at times of difficulty and crisis, although in the circumstances it was fully understandable that Prince Charles Edward reserved the most senior command for himself. In spite of the prince's naïvety, self-centredness and military ignorance, both his name and undoubted personal charm were invaluable in persuading men to join his hazardous enterprise. But with the odds so heavily weighted against his venture succeeding he needed effective field command which, by temperament and experience, he was certainly not able to provide himself.

If only the prince had given Lord George full support in military matters the clumsy system of joint commanders might have been made to work, for the Duke of Perth was so devoted to the prince's cause that it is likely he would have put aside his personal ambitions. Unfortunately the command hierarchy did not devolve solely on the three of them, for the prince brought with him a number of familiars of Irish descent with pretensions of their own. Among these was the prince's former tutor, Sir Thomas Sheridan, an opinionated old captain of Carabineers, Sir John MacDonald and Colonel John William O'Sullivan, 'a soldier, on his own account, of some distinction but generally perceived by most who knew him as an intemperate and bombastic fool'.[37] Ambitions aside, like the prince they had far less to lose than Lord George and his Athollmen, or for that matter than the clan leaders, particularly those like Lochiel or Keppoch, who had come out in the previous risings.

The prince gave his household companions military posts far beyond their competence and unforgivably, in their envy of Lord George's greater ability, they took every opportunity to blacken his name with their master. The combination of their gross inefficiency and Lord George's scalding impatience with it ensured the unlikelihood of relations between them ever improving. Sir Thomas Sheridan attempted to act in the capacity of both foreign and military secretary. He was incapable of carrying out either role effectively and as a result the extent of French help was less than the Jacobites could have expected. Sir John MacDonald served as an aide, but he was not only old but so frequently intoxicated that he was unable to carry out his duties. By far the most influential, as far as Lord George was concerned, was John William O'Sullivan, the prince's self-styled military adviser, quartermaster and adjutant-general, who clashed with Lord George on virtually every important occasion. They were as oil and water: where Lord George was resolute, O'Sullivan was ever absent at times of danger; above all he was incompetent. After acting as tutor to the son of the French marshal, Maillebois, a commission had been found for him in the French army, but after 20 years of foreign service he remained a captain. To rely on incompetents was bad enough but as Lord Elcho observed, 'the prince was naturally of a suspicious turn of mind'[38] and his inner cabinet of mediocre Irishmen were far wittier and more obsequious companions than the blunt, determined but ever-resourceful Lord George. To their disgrace they both encouraged and fed any antipathy the prince showed for Lord George. The unfortunate results from such plotting soon began to manifest themselves during the military campaign and at its conclusion they had disastrous consequences. When the climacteric came the prince had virtually lost all faith in Lord George's loyalty although, in fact, he remained unfailingly true if no longer affectionately disposed towards his wayward master.

As a boy, Lord George was the most physically robust and unruly of five sons born to the Duke of Atholl at the family seat of Blair. Although a lifelong Protestant, when Lord George ran away from school he was taken in by his uncle, whose wife Lady Nairne, a staunch Jacobite and Catholic, exerted a powerful influence over him. Having taken a junior commission in the army of Queen Anne and later in that of George I, in 1715 he gladly exchanged it for a colonelcy in the army of the old Pretender. During the 1715 campaign he became renowned for his strict discipline and rare organising ability. He was absent from the defeat at Sheriffmuir, but was involved four years later in the next Stuart uprising, this time as a major-general under his brother William, who acted as the force commander.

After the failure of this campaign Lord George, among other Jacobites, was banished to the Continent where he served King James for a further eight and a half years. During that time the king sent him to complete his education at the Paris academy and saved the headstrong young man from several serious escapades, notably his involvement in a foolish duel with Campbell of Glendaruel for which ever afterwards he had Lord George's unswerving loyalty. In 1724 Lord George's father fell seriously ill and King James granted him leave to visit the duke, while after his father's death, the king approved his seeking a pardon from the Hanoverian authorities. This was duly granted and Lord George took a lease on Murray lands near Tullibardine castle. Although his interest in military affairs remained unabated most of his energy was now directed to organising his own and other estates. Never a dissembler he still refused to take a formal oath of allegiance to the Hanoverians but, fourteen years after his pardon, with the Stuart fortunes at their lowest ebb, the Atholl family appealed to him to help organise his brother John's parliamentary campaign. For such a public role he had no option but to take the oath of allegiance, although he heartily detested the current Whig administration at Westminster which he judged as venal where 'All seems to centre on self-interest'. In truth, Lord George's heart remained with the Stuart cause and with his old master, and he persuaded himself, for instance, that a return by the Stuarts would be accompanied by a rise in moral standards, led by the example of King James himself.

In 1741, soon after belatedly taking the oath of allegiance, he was approached by the Jacobite representative in Scotland, Lord John Drummond, brother of the Duke of Perth, and although the discussion at that time was general, Lord George acknowledged that for King James he would still 'wholly give himself up to his duty, venture his life to his service, and ever remain his faithful servant'.[39] However, less than three years later the news of young Prince Charles Edward's landing at Moidart on 25 July 1744 with just seven followers did not bring Lord George's automatic support. His prime sympathy lay with the prince's father, and the debacle of 1719 and its failure to attract support remained strongly in his mind. There were, too, all the years of hard work he had put into reviving the Atholl estates. All this was bound to be lost if he turned his coat and, if the rising did not succeed, the consequences to his family would be disastrous. Any risk of Lord George standing in isolation ended with the return of his elder brother William, the long-exiled Duke of Atholl who ordered his clansmen to take up their swords for the Stuart cause. More pressure came by way of a personal letter from the prince, requesting Lord George to help him. At this, whatever the fearful risks and the grave effects to his loved ones, he felt he could hold out no longer. He wrote in justification to his brother James, who remained true to the Hanoverians: 'My life, my fortune, my expectations, the happiness of my wife and children are all at stake (and chances are against me), and yet a principle of (what seems to me) honour, it is only with respect to you. I owe obligations to nobody else – I mean the Court of London. If you find you cannot forgive me, yet sure you will pity me.'[40]

Lord George's decision was a massive boost for the prince's landing, for he was recognised not only as a man of strong and upright character, with a broad grasp of affairs, but above all (despite his relative lack of experience) as someone with the gift of genuine military leadership. Winifred Duke goes as far as to say that only the adherence of Lochiel to the prince's cause, followed by that of noble and unselfish men like Lord George and Lord Pitsligo, prevented Charles Edward being forced to make an ignominious return to France.[41]

Whatever his nominal position as joint commander with the Duke of Perth, from the time Lord George joined the Jacobite forces he seized the initiative, 'taking charge of everything and attending to everything',[42] demanding firm discipline from the Highlanders. Here he was on sure ground for he was not only familiar with the relationship of a clan chief to his men but he also understood that a force commander exercised as much authority over them as a chief, and must always act in the manner expected by the other chiefs.

To foster his public image as a commander of Highland soldiers he decided that while in Scotland he would wear the kilt, but his interest in them did not stop there. As a conscientious leader he concerned himself with their food and equipment and ensured that they did not suffer unnecessary hardships. To help discourage plundering, a practice bound to alienate those whose support was needed, he proposed a commissariat committee to co-ordinate the Highland army's supply system. Predictably this brought him into immediate conflict with the prince's quartermaster, General William O'Sullivan.

In the early stages of the campaign Lord George was warmly disposed towards his young royal master, delighting in the energy and enthusiasm he showed and approving his willingness to share in their long marches. This could not fail to have an effect on the prince yet, from now onwards, he was systematically turned against Lord George. The prince's secretary, Murray of Broughton, for instance, continually questioned Lord George's adherence to the Jacobite cause when he had previously served the Hanoverians, reminding the prince that Lord George had taken oaths of allegiance to the government and because of this he 'had been looked upon for some time as no friend to the cause'.[43]

In the meantime, the bold adventure had begun and the Highland army with Lord George at their head moved south, crossing the Forth near Stirling. After taking Edinburgh they moved on to Prestonpans where they met General Cope commanding an English army of about 2300 men, many of them raw recruits but supported by regulars of the 13th and 14th Dragoons and armed with six cannon. The Jacobites had slightly higher numbers but they were quite without artillery and their cavalry were limited to a mere forty horsemen. The English occupied a strong defensive position, but Lord George devised a plan of attack that included a turning movement which exposed the Jacobites' flank to the enemy. This however brought indignation from O'Sullivan since it violated his text book theory of war. Working on knowledge of the ground provided by a sympathiser, the rebel army, with Lord George leading the left wing and the Duke of Perth the right, made a successful approach march. Shortly before dawn on 21 September 1745 in swirling mist the Highlanders successfully interposed themselves across the English flank.

As the sky lightened General Cope realised he had been thoroughly outmanoeuvred. He endeavoured to swing his whole battle line to the left, at the same time shouting abuse against the Jacobite forces, calling them 'a parcel of rabble, a parcel of brutes'.[44] Shortly after the words were uttered the 'brutish' Highlanders were rushing forward towards Cope's army. His cavalry broke first, followed by his gunners, and finally the infantry succumbed to the flailing broadswords and Lochaber axes. In barely fifteen minutes it was all over; Cope lost 300 men killed on the field and 1600 were captured. For a death roll of just forty soldiers and six officers, the Jacobites now controlled Scotland, with the exception of government garrisons holding out in Edinburgh and Stirling. The prince and his army made a triumphant entry into the Scottish capital although Lord George took no part in it. He had returned to the battlefield to make arrangements for feeding the prisoners and taking possession of the enemy guns and baggage. Here he clashed again with O'Sullivan, 'who put round a malicious story that Lord George had sent away a number of carts laden with booty for his own purposes'.[45]

After Prestonpans the prince was anxious to move immediately into England and harry the government before it could gather its forces but, as was usual after any successful battle, many of the Highlanders went home, some with their plunder, others ostensibly to bring in the harvest. Although speed and surprise were undoubtedly important factors and the prince was convinced his Highland army was invincible, his commander knew it was unbelievably rash to consider invading England with a mere 1500 followers, unless they could be sure that large numbers of men from the northern counties stood ready to join the Stuart cause. Lord George was aware of how things had changed since the beginning of the century and that in the 1740s the reaction to foreign intervention on behalf of the Stuarts was likely to be far less positive.

In retrospect the army's six week stay in Edinburgh while it awaited reinforcements proved disastrous to the rebellion, nor did they gain any supplementary help from abroad. During this time the prince held a daily council of war and throughout these meetings it was Lord George, with a grasp of affairs far superior to either O'Sullivan or the Duke of Perth, who usually 'brought the majority over to his opinion'.[46] With good cause he frustrated the prince's grand but illusory designs based on his conception after Prestonpans of the Highlanders' fighting ability. 'Ever after (he) imagined they would beat four times their number of regular troops.'[47] Sadly this only helped to confirm in the prince's mind the calumnies spread by Murray, the prince's secretary, about Lord George's loyalty and to increase his own dislike of his blunt and outspoken general.[48]

Both reason and perceived wisdom were on Lord George's side for, despite the prince's promises, no French nor Spanish appeared to swell his little army, while Dutch forces had already arrived in England to oppose them and other English forces from the continent were steadily massing. In a worsening situation some of the chiefs went as far as to say they wished to have nothing to do with any invasion of England.

It became clear to the senior commanders that in spite of mounting problems and Charles' failure to make contact with his potential supporters in England, unless the army invaded England soon the opportunity would be lost. The order was accordingly given. The prince proposed marching straight on Newcastle to seek out General Wade, who headed an army almost twice their size. Lord George was alarmed at risking everything against such superior forces on ground of their own choosing, and favoured taking Carlisle, thereby forcing Wade into a long march if he wanted to intercept them. At Carlisle it was hoped they could enlist support from the English Jacobites. This became the chosen option.

In the end General Wade's army was so weakened by sickness that it might have been defeated, but logic was undoubtedly on Lord George's side. As the Jacobites approached Carlisle, Lord George was offered the army's supreme command but, because of his inexperience in siege warfare, he inexplicably deferred to the Duke of Perth over the positioning of the batteries there. At this, the prince took the opportunity of sending all his orders to Perth rather than Lord George and although the city soon fell, relations between the prince and Lord George Murray deteriorated to such a degree that Lord George tendered his resignation as army commander, although still offering to serve the Jacobite cause as a volunteer. The prince immediately accepted his resignation (which was exactly what his secretary, Murray, wanted), but the army became so alarmed at the demotion of its most capable leader that the prince – much against his own judgement – was forced to ask him to take back his commission. Both at Carlisle and after, the expected English recruits failed to materialise and only at Manchester did any volunteers join the Jacobites. Even then there were only 200 of them. If the militia and volunteer regiments on the English establishment were included, the 4500 strong Scottish army now had 60,000 men in arms against it.

At Derby, although the bells were rung for the prince as he entered the town, only three recruits joined him while the government forces were moving closer. Finally on 4 December, in despair at their inactivity, Lord George presented himself to the prince with the challenging words, 'It is high time to think about what we are to do'. On the next day a grand council of war was held and, to the immense disappointment of the prince, the momentous but inevitable decision was made to turn back for Scotland. Lord George took a prominent part in the discussions about the threats provided by the approaching English armies, one under the Duke of Cumberland, the other under General Wade. Lord George said the Scots had now done all that could be expected of them. They had marched into the heart of England without any party declaring for the prince or any French troops being landed to support them. If there was an invitation on behalf of English Jacobites for the army to go to London or to any other part of England they were ready to go; if not, the army must withdraw to prevent it being sacrificed. The only alternative now open to them was for a sudden and speedy retreat. Lord George undertook to bring the army 'safe back to Carlisle by the very same road they came' and promised he would always take the rearguard station. After moving so close to London once they were safely back in Carlisle the French and all Europe must have a good opinion of them and send help.

Despite such brave words it is uncertain how much confidence Lord George had in such continental reinforcements, although there can be no doubts about his conviction that the army should move back to safety. Of those attending, only the Duke of Perth, seeing how set the prince was on advancing, tried to persuade the others to consider attacking Cumberland's army. The prince heard all the arguments with the greatest impatience, fell into a passion and gave 'most of the gentlemen that had spoken very abusive language and said that they had a mind to betray him'.[49] Of the prince's familiars, Murray of Broughton, argued strenuously for the retreat and was supported by General William O'Sullivan. However, when they found it was carried by a great majority they later tried to reinstate themselves with the prince by saying the only reason they agreed to the retreat was because they knew it would certainly be put into execution. It is difficult to believe that such arguments put forward by pusillanimous men would fully convince the prince, yet undoubtedly from this time onwards the chances of the prince and Lord George, his most able leader, working together in any sort of harmony had gone.

Despite the prince's strict instructions that no cannon nor ammunition should be left behind and the immense difficulties this was to cause in the winter conditions, Lord George successfully brought about the army's safe withdrawal from England. This he did as a result of his unshakeable resolution combined with tactical flair, both qualities which were in evidence when he inflicted a sharp reverse on Cumberland's cavalry as it harried them just short of the border. On 20 December 1745 the Highland army crossed back into Scotland, where, as the chiefs had foretold, it received considerable reinforcements, mostly clansmen from the north but also a small but useful force of 800 men from France under Lord John Drummond, including six cannon.

The Jacobite army was now 9000 strong and Lord George, eager to take advantage of the improved position, was all for attacking the government forces of roughly equal strength that were near Falkirk, under General Hawley (Cumberland's second in command) who had taken over troops from General Wade. Lord George knew they had to act fast for the government forces were sure to be augmented soon and would seriously outnumber the Jacobites. So it was agreed and Lord George ordered Lord John Drummond to make a feint towards the government positions which, as he hoped, succeeded in bringing about considerable confusion. On 17 January 1746, using his knowledge of the ground, Lord George led the army's main body over the river Carron at Dunipace, in order to occupy the ridge of Falkirk Muir from where he was sure he could dominate the enemy. The government forces were taken off guard and their commander arrived on the battlefield only at the last moment, having been beguiled by Lady Kilmarnock (a staunch Jacobite) into a heavy and bibulous lunch. To Hawley's credit, when he appeared he did not hesitate; after ordering his dragoons to contest the ridge he sent his foot soldiers and artillery to follow them up it. Upon the ridge sleety squalls broke over both armies, weather familiar to Highlanders who had the sleet pattering on their backs, but it struck directly into the faces of the government troops, half-blinding them as they struggled upwards. It was not until the two sides were almost at the high point of the ridge that they caught sight of each other.

Up to this point everything had gone the Highlanders' way; as Lord George acknowledged, 'The Highland army had all the advantages that nature or art could give them.'[50] There followed a pause during which Lord George's three MacDonald regiments advanced slowly in line to let the other regiments take up their positions on the left.

Lord George chose to fight on foot and with his broadsword and targe (illustrated in somewhat romantic fashion by his portrait on plate 10) he walked down the front of the MacDonald lines ordering his men 'to keep their ranks, and not to fire until he gave the order'. Shortly before this he had sent his two mounted ADCs, Colonel Kerr and Major Anderson of Whitburgh, to find out whether the enemy dragoons facing him had infantry support or not. To his satisfaction he was told they had not.

Meanwhile the Jacobite centre and left wing came into position and formed up in line alongside the MacDonalds. On the extreme left were the Stuarts of Appin facing a small but steep ravine while between them and Lord George's MacDonalds came the Camerons, Frasers, MacPhersons, Mackintoshes, Mackenzies and Farquharsons. In the second line from left to right were the regiments of Lord Lewis Gordon, Lord Ogilvy and the Atholl Brigade. The reserve arrived later, for these troops had accompanied Lord John Drummond on his first march. The reserve was under the command of the prince.

Unbeknown to Lord George the prince's command system had broken down. A commander had not been appointed over the army's left wing although Lord George had assumed all along that it was Lord John Drummond. After the prince, responsibility for the lapse lay with his adjutant General William O'Sullivan who should have been riding through the lines monitoring the battle.

In any case Lord George had enough to occupy him. His infantry faced three full regiments of dragoons against which the Jacobites had no equivalent horse. Fortunately they were not yet supported by infantry. Hawley's infantry regiments were, in fact, toiling up the slopes approaching the ridge when the storm which had threatened all day broke over them. In the most adverse conditions Wolfe's regiment hastily formed in line while the rest, Cholmondeley's, Pulteney's, the Royal, Price's and Ligonier's regiments filled in on its right and the second line regiments Blakeney's, Munro's, Fleming's,

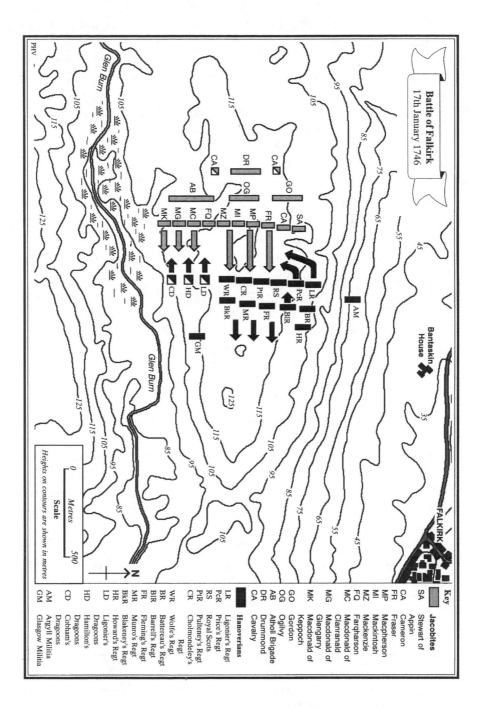

Battle of Falkirk
17th January 1746

Key

Jacobites

SA	Stewart of
	Appin
CA	Cameron
FR	Fraser
MP	Macpherson
MI	Mackintosh
MZ	Mackenzie
FQ	Farquarson
MC	Macdonald of
	Clanranald
MG	Macdonald of
	Glengarry
MK	Macdonald of
	Keppoch
GO	Gordon
OG	Ogilvy
AB	Atholl Brigade
DR	Drummond
CA	Cavalry

Hanoverians

LR	Ligonier's Regt
PcR	Price's Regt
RS	Royal Scots
PtR	Pulteney's Regt
CR	Cholmondeley's
	Regt
WR	Wolfe's Regt
BR	Battereau's Regt
BIR	Barrell's Regt
FR	Fleming's Regt
MR	Munro's Regt
BkR	Blakeney's Regt
HR	Howard's Regt
LD	Ligonier's
	Dragoons
HD	Hamilton's
	Dragoons
CD	Cobham's
	Dragoons
AM	Argyll Militia
GM	Glasgow Militia

Scale

0   500

Metres

Heights on contours are shown in metres

→ N

Bantaskin
House

FALKIRK

Glen Burn

Barrell's, Battereau's and Howard's (Old Buffs) took up positions behind them.

The opposing lines were by no means opposite each other. On the Jacobite right Lord George's infantry outflanked their mounted opponents who could not extend due to a belt of wet and broken ground while on the left the situation was reversed although three of Hawley's regiments, Price's and Ligonier's with Battereau's in the rear, could not use their superior numbers to work round the Jacobites' left flank because they faced the ravine. O'Sullivan, alarmed by the strength of enemy numbers on the left, ordered up Lord Ogilvy's regiment from the rear but it is doubtful whether it was in time to play any worthwhile part. There was still no overall commander for that flank.

By the time the opposing forces had taken up their respective stations it was nearly 4 o'clock in the afternoon. On such a winter's day the light was fading quickly when the confident and impatient Hawley sent orders for Colonel Ligonier and his dragoons to begin attacking the MacDonalds. The three regiments advanced at a good trot in very good order. Lord George waited until the horsemen seemed perilously close before ordering what proved to be an accurate and damaging volley into their ranks. More than eighty troopers were killed outright with many more injured and most turned and fled crashing into their own foot and scattering them. To its credit Ligonier's dragoon regiment continued to advance but as its troopers reached the Highland lines their horses' bellies were dirked by men lying in the ground and their riders dragged off and killed. The dragoons were pursued enthusiastically by the Highlanders and two of the MacDonald regiments were now quite beyond Lord George's control.

The success on the left was not lost on the Jacobites' centre formations and finding it almost impossible in the heavy sleet to reload their muskets they flung them away and charged forward swords in hand in what O'Sullivan extravagantly called was 'perhaps one of the boldest and finest actions that any troops of the world could be capable of'. They were followed by many from the second lines. Already disorganised by the fleeing dragoons four of Hawley's six front line regiments, Wolfe's, Cholmondeley's, Pulteney's and the Royal gave way and as they ran (with the exception of Barrell's regiment) they were followed by the second line.

Fortunately for Hawley, Barrell's regiment joined with Ligonier's infantry and Price's regiment who had stood inactive facing the ravine and together they moved back up the slope in a leftwards direction. Here they poured accurate cross fire into the flank of the pursuing Jacobites and 'threw them into great disorder'. At this an order went out for the Highlanders to stop their pursuit and many became uncertain of what to do next. On both sides many men thought the battle lost.

On the ridge above, Lord George Murray, along with some of Keppoch's regiment, had been joined by the Atholl Brigade and they stood there in perfect formation, eager to complete the victory. Lord George asked permission to advance his reserve but before it was granted the Jacobites faced a new threat. Cobham's dragoons who were least affected by the MacDonalds' charge moved up the hill to the Jacobites' rear where they were checked by the Irish piquets from the reserve. At this point Hawley's men, seeing no further prospects of success, formed a strong rear guard and moved towards Falkirk from where they continued their retreat to Linlithgow. Lord George had moved his men downwards, and to his surprise he was joined there by Lord John Drummond, but uncertain of the battles' fortunes elsewhere he halted them at the base of the ridge.

Fought in swirling snow and fading light the battle was confusing for both sides. At its conclusion the Jacobites held the field but a great chance had been lost. After Lord George had given them a powerful advantage by his skilled approach march and the conduct of his MacDonalds against their opposing dragoons, the government forces should have remained at a disadvantage throughout. The charge of the Highlanders from the Jacobite central formations could have decided the day but it became uncoordinated and allowed Hawley's men to regroup. With Lord George's inability to communicate with an equivalent commander on the Jacobites' other flank he decided he must keep his reserve regiments steady in order to match the enemy's still unbroken ranks. With greater knowledge of events he could have loosed his men and gained a far more crushing victory.

The tragedy of Falkirk for the Highland army was that, while it inflicted a definite reverse on the government's troops, it did not demoralise them and their combined strength continued to increase.

It was entirely due to Lord George that the rebels followed up their success as far as they did, namely by taking possession of Falkirk. The prince, who earlier had advocated the most hazardous of expeditions into England, vetoed Lord George's proposal to pursue Hawley's disorganised forces, preferring instead to give him the task of besieging the formidable castle of Stirling which, while a powerful symbol, could bring the Highlanders no strategic benefits. It was a decision based on resentment more than anything else. The task was made the more difficult because, although the Highlanders were awesome in pursuit, they actively disliked siege warfare and had inadequate cannon to achieve a quick result. One of the young officers, James Johnstone, was furious with the decision and wrote: 'We should have kept continually at their heels; we should never have relaxed until they were no longer in a condition to rally . . . The absurd wish to possess an insignificant castle which could be of no use to us produced a series of effects which ruined the prince's enterprise and brought a great many of his partisans to the scaffold.'[51]

The sad truth was that by now virtually any suggestion from Lord George was not only criticised but vetoed by Charles and his cabal of advisers. After Falkirk some of the Highlanders again departed with their booty, and as the strength of the Jacobite army fell and Hawley reorganised his shaken formations, the rebel commanders learned that Cumberland was approaching with an army twice their strength. Against this twofold threat the Highland chiefs knew they must move further north into the Highlands, a decision which incensed Charles and for which he characteristically blamed Lord George Murray. Although the prince finally agreed to it he washed his hands of the consequences.

When the retreat began, a rash of conflicting orders made it appear more like a flight than an ordered withdrawal. Lord George himself was almost captured by an enemy sally from Stirling Castle. During the acrimonious council of war that followed, Lord George proposed a stand at Atholl which the prince immediately refused, so the decision was taken to retreat to Inverness; it was agreed that the cavalry together with the Low Country regiments would take the coastal route while the prince and clans moved through the Highlands. In bitter weather with snow often up to their thighs and their eyebrows and heads covered in icicles Lord George's men eventually reached Elgin. Before them, in Inverness, Lord Loudoun's Government militiamen slipped away into Sutherland. Attempts to pursue them were unsuccessful and Lord George moved his men back to Dingwall. He now planned to dislodge the hated Campbell Militia from Atholl and by seizing his family's seat at Blair castle he intended to throw out a challenge to Cumberland which he hoped would lure him from the Aberdeen region into wilder country much more to the liking of the Highlanders. Moving back into the Grampians he set out for Rothiemurchus and then over the hills to Dalwhinnie. Dividing his men into thirty small groups they moved fast across the inhospitable country and just before daybreak each company seized the thirty houses and inns in Atholl occupied as Government outposts. Lord George went on to beseige Blair Castle but after fifteen days just when he was close to success, he was ordered by the prince to return to Inverness: if Cumberland ignored the intended bait of Blair Castle he could be at Inverness in a day or two and every soldier would be needed to face him there.

On 12 April Cumberland crossed the River Spey unopposed and pitched camp at Balblair, west of Nairn. At this Lord George ordered his two ADCs, Colonel Keir and Major Kennedy, to reconnoitre a site between the two armies as a possible battleground; they found a patch of rough ground near Dalcross castle which they reported suitable. Later the prince sent O'Sullivan out who selected a different site to the south-east of Culloden house, where he considered a wide morass would apparently protect the Jacobites' left wing. The prince accepted this without bothering to consult Lord George, and Lord Elcho, for one, had no doubt it was the wrong choice. 'There was but one party to take, which was to have crossed the Water of Nairn, which was upon the right and marched up a hill where the Duke's army could not have followed, and have waited there until night, and then attacked him.'[52]

Stuart Reid, in his efforts to paint a more balanced picture of the prince and his mediocre advisers, has pointed out that Lord George's choice of battlefield site took much account of 'the need to find a battlefield from which it would be possible to execute a successful retreat',[53] while O'Sullivan was intending to fight. Reid goes on to point out that to make full use of their renowned charge the Highlanders needed a clear run at their opponents and the battles of Prestonpans and Falkirk had taken place on grounds that were as equally featureless as Culloden. Yet this was not the full story. In both the earlier cases clever manoeuvring by Lord George had led to a degree of surprise that gave him both a moral and physical advantage over his opponents. At Culloden there was no chance of this. While the Highland army had enjoyed equal, if not slightly superior, numbers in the previous two battles it was now heavily outnumbered. The government troops were well rested and had been drilled in a new use of their bayonets to counteract the Highlanders' range of hand weapons. Additionally on the field of Culloden heath the Highland army would have to make its way over relatively open ground, which could be swept by cannon fire supplemented by muskets positioned along one flank. General O'Sullivan could not have foreseen the circumstances that would so tax the physical strength of the rebel army immediately prior to the battle, although it was the highly unfavourable nature of Culloden heath that led Lord George to consider the hazardous and difficult expedient of attacking Cumberland's camp. As Lord Elcho justly observed, the rebels needed some device to level the adverse position adopted by O'Sullivan, but the basic cause of the tragedy stemmed from the prince's willingness to accept O'Sullivan's opinion without considering the possibility of any counter proposals.

At dawn on 15 April the clansmen were drawn up in battle formation on Culloden heath until 11 a.m. when the prince ordered them to refresh themselves by sleep or otherwise.[54] The Jacobite forces were not only outnumbered and on an adverse site, but in spite of the prince's instruction they had no food supplies due to the breakdown of the commissariat arrangements under John Hay, the brother-in-law of the prince's secretary, Murray of Broughton. There were adequate provisions but these were still in Inverness. To any even-minded observer the half-starved, thinly peopled ranks – a great many Highlanders had not yet rejoined – drawn up on the open heath must have seemed a poor match for Cumberland's army and among others the prince started to consider various schemes, including a raid upon Cumberland's camp climaxed by a dawn attack. The officers were appalled at the prospect of such an exhausting march prior to meeting a superior and alerted army in broad daylight. Unsurprisingly a feeling of despondency, even desperation, grew among the chiefs and supporters of Lord George. Their expectations had never included meeting the enemy on 'a large plain muir; and although in some places it was interspersed with bogues and deep ground yet for the most part it was a fair field, and good for horse'.[55] As Lord Elcho remarked bitterly, 'The persons capable of serving (the prince) were suspected and neglected and those on whom he placed his trust had not the ability to be useful to him.'[56]

For his own part, Lord George became convinced that almost anything would be better than remaining at Culloden and he went to the prince, saying he would agree to attack Cumberland's camp by stealth but in a night attack rather than at dawn. 'For as regular troops depend entirely upon their discipline, and on the contrary the Highlanders having none, the night was the best time to put them most upon an equality.' Lord George agreed to take on the most difficult part of the operation, which was the longest march ending with an attack on the rear of the enemy camp, while the Duke of Perth attacked the front and the prince took a supporting role with the second line. He was not sanguine about the outcome: 'I was with many others for a night attack. But that was only of two evils to choose which we thought the least. We thought that it was better than to fight upon that plain muir ... and no attempt could be more desperate than their present situation.'[57]

The rebels moved off at about eight o'clock that night, not being able to start earlier in case they alerted the enemy. According to O'Sullivan as the march began the prince came and put his arm round Lord George's neck saying, 'Lord George, you can't imagine, nor can I express to you, how acknowledging I am of all the services you have rendered me. But this will crown all. You'll restore the King by it.' However, it was too late for a reconciliation. Lord George, burning with resentment over his own treatment and the state to which his kinsmen had been reduced, did not answer. They walked in silence together until Lord George took off his bonnet, made a stiff bow and the prince departed.

From the beginning things started to go wrong. Although Lord George's Highlanders kept moving at two miles an hour the second column constantly fell behind. Whereas the guides knew the ground well, they were less skilled in estimating how long the ten mile march would take, especially as the indirect route adopted was far more than ten miles. From the rear the prince despatched a constant stream of messages telling Lord George to wait. There were some fifty in all, an excessive number in the circumstances, especially as the Royal Scots and Irish picquets who were failing to keep up were only a few hundred strong, and in any case designated for the reserve.

The weather conditions were adverse: the Macintoshes who acted as guides found the night so foggy they could hardly distinguish a white horse from a black one. Lord George's orders were that he would fall on the enemy camp before the second column came up and, although it was hoped the second attack would follow quickly upon the first, it meant his 1200 men engaging an enemy about eight times stronger. To make matters worse many of the attackers left the ranks and threw themselves on the ground, most probably through lack of food. By 2 a.m. it was clear the plan had miscarried. At the existing rate of progress the enemy would have the Highlanders in their sight for at least two miles before they could come at them and in any case their numbers were diminishing with every forward movement. Lord George concluded that to fall upon Cumberland's army in daylight with such few men would be madness and he therefore gave the order to withdraw.

It was a decision that predictably earned the prince's renewed anger, although once they began to retrace their steps he was powerless to reverse it. After the endless march back the thought in most men's minds was to obtain some sleep, but just two hours into their rest a message came that Cumberland's army was on the move with its vanguard only two miles away. The Highlanders were called to battle and with such speed that no discussion was permitted over an alternative site nor would the prince discuss any plans in the event of a defeat. To some of the Highland chiefs it even 'seemed as if the Irish and officers from France weary of the campaign and hoping for a miracle urged the prince to give battle.'[58]

Despite Lord George's anger at the events and his near despair about the likely outcome, he and his men took up their allotted position on the right wing; it was the only sector to be commanded by Lord George that day, for the prince had assumed the role of overall battlefield commander. On entering the field Lord George realised that the stone walls bounding both its sides would prevent the Jacobites stopping any attempt by the enemy to outflank them so he decided they should be torn down. However, O'Sullivan had been slow in setting up the army in line of battle and as this 'would have broke the line and the enemy forming their line of battle near that place, it was judged by those about him too dangerous to attempt.'[59] Not only did the prince's favoured commander make the fatal decision to let the walls stand but, when the English cannonade opened, the prince himself was too far back to exercise the necessary control. All his hopes depended on Cumberland attacking first, but when he did not oblige the prince delayed for half-an-hour, giving Cumberland the opportunity to continue his destructive firing and his men to improve their defensive positions. The Campbells were particularly active, beating down part of a low wall to enfilade the Jacobites' right wing, while Major James Wolfe's detachment also moved forward into an enfilade position. When the prince finally ordered the attack his message went first to the Duke of Perth, whose wing was set further back than Lord George's. The officer charged to carry a similar order to Lord George was killed on his way and it was left to O'Sullivan to transmit the order.

Once the order was received Lord George made directly towards his objective but the Highland centre veered towards the right flank in a confused mass and so closely pressed were Lord George's Frasers, Stuarts, Camerons and Athollmen against the long stone dyke to his right that they could barely swing their swords. All the time they were heavily galled from the musket fire of 200 Campbells supported by the men of Wolfe's regiment who were working in conjunction with a three gun battery set on the Urchill enclosures. Even with large gaps being torn in their ranks the Highlanders succeeded in brushing aside the forward regiments, but broke against the government's second line. As Winifred Duke has said of that gallant but doomed charge, 'There are few incidents in military history finer than the fierce futile dash made through a blinding, bewildering haze of powder and sleet, of the right wing of the prince's army, headed by Lord George Murray. His escape from death was miraculous for his horse plunged and reared to such an extent that he was forced to dismount, lost his bonnet and wig and had his clothes torn in innumerable places.'[60] Lord George retained the presence of mind to struggle back for reinforcements that might yet turn events in the attackers' favour, while the prince, 'who was best placed to see the course of the battle, remained inert, irresolute and immobile, wholly incapable of judging where the regiments in the reserve could best be sent.'[61] It was also Lord George's prescience in sending FitzJames' horse and Elcho's Life guards to the right flank that the whole army was not encircled and destroyed.

Meanwhile, on the left the Highlanders were advancing more slowly and they were still one hundred paces from the enemy when they saw the right wing in full retreat, whereupon they began to retreat themselves. As Lord George hurried forward with his reserves he saw from the men streaming back that it was too late. The bayonets of Cumberland's army (seventeen inches long at this time) together with their superior numbers had prevailed over broadswords wielded by half-starved and exhausted men. As for Lord George, although his regiment had suffered the most casualties he was still able to bring them off the field in good order, together with his reserves.

The prince's first essay in supreme command on a field selected by John William O'Sullivan had ended in disaster. For Charles there was the prospect of sanctuary on the Continent but for so many of his Highlanders, some of whom had been pressed into service by their clan chiefs, there were only the sabres of the pursuing dragoons or, after being dragged from their hiding places and flung into loathsome jails, the prospect of being transported or shot. As for Lord George – whom Colonel Keir reported not only at Culloden but on other battlefields as exposing himself to danger whenever occasion offered, 'a leader who went on with the first and came not off till the last', he determined to fight on. Along with Lord Perth and Lord John Drummond he kept some 1500 men under arms, and when they reached Ruthven sent a despatch to the prince informing him of their assembly. Lord Elcho made an impassioned plea for the prince to join them as they set about regrouping their strength in the mountains, but the prince's advisers were against it and he went on to Glengarry. At this point Lord George, doubtless grieving for the friends he had just lost in battle, and faced with the ruin of all his hopes and endeavours, wrote the prince a scalding letter of criticism on the conduct of the campaign:

> I hope, Sir, you will upon this occasion pardon me if I mention some truths which most of the gentlemen of our army seemed sensible of.
>
> It was surely wrong to set up a Royal Standard without having positive assurance from his most Christian Majesty that he would assist you with all his might. As for what regards the management of your army, we were all fully convinced that Mr O'Sullivan, whom your RH trusted with the most essential things in regard to your operations, was exceedingly unfit for it, and committed gross blunders on many occasions. He whose business it was, did not so much as to visit the ground where we were to draw up in line of battle. In short never was more improper ground for Highlanders than that where we fought . . . The last three days (which were so critical) our army was starved, and this was great cause of our night march proving abortive . . . had our field of battle been right choice, and if we had got plenty of provisions, in all human probability, we would have done by the enemy as they have unhappily done by us.[62]

History is not kind to those who complain but in this case the letter represented a great shout of anger and frustration at a prince who from an early stage would not trust such a loyal follower – whom Chevalier Johnstone for one knew 'was the only person capable of conducting our army'[63] – a prince who increasingly spurned him in favour of incompetents who would inevitably lead them all to disaster. Ten days after assembling at Ruthven Lord George received the prince's chilling command that ended the campaign. 'Let every man seek his safety in the best way he can.'

Lord George went into hiding for eight months in the hope of further military initiatives, but eventually he sailed over to the continent to make his peace with King James. There he found the prince determined never to be reconciled and actively trying to do him harm. But whereas the prince in his bitterness and disillusion became a habitual drunkard and wifebeater, who even refused to visit his father on his deathbed, Lord George showed far more resolution. For fourteen years he lived away from his native land, unable to watch his children grow up, but conscious of the effect on his eldest son of having a traitor for a father. When Lord George was joined by his wife his later years were made more tolerable, but the opportunity to take any further part in public affairs had been irretrievably lost. Lacking a challenge, his health began to deteriorate until, with his wife at his side, he died at Medembilk (north Holland) in his 66th year.

Lord George Murray had the attributes necessary for a true commander. He was personally brave, amazingly energetic with an urge to seek out his enemy. He was equally correct in his treatment of his own men and enemy captives. Like his two predecessors Montrose and Dundee, he sought the battlefield conditions that best suited the Highlanders' soldierly qualities. It was Lord George Murray's fate to serve under the most charismatic, if morally the weakest, of the three Stuart claimants to the British throne, a prince whose mind came to be poisoned against him. If equal trust had existed between Lord George and the young prince, Chevalier Johnstone, for one, was sure they could have worked together to great affect because Lord George was generally acknowledged as 'having a natural genius for military operations.'[64]

Lord George Murray's very strength of personality and serious mein did not recommend him to a prince who reputedly appeared shy and diffident in his company. His forthright style of address, his vigorous and unyielding logic used to bring others round to his thinking, his justifiable pride when successful, his haughtiness when frustrated, his disapproval of jobbery and loose living, his refusal to pander to anyone regardless of rank, repelled his weak master and drove him ever further into the clutches of smooth-tongued flatterers such as Sheridan or O'Sullivan. Like Montrose and Dundee, Lord George Murray might have benefited from a sense of humour. He would also have been well advised not to display so openly his criticism of his royal master.

On the other hand if Lord George had not been so entirely honest, straight and forceful, so grave in his actions to the point of recklessness, so impatient when others were prevaricating, he would have been a lesser commander. It was his tragedy that because of his great virtues he frightened his insubstantial master and that, unlike Montrose and Dundee, was unable to demonstrate his full talents on the battlefield, talents that were superior to those of his opponents and that even as late as the 1740s, could conceivably have led to the reinstatement of the Stuarts on the British throne.

As it was, Culloden led to the dismembering of the clan system and the ruthless destruction of their unique way of life. It rang the death knell to the hopes of any Stuart revival, while over the next fifty years startling economic and social advances would become evident in Scotland as a whole. Twenty years after Culloden the English prime minister, William Pitt, would congratulate himself on recruiting hardy clansmen into the British army. But henceforth any would-be Scottish commander would have to look outside Scotland where, after the war with America, the most promising military opportunities would appear to lie with Britain's great struggle against revolutionary France.

≈

CHAPTER SIX

BRITAIN AGAINST NAPOLEON – ABERCROMBY AND MOORE

'A coward turns away, but a brave man's choice is danger'

Euripides, *Tauris*

R ALPH ABERCROMBY WAS ELEVEN years of age at the time of Culloden but by the time his family purchased a cornetcy for him, when he was twenty-two, a military career for any aspiring Scot meant one thing only, service in the British army. Any opportunity of serving the Stuarts had almost totally disappeared. This was, of course, also true of John Moore, born twenty-seven years later. Both served in the decade of peace between the end of the American revolutionary war and the start of the French Revolution, years when the reform of the British army was long overdue.

Both men had to contend with serious shortcomings among their troops, and their reforms in British army organisation, together with their quality of leadership on the field of battle, opened the way for the period of triumph under Wellington and the defeat of republican France.

Sir Ralph Abercromby (1734–1801)

If battlefield victories are taken as the criterion for success then Sir Ralph Abercromby's military career might be thought less notable than those of some other Scottish captains. But as his son put it, at the commencement of the French revolutionary wars, when victories were scarce: 'It would surely have a deep interest for those who can appreciate the virtue of an officer advanced in life who devotes himself to the service of his country from the day that war is declared to the day of his death, who is discouraged by no disappointment or defeat, who shrinks from no climate, who surrenders at a critical moment a high and honourable position, because he would not consent to oppress the people by violating the principles of law and the Constitution, and who closed his life in the last, the most difficult, and the most arduous service of that war in which he had throughout borne so distinguished a part. . . .'[1]

It is fully understandable that Abercromby has attracted less interest than the Duke of Wellington, whose battlefield exploits with the forces Abercromby helped to revitalise earned him deserved fame. It is probably appropriate that he should receive less attention than Sir John Moore, who developed certain of Abercromby's reforming ideas and was almost certainly the greater battlefield commander. Yet at the time of his death his contemporaries acknowledged Abercromby as a great soldier and posterity seems to have been kinder to him than to John Moore.[2] Abercromby died overseas and was buried at Malta in the crusader fort of St Elmo but subsequently a monument was erected to him in St Paul's Cathedral and a peerage conferred upon his wife. In his native country, among other marks of remembrance, Abercromby Place in Edinburgh's New Town was named in his honour. Abercromby himself would probably have been more delighted by the many taverns named after him by his ex-soldiers turned landlords than in any formal monuments. Apparently only the legendary, generous Marquis of Granby exceeded him in this respect. Such tributes were appropriate for a man with a special regard for ordinary soldiers and who helped lift the British army from its widespread disorganisation and low morale to a high state of efficiency.

Abercromby's work by no means stopped with the lower ranks. It was under him during the Helder campaign when the British invaded Holland in support of Austrian and Russian armies fighting revolutionary France that young Arthur Wellesley, the future Duke of Wellington, learnt much about conducting a successful retreat. Six years before in 1793, when Abercromby first came into prominence as a senior commander during the British army's earlier invasion of Holland (the Flanders expedition) it had but one other capable general, Cornwallis. When Abercromby died, after serving in every important campaign since Flanders, he had nurtured a pack of worthy successors who were subsequently to distinguish themselves, among whom were John Hope, Edward Paget, Rowland Hill, Thomas Graham, Thomas Picton and, above all, Sir John Moore. The latter applied many of his mentor's ideas, notably with regard to training and novel tactical principles together with an increased emphasis on the care of individual soldiers.

In Egypt, for instance, Abercromby developed the missile fire of infantry which so often won victories for Wellington in the Spanish peninsula.[3] Abercromby, an initiator and reformer, was also a good battlefield general, which was remarkable considering the extreme short-sightedness that afflicted him all his life: '. . . so much so as to require the use of a glass in the ordinary affairs of life – in reading, in writing, and in recognising his acquaintances'.[4] By rapid use of a telescope Abercromby was able to observe ground and discern the movements of enemy formations both quickly and well, but to a much greater degree than normal-sighted commanders he relied upon the assistance 'of good executive generals, quick to grasp his intentions, to act on their own responsibility and to carry out his intentions with singleness of purpose during the many phases of a fight'.[5] Abercromby's aides de camp also tended to have greater mandates than those serving other commanders in providing him with rapid briefings of battlefield developments. Notable for this was his son John, later General Sir John Abercromby.

Occasionally Abercromby's short-sightedness led him to give a flawed command, but more often than not it offered his subordinate commanders marvellous opportunities to gain experience and observe their senior commander's processes of decision-making. John Moore, for one, benefited greatly in this respect and from an early stage was given extensive individual responsibility. Notwithstanding, it was with deceptive ease that Abercromby retained full control over such ambitious and spirited men. While well known for his comparative gentleness with his officers, where matters of professional loyalty were concerned he could rebuke both Wellesley and Moore, notably when the latter showed petulance during his time in the West Indies, and he could be very stern indeed with officers who failed to come up to his expectations. Sir Ralph's head was large and his eyes wide-spaced and as he looked out myopically from under his thick, shaggy eyebrows, he gave the idea of a good-natured lion but one that could roar when needed. Abercromby's short-sightedness also meant that while he always taught commanders not to expose themselves to danger unnecessarily he was never able to follow his own good advice. However, this was probably due to a natural rashness, not just to his poor sight. It was an example not lost on Moore. Abercromby felt a compulsion to see and feel the heat of battle. As Lord Dunfermline described it: 'When the fight began he seemed to be uneasy and impatient until he reached the point where the struggle raged most fiercely and then he was at ease and became more collected, clear and decisive in giving his orders as the perils around him increased.'[6] Wellington forced himself never to yield to the same impulses, always retaining a position from where he could both watch and control the progress of his battles.

Far more serious than any deficiencies in his sight was the fact that he led British forces that were seriously inadequate. During most of his career Abercromby was made to take the brunt of false military economies, together with shortcomings in parliamentary direction which made 'England the distrust of her allies in the West. Time after time he was sent away with a rabble of raw recruits upon expeditions ill-projected, ill-conceived and ill-prepared and time after time . . . he contrived to get out of them the work of soldiers.'[7] It is therefore all the more creditable that Abercromby at length achieved a notable military success and became one of the few British commanders to carry out a successful opposed sea landing.

Inevitably Abercromby's achievements were eclipsed by the drum roll of Wellington's battlefield triumphs, but even so it is safe to say that Abercromby has been a neglected figure. Written accounts about him are limited to a single memoir by his son, along with features within compendiums on British commanders and infrequent references in military publications. The reason for this is surely the military setbacks associated with so many of his campaigns, despite his personal successes there. But there is something else: Abercromby was a somewhat elusive subject for commentators: strongly independent he never courted publicity. He was clear about his own principles of conduct, both public and private, and his forthright criticism when he perceived something was wrong was never designed to bring him fair weather friends. This worried him not at all for he came alive on campaign, where despite his high demands, he displayed a genuine warm-heartedness towards his officers combined with a respect and affection for his private soldiers that was virtually unheard of at this time. His men would also be in no doubt that, in common with other outstanding military figures, they accompanied someone who relished action.

Ralph Abercromby had a good start in life. He was fortunate to come from a relatively powerful and well-respected family. The Abercrombies were both Whigs and strong Presbyterians, major landed proprietors at Tullibody in Clackmannanshire and bitter opponents of the Stuarts. His father, George Abercromby, married a member of the powerful Dundas family apparently renowned for her intelligence and energy as well as for her looks. Three of her sons, including Sir Ralph, were to rise to positions of eminence. The marriage gave the Abercrombies valuable connections, notably with Sir Henry Dundas, Secretary for War during the final phase of Abercromby's career.

Born in 1734, Ralph Abercromby was first educated at Rugby School before going on to study law, in the manner of his father and grandfather, at the universities of Edinburgh and Leipzig. Much to his father's disappointment he rejected a career in law for one in the army. The family made the best of his decision and in 1756 a cornetcy was purchased for him in the Third Dragoon guards. He accompanied the regiment to Germany where he came to the attention of General Sir William Pitt, its senior officer who made Abercromby his ADC. During the Seven Years' War (1756–63) when Britain united with Prussia against France and Spain, Abercromby counted himself fortunate to see much active service in Europe and was promoted lieutenant in 1760 and captain in 1762.

At the end of the war he accompanied his regiment to Ireland. Apart from a reputation for personal independence he was already known for his firm discipline, and for the close attention he gave to the needs and health of his soldiers. While serving in Ireland he married a Miss Menzies from Fernton, Perthshire. They were very happy together, although his wife never joined him permanently in Ireland, preferring to stay at home and devote herself to Abercromby's widower father and their own growing family. In Ireland, Abercromby became a major in 1770 and the commanding officer (lieutenant colonel) of his regiment in 1773. While in Ireland, he was elected as member for the county of Clackmannan, a seat traditionally held by the Whig party (at that time regular soldiers were allowed to stand for Parliament). This followed a bitterly fought election against a Colonel Erskine who was supported by the local Jacobite families. The contest ended in a duel between the contestants without injury to either side (with his short-sightedness Abercromby probably made a somewhat poor, if determined, duellist). Abercromby's election apparently owed much to the influence of his relative, Sir Henry Dundas. When he entered the House of Commons the jobbery and cabals prevalent at that time held few attractions for him since he saw himself primarily as a serving soldier pledged to support his country. He was not prepared to defer his judgement on matters of national interest to a party leader, nor for that matter to his sponsor Dundas; he resolved not to be re-elected and declined the seat in favour of his brother Burnet.

In 1781 Abercromby had been made colonel of the 103rd or King's Irish infantry, but this regiment was disbanded in 1783 and he retired on half pay. By now he had been in the army for some twenty-seven years, twenty-one of which he had spent in Ireland. After his early period of military action during the Seven Years' War, his had been an unremarkable career, seemingly unaffected by the American Declaration of Independence in 1776 and the subsequent campaigns by the British army in the Americas that ended with General Cornwallis' surrender at Yorktown in 1781. It seems hardly credible that such an able, ambitious and relatively well-connected soldier with a strong love of adventure should have spent so long in Ireland engaged on regimental and staff duties. However, like some other officers on the British establishment, Abercromby sympathised with the Americans in their struggle for independence and determined he would never fight against them on that issue. He was a great respecter for the moderation, sound judgement and disinterested patriotism of General Washington. In this he was not alone: Lord Effingham, for instance, resigned his commission when his regiment was ordered to America and Admiral Keppel refused duty against the Americans.

What Abercromby's stand demonstrated was his constancy to his principles even when they seriously hampered both his military and political advancement. As a devoted soldier he would have wanted nothing more than for his regiment to be able to show its mettle upon active service and it must have been particularly galling for him to see his brothers, who had no such scruples, proceed to America. One of them, James, was subsequently killed at Brooklyn, while Robert commanded his regiment whilst it was on duty there.

After moving onto the half pay list in 1783 Abercromby lived quietly in Edinburgh, devoting himself to his wife and the education of his children. It was not a task he was destined to complete. Although he had chosen to stand aside during the American struggle, operations against France would be quite another matter. While he almost certainly had considerable sympathy with some of the French revolutionary ideas respecting human liberties, when that country declared war against Britain he was committed to France's defeat. In 1787 he had been made a major general and six years later, on the outbreak of war, he applied immediately for a command. He was now in his sixtieth year but his family's position worked in his favour and in 1793 Abercromby went to Flanders with an auxiliary force sent to support Britain's allies in the Low Countries. It was commanded by the Duke of York with Abercromby as a brigade commander. The calibre of Abercromby's soldiers was abysmal, 'the newly-raised recruits were in general unfit for service and inadequate to the fatigues of a campaign, being mostly either old men or quite boys extremely weak and short'.[8] Sir Henry Calvert, ADC to the Duke of York, followed up this description of these late 18th century soldiers by comparing them with the rag-tag of 'Falstaff's men' from Shakespeare's Henry IV.

The campaign did not bode well for the British, with their poor troops and such an undistinguished royal commander. However, by considerable efforts Abercromby succeeded in bringing his own brigade into some kind of condition. In Flanders, despite having no experience of active service since his early years, Abercromby increased his personal reputation in every engagement he entered. In May 1793 'the Gazette' referred to the allied attack on the French camp at Furnes and stated that 'The British troops who had the opportunity of distinguishing themselves were the Brigade of the Line, namely the 14th and 53rd regiments, with the Battalion formed from three light infantry and grenadier companies commanded by Major-General Abercromby.'[9] He was also in command of the British troops who successfully stormed the French Fortress of Valenciennes. The allied fortunes in Flanders were soon to deteriorate and Abercromby was then faced with organising a series of withdrawals which he did with considerable skill and perseverance. The Duke of York

William Wallace
Renfrew Council (Paisley Museum)

King Robert Bruce
Scottish National Portrait Gallery

IACOBVS · 4 · D · GRATIA
REX · SCOTORVM

King James IV
Scottish National Portrait Gallery
ARTIST UNKNOWN

James Keith
Scottish National Portrait Gallery
ANTOINE PESNE

James Graham, Marquis of Montrose
Scottish National Portrait Gallery
ATTRIBUTED TO WILLEM VAN HONTHORST

Alexander Leslie, 1st Lord Leven
Scottish National Portrait Gallery
ATTRIBUTED TO GEORGE JAMESONE

David Leslie, 1st Baron Newark
from a private Scottish collection, by arrangement
with the Scottish National Portrait Gallery
ARTIST UNKNOWN

John Graham of Claverhouse, Viscount Dundee
Scottish National Portrait Gallery
DAVID PATON

General Hugh MacKay of Scourie
Scottish National Portrait Gallery

Lord George Murray
the Blair Castle Collection, Perthshire
ARTIST UNKNOWN

Sir Ralph Abercromby
Scottish National Portrait Gallery
JOHN HOPPNER

Sir John Moore
Scottish National Portrait Gallery
JAMES NORTHCOTE

Sir Colin Campbell, Lord Clyde
National Portrait Gallery, London
ROGER FENTON

Sir Hector MacDonald, 'Fighting Mac'
the Dingwall Museum Trust
ARTIST UNKNOWN

Douglas Haig
Scottish National Portrait Gallery
JOHN SINGER SARGENT

David Stirling
Imperial War Museum

abandoned Flanders and retired into Holland where the severe wintry weather hampered defence as the many river barriers were covered by thick ice. In the circumstances there seemed no alternative but to evacuate Holland as well. At this stage the Duke of York returned to England and left the force under the command of General Harcourt who proved unequal to the crisis. As a result the chief responsibility for getting the army back to Britain, in Arctic weather conditions and pursued all the time by the French, fell upon Abercromby as the rear column commander. Robert Brown, a corporal in the Coldstream guards, wrote of the extreme conditions during the retreat: 'The frost was so intense that the water which came from our eyes, freezing as it fell, hung in icicles to our eyelashes; and our breath, freezing as soon as emitted, lodged in heaps of ice about our faces, and on the blankets and coats that were wrapped round our heads.' On the next day they halted. 'And in the morning waggons were sent out with a number of men to search for those that were left behind. A great number were found in the route of the column; but a greater number who had straggled farther off were never heard of more . . . One or two men were found alive, but their hands and feet were frozen to such a degree as to be dropping off by the wrists and ankles.'[10]

Abercromby was never to forget the deterioration in discipline that occurred during that retreat and the necessity of having good officers and sergeants if men were to be saved. When he returned to Britain in 1795 it was to his genuine surprise that he found his ability as a commander who could keep cohesion during a prolonged withdrawal and get the survivors safely away had finally been recognised. He was promoted to full general and made a knight of the Bath. In one bound he had, in fact, become the country's foremost soldier.

He was to enjoy little pause as the government turned to other ways of attacking its enemies, in the first instance by attacking the French and Dutch territories in the West Indies. Here Abercromby enjoyed considerable success. He started by successfully invading the island of St Lucia using a force commanded by Sir John Moore whom he left to govern the island before proceeding to take Demerara and relieve Port St Vincent. Characteristically, during the campaign he also set about improving the conditions of service for his soldiers in a part of the world renowned for its high rates of sickness. He instigated lighter weight uniforms and established mountain stations where men could rest and convalesce.

Abercromby returned to Britain during the summer of 1796 but not for long, and by the end of the year he had taken Trinidad, although he failed to capture the strongly fortified positions at Porto Rico with the inadequate numbers of troops under his command. In the following year he resigned his command, nominally for reasons of ill health, but in reality because he resented the demands of having to keep cumbersome accounts of petty expenditure required by London; the endless book-keeping prevented him from supervising his men as closely as he wished. Despite his premature return Abercromby's short and belated career as a senior commander had prospered far better than he could have expected, given his independent stance and need for plain speaking together with the common burden of any commander of that time, namely the low calibre of British troops and the deficiencies in their support arrangements. In fact, when he returned from the West Indies his reputation was enhanced.

Abercromby's next appointment was to Ireland as military commander there. This was no sinecure for the country was plagued by serious internal unrest and there was a strong possibility of an invasion from France. From his past experience Abercromby had a thorough knowledge of the country and he had barely landed when he clashed with the civil authorities over how the military should be used to quell civilian disturbances. It was his plan to concentrate the army into large bodies, including artillery, in order to re-establish much-needed discipline and enable them to cope more effectively with any enemy invaders. His proposals, however, were opposed by both magistrates and landowners, who wanted the troops scattered across the country; if, through a mixture of oppression and intemperance, they helped to cow the people so much the better. In the circumstances a break between Abercromby and Lord Camden, the lord lieutenant was inevitable. On 26 February 1798 Abercromby issued an uncompromising Order of the day that opened with the unflinching words: 'The very disgraceful frequency of courts martial, and the many complaints of irregularities in the conduct of the troops in this kingdom, having too unfortunately proved the Army to be in a state of licentiousness which must render it formidable to every one but the enemy. . . .'[11] The commander-in-chief went on to demand the most unremitting attention to both discipline and order and he forbade any troops to act without his authority. At the same time Abercromby wrote to Dundas, the Secretary of State for War, informing him that the breach between him and the lord lieutenant's advisers made it impossible for him to stay on.

In London, William Pitt, the British prime minister, had little option but to support the Irish establishment, although in any case Abercromby had already resigned before the name of his successor had been decided. After obeying a series of government directives that had taken him and his ill-equipped British troops on a number of unsuccessful forays against France, Abercromby had come to a sticking point. Significantly this was over the principles of human rights for Irish citizens and the use of troops against them. The government chose to appear both shocked and amazed at his objections. In the event Abercromby had the satisfaction of seeing the irresolute Lord Camden recalled from Ireland and replaced by Lord Cornwallis, but he was disgusted by the lack of support given him by London. As Abercromby never forgave Pitt, so Pitt never forgave him, 'for men, as Tacitus observed centuries before 'are slowest to pardon those whom they have injured'.[12] King George III certainly let Abercromby know he believed him to have been ill-treated and told him he would now be sent to Scotland as commander-in-chief, where people would treat him with due respect.

Within twelve months Abercromby's military skills were again in demand, and this time he was sent to Holland as commander of the British army's first division with the purpose of restoring the independence of that country. The Dutch were expected to rise against the French in support of the British forces and the Russians had promised additional military assistance. Once more the Duke of York was appointed as senior commander. Like most British military initiatives at that time the plans miscarried and the ships carrying the troops were in full sight of the Dutch coast for six days thus destroying any chance of surprise. Abercromby acted as vanguard commander and he selected the port of Helder at the northernmost point of Holland as his target. The landing was hazardous due to heavy surf but Helder was taken. With a secure port for his base he moved forward to Potton on the Zeider Zee to await Russian re-inforcements and for the Duke of York to assume command. Before either arrived the French attacked Abercromby with superior numbers but they were successfully driven off. On 13 September 1799 the Duke of York took command and 16,000 Russian troops joined the British. Six days later a Russian attack miscarried and

Abercromby was ordered to draw his own men back. The main allied attack took place on 2 October upon the port of Egmont op Zee near Alkmaar. During it Abercromby's column distinguished itself and the Duke of York's despatch afterwards was strongly in Abercromby's favour, 'Animated by the example of Sir Ralph Abercromby, and the general and other officers under him, the troops sustained every effort made upon them by an enemy their superior in numbers and much favoured by the strength of their position.' In the fighting Abercromby had two horses shot from under him. Outnumbered as the British and Russians were, each engagement tended to make things worse. The momentum of the campaign declined and the Duke became convinced that the conquest of Holland was beyond the capability of his forces. In three actions the British lost 10,000 men while the numbers opposing them increased. In the end there was no choice but to evacuate the country. Abercromby's opinion about the unrealistic objectives for the campaign can best be gathered from his conduct when he returned to England. After his ship docked at Shields, he completely ignored his superior authorities in London and went straight to Scotland to resume command there.

A general sense of relief greeted the withdrawal of the army from Holland. George Canning, Under Secretary in the Foreign Office, spoke for many when he said, 'We have our army again for better times and seasons.' Many men were lost, though, and no-one could call the Helder expedition a success. However, a royal duke while only an average commander, could hardly be held responsible for any shortcomings in leadership and it was Abercromby who was made the scapegoat, although he was offered a peerage. This he contemptuously declined, since he was unwilling that 'his name should be permanently associated with an expedition the result of which was so humiliating to the country'.[13] If a peerage had been offered him for his initial attack on the Helder he would most probably have accepted, but that did not suit his political masters.

While Pitt could not have found Abercromby the easiest of commanders to deal with, his ability was such that on 22 April 1800 he was once more brought from Scotland for overseas service, as commander-in-chief of the so-called British Mediterranean forces. At sixty-six years of age, when the vast majority of men would have been considering retirement, he was finally given the opportunity to command a genuine army and in May 1800 Abercromby set sail with just under 20,000 men in 143 ships. Amazingly the purpose of his force had not yet been determined. From the beginning there were problems; any hope of assisting in a successful invasion of France by landing troops in Italy was ended by Napoleon's defeat of the Austrians at Marengo and his acquisition of Liguria, Piedmont and Lombardy in northern Italy. Abercromby was ordered to make for Gibraltar, where it was decided he should join in the task of defending Spanish naval arsenals from the French. The initial plan was to land troops on the Bay of Cadiz and there secure a safe anchorage from which the British fleet could operate, but after the troops had rehearsed their landing in some detail Abercromby's admiral, Lord Keith, ruled the anchorage unsafe and Abercromby had no choice but to return to Gibraltar. After a year's campaign marked by orders and counter orders nothing positive had been achieved. Lord Cornwallis was among those in Britain who watched Abercromby's naval antics, and he wrote: 'What a disgraceful and what an expensive campaign we have made at this time. Twenty two thousand men, a large proportion of them not soldiers, floating round the greater part of Europe, the scorn and laughing stock of friends and foes.'[14] Like General Archibald Wavell in World War Two who seemed to jinx any aircraft he boarded, it seemed that Abercromby had only to set foot on a ship for the wind to rise. Grenville, the English Foreign Secretary, was driven to declare that 'If I were a seaman, with half the superstition which belongs to them, I should certainly throw him overboard as a second Jonah.'

When Abercromby reached Gibraltar on 26 October 1800 he found new instructions from his Secretary for War, Henry Dundas, which were to expel the French from Egypt, where the Emperor's troops had been stranded since Nelson's victory at the Battle of the Nile. Abercromby was told the French strength was approximately 13,000; it was, in fact, nearer 24,000. He reached Malta on 19 November and with his strategic grasp wrote home with the proposal that Malta instead of Minorca should be made the headquarters of the Mediterranean army. On 13 December, Abercromby sailed from Malta for Mamorice Bay in Turkey just north of Rhodes. He chose this particular location for two reasons: it was only a few days' sail from Egypt and suitably placed to pick up expected Turkish reinforcements (these did not arrive but by now nothing would deflect Abercromby from attacking the French). Accompanied by

John Moore he reconnoitred the coast and selected the crescent-shaped beach at Aboukir Bay near Alexandria as his landing point.

While waiting for suitable weather Abercromby made determined attempts to build up his troops' fitness and confidence after their long period on ship. In conjunction with the Navy, he rehearsed them again and again in techniques of disembarkation in the face of an enemy. The British had 15,330 men – far too few for such an operation including 1000 sick and 500 locally enlisted Maltese, against the French strength of 24,000. In spite of the force imbalance, under Abercromby's direction General John Moore and Captain Cochrane of the Royal Navy worked out a detailed landing procedure. Foremost in approaching the beach would be forty-eight flat boats packed tightly with fifty soldiers apiece: their muskets unloaded and carrying on their backs sixty rounds of ammunition, three days rations, full water canteens and either blankets or greatcoats. 'Behind them followed 84 cutters also crammed with soldiers. In a third line were 37 launches with a fourth line being made up by 14 launches filled with seamen, gunners and field pieces. On each flank were three vessels of light draught with their broadsides trained on the land.'[15] In all the assault party numbered 5500 invaders. Not knowing the exact site of the landing, the French, under General Menou, had their main forces some way inland but 1600 foot and 200 horse supported by 15 guns directly covered Aboukir beach.

At 2 a.m. on 8 March 1801 the troops climbed into their boats and, after moving closer inshore, spent a further two hours getting the craft into straight lines. At 8 a.m. exactly, the sailors began to pull for the shore. The plan was for them to ground simultaneously and for companies and even battalions to land in their battle formations. In the event all the punctilious planning came into its own. As they approached the beach 'grape shot and musketry came down upon them like hail, and many casualties were sustained; yet the confusion created proved so trifling as scarcely to deserve notice'.[16] On the right John Moore had three battalions ashore. These were rapidly formed up and under his lead the beach's key strongpoint was taken within twenty minutes. On Moore's left the invaders were charged by French cavalry but they successfully drove them off. The disembarkation was a classic of its kind; firm lodgement was made and the main force was able to follow on without delay. The British army in its history has made five great contested landings: at Louisburg in 1758, at Helder

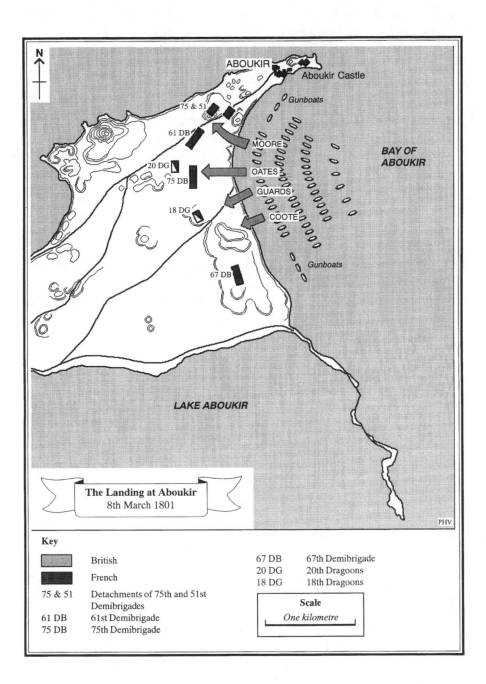

ABOUKIR

Aboukir Castle

Gunboats

75 & 51

61 DB

MOORE

*BAY OF
ABOUKIR*

20 DG

75 DB

OATES

GUARDS

18 DG

COOTE

67 DB

Gunboats

LAKE ABOUKIR

PHV

The Landing at Aboukir
8th March 1801

Key

	British
	French

75 & 51	Detachments of 75th and 51st Demibrigades
61 DB	61st Demibrigade
75 DB	75th Demibrigade

67 DB	67th Demibrigade
20 DG	20th Dragoons
18 DG	18th Dragoons

Scale
One kilometre

in 1799, at Aboukir in 1801, at Gallipoli in 1915 and at Normandy in 1944. That at Louisburg owed much to luck and Helder was a somewhat confused affair, but the principles laid down at Aboukir became the basis for both the Gallipoli and Normandy landings.

After the initial success events began to go less well. The French had constructed a succession of strong defensive positions and Abercromby, having started a series of forward movements followed by assaults, realised the enemy's superior cavalry and artillery were taking too heavy a toll of his men. After suffering 1200 casualties (double those sustained during the landing) the British set up defensive positions about four miles from Alexandria. At this point the solicitous Abercromby asked the French for a short truce – which was granted – during which both sides could tend their wounded. George Gleig, soldier, writer and future Chaplain General, for one, was critical of the British follow-up attacks and thought that Abercromby's eyesight problems, compounded by the clear atmosphere of Egypt, had made him misjudge distances and order an advance he would not normally have hazarded. Whatever the truth, the next attack came from the French who had collected 10,000 men including 1400 cavalry and 46 guns. General Menou's plan was to fall on the British before daylight, but the percipient Abercromby ordered all his troops to sleep in their equipment and to stand under arms half-an-hour before daylight. As a result General Moore was able to repulse the French, who suffered immense loss, including three of their generals. However, in the half light the battle became confused and three regiments of French cavalry broke through the British lines and galloped round their rear. There they came upon Abercromby who, typically, was well forward in his eagerness to follow the progress of the battle. For a moment they surrounded him and a French dragoon managed to seize the bridle of his horse, until he was shot down by an English soldier.

In the mêlée Abercromby sustained a sabre cut across his chest but his uniform took the brunt and it only grazed his flesh. General Moore, who was at the point of danger himself, was led to comment, 'while Sir Ralph had always been accused of exposing his person too much I never knew him carry this so far as in this action'.[17] When, at the end of the attack, Sir Ralph's damaged clothing was noted he was asked whether he was injured, and he replied: 'Yes, by a spent ball, but it gives me no uneasiness.' At first he refused treatment but, after complaining of feeling faint, he sat down on the ground. Up to this time he had given his orders in his usual manner and continued to walk with a firm and steady step. However, when he was examined by a surgeon, in addition to his superficial chest wound he was found to have a wound in his thigh. He agreed to be taken to Lord Keith's flagship and as he was placed on a bier an officer took a soldier's blanket and put it under his head for a pillow. At this the patient asked: 'What is it that you are putting under my head?' The officer replied that it was only a soldier's blanket, on which Sir Ralph retorted, 'Only a soldier's blanket! A soldier's blanket is of great consequence, and you must send me the name of the soldier to whom it belongs, that it may be returned to him.'[18] The soldier had his blanket returned but the surgeons found the ball had lodged deep in the General's thigh bone and could not be removed. Gangrene set in and, six days later, in his 68th year, Abercromby died.

For the man who had known so many disappointments death came at his moment of triumph. At Aboukir under his command the much criticised British troops accomplished a text-book landing from the sea, and followed it by inflicting a heavy defeat on quality French regiments that had served under Bonaparte. French captives declared their work in Italy had been child's play compared with the three actions against the British in Egypt. In the course of the battle the French lost 5000 men as compared to 1500 British casualties. Although Abercromby was not to see it, as a direct result of his victory, Turkish and other national troops joined the British, which so demoralised the French that on 30 August 1801 their army in Egypt finally capitulated.

Following a period of terrible deterioration, at Aboukir, Sir Ralph Abercromby gave the British army back its pride together with what would become known as its renowned steadiness. Aboukir marked the peak of his career as a commander, one that his son acknowledged had been chequered by much adversity. In its early stages he was compelled to work with both bad men and poor officers and he never fully trusted his political masters who too often gave him contradictory if not unrealistic tasks. In Holland Abercromby twice experienced defeat and in the West Indies he saw the havoc caused by disease when it was not controlled. Not all politicians fully appreciated his qualities. He was accused by the Foreign Secretary, Lord Grenville, of being pessimistic and obstructive and he acknowledged to his son that he always stated his difficulties frankly and unreservedly to ministers. Before the Helder expedition, for instance, he highlighted serious problems over shipping and anticipated others on disembarkation due to deficiencies in the forces' land transport. Whether awkward or not Abercromby knew what was needed for military success. With the second Dutch campaign his plan to land at the Helder with one strong corps instead of making multiple landings was eventually accepted and it proved successful. Once ashore he was unjustly criticised both for halting his forces on the Zype Canal in face of the vigorous French reaction to the landing and for his gloomy assessment about the campaign's future prospects to his commander, the Duke of York. In the event as Abercromby had foreseen the allied forces in Holland proved quite inadequate for the tasks set them.

What Abercromby never lacked in any degree was courage whether it was landing on an exposed Dutch coast, attacking the defended beach at Aboukir or investing French strongpoints in front of Alexandria. He also had the moral courage to say no to politicians when their ideas or suggested plans seemed unrealistic. He was not afraid of resigning if he thought the issue warranted it: he refused to serve against the Americans, he quickly terminated his Parliamentary career, he registered his objections when saddled with unrealistic accountancy demands in the West Indies and he declared his opposition to flawed military practices in Ireland. Some of his critics might have thought he was somewhat too fond of resigning and over careful with his men. At Aboukir, however, despite the enemy's superior numbers and the hazards of a beach landing against prepared positions he was determined to go ahead. By then he believed the regeneration of the British army which he had begun during 1794 in Holland made it more than a match for the French.

After Flanders Abercromby's career had been dedicated to 'restoring discipline, professionalism and self-confidence to an army eroded by dispersion, neglect and failure.'[19] With him discipline was not that of the mindless martinet, it came through shared responsibility and mutual regard. In 1799 Parliament authorised volunteers from the militia to join the regular forces and Abercromby immediately saw such men as a great acquisition to the army, if only they were treated properly. He confided his ideas here to his brother-in-law Colonel Alexander Hope: 'The militiamen are rather a better species of man, they understand the use of arms, and can move tolerably well, but they have not been accustomed to due subordination, to this they must be led by degrees, they must not be treated with too much harshness and severity . . . if they are used with judgement and discretion, you will have a fine army.'[20]

He knew it was not just soldiers who needed moulding, a new generation of devoted officers needed bringing on and in their turn they loved Abercromby for his professionalism compared with most of his contemporaries. Alexander Hope, for instance, remembered him as 'My old commander and first master'.[21] Abercromby knew his military business and when campaigning although undoubtedly tenacious he was not quarrelsome. His success at Aboukir, for instance, owed much to his excellent understanding with the Royal Navy and the joint training carried out with them beforehand.

Over the years Abercromby also concerned himself with the technical performance of the British army. At Aboukir his control of the infantry's fire power was particularly effective while earlier at Minorca he had asked John Moore to think about the need for British battalions to be trained as skirmishers, on the lines of the French *voltigeurs*.

Understandably the men who shared the hazards of the battlefield with him knew Abercromby best both as a man and commander. Their feelings were summarised by Captain (later General) Sir Henry Bunbury, whose memoirs contained the following reference to his past military teacher: 'There was an absence of selfishness in Abercromby, a liberality of feeling, and an independence of spirit which entitled him to the highest respect as a gentleman; while his justice, his intrepidity, and experience assured to him, as a commander, the attachment and confidence of his troops.'[22]

Sir John Moore (1761–1809)

Johnny, or Jack, Moore, as the son of a Glasgow doctor and writer, came from relatively humble if secure beginnings. There were eleven children in the family although the early death of three boys made Jack the eldest son. When young the family considered him fiery and intractable and, although he learned to control his temper, the high spiritedness never left him. By his teens Moore had become undeniably handsome: tall and graceful with hazel eyes and brown hair, and according to his brother James he had become easily approachable, 'the expression of his countenance cheerful and benign'.[23]

From the age of twelve Moore was certain he wanted to be a soldier, an ambition that was helped by the chance friendship that developed between him and the Duke of Hamilton when Moore's father was appointed to restore the health of the young nobleman. Together they went on a European tour under the tutelage of John Moore senior, and their affection was cemented by an accident which occurred when, while playing at soldiers, the Duke pierced John in the side with a sword. Fortunately the blade bounced off his ribs and, although blood flowed freely, Moore made little of it. It was as if he knew he would receive far more serious wounds during his career. With help from his friend's mother, the Duchess of Hamilton, John Moore obtained an ensigncy in the 51st regiment of foot at the early age of fifteen, but even then 'he was man enough to assure his father that the fees for the ensigncy would be taken off his pay.'[24] Moore joined his regiment at Minorca but he was soon restless and looked for the chance of active service, which at this time promised to be in America.

After the surrender of General Burgoyne at Saratoga and the entry of France on behalf of the colonists, several new battalions were raised both in England and Scotland and, on 10 January 1778, the seventeen-year-old Moore was gazetted lieutenant in the 82nd of foot, a Scottish regiment raised by his friend and sponsor the Duke of Hamilton. Moore went with it to Nova Scotia where it was intended to establish a base in Penobscot Bay, close to Halifax. Here Moore showed remarkable coolness and bravery during a skirmish with the Americans. The British commenced to build a fort to dominate the anchorage but it was still far from complete when they were attacked by far superior numbers of Americans. The American long boats grounded opposite the 82nd Regiment where Moore stood with twenty men. After firing a volley most of the British withdrew with the exception of Moore and his platoon. He was eventually ordered to pull back by a Captain Dunlop of the 82nd but not before only six of his men remained unwounded. This was Moore's first taste of action and he confessed to his father that he was 'devilishly frightened' although he acknowledged that he was the only officer who did not leave his post 'too soon'. Before the British surrender at Yorktown which virtually ended the war Moore had been joined by his brother James who at seventeen was a military surgeon's mate while he himself had become an acting captain. After the surrender Moore returned home and, with little soldiering available, was reduced to half pay. The Duke of Hamilton now persuaded him to enter Parliament but, characteristically, Moore agreed only on condition that he would not be bound to a particular political party, although he admitted he much admired William Pitt.[25]

For six years he was an unassuming but keenly observant MP, although his heart remained in soldiering and he continued his military studies. In 1788 there was some expansion of the army and he was appointed major to one of two new battalions of the 60th rifles before returning to his original regiment, the 51st, as he had heard it was likely to be sent overseas. At that time the 51st was stationed at Cork and as its colonel was by no means keen to leave the comforts of Irish society for foreign service, Moore was able to purchase the incumbent's commission and with it command of the regiment. The price was £1000 and the loan provided by his father had to be repaid.

During the wet Irish winter at Cork the 51st had no opportunity to relax since Moore was preparing his battalion for active operations, a procedure which must have come as a shock to some of the officers. After a lieutenant had gone rioting in Cork and had been absent from his guard all night Moore ordered him to dispose of his lieutenancy immediately or risk a court martial. He weeded out other inefficient officers and went on to tackle the high levels of drunkenness among the soldiers. While a firm disciplinarian he was ever sparing with the lash and, although training was hard, he attempted to make it enjoyable by introducing competitions for marksmanship and weapon training. He insisted on individual fitness, but there were few willing to join the young colonel in his daily 6 a.m. swim in the cold Irish Sea.

Moore and his regiment were ordered to Gibraltar and arrived there on 25 March 1792. During the rest of that year and all the following one Moore suffered the frustration of other soldiers at the commencement of the war with Revolutionary, then Napoleonic, France. Despite having command of the sea Britain could find no worthwhile mission for its ground troops.

To his delight he and his regiment finally had a chance to show their paces when in conjunction with the Royal Navy under Lord Hood it would invade French-held Corsica, at that time considered a key position in the Mediterranean. Despite clashes with the imperious and irascible Hood, along with his champion Captain Horatio Nelson, Moore distinguished himself militarily.

Hood sent Moore to Corsica (along with Sir Gilbert Elliot, lately commissioner at Toulon) to see how far an attack with their small forces would be practicable. His report was clear and bold, recommending the seizure of San Fiorenzo by taking its fortified tower (its Mortella) and freeing Mortella Bay for the security of the fleet. The report was accepted by both Hood and General David Dundas, now appointed as army commander. After the navy had neutralised the tower, Moore at the head of the Royal and 51st Regiments took the massively strong redoubt guarding San Fiorenzo. Hood himself told Moore's friend Major Koehler, the Deputy Quartermaster General, 'We should never have had any footing in Corsica, but for the perseverance of yourself and Colonel Moore.' The advance continued and Moore himself led his men into a breach that had been made in a formidable fort guarding the important town of Calvi. Fearlessly charging into the breach Moore suffered his first wound, a shell splinter to the head. This was relatively superficial but if it had struck an inch or two further down it would have decapitated him. He wiped the blood from his eyes and completed the occupation of the fort. After this all Corsica was soon in British hands.

Although outstanding militarily, Moore showed naivety in his vigorous opposition towards Sir Gilbert Elliot, now appointed British viceroy in Corsica. The viceroy was certain his office gave him the widest authority over the military, an opinion which Moore contested and he further infuriated Elliot by the close camaraderie he developed with leading Corsican patriots. Moore was sent home in disgrace for meddling in the politics of the country, but his criticisms of Elliot's misguided policy were soon justified when a rebellion broke out on the island and the French quickly recaptured it. On Moore's return to London he was summoned by William Pitt to account for his conduct. The Prime Minister was impressed by his spirited defence, together with the warm recommendations of senior soldiers on his behalf. As a result Moore learned from Henry Dundas, fellow Scot and Secretary for War, that he would be promoted to the rank of temporary brigadier general for service in the West Indies.

In the West Indies Moore was fortunate to come under the command of Sir Ralph Abercromby. At St Lucia, the young lion distinguished himself on several occasions, notably when after the main landing force was delayed he pushed forward to catch the French garrison off balance by leading an attack on the dominating heights of Morne Chabot. During this action he admitted he had never made greater efforts nor ever run more personal danger. As a reward he was made governor of the island, a sedentary post he would have liked to refuse. Like so many others Moore caught yellow fever and the physicians gave him up for dead, but his recovery was apparently brought about when his devoted staff officer and friend, Major Paul Anderson, poured strong wine down his throat. Moore returned to England and because of his sound constitution, by the end of the sea voyage his health was restored.

In late 1797 Moore again joined Abercromby who was by then commander-in-chief in Ireland, although Abercromby's stay there was short-lived after his clash with the civilian authorities. Abercromby had found the Irish militia were poorly trained, brutal and too often corrupt. Moore quickly set about improving this state of affairs by weeding out poor officers and adopting a system of training that involved mutual trust throughout all ranks. He was appalled too at the religious bigotry in Ireland. His father, aware of the dire effects that serious religious divisions had caused in Scotland, had taught his son that whereas religion should be an intrinsic part of a Christian's lifestyle it should also be kept private. Throughout his life Moore's beliefs were steady but largely understated. In Ireland he told his men that the Government had entrusted both Roman Catholics and Protestants with the country's defence and that to boast or be unduly proud of your religion is absurd: 'Any man might fairly pride himself upon being just or honest, but not on his religion'.[26] During the Irish Civil War of 1797 Moore was prominent in showing his 'usual enterprise and activity' in leading troops against the rebels and in the process he not only revealed his tactical awareness but his pronounced ability to act quickly.[27] During an advance towards Taghmon near Wexford three of his companies were surrounded and in danger of being annihilated. He rallied the panic-stricken men, turned them about and led them into the attack at which 6000 or so rebels fell back before him. Abercromby had been succeeded by General Lake (who did not impress Moore) but he was himself quickly replaced by Lord Cornwallis, who continued with the policies that Abercromby had advocated; this was to Moore's approval and the two became firm friends.

In 1799 came the Helder campaign, the invasion of Holland to liberate it from the French where John Moore acted as a major general under Abercromby, the commander he admired so much. The British forces had been hastily assembled and the expedition itself proved confused. Characteristically Moore distinguished himself by his personal leadership and complete disregard for his own safety. He was always at the centre of things, from the earliest stages when Abercromby's advance guard landed at the Helder and established a firm bridgehead there. Moore had a finger shattered in this action.

On 2 October 1799 Moore commanded the British troops that supported a Russian attack on Bergen. Moore's regiments repulsed a dangerous attack upon the flank of the British column and were constantly in action as the French fell back. In this engagement Moore suffered another injury, a glancing wound to his thigh. Near Egmont op Zee the French turned and attacked. Moore was with his leading regiment, the 25th, which was giving way when Moore was again wounded, this time seriously. A bullet entered behind his ear and ploughed through the cheek below his left eye. He could easily have been killed outright or quickly died of his wounds, but miraculously the eye appeared undamaged, neither the jaw nor any other bone had been broken and the bullet exited cleanly.

Moore was evacuated to Britain and although the campaign ended in a disappointing armistice Moore's own reputation had been enhanced. The military secretary to the Duke of York, Sir Robert Brownrigg, wrote to Dr Moore on 4 October 1799, 'His conduct in the serious action of the 2nd, which perhaps may be ranked among the most obstinately contested battles that have been fought in this war, has raised him, if possible, higher than he before stood in the estimation of this army . . . and you may boast as having as your son the most amicable man, and the best General, in the British service'.[28] This was followed by a breezy letter from Sir Ralph Abercromby in which he seemed remarkably dismissive of Moore's serious wounds: 'Although your son is wounded in the thigh and in the cheek, I can assure you he is in no sort of danger; both wounds are slight . . . The General is a hero, with more sense than many others of that description. In that he is an ornament to his family, and to his profession.'[29]

By June 1800 Moore was once more in the thick of action, again under Abercromby, this time in the Mediterranean. Throughout a complicated campaign he repeatedly showed both his military skills and training ability. Moore deserved most credit for the meticulous rehearsals before the sea landing at Aboukir. Once ashore he identified the defenders' key ground and swiftly took it. In the heavy fighting that followed Moore's formations took the brunt of the action but even in the confusion of battle Moore maintained his tight control. In the fighting he sustained a further injury, this time a bullet in his thigh. Moore doubted whether the British had sufficient numbers to take Alexandria but when the French commander capitulated on 30 August 1801 Moore was appointed commander of the city. This static role did not please him and he was allowed back to England to visit the bedside of his dying father.

In 1802 the Treaty of Amiens brought peace to Europe and a respite for its soldiers, yet while Moore was still recovering from his wound this restless dynamo of a man was turning over in his mind ways of reforming military training. By 1800 at Abercromby's prompting the British army's experimental Rifle Corps had been created expressly to match the French *voltigeurs* – their skirmishers or sharp shooters. In some respects the Rifle corps was to resemble 'the Freischärler', or free hordes, that had been used in Europe during the Seven Years' War.[30] It was further intended to develop a light company of mobile troops and for each of its foot regiments to be armed with the Baker rifled gun that gave reasonable accuracy up to a range of 300 yards. In the autumn of 1802 Moore ordered the Rifle Corps to move to Shorncliffe. This became their permanent training camp, and over the following year he created the Light Infantry Brigade. A new rifle regiment was formed and two other infantry units were reorganised on light infantry lines. Together with some cavalry and artillery the whole brigade which was destined to become the army's spearhead in war came under Moore's direct command.

Moore was not a revolutionary innovator: his patterns of training owed much to an earlier manual produced by General Dundas, which Moore amended after watching Colonel Francis de Rollenburg's 60th Royal Americans when he had them under his command in Ireland. Even more important than the actual military exercises, however, was Moore's moral training of the men, which *was* revolutionary. Everything at Shorncliffe was based on treating the soldier as a human being. The training of officers and soldiers ran concurrently, young officers drilled and worked side by side with their men and all the training was for war. Feeding was regulated to promote comradeship: 'comfort and unanimity at meals whether it be among officers or soldiers is the source of friendship and good understanding'.[31] All soldiers were to take their turn at cooking for their messing group of between ten and fourteen men and each mess was to have two table-cloths and knives and forks for everyone in that mess. Good shooting was achieved by competitions where men could emulate each other. A system of comrades was introduced whereby two men would be in the same file on parade and go on the same duties with arms. This resembled 'the buddy system' adopted by some western armies in the late 20th century. In some ways the egalitarian principles (which operated within the military structure of command) and Moore's recognition of the common human dignity shared by all soldiers can be thought of as being in the direct Scottish tradition.

Moore reckoned that men must be made proud of their profession for discipline will never truly succeed 'unless a general anxiety that it should do so lies in every man's breast to a certain degree, and unless his officers are animated with an equal desire of their regiment doing honour to the army they are in'.[32] No floggings were carried out at Shorncliffe. Moore wanted spirited soldiers but also men who were self-disciplined, sober and clean both in their appearance and their living habits. He recognised the military value of competitive games to help soldiers leave the tobacco-filled atmosphere of inns and end their perpetual gambling. All his riflemen had to be able to swim and all ranks were ceaselessly trained in infantry tactics, including the use of ground cover and the principle of never moving without covering fire. Moore, whose brain assimilated everything rapidly, made speed the keynote at Shorncliffe; such fit, quick-thinking, fast-moving men would be sure to outwit any enemy.

In 1924 Colonel (Boney) Fuller, himself a noted military reformer and stern critic, wrote that Moore's 'regulations' excelled any he had encountered, ancient or modern. 'Based on comradeship, humanity and common sense, they defeat criticism, and the astonishing thing is that they were produced at a time when the British Army lay utterly exhausted under the heel of chaos.'[33] The Light Brigade was, of course, only a small portion of the army, a *corps d'élite*, but Moore's principles were demonstrated by the brigade under its commander General John Crauford during Moore's retreat towards Corunna when it acted as the army's rearguard and its cohesion and readiness for instant action acted as a model for the rest. Roger Parkinson relates how outside the town of Benavente the Light Brigade held the river bridge against much superior numbers of French cavalry for over a day until explosive charges could be laid for it to be destroyed.[34] Under Wellington in the Peninsula the example set by light infantrymen (now expanded to divisional strength) did much to penetrate the hide-bound structure of the army as a whole.

As for Moore, the active soldier, his experiences in the four years before his final campaign, ending at Corunna, need only be briefly told. Made Knight of the Bath in 1804 and lieutenant general in the following year, he was acknowledged to be the country's best general. Notwithstanding, given Moore's uncompromising principles, when he was not actively campaigning he was all too likely to clash with his civilian masters. Made second-in-command, then commander-in-chief of the Mediterranean theatre, he spoke his mind about what he saw as the British government's rash support for Queen Maria Carolina, the Queen of Naples, and her opportunistic claims to lands in Italy. With the French invasion of the Iberian peninsula Moore was given the task of evacuating the Portuguese royal family, but the instruction came too late and he returned to England on 1 January 1808.

There followed an amazing interlude. With 12,000 men Moore was sent by sea to help the King of Sweden, Britain's only ally in the Baltic. Moore's instructions were remarkably vague and to his consternation he found the Swedish king more than half mad. The king ordered Moore to undertake a succession of unreal operations against Sweden's neighbours and unsurprisingly, Moore, who was never able to hide his scorn and disbelief, refused and was put under arrest. Moore however escaped, and took his troops with him without asking permission from London.

Moore's frustration in Sweden was the greater because, with the French invasion of Spain, he foresaw that a British army would have to be sent to the Peninsula and, if he was away, it was likely to be commanded by his rival Arthur Wellesley, the future Duke of Wellington. In the event, the Duke of York, who was commander-in-chief at this time, objected to Wellesley's appointment on grounds of inexperience. This was no relief to Moore who was informed by Lord Castlereagh, the Secretary for War, that command in Spain would go to Sir Hew Dalrymple and Sir Harry Burrard, generals who were undoubtedly senior to both Moore and Wellesley but well past active soldiering. After Sweden, it was felt that Moore had to be put in his place. Although he registered a protest he was not prepared to miss the operations even when acting in a relatively junior capacity, especially as Wellesley had already set out before him.

Before landing in the peninsula Moore learned that the Spanish had gained a victory over the French and that Wellesley had gained a further victory over them at Vimeiro. To Wellesley's anger he had not been allowed to follow up his success and, what was worse, the British commanders had then allowed the defeated French free passage back to France in British ships. The disillusionment in Britain over such weak leadership and the subsequent court of inquiry led to the only possible decision. Moore was appointed to command the 30,000 British infantry and 5000 cavalry 'in the north of Spain to co-operate with the Spanish armies in the expulsion of the French from that kingdom'.[35] Moore wrote delightedly in his journal, 'There has been no such command since Marlborough for a British officer.'[36]

Given the state of the British military establishment and with Moore's luck it was unlikely to be a straightforward operation. His orders were to leave 10,000 troops in Portugal and with his other 20,000 join up with another British force of 14,000 infantry and 4000 cavalry which was to be landed at Corunna. These were commanded by another Scot, Sir David Baird. Moore was told to co-operate with the Spaniards, even to place himself under their supreme command if so required; with such instructions a divergence between Spanish political interests and Moore's concern for his troops could only be a matter of time.

After previous abortive operations in Holland and elsewhere, this signal opportunity for the British to play a significant part in the land struggle against Napoleon had obvious attractions. Spain, however, presented immense difficulties for the army commander. The country was extremely backward politically and economically. Its central government was weak and the prevalent custom for provincial councils to ignore instructions from the central Junta was bound to bring about serious friction. The armies raised by the provincial councils had no shortage of generals, all of whom were jealous of each other. Worse still their soldiers were ill-treated and badly equipped. While before Moore's arrival the Spaniards had confounded everyone by defeating the French, the French had as yet only sent in third-line troops and their reinforcements were bound to be of a very different calibre.

The size and nature of the country itself presented additional problems. If Spain and Portugal are viewed together as a rough square with 400-mile sides, the Spanish capital, Madrid, is in the middle, Lisbon 300 miles to the left, Corunna at the top left hand point and the Pyrenees over 400 miles away. Any army in the peninsula had to be prepared to cover large distances, but the so-called roads were few – in most cases no more than earth tracks that crossed bleak countryside or ascended high mountain passes to be intersected, at intervals, by large rivers. In the autumn the weather was most adverse with customary torrential rains; in the winter these turned to snow, accompanied by bitter winds.

Such conditions would have taxed any army but Moore possessed no supply nor transport services. While the French took what they wanted from the local population the British had to commission everything. All their supplies were short: food, forage and the vast number of oxen-drawn carts that were required to carry the necessities. The British Treasury kept Moore short of funds and his soldiers had, therefore, to carry the bulk of their equipment on their backs. In such adverse circumstances Moore forbade women and children to accompany the army, although a number still did so.

In normal circumstances English naval supremacy would have

enabled Moore to have moved his army by sea, but with the frequent autumnal storms he considered the risk too great. His first object was to unite the two armies, which involved a 250 mile march northwards for Moore while Baird moved the same distance south. Because of the terrible roads Moore was forced to send his heavy artillery on a roundabout route through Madrid adding 100 miles to its journey. The artillery required a powerful escort amounting to 4000 troops, including cavalry. This was put under the command of General Hope (the future Earl of Hopetown).

The race was on. The oncoming French hoped to catch the English while they were divided, while Moore did everything possible to unite his forces before he had to face the enemy. The French were believed to have received reinforcements of 10,000 men and, unbeknown to Moore, eight days after he set off on his journey, Napoleon had joined the French forces moving towards Madrid. As Roger Parkinson put it, 'Sir John Moore walked to his horse to lead the stab into enemy territory; with too few men, too late in the year, along unfit roads, with his forces scattered, hampered by lack of finance and heavy equipment, unable to rely on his Spanish ally – and against an experienced enemy far superior in numbers.'[37] It was a daunting prospect for anyone, even as fine a soldier as John Moore.

By mid-November Moore's forces had covered their 250 miles and reached Salamanca, only to learn that one Spanish provincial army had been wiped out, to be followed by another two caught by Napoleon and his grand Armée. While Hope was still 100 miles away and Baird twice that distance after being delayed by a provincial council, French detachments reached the place where Moore had ordered his forces to meet. To make matters worse the French cavalry were only about sixty miles away from Moore's troops at Salamanca.

To preserve his forces Moore seemed to have only one option, withdrawal. He therefore ordered Baird to halt his corps at Astorga ready for a return to Corunna, while he remained at Salamanca. On 26 November Moore learned that a fourth Spanish army had been defeated, and any hope of support from his Spanish allies was reduced to one last army under the command of a general, Castaños, which was thought to consist mainly of peasantry rather than trained troops. Moore doggedly held on at Salamanca despite the overwhelming arguments for withdrawal and despite the shower of over-optimistic messages from Hookham Frere, British envoy extraordinary in

Madrid, urging him to continue his march into Spain. News that the army under Castanos had, in fact, been destroyed confirmed Moore's pressing need for withdrawal; summoning his staff he told them of his decision. Orders went out for Baird to fall back on Corunna and for Hope to join Moore by a series of forced marches. The following morning Moore sent a brief despatch to Castlereagh telling him of his decision. Yet, while he waited for Hope, he was told reports of the enemy strength round Madrid were probably inflated and that the remnants of the broken Spanish armies were uniting close to the city.

Further reports came from Frere and the Central Junta about the improving conditions of the Spanish forces. Moore very much doubted their truth but, after uniting his forces, he decided to make a final offensive move in order to give the Spanish more time to organise their resistance. He wrote to Castlereagh: 'I shall never abandon the cause as long as it holds out a chance of succeeding – but you must be sensible that the ground may be, in an instant, cut from under me.'[38] On 9 November Moore went further and told Castlereagh, 'I shall threaten the French communications and create a diversion if the Spaniards can avail themselves of it.' Unknown to him Madrid had already fallen.

After uniting with Baird, Moore planned a quick dart against Marshal Soult. In a letter to his confidante, Lady Hester Stanhope, Moore showed he was in no doubt about his hazardous position: 'We are in a scrape; but I hope we shall have spirit to get out of it. You must, however, be prepared to hear very bad news.'[39] In a series of forced marches the British went ever deeper into enemy territory. After preliminary clashes with Soult, Moore learned that his object of drawing the French from the south had succeeded. Napoleon had decided to lead his whole army in a northwards direction against the British and, what was more, he was already three days' march along the road.

On 23 December Moore started withdrawing and in his diary he once more gave his reasons for thrusting north: 'I was aware that I risked infinitely too much; but something, I thought, was to be risked for the honour of the service and to make it apparent that we stuck to the Spaniards long after they themselves had given up their case as lost.'[40] Napoleon boasted of crushing Moore's little army – the French strength was something in the region of 300,000 men. However, even

Napoleon proved fallible by advancing too far to the east and Moore's men beat them to the mountain defiles. Napoleon thereupon turned back for Paris, leaving Soult with an army of nearly 50,000 to pursue Moore, whose force by now was reduced to half that number.

Moore had achieved more than could have been expected of him by, against all the odds, giving the Spaniards a breathing space and demonstrating Britain's willingness to help her ally, but his army, which had so relished the prospect of fighting, showed signs of cracking under the terrible weather conditions and the strain caused by the protracted withdrawal. In their discomfort and near despair some men became crazed for drink, whatever the consequences. Moore, like Lord George Murray sixty years before, placed himself at the rear with the reserve, issuing communiques condemning their behaviour. After two days rest at Benavente the army moved towards Astorga some thirty-five miles away along the same route as the Spanish troops who were not only verminous, half-naked and starving, but completely out of control. Their example had its effect on the poorer elements of Moore's own forces. As the British left Benavente the cavalry, under their brilliant commander Sir Henry Paget, repulsed their French opposite numbers and bought valuable time for the main body. Following another punishing march Moore reached Astorga only to find his stores had been plundered. Here he was forced to leave his sick behind in order to save the main body for its grim journey north from Astorga via Bembibre to Villafranca.

Now came the most terrible phase of their march, through sixty miles of mountain passes before they reached the barren plateau guarding the coast. In blizzard conditions the track lay under deep drifts, and because the freezing winds sapped the energy of even the strongest, many baggage carts had to be abandoned. Without replacement shoes, men were forced to go barefoot – their progress marked by bloody footprints on the snow. Moore struggled to keep his army's cohesion – and to keep it moving. Despite their indiscipline he was still unwilling to condemn his suffering men to the lash, or worse. For an enlightened commander, like himself, his communique of 6 January makes tragic reading. 'The commander of the forces is tired of giving orders which are never attended to; he therefore appeals to the honour and feelings of the army he commands; and if these are not sufficient to induce them to do their duty, he must despair of succeeding by any other means.'[41]

At Lugo, before it retreated again, the army showed it retained its warlike spirit, turning against its French pursuers and inflicting 400 casualties on them, with Moore in the thick of the action shouting encouragement. Most importantly this sally gave him the opportunity to make the downhill track to Corunna without close interference. Before the main body reached Corunna, however, Moore's scouts returned with the terrible news that only a few transports lay at anchor in the harbour; the main fleet had been delayed. Before he could get his army off safely Moore would have to fight a defensive battle.

At Corunna, on 13 January, Moore wrote his last letter to Castlereagh. In his exhaustion it was misspelt, smudged and almost illegible. He told Castlereagh that he was sending him General Stewart to give him the full details of the campaign. He mentioned the risks he had taken and the poor behaviour of the army during the retreat, although he ended with the proud words, 'but when there was a prospect of fighting the enemy, the men were then orderly and seemed pleased and determined to do their duty'.[42] Despite this he felt bound to warn Castlereagh that 'my position in front of this place is a very bad one'.

Having embarked the cavalry and heavy artillery on the ships available Moore prepared the defence of the harbour with his four infantry divisions now much wasted and totalling just 15,000 men. He placed two divisions on a ridge with an open valley to the right, while the other two were commanded to move into the adjoining valley and conceal themselves. The French refused to attack his prepared positions and so, on the 16th he finally ordered one of his rear divisions to make for the harbour. At the sight of its withdrawal the French started to come forward at which to a man the division turned about and marched back to the sound of the guns. Moore, in a clean uniform and on a good horse, was in full control. Observers said that on that afternoon, Moore, in a state of near exultation because the French had decided to give battle, was everywhere, severally leading a counter-attack, ordering a diversion or plugging a gap in the line. His first two divisions succeeded in holding the French on the ridge, while in the valley the French attack was checked by the other two. The British started to gain ground and the prospect of victory lay before them. At the moment of success a round shot struck Moore and threw him off his horse. He made no cry and his face did not change. When his aides turned him on his back they saw his left shoulder was carried away, exposing his lung; and one arm hung by a strip of flesh. There was nothing the surgeons could do.

But had Moore already achieved his purpose? He certainly bought time and had succeeded in leading his army across Spain in winter, in spite of the superior French forces snapping at their heels. At the end of an heroic march he was able to repulse the French and therefore preserve his army for a fresh campaign. Meanwhile, without their commander the British counter-attacks died down. The battle closed with both forces in much the same positions as when it started, but the French were too weakened to impede the British army's move to the ships of the main fleet that had now entered the harbour. Throughout the night and the next day the British embarked and on the evening of the second day Moore's aides took their general's body to a bastion on the city ramparts where they buried him in his cloak within a shallow grave. When the French occupied Corunna Moore's opponent, Soult, with notable gallantry, ordered guns to be fired over the grave and then set up a monument to the man who had first outmarched and finally outfought him.

From the time that Moore's ragged and verminous men returned to England controversy surrounded his three month campaign. In retrospect it can be seen that Moore's thrust against the French communications, which he himself considered too hazardous in normal circumstances, had far-reaching military and political consequences. Had it not been for Moore, Napoleon would have subjugated all Spain and Portugal. By taking such risks Moore gave the Spanish guerrillas time to become organised and for the British flag to be kept flying over Lisbon. Three months after Corunna most of the army that Moore saved would re-land at Lisbon to take part in the five year campaign that ended with Spain's liberation and Napoleon's defeat. Years later Wellington, the successful commander of that second campaign, acknowledged his debt to Moore when he remarked to his Military Secretary, Lord Fitzroy Somerset, 'D'you know Fitzroy we'd not have won, I think, without him [Moore].'[43]

The principles that Moore devised for training were also an unquestionable help to Wellington, not only in the outstanding conduct of the light division when it came under his command, but also in the flexible tactics of which Wellington made such good use in the peninsula. On the fifty-third anniversary of Waterloo Colonel George Gawler, who had witnessed the battle and the earlier peninsular campaign, wrote

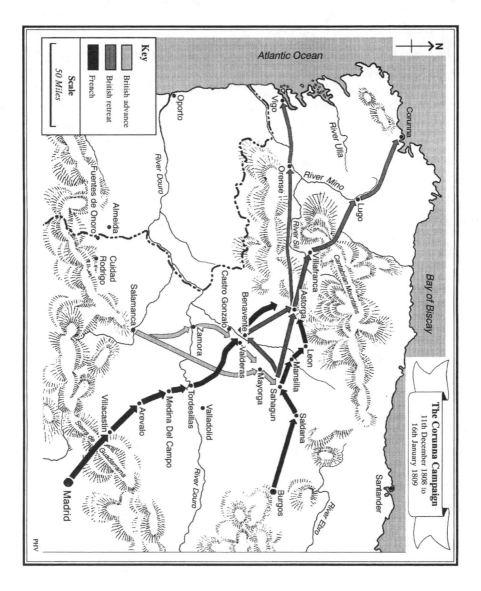

to his son, 'Good common-sense heads in England devised, first under Sir John Moore at Shorncliffe, pliable solidarity. With this system the old duke out-numbered every army opposed to him, and never lost a battle.'[44]

Whatever his legacy, Moore had both high ambition and high personal ideals. One of the British army's foremost historians, John Fortesque, wrote of him, 'The inwardness of the man was as fair as the outward semblance, for he was the soul of honour, a hater of all crookedness and meanness, straightforward, generous, gentle, fearless, pure and true, a man of clean hands and of a clean heart.'[45]

Such magniloquence seems more appropriate for a saint than a soldier and Moore was certainly no saint but it cannot be denied that with his sharp mind, abetted by deep professional knowledge, he was usually proved right, not only against military opponents but with his political masters, too. Always an inspired tactician and outstanding leader of men, by the time of Corunna he had become an able strategist, the requirement of any senior commander.

On the other hand Moore, the indomitable, could fairly be said to have tempted fate too hard. As a result he rarely went into a major action without being wounded. He never thought of changing; knowing his worth with men far less sure than himself, he continued to take the highest risks. His death wound at Corunna was a direct result of such belief. Nonetheless, Moore can be considered an unlucky commander. If he had survived Corunna, he, not Wellington, would surely have led the fight against Napoleon. He was also unlucky in that he did not have the same time as Wellington to rid the army of the incompetent soldiers that were swept into the British ranks in the late 18th century. In this respect it is true, if harsh, to say that his retreat to Corunna undoubtedly cleared out more incompetents than good men, something that could again only help Wellington.

Finally, whatever his actual virtues Moore can be seen as a legendary, prickly man, magnificent when in a crisis but essentially a northerner, contemptuous of fools or slackers and no less critical of them if they came from London's Horse Guards and War Office. Restless, ever seeking glory on the field of battle, he never compromised as he eagerly anticipated the next phase of his triumphant career. But Moore the happy warrior also possessed an understanding of the dignity owed to all men, especially fighting men, a characteristic the greatest Scottish commanders bequeathed to the British military system.

CHAPTER SEVEN

VICTORIA'S WARS – CLYDE AND MACDONALD

'Ship me somewhere east of Suez, where the best is like the worst, Where there ain't no Ten Commandments and a man can raise a thirst.'

Rudyard Kipling, 'Mandalay'

AFTER WELLINGTON'S CROWNING SUCCESS at Waterloo the European states met at the congress of Vienna and consolidated the balance of power. The still-fresh memories of the long and costly wars against Revolutionary and Napoleonic France served to remind them about the importance in not pursuing their national interests regardless of others.

As a consequence the Continent was to enjoy many years of peace, and ambitious soldiers, including those from Scotland, had to content themselves with campaigns across an expanding British Empire. By the turn of the half-century things were changing and Britain's armies were not only involved in fighting against the Russians in the Crimea, but faced a massive and determined rebellion in India. By the final years of the century war came back into its own, with new and terrible clashes between the great powers bringing an escalation of military activity that would lead to the world wars of the 20th century along with their ultimate tests of military leadership for western commanders.

In the second half of the nineteenth century two Scottish commanders, both from humble backgrounds, were to gain fame for their mastery of the battlefield. They were Colin Campbell, who became Lord Clyde and a field marshal, and Major General Sir Hector Archibald MacDonald who thrilled all Scotland with his martial exploits. As with Abercromby and Moore their loyalty to the British establishment was total, in their case towards a Queen who was both surprisingly knowledgeable in military affairs and warmly disposed towards the commanders who devoted their lives to extending her Empire across the face of the globe.

Colin Campbell (Lord Clyde) (1792–1863)

Colin Campbell was the eldest of four children born to a Glasgow carpenter, John MacLiver and his wife Agnes Campbell. Colin had good military antecedants; his paternal grandfather was laird of Ardnave in Islay, who had 'been out' in the '45 and was forced to forfeit his estate as a result; his mother was a Campbell who could trace her direct ancestry back to the 2nd Earl of Argyll who fell at Flodden. Although the family had a proud military tradition it had little money at this time, yet Colin started off well enough when his uncle, Colonel Campbell, introduced him to the Duke of York, the British Army's commander-in-chief. The Duke duly promised Colin a commission but mistakenly entered his name in the lists as Colin Campbell, rather than Colin MacLiver. His uncle advised him to ignore the error and from that time on for all practical reasons he remained a Campbell.

Like Sir Ralph Abercromby, Campbell's career falls into two distinct parts. The first started when he was fifteen and a half years of age and was to last for forty-four years while the second, which he undertook after emerging from retirement, lasted just five years although this was the time when his abilities as a senior commander became fully apparent. As one would expect the two phases, while convenient in tracing his career, were by no means self-contained. The leadership qualities he showed in the second were forged and tempered during the struggles and disappointments of the first while the physical toil of the earlier years would also leave their mark.

As a young officer he took part in much active fighting, suffered several serious wounds and had many lucky escapes. These wounds were by no means his only physical problem, although after suffering them he was never fully free from pain; when still under twenty he contracted a fever which continued to flare up periodically for the rest of his life. It was still affecting him almost forty years later, laying him low, for instance, during 1849 just before a most hazardous engagement against the Sikhs at Chillianwala. During his early years

Campbell served under the two leading soldiers of his day, Sir John Moore and the Duke of Wellington. With such ambitious leaders young officers were tested to the limits of their physical endurance. In 1809, under Moore, he took part in the terrible retreat to Corunna during which one officer and 148 men of Campbell's own battalion died. In later life he was to describe what that meant to him; and how he had marched through the snow with bare feet when the soles of his boots were completely worn away. At Corunna, he was unable to remove them 'as from constant wear and inability to take them off the leather adhered so closely to the flesh of his legs, that he was obliged to steep them in water as hot as he could bear, and have the leather cut away in strips'.[1] Fortunately Campbell's legs were not to suffer any permanent damage from this experience.

Apart from the physical costs of 19th century soldiering Colin Campbell suffered from another considerable handicap. After a promising start financial limitations were to impose a serious curb on his rate of promotion. In 1813, as a result of his distinguished conduct under Wellington at San Sebastian, he was promoted to captain, but twelve years were to pass before he was able to purchase his majority, for which he was forced to take out two loans, one of £600 from a friend and a further £200 from his army agents. From his appointment as captain he continued to assist his father with an annual payment of between £30 and £40 out of his meagre pay. After a further seven years he succeeded in purchasing a lieutenant-colonelcy but, largely for reasons of finance it had to be an unattached one. In that instance the required amount was provided by a relative – although he almost certainly had to pay her back. Campbell was finally made full colonel in 1846 when he was appointed aide-de-camp to the Queen for his service in China. Towards the end of his 'first career' he was promoted to temporary brigadier general when required to help form an army for active service in the Punjab. In spite of his virtually unrivalled battlefield experience compared with his peers this failure to obtain brevet rank was an important factor in him not having a brigadier's command before the age of fifty-five.

Colin Campbell entered the army at a good time for a young, ambitious officer. Napoleon had made himself master of nearly all Europe, but when the Spaniards and Portuguese rose in revolt, 9000 British soldiers under the command of Sir Arthur Wellesley were despatched to the Iberian peninsula in support. On 19 July 1808 the teenage Campbell was a lieutenant in the 9th Regiment of Foot (on the strength of its second battalion) when it joined Wellesley after landing in western Portugal off the Bay of Peniché near Lisbon.

Campbell wrote home that he 'lay out that night for the first time in his life'. Wellesley had already been in Portugal for eleven days during which time he had got the better of two skirmishes with the French. On the 21st Campbell was present when Wellesley again defeated the French, this time on the heights of Vimiero. Campbell's company was in the battalion's rear when it came under steady fire. At this point one of the company's more senior officers gave him his baptism of fire taking the youth along the face of the leading troops in full view of the enemy riflemen, a kindness that Campbell referred to gratefully in later years. After Vimiero the French evacuated Portugal and Campbell was transferred to the 9th's first battalion which went to Salamanca in November to join General Moore and his army to help expel the French from Spain. Not only did Campbell take part in the memorable retreat to Corunna but his battalion fought in the battle against the French there, provided the fatigue party which dug Sir John Moore's grave in the city ramparts and was the last to re-embark.

After about six months in England Campbell and his battalion formed part of the force under the Earl of Chatham which was sent to the Netherlands to take the fortress of Antwerp and destroy the French fleet lying at anchor in its harbour. The so-called Walcheren expedition proved disastrous: the French fleet escaped and Campbell's battalion stayed on the island of South Beveland (opposite Walcheren) until it re-embarked by which time most of them had the serious fever which killed a sixth of the force and affected the survivors for the rest of their lives.

On his return Campbell reverted to the second battalion which in 1811 saw action in the battle of Barrosa at the southern tip of Spain. Their Spanish allies stood by while the British fought against the French who were more than double their strength. The British prevailed but it was a hard fought action and Campbell's diary referred to his part in it. 'At the battle of Barrosa, in 1811, the present Lord Lynedoch was pleased to take favourable notice of my conduct when left in command of the two flank companies of my regiment, all the other officers being wounded.' During 1813 the twenty-year-old Campbell, now back with the 9th's first battalion, joined with the Duke of Wellington's forces in their great advance towards the Pyrenees before entering the French heartland. He was in the thick of the fighting at Vitoria and distinguished himself at the seige of the northern seaport fortress of San Sebastian close to the French frontier. At San Sebastian Campbell attempted to enter a breach made in its great surrounding wall. As Napier described it: 'It was in vain that Lieutenant Campbell, breaking through the tumultuous crowd with the survivors of his own detachment, mounted the ruins – twice he ascended, twice he was wounded, and all around him died.'[2] His conduct was not totally without reward, however, since from this time he was marked out for his great spirit and powers of junior leadership. Before the wounds healed he discharged himself from hospital and took part in another successful attack against the French in which he was again wounded. For leaving hospital unofficially he received a severe reprimand from his commanding officer.

When Campbell returned to England, he carried with him a letter from his general to be delivered to the Military Secretary which recommended him 'as a most gallant and meritorious young officer'.[3]

In 1819, after a period of leave to allow time to recover from his wounds (which were serious enough for him to be granted a temporary pension of £100 a year) he spent a short spell in Nova Scotia and then Gibraltar with the 60th Regiment before it was reduced and he was transferred to the 21st Regiment, the Royal North British Fusileers with whom he went to Barbados in the West Indies where he was to remain for seven years. He acted first as ADC to General Murray, Governor and Military Commander, although in 1825, following his promotion to a major, he was given the responsible appointment of Brigade Major to the forces there. Despite periodic attacks of fever, it was a happy period that brought him many enduring friendships.

When Campbell returned home from the West Indies he again bore letters of the highest praise. He continued in the 21st and served with it in Windsor and then in Ireland but despite his ability and letters sent on his behalf by Lord Lynedoch to the Military Secretary, it was a time of frustration. He sought promotion, but finding no prospect of a vacancy in his own regiment he set about purchasing an unattached lieutenant-colonelcy. For a regular officer this was a less attractive option. After obtaining it in October 1832 there followed a series of false hopes for employment and following what must have seemed like endless delays he was, in 1835, finally appointed commanding officer of the 98th regiment then on overseas service at the Cape.

Even now there was delay for he did not assume command until the summer of 1837 when it returned. Campbell immediately set about training his regiment according to the principles devised by Sir John Moore at Shorncliffe. In 1839 an opportunity came for Campbell to see how effective his directives had been. The regiment was ordered to Newcastle on Tyne to undertake internal security duties, in particular to check any disorder caused by the radical Chartists. Campbell, the ardent soldier in war, now showed a much more circumspect side to his personality. He personally attended Chartist meetings and concluded that most of those who were there 'advocated moral rather than physical arguments' to gain their objectives.[4] Colin Campbell's commander in Northern District, Sir Charles Napier, already had a high opinion of him. 'I have sent Campbell, Ninety-Eighth (to Newcastle) from Hull. The colliers had better be quiet; they will have a hardy soldier to deal with; yet he will be gentle and just or he should not be there.'[5] Campbell showed he was both wise and fair in his dealings with such men and in his district the disaffection gradually abated.

Sir Charles Napier was also aware of Colin Campbell's zeal in promoting the interests of his regiment. The Scot prided himself on his troops' professionalism as well as their high standard of discipline and low crime rate. He was eager to keep them under his direct control and continually tried to have those who were away on detached duty in the Isle of Man returned to him on the mainland. To his request that they should be quartered in Tynemouth Castle, Napier sent him a letter of most gracious rebuke. 'Pray tell Campbell he has no conscience. I am daily fighting battles with the cavalry for keeping two headquarters at Leeds to preserve the command for him at Newcastle . . . and now he growls about his company at the Isle of Man. So tell him to be quiet and not growl, and trust to me for doing all I can for my friends of the 98th. His officers are right good, but so would they be in any regiment that he commanded. Send him this letter, for I have not time to abuse him myself and he cannot expect a civil letter.'[6] The problem for Napier was that Colin Campbell, while probably his best commander, was junior to most of his other commanding officers, particularly to some in charge of cavalry units. This seemed to be confirmed when Napier, after receiving Campbell's far from obsequious reply to his admonishment, wrote: 'You say you are not a grumbler though you have the appearance of one. I have sixteen regiments under my command, and wish every one was commanded by such a grumbler.'[7] The warmth and respect shown by Sir Charles Napier for Colin Campbell was palpable and for such a superior Campbell himself would march to the ends of the earth. Yet a man who took both himself and his regiment so very seriously needed careful handling and in the future some of his superiors would be far less appreciative of his qualities.

In 1842 the 98th were ordered to China for one of the so-called Opium wars during which the Imperial Chinese authorities were forced to accept opium – a drug they had earlier declared illegal – in exchange for their goods, notably tea and silks. In spite of the undemanding military operations there Campbell was driven almost frantic by the high rate of sickness suffered by his battalion after its six months at sea. By December 1842 he had lost 283 men and a further 231 were sick. With the end of hostilities, Campbell was made Commandant of Hong Kong until 18 January when he was appointed an acting brigadier in Chusan. At this point he moved his battalion from Hong Kong to the healthier climate at Chusan. By now its death toll alone had risen to 432. For his work in China Campbell was nominated to the companionship of the Bath and made ADC to the Queen, the first public recognition of his abilities. Campbell stayed in China with the 98th until 1846. He successfully restored his battalion to health and brought it up to a high level of training. At the same time Campbell earned the full respect of the Chinese authorities for his wise and restrained approach as governor. In 1847 he handed over the command of the 98th and was posted to India as a brigadier second class, and commander of Lahore state. His commander-in-chief, Lord Gough, greeted him cordially enough, as did the Governor General, Lord Hardinge. Nonetheless on this posting he was not to enjoy anything like the same relationship with his superiors as he had done with Napier. Despite being promoted to temporary brigadier general, his five years in India – marked by the serious Sikh rebellion – proved less happy than any of his previous postings; he suffered badly from periodic attacks of his old fever, and on several occasions expressed a wish to return home.

In 1848, however, a major insurrection led by Moolraj Singh, governor of Mooltan state in the Punjab put all such thoughts aside. By the end of September the outbreak was spreading fast among the warlike Sikhs. With the prospect of action Campbell became a new man. He was given temporary promotion to the rank of brigadier general and made commander of a strong brigade from the British garrison at Lahore. The plan put forward by Lord Gough was to assemble an army and strike at the heart of the insurrection in the northern part of the Punjab. Campbell's senior there was Brigadier General Cureton, who constantly deferred to orders from the commander-in-chief. To Campbell's frustration Lord Gough decided to take direct command and according to Campbell's diary, he proved limited as a field commander, both in failing to reconnoitre before offensive action and in not using his artillery to its fullest advantage. On 19 November 1848 in clashes between opposing cavalry detachments General Cureton was shot and killed. Campbell was offered the vacant post of adjutant general but unhappy with the conduct of the campaign, he refused and for good measure stated his previous wish to get back to Europe. This was refused and a period of relative inactivity followed during which Campbell suffered a renewed bout of fever triggered off by his insistence on sharing his troops' primitive conditions on campaign. In January 1849 it was decided to renew the pursuit of the rebels. Campbell recommended a preliminary reconnaissance but his advice was not taken and as the British advanced they were surprised to discover the enemy's main army drawn up for battle on a plain before a village called Chillianwalla. The British deployed opposite them for what was expected to be the decisive action of the war.

The battle ground was difficult and in the Sikhs' favour with a swathe of jungle scrub lying between the two armies in which the Sikhs had posted observers and sharpshooters. Lord Gough found himself committed to a frontal attack and as it was late in the day he would have one hour only for a preliminary bombardment before he started moving forward. General Gilbert commanded Gough's right hand infantry division with Campbell on the left. Campbell's division had two brigades: Brigadier Pennycuick commanded the one on Campbell's right and Brigadier Hoggan was on the left. Due to the jungle Campbell decided he could not personally superintend more than one brigade during the battle. He opted to stay with Brigadier Hoggan as he was as 'blind as a bat', and took direct charge of it. Under Campbell's strong leadership the brigade advanced without too much difficulty firing as it went, a potentially hazardous but most effective procedure which Campbell had practised beforehand. His armed volleys succeeded in putting the opposing cavalry to flight and his troops went on to roll up the opposing enemy line and capture thirteen guns until they joined up with units from General Gilbert's division. Unfortunately Campbell's right hand brigade met a far different fate, coming under accurate fire from both infantry and the Sikh artillery which was unsubdued. As a result it sustained heavy losses, including its commander, together with twenty-two other officers and almost 500 soldiers. After the battle Campbell wrote proudly to his sister: 'The numbers of the enemy were fivefold greater than ours, and they had the advantage of a very strong position. The portion of my division, which I conducted myself during the attack, was most successful . . .'[8] This was undoubtedly true and as darkness fell the British held the field but in Gilbert's division, Brigadier Mountain's command had suffered even worse than Pennycuick and the 2400 men killed and wounded in the action brought shock and alarm both in Britain and in the Indian press. During the assault Campbell was wounded in the arm from a sword cut inflicted by an artillery man defending his gun. Campbell had obviously been at the head of things and his small pocket pistol took the full force of a bullet which might otherwise have killed him.

However, such personal bravery by no means protected Campbell from criticism, with some authorities attributing the disaster suffered by Pennycuick's brigade to the lack of precautions taken by his divisional commander. Campbell vigorously refuted such charges; a staff officer had apparently countermanded his orders for the artillery to provide close support, while Pennycuick's brigade had advanced so quickly that it put itself across the guns allocated to give covering fire. After the initial shocked reaction there was a reassessment of the battle, and no less an authority than the Duke of Wellington stated that Campbell had saved the army from destruction in 'one of the most brilliant exploits that had ever signalised a British Regiment'. Despite the eminent source, such praise seemed decidedly extravagant although, due to the battle's late start, the difficulties posed by the ground, and the failure by cavalry and infantry elsewhere, the conduct of Campbell's brigade was outstanding, and without him defeat would have been probable.

After Chillianwala the British received reinforcements and went on to defeat the Sikhs at Goojrat where Campbell's advice to the commander-in-chief, about making the fullest use of their superior artillery, proved of vital importance. After Goojrat the Sikhs started to lay down their arms and by 21 March the campaign was over. Despite being awarded a knighthood for his services, about which Sir Charles Napier said 'no man had won it better', Campbell was plainly not happy with the criticisms directed against him, particularly from the Indian press over Chillianwala. However unfair and exaggerated some of these might be, he again voiced a desire to leave India. His wish was not granted for in November 1850 he was made divisional commander of the Peshawur District on the troubled north-western frontier, where he remained for a further three years.

The initial outcry over Chillianwala brought changes in the high command. To Campbell's delight Lord Gough was replaced by his old friend Sir Charles Napier, but before Campbell went to Peshawur, Napier was himself replaced by Sir William Gomm. Campbell and Gomm were well known to each other having served together in the Peninsula. More importantly for Campbell, however, than the replacement of the commander-in-chief, was the arrival in 1847 of Lord Dalhousie as Governor General.

In 1851 Dalhousie visited Campbell at Peshawur to discuss the army's proposed stance towards the turbulent tribes on the border, particularly the fierce Momunds. Dalhousie was in favour of inflicting summary punishment on them by firing their villages but Campbell, finding their hill positions extremely strong and concerned that his troops would be likely to suffer excessive casualties trying to shift them, proposed a considerable strengthening of the border outposts. It was only with reluctance that Dalhousie concurred with Campbell's initial decision to go on the defensive (a decision fully and warmly approved by the commander-in-chief). When Campbell subsequently became aware of the strong hostility towards the British Government from the more powerful Swat tribe with its 6000 hostile tribesmen it was his turn to advocate a powerful offensive but the Punjab Board of Administration, supported by the Governor General refused his request for extra troops and transport and he was obliged to return to his base at Peshawur.

At Peshawur the Governor General's dissatisfaction with Campbell's conduct of military operations materialised in a formal censure that was damning in its reference to his 'over-cautious reluctance' against the marauders during March 1852. It was followed by the further charge of placing himself in an attitude of direct and proclaimed insubordination to the authority of the Governor General.

From all accounts Campbell was genuinely surprised he should be accused of insubordination. It was a patently unfair charge against an experienced commander who, unlike the Governor General, had conducted a careful reconnaissance of the ground involved. In writing to Sir William Gomm, Campbell concluded with heavy irony that 'There is a limit at which a man's forbearance ought to stop, and that limit has in my case been reached'. He resigned his command on 25 July 1852, although before leaving India he received official acknowledgement of the skill with which he conducted his final operations. It recorded the Governor General's regret 'that any incident should have occurred to deserve a censure of any portion of Sir Colin Campbell's conduct' and it 'acknowledged in the most ample terms the ability, the personal intrepidity and activity, and the sterling soldiering qualities which this distinguished officer had displayed in the military command of the troops at Peshawur upon every occasion in which they had taken the field'.[9]

However much the Governor General was prepared to be gracious after the event, his criticisms of 'over-cautious reluctance' had caused the peppery Campbell to go. This appeared to be what Dalhousie wanted, since he consistently under-rated Campbell's ability as a commander. Predictably Sir Charles Napier wrote to Campbell on 18 April 1852 in a warm and generous fashion about what Napier described as 'an ill-judged expedition and one of relatively little consequence as a fighting soldier . . . I am so angry at the attacks upon you in the Indian newspapers that I cannot resist saying to you that I firmly believe, had you not commanded, some disaster would have befallen the force.'[10] However, nothing would change Campbell's decision and during the summer of 1853 he began his return journey to Britain. Before leaving he declined a farewell banquet organised by the officers of Peshawur garrison on the grounds that to accept 'would be contrary to the Queen's regulations'. In spite of his clash with Dalhousie Campbell must have been fully aware of his impressive successes over a long and adventurous career. He had distinguished himself against widely differing enemies through ascending levels of command. However, while in his later stages he had commanded at divisional level, as the old soldier of sixty-one prepared to go on half pay after forty-two years of service, his substantive rank was still only that of colonel.

*   *   *

In an amazing and unexpected turn of events during the last nine years of his life Campbell would return to serve his Queen first in the Crimea and then in India. Involvement, however, was no guarantee of success, since for the British high command as a whole, the Crimean war was nothing short of disastrous. To his credit Campbell, an old man by conventional military standards, was to prove the great exception. When called again to be commander-in-chief in India he would go on to lead a successful campaign there.

On 10 February 1854, just eleven months after returning from India and before war was officially declared in March, Campbell found himself one of the first senior officers selected for employment. This was with the British expeditionary force already stationed in the East to co-operate with French forces in defence of Turkey against Russia.

Lord Hardinge, who knew him well from their recent time together in India, told Campbell he would command one of the two infantry brigades of the First Division which along with four other divisions would proceed to the Crimea under the command of Lord Raglan. He was to command the Highland Brigade and the Duke of Cambridge would command the Guards Brigade of the First Division. With the royal duke as his fellow commander Sir Colin lost the chance of being made senior brigadier, although compared with him the Duke of Cambridge was woefully inexperienced. Similarly, although Lord Raglan had lost his arm from what was generally thought to be the last shot of the Waterloo campaign, he had experienced no active service since then. Campbell had never commanded Highlanders before but he felt he understood their character, and he was delighted when his own military efficiency and wide knowledge of war speedily won both their respect and affection. In their turn they would come to see him not only as their brigade commander but as the chief of a special clan, one united for the purpose of war.

In July the move to the Crimea began with the capture of Sebastopol as their first objective. The troops were landed about twenty-five miles from Sebastopol and on 19 September together with their French and Turkish allies they began to march on the city. The French and Turks were first to come into contact with the Russian defenders and soon found themselves bogged down under heavy artillery fire. Lord Raglan decided the British must assume the offensive by crossing the river Alma and seize the fortifications on its further side. As the

Highland Brigade halted before the Alma their veteran commander addressed them in terms both practical and proud, terms they could well appreciate. 'Now men, you are going into action. Remember this, whoever is wounded – I don't care what his rank is – must lie where he falls till the bandsmen come to attend him. No soldier must go carrying off wounded men. If any soldier does such a thing his name shall be stuck up in his parish church. Don't be in a hurry about firing. Your officers will tell you when it is time to open fire. Be steady, keep silence, fire low. Now men, the army will watch us; make me proud of the Highland Brigade!'[11] The threat of posting men's names in their parishes showed the closeness of kinship within those in the brigade at that time.

The Alma was an infantryman's battle. In the British sector the light division formed the extreme left of the British forces and the first division was in immediate support behind it. The light division advanced against a great Russian redoubt immediately to its front which was protected by artillery on both its flanks along with more batteries stationed on the heights above. Large numbers of Russian troops supported their artillery. After taking the redoubt the light division were checked, their casualties rose alarmingly and the redoubt fell into Russian hands once more. As Campbell was wading the Alma with the 42nd he quickly took in the serious situation and ordered them up to the plateau on which the redoubt stood where 'they came upon the enemy and opened fire while still advancing in line'.[12] Another mass of enemy troops came forward but these were also driven back with heavy losses. When the 42nd halted, the 93rd came up on their left flank and succeeded in dispersing another large enemy force. As new detachments of the enemy came up against the left flank of the 93rd the 79th made its appearance over the hill and sent them down the hillside in confusion. The movement of his battalions in support of each other was a triumph for discipline and timing, the marks of good leadership. Campbell proudly wrote to Colonel Henry Eyre: 'The Guards during these operations were away to my right, and quite removed from the scene of this fight, which I have described. *It was a fight of the Highland Brigade.*'[13]

After the battle Lord Raglan, accompanied by the Duke of Cambridge, warmly congratulated the Highlanders. As Sir Colin Campbell wrote: 'When I approached him I observed his eyes to fill and his lips and countenance to quiver.'[14] Raglan was unable to speak and Campbell filled the uneasy interval by asking the commander-in-chief whether he could be allowed to wear the Highland bonnet for the rest of the campaign. Campbell himself was full of pride for his men and he reported to Colonel Eyre that: 'My men behaved nobly. I never saw troops march to battle with greater sang froid and order than those three Highland regiments. Their conduct was very much admired by all who witnessed their behaviour.' The Alma was not a complicated action but by seizing the initiative, the three battalions of the Highland Brigade not only protected the left wing of the British army and recovered the great redoubt but in doing so put to flight eight Russian battalions and compelled four more to retreat. The opposing troops were from the elite of their army and before he died of his wounds the Russian General Karganov gave grudging admiration to Campbell and his Highlanders whom he called, 'the savages without trousers'.

Campbell's next task appeared to give him less opportunity for distinction. He was appointed commander of the troops defending the port of Balaclava, a task he approached with his customary energy and determination, spending all his daylight hours in trying to improve its decrepit defence works which he acknowledged they held, 'by sheer impudence'. In the process he made a firm friend in General Vinoy, his French counterpart there. It was exhausting work, made the more urgent by the strong expectation of a Russian attack, which came nine days after the allies had begun improving the positions. Sir Colin's own share of the action was appropriately with the 93rd Highlanders.

On 25 October 1854 the Russians mounted attacks on the double line of defence works which Campbell had constructed to protect the port. In the Russians' early attacks the Turkish defenders were driven back from the outer defences, a chain of forts dividing the southern or inner plain before the city from the exterior or northern valley, but they rallied on either side of the Highlanders who were occupying rising ground in front of a gun battery. At this time the 93rd were seriously deficient in numbers through having over 100 invalids. When the Russian artillery began to inflict casualties on his men Campbell ordered them to retire behind the crest of the hill. Meanwhile the Russian cavalry, soon to be engaged by their British opposite numbers, continued to advance up the North Valley to their left. Four squadrons detached themselves and made their way towards Campbell's Highlanders. When they were within about 1000 yards he had his men return to the top of the hillock. Well knowing the importance of Balaclava and the limited numbers of infantry to guard it he told his Highlanders: 'Remember there is no retreat from here men. You must all die where you stand.' To which came the reply, cheerily given, 'Aye, aye, Sir Colin, we'll do that!'[15] In fact, the erratic charge of the Russian cavalry did not disturb the resolution of either Campbell or his men. As the Russians came closer some of the young Scots were even anxious to rush forward with the bayonet but they were curbed by Sir Colin's angry shout, '93rd, 93rd, damn all that eagerness!' When the horsemen came within long musketry range the Highlanders opened fire, making the cavalry wheel to the left where they threatened the Scots' right flank. Campbell moved the grenadier company of the 93rd to oppose them and the cavalry retreated.

At this moment in the North Valley the main body of the Russian cavalry advanced against the British Heavy Cavalry Brigade and the 93rd from their vantage point were able to cheer on the cavalry's success quite unaware of the Light Brigade hidden from their view. The 93rd gave a round of cheers for the cavalry and Campbell was unable to resist riding over to congratulate them saying, 'Greys, gallant Greys, I am sixty-one years old and if I were young again I should be proud to be in your ranks.'

While the Russian cavalry were regrouping their broken ranks they placed a field battery of eight guns in a commanding defensive position at the eastern end of North Valley. Following this, as a result of a garbled message taken by a Captain Nolan from Lord Raglan to Lord Cardigan, commander of the Light Brigade, they set off on a suicidal charge down the full length of North Valley towards the covering battery, fired on by artillery the whole way. Of the 673 horsemen who set out only 195 were fit six hours later and nothing positive was achieved. W. Barry Pemberton in his *Battles of the Crimean War* was firmly of the opinion that with 'Sir Colin Campbell in supreme command it is unlikely that the Light Brigade would have been sent to its destruction.' Given his past record one can hardly believe that Campbell would have given the imprecise instruction that led to the debacle.

In a war of frustrating and muddled actions Campbell's and the 93rd's resolute stand against cavalry, by adopting a formation just two ranks deep, was seized on gratefully. It gave the British a new phrase, coined by W. H. Russell, *The Times*' noted war correspondent, the 'thin red line tipped with a line of steel', later to be shortened to 'the thin red line'.

Campbell himself made virtually nothing of the fleeting encounter. For him there were another six weeks of ceaseless activity and vigilance within Balaclava's defence lines until, on 5 December, the Russians finally withdrew. Campbell's energy had been amazing: he wrote to his friend Colonel Henry Eyre in February 1855 that until the first week of January he never had his clothes off to sleep. Apart from the state of the defences Campbell was always concerned to improve his men's living conditions, as exemplified on a celebrated occasion when the Highland Brigade were still under canvas. He heard of a ship in Balaclava port that was loaded with wooden huts, but was told there was no means of transporting them the five miles required. Campbell thereupon ordered out all his regiment in fatigue dress and marched them the five miles to Balaclava 'where everyone, officers and men, carried them piece by piece to be erected into comfortable huts'.[16]

Campbell was far less successful where his own career was concerned. In February 1855 he succeeded the Duke of Cambridge in the command of the 1st Division but he had not been allowed to accompany his Highland Brigade on an expedition to Kertch. When it returned and plans were made for the first unsuccessful assault on Sebastopol itself it was held in reserve. In June Lord Raglan died and before the final assault upon the Sebastopol Redan when Campbell and his Highlanders *were* involved the Russians withdrew, much to their anger. More frustrating still, after the unexpected death of the commander-in-chief, the overall command went not to Campbell but to General James Simpson, who had been sent out from England as chief of staff. It was under Simpson's uninspired direction that the British had experienced so many difficulties before Sebastopol despite suffering considerable casualties. When General Simpson asked to be relieved from his post as commander-in-chief Campbell's name was raised but again he was passed over, this time in favour of General Sir William Codrington, undoubtedly younger but a far less experienced and able commander. Meanwhile, Campbell had been offered command of Malta – or as he put it bitterly, to 'become schoolmaster to the recruits in Malta'.[17] Campbell was understandably hurt and angry at such treatment and set off for Britain to offer his resignation, for the second time in two consecutive campaigns. By now his abilities were so much more widely known that, on arriving home, Campbell was commanded to attend the Queen at Windsor, where she treated him so warmly that he was persuaded to return to the Crimea ready, as he gallantly said, 'to serve under a corporal if she wished it'. In reality he was to resume command of the Highland division until, shortly afterwards, the war came to an end. On his return Sir Colin Campbell was showered with awards and, on 30 June 1857, his home city, Glasgow, gave the old warrior its freedom, together with a sword of honour.

Once more he was to have scant time for leisure. Northern India was already in revolt. There were many issues of contention against the British Raj, including the recent wars against the Afghans and Sikhs, the annexation by the Governor General, Lord Dalhousie (Campbell's old adversary), of states whose rulers had no direct heir, the abolition of Suttee (widow burning), infanticide and thuggism and the require- ment for English to be the official language. The revolt however had a military origin. After isolated shows of disaffection in other garrisons of the Bengal Army it began at Meerut during May 1857 where Indian soldiers had been placed in irons for refusing to accept the cartridges for the new breech-loading Enfield rifles. These had to be bitten off before insertion and in their crass ignorance the British manufacturers had supplied a fat for them of mixed beef and pork, meats that were anathema to both Hindus and Muslims. At Meerut the Indian soldiers shot their English officers and made for Delhi, the capital of the Mughuls, where there were no English troops. There the Indian garrison joined them and the aged Mughul king, Mohammed Bahadur Shah, was proclaimed as their leader. From Delhi the mutiny became a full scale revolt. In June it spread to Cawnpore, where the British were massacred, and Lucknow, which held out. The revolt was particularly serious as the British garrisons in India had been reduced to 23,000 men due to troop withdrawals for the Crimea compared with the 130,000 Indian troops that remained.

On 11 July, the very day the War Office learned of the death from cholera of General George Anson, the Indian commander-in-chief, Campbell was offered the post. He accepted it, declaring with almost boyish zest that he was ready to start the same evening, if necessary. On his return from the Crimea, Campbell had appeared melancholy and listless, but when the new challenge came both his energy and enthusiasm revived amazingly. The slights suffered in the Crimea were forgotten and, as he left London, the sixty-five-year-old soldier wrote: 'Never did a man proceed on a mission of duty with a lighter heart and a feeling of greater humility, yet with a juster sense of the compliment that had been paid to a mere soldier of fortune like myself in being named to the highest command in the gift of the Crown.'

So began Campbell's last military phase in which, as commander-in-chief, he restored India to British authority. Fortunately on his arrival the British possessed certain strong advantages. The rebels were by no means united; the Sikhs were so hostile to the Muslims that they supported the British against the Mughul restoration; the Punjab was kept quiet by the 10,000 British troops there and on 20 September a small British army succeeded in storming Delhi where the Bahadur Shah surrendered. But Delhi was beleaguered by large numbers of rebels and the hard fighting was to come.

On his arrival the sometime irascible Campbell effortlessly shouldered the mantle of commander-in-chief, alternately praising and heartening his subordinate commanders. As he wrote to Colonel Robert Napier, General Sir James' Outram's Chief of Staff at Oudh: 'I am delighted to find you where you are at present, and most thankful for my own good fortune and that of the service in having the benefit of Sir James Outram's and your assistance exactly in the situation where the abilities and sound judgment of both will be of the greatest value.'[18] Similar letters were written to Brigadier Henry Havelock and Sir Charles Outram, trapped in Lucknow, and to Brigadier Wilson who commanded the force at Delhi. Based at Calcutta, Campbell found he was lacking in virtually every means of war: horses, ammunition, food supplies, and above all guns and gun carriages. He spent two months remedying this amidst an increasing clamour for him to take the field. But Campbell would not move until he knew he could win and on 9 November 1857, leaving General Windham behind with a weak force to hold Cawnpore, Campbell set forth on his campaign to recover India. With 3400 mainly British troops and, equally important, an arsenal of thirty-two guns, he started out to relieve Lucknow and take off the non-combatants who were confined there, wounded soldiers together with women and children. To his delight, his European troops included the 93rd Highlanders, who greeted him with loud cheers that earned the response, 'Ninety-Third, you are my own lads, I rely on you to do yourselves and me credit.'[19] However, his army was not very large and at Lucknow it was opposed by much superior numbers. But the British had the advantage of a common purpose and a determined commander who had brought together impressive artillery support.

On 16th November, acting on information brought by an ex-civilian clerk named Kavanagh who dressed as an Arab and passed through the enemy positions, Campbell successfully battered his way into the beleaguered Embassy at Lucknow and united with Outram and Havelock. It had cost him 45 officers and 496 men. From Lucknow with not much more than 3000 men he withdrew through a countryside thick with enemy troops carrying with him 400 women and children, together with 1000 sick and wounded men, towards Cawnpore where it was planned to take them by steamer to Calcutta.

As the column moved forward the sounds of heavy firing told them the garrison at Cawnpore was under attack. In fact General Charles Windham and his forces were in extreme difficulties. Windham had taken up a position between the town and the River Ganges where his force of 1400 men and eight guns was being attacked by 14,000 men with 40 guns. Riding at the head of his column Campbell relieved them just in time and after securing the river bridge he began to get his convoy of invalids and non-combatants away. After achieving this he set about attacking an enemy of roughly 25,000 who were posted in old cantonments just outside the city. Following a feint that succeeded in deceiving the enemy his 5000 infantry, 600 cavalry and 35 guns proved markedly superior to their remaining 20,000 opponents. The risks Campbell took to relieve the residency at Lucknow, followed by his defeat of much more numerous enemy forces at Cawnpore, gave him the opportunity to pursue his main strategic aim, the liberation of India.

By December Campbell had built his forces up to around 25,000 men, and the key decision was how best to use them in the vast sub-continent. Campbell proposed moving north, which meant a march into the northernmost Rohilcund area to safeguard Delhi, but Lord Canning, his civilian superior, decided that the more westerly province of Oudh with its occupied city of Lucknow should be taken first. He gave his reasons to Campbell: 'I do not underrate the importance of recovering and pacifying the whole province as soon as may be, but I estimate the early possession of Lucknow as of far greater value – of value far and wide, from one end of India to the other.' Campbell and Canning had an excellent relationship and, despite his own plan to begin attacking in the north and follow it with a great sweeping movement against Lucknow during the cooler autumn weather, he willingly gave way to Canning's counter proposal.

Campbell's force was a well-balanced one, consisting of a cavalry division with three infantry divisions and strong artillery support. A further infantry division was promised from Nepal giving him a total of 31,000 men and 164 cannon in all. As he built up his forces Campbell, in typical fashion, set about confusing the enemy and sent his men racing about in different directions to very little purpose, regardless of the inevitable criticisms from the press. Many of his own troops were equally confused, although Lieutenant Ames of the Rifle Brigade wrote home explaining that he believed Campbell was pushing all the rebels into one big net and would soon scoop them up. He also guessed correctly this would be at Lucknow.[20]

The great assault of Lucknow took Campbell twenty days, from 2 to 22 March 1858. Although he assembled forces that were larger in number than any yet seen in India, when measured against the nature of the task this strength was by no means excessive. Lucknow city was approximately the size of Paris and at the time it had a garrison of 120,000 men, of whom 33,000 were trained soldiers supported by 87,000 rural levies. Like any city its major buildings could act as powerful strongpoints and an obstinate enemy could be expected to defend it street by street. Campbell's strategic plans revealed his determination not to let the action develop into prolonged street fighting, which was very likely to bring unacceptably high levels of casualties. He always conserved his forces and in any case every fit man would be needed to complete the concluding phases of the campaign.

The Lucknow defences appeared impressive; the rebels had used 15,000 labourers to construct three defence lines that both adapted existing buildings and joined them to others. The outer line, whose centre was a strong artillery position in the Hazrat Gunge palace, stretched across the city to join with the Gumti river on the north and the canal to the south which was linked to the Gumti. The second and much shorter line was a continuous rampart with intermediate bastions that joined the palace of Imambara to that of Moti Mahal. The third constituted the great central stronghold of the Kaiserbagh, flanked by entrenchments whose walls had been loopholed and strengthened.

Campbell's assault has been described aptly by Bruce Watson as 'a

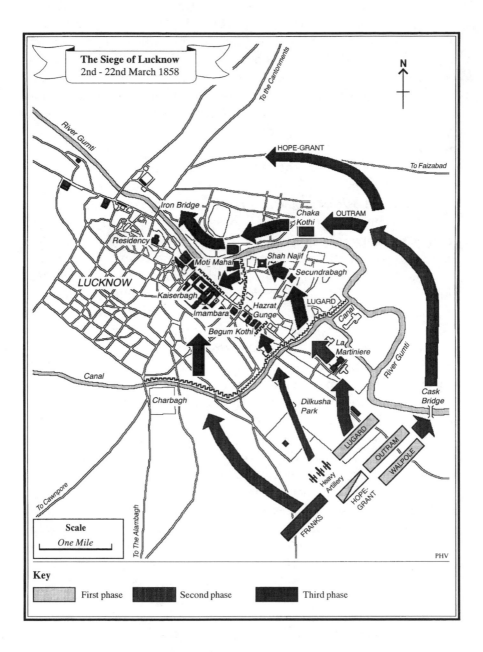

The Siege of Lucknow
2nd - 22nd March 1858

N

To the Cantonments

River Gumti

HOPE-GRANT

To Faizabad

Iron Bridge

Chaka Kothi

OUTRAM

Residency

Moti Mahal

Shah Najif

Secundrabagh

LUCKNOW

Kaiserbagh

Hazrat Gunge

LUGARD

Imambara

Begum Kothi

La Martiniere

Canal

Canal

River Gumti

Charbagh

Dilkusha Park

Cask Bridge

LUGARD

OUTRAM

WALPOLE

Heavy Artillery

HOPE-GRANT

To Cawnpore

FRANKS

To The Alambagh

Scale

One Mile

PHV

Key

First phase

Second phase

Third phase

rolling siege',[21] involving three main phases. The first was the initial entry to the city. This was in the form of a pincer movement, with the attacking units supported by powerful enfilade fire. Campbell was with the main force of General Edward Lugard's infantry division, supported by a cavalry division under Colonel Hope Grant and powerful artillery detachments. As it moved close to Kilkusha Park to the south of the city Campbell ordered General Outram's third infantry division to move up the eastern boundary, from where he could outflank the outer defence line and provide fire support for the main attack.

The second phase was the capture of the outer defence line. While Campbell kept up heavy fire on the canal defence line and the defended palace of La Martiniere, on 6 March 1858 Outram crossed the Gumti river by using two cask bridges constructed by the engineers, and marched northwards along it. From there he placed his twenty-two siege guns to enfilade the Chaka Kothi, the grandstand of the former racecourse and the pivotal point of the outer defence line. When this was accomplished, there followed the first main assault. As Walpole attacked from the west, Outram, working from the east flank, captured the Chaka Kothi. They joined forces inside the first defence line and turned their guns southwards, preventing intervention from rebels holding out in the college fortress of La Martiniere, which Campbell then captured without much trouble.

The third and most important phase of the siege came with the assault on the great central strongholds. Having brought his heavy artillery across the canal Sir Colin used it to bombard the southernmost palace the Begum Kothi, followed by the Kaiserbagh. Meanwhile Lugard's infantry took the eastern fortresses at Secundrabagh and Shah Najif, while from across the river Outram's troops attacked the rebels guarding the bridges across the Gumti. This allowed Campbell to concentrate on attacking the Begum Kothi, a complex of fortifications defended by 5000 rebels, which he had isolated. A breech was made in its outer walls and to Campbell's delight on 10 March the 93rd surged through it; after two hours of bloody fighting in which the Highlanders, aware of past outrages, showed little mercy, the fortress was in Campbell's hands.

From 11 to 15 March the British prepared for the final assault. Heavy artillery opened a breach in the wall of Imambara Palace and after a short but vicious fight British and Sikh troops gained entry. They did not stop there but continued, 'bouncing through the buildings that joined it to the still larger neighbouring palace of the Kaiserbach', which was also quickly taken.

From 12 to 14 March General Outram was at the Iron Bridge east of the central complex. He had asked to cross the Gumti but Campbell stopped him moving to avoid unnecessary casualties, although the crossing would have closed the pincers and cut off many of the fleeing enemy. The press, including W. H. Russell, were critical of such ultra caution, and later Sir John Fortesque joined the critics by calling the decision 'ill-concerned thrift', on the grounds that those who had been allowed to escape would be expected to fight (and inflict casualties) in later battles.[22]

With the taking of the Kaiserbach the battle was to all intents over, although mopping up operations took a further week, with Outram belatedly joining in by crossing the river and taking the residency. At this point Campbell did attempt to close the net when he ordered Brigadier Campbell (no relation) to take the Moosabagh Palace some four miles north-west of Lucknow and, together with some of Hope Grant's cavalry, cut off the rebels' retreat northwards. Brigadier Campbell apparently lost his way and the chance was missed.

Despite this setback Campbell undoubtedly achieved his objective. By meticulous use of fire and movement he had taken the heavily defended city of Lucknow at the cost of just 127 killed and 595 wounded. More than 3000 rebels were killed, although many thousands succeeded in escaping. It was, as one would expect with Campbell, a deliberate operation. With General Outram's forces covering the east flank the main body moved from strongpoint to strongpoint until they seized the vital one of the Kaiserbach. Before assaulting they softened up the defenders with their heavy guns and convinced them they had no hope of stopping the invaders. Despite the criticisms of Campbell for allowing so many to escape, those who did so were by no means the threat that many expected: in a great many cases they just melted away.

With the capture of Lucknow the campaign moved into a new phase, for which Campbell organised his army into several mobile columns, the strongest under General Sir Hugh Rose, to undertake operations in central India. Campbell continued to be as methodical as ever; as the columns advanced and drove the enemy from their strongholds, auxiliary troops were installed as garrisons and the due representatives of the civilian authority quickly restored. It was not until May 1859 that the rebellion could be said to be over finally when the huge tracts of Oudh Behar, Goruckpore and Romilcund had been returned to a state of relative calm.

In June 1858, to mark his services in India, Sir Colin Campbell was awarded a peerage: having no property in Scotland he agreed to take the title of Lord Clyde, to commemorate the great river of his native city. When the Duke of Cambridge suggested Lord Clyde of Lucknow he refused, giving as his reason that Sir Henry Havelock, whose earlier heroism at Lucknow was so marked, should be the only man to be distinguished by the name. In fact, Campbell proved most reluctant to make any use of his new title and continued to sign letters to his friends with the name C. Campbell.

Whatever titles might be awarded him, Colin Campbell still wanted to be where he was most comfortable – with his fighting troops. Although he was forced to remain at Allahabad until 1 November when Lord Canning promulgated the act that signified the Crown's direct government of British India, he departed as soon as possible to continue campaigning. On 17 December 1858 during an engagement with rebels at Burgidiah Campbell's horse fell and threw him violently to the ground, injuring him severely: one shoulder was dislocated, a rib broken and blood poured down his face. Typically, as soon as his dislocation was put back he walked to the front as if nothing had happened. That evening another incident directly witnessed by W. H. Russell occurred that was characteristic of the man. 'It was cold and with his arm in a sling he sat before a bonfire on an old charpoy bed that had been brought out to feed the fire. An adjutant brought some news and he rose to greet him. As he got up a tired Baluchi soldier flung himself full length on the bed. He was jerked off by his comrades but Clyde interposed. "Let him lie there; don't interfere with his rest," and was himself content to take another seat on a billet of wood.'

In fact, his injuries from the fall led to some inflammation of the lungs and he was forced to leave the active campaigning to others. From Oudh, Hope Grant and the cavalry watched matters on the frontier, while Hugh Rose pacified Calpee.

Clyde eventually left India on 4 June 1859, having handed his military responsibilities over to Hugh Rose. In Paris he was given an audience by the Emperor Napoleon III, and there he heard he had been given a colonelcy of the Coldstream Guards to complement his colonelcy of the 93rd Highlanders. He also learned that the freedom of the City of London had been conferred on him in his absence.

During his many campaigns he never had much time for relaxation, now that he did, his health began to give way. There had been signs of this during his last year in India, as the fever and ague that he contracted all those years ago in Walcheren eroded his strength. The last time he appeared at the head of troops in the field was when he inspected a Volunteer review on Easter Monday 1862, at which 20,000 men paraded on Brighton Downs. He was still acute enough to praise the steadiness and intelligence shown there by the civilian soldiery.[23] That autumn, on 9 November, Clyde was given the ultimate military tribute when, to mark the occasion of the Prince of Wales' twenty-first birthday, he was, among others, raised to the rank of field marshal.

With no close family ties in Scotland, in the following June Clyde went to Chatham where he lived with his dearest friends, General and Mrs Eyre. There, as he grew weaker, his memories would tend to revert to those Highland soldiers who in past days had always been so eager to follow him. Clyde died on 14 August 1863 and, in typical fashion, it was his wish that he should be interred at Kensal Green cemetery in a private ceremony. The government, however, decided that such an outstanding soldier should have his remains placed in Westminster Abbey, although they agreed the ceremony should still be private.

Clyde spent over half a century fighting Britain's wars across the world: from Corunna in western Spain to Walcheren in the Netherlands, back to Spain again at Barrosa then along to Vitoria and San Sebastian close to the French border; from Chinese Chusan to Chillianwalla in Northern India, then to the Crimea with battles at the Alma and Balaclava. However, it was not until he returned to India at the time of the Great Mutiny that Clyde was fully recognised as a senior commander.

By any yardstick this came at a late stage in his career and if it had been up to Lord Dalhousie he would never have been given the chance. Dalhousie saw him as a prickly customer with clear limitations as a commander. Even after his successes with the Highland Brigade and latterly as a Divisional commander in the Crimea he was twice passed over for the post of commander-in-chief there. In India when Clyde finally reached that pinnacle his 'safe and sure' policy did not escape criticism. In such circumstances one is led to wonder why he was so long out of favour and what the authorities considered were the true qualities of a senior commander.

Clyde was certainly a strong character who could fairly be described as a soldiers' soldier. He was a vigorous trainer and keen tactician always prepared to share his troops' dangers while solicitous for their welfare and jealous with their lives. A man of high personal integrity he was contemptuous of luxury and ease. At the time of the mutiny he would never consider taking any riches from the royal palaces that were sacked and whose contents were seen as just proceeds for the victors. While short of funds for most of his career, when he reached high rank, and was well paid, he delighted in finding reasons to give money away. When he finally relieved the beseiged Residency at Lucknow a celebratory meal was arranged using food and fine champagne saved for the purpose. His reaction was to enquire frostily why the food had not been handed over (before) to the troops and he had sat with his arms folded throughout the whole dreadful repast like a ghost at a feast.[24]

Such high-minded behaviour could be viewed in certain circles as priggishness especially when it was accompanied by his quick temper but W. H. Russell was pleasantly surprised to find Clyde an excellent conversationalist and fine host. He was something of an intellectual soldier and keen linguist who so loved the French language that when shortly before his death he requested the Bible to be read out loud, he asked whether it could be read in French. Clyde possessed his countrymen's capacity to relate effortlessly with people of different nationalities and from different stations in life from the Queen to humble Indian soldiers. Along with this he was capable of affection and he possessed a true sense of theatre. When Clyde addressed the Highland Brigade at the end of the Crimean War he told them with unashamed emotion, 'Our native land will never forget the name of Highland Brigade and in some future war the nation will call for another one to equal this, which it can never surpass.'[25]

While significant, such qualities do not necessarily make someone a good senior commander. There can be no doubt that Clyde was an outstanding brigade commander; he demonstrated it both in the Crimea and in India. His harshest critics might say he performed as a fine brigade commander at Chillianwala when his designated responsibility was over a division.[26] Clyde cannot escape some criticism for his performance at Chillianwalla although he was a fledgling divisional commander at the time, but following his good leadership in the Crimea, when he became commander-in-chief in India he came into his own, demonstrating a sure grasp of both the strategy and tactics required. While he was undeniably cautious, by any standards of comparison the performance of Lord Raglan and the two other commanders-in-chief in the Crimea fell far short of Clyde's leadership in India.

For his battlefield skills in the Crimea and as commander-in-chief in India, Clyde earns the right to be considered as one of Queen Victoria's best senior soldiers during that non-vintage period between the end of the Napoleonic War and the outbreak of the second Boer War in 1899. That his recognition was so long coming was probably because he spent most of his career fighting overseas within the close social confines of his regiment and because he felt he could not afford to marry and therefore lacked the extended social circle a wife was likely to have provided. Additionally as a strong-willed perfectionist he was not the easiest of men to work with although once confident of a chief such as Sir Charles Napier or Lord Canning, he could prove himself the most devoted, unstinting and able of servants. On the other hand if he did not respect a superior he could be not only 'irascible and given to strong language' but only too willing to resign. It is also tempting to think that some measure of his belated recognition might have been due to him being a Scot and never part of the privileged group of officers based in London. The historian Kinglake certainly thought so when he wrote, 'After serving with all this glory for some forty-five years, he returned to England, but between the Queen and him stood a dense cloud of families which made it out to be right that people who had seen no service should be invested with high command, and that Sir Colin Campbell should be only a colonel.'[27]

Major General Sir Hector Archibald MacDonald – 'Fighting Mac' (1853–1903)

No one would consider placing Hector MacDonald within the front rank of Scottish military leaders. At the time of his suicide, which occurred amid vague and damaging rumours regarding his personal conduct, his battlefield responsibilities had never risen beyond the command of a brigade. Yet 'Fighting Mac' was a public hero, the symbol of Scottish martial virtues – and justly so, for his achievements were remarkable. There was his progression from private soldier to general, advancement virtually unknown in the Victorian army. While a very small proportion of senior ranks from the Sergeants' Mess did succeed in gaining a commission, normally they were destined to be either quartermasters or regimental adjutants.[28] They were usually too old to progress towards high rank and, if not too old, then past prejudices together with their own humble backgrounds tended to put them at a severe disadvantage with other officers of their generation. A handful like MacDonald progressed further, the most notable and often quoted example being another soldier of Scottish extraction, Field Marshal Sir William (Wullie) Robertson, who enlisted in the 16 Lancers during the 1870s and was gazetted lieutenant at the age of 28. But Robertson was above all a staff officer, whereas 'Fighting Mac' – as the sobriquet implied – was a battlefield soldier.

MacDonald was born a crofter's son at Mulbuie in the far north of Scotland. He was the seventh boy born to his parents in nine years of marriage. At the local parish school MacDonald was given rudimentary instruction by the local dominie, Alexander Treasurer, who lost his post when the 1870 Education Act required country schoolmasters to have higher educational standards. Young Hector certainly made an impression on the schoolmaster, for he recalled his young charge's prominent role during the perpetual and ritual 'battles' between boys from different regions of the parish. Although the MacDonalds were to expand their croft over the years, only the eldest son could reasonably expect to be granted it. In any case,

Hector never showed any interest in the land; and at thirteen he began working as a stable boy at the National Hotel in Dingwall, the county town of Ross-shire. He was popular with the Robertson family who ran the hotel and it was apparently at their instigation that he became an apprentice draper in a local store.

When he quickly became dissatisfied with the restrictive nature of the small establishment his parents sent him as an apprentice to the Royal Clan and Tartan Warehouse in Inverness, but MacDonald hardly fitted the image of an average shop assistant. 'He was moir like a smith than a draper',[29] according to a shop girl who remembered him as broad and strong and tough looking. The Tartan Warehouse was far larger than its Dingwall equivalent and in Inverness it was hoped there would be more ways of absorbing his restless energy than were available in the sleepy county town. However it was not part of the family's plans for him to join the Inverness Highland Rifle volunteers, many of whose members went into the regular army. At the time military interest was heightened by events on the Continent, particularly the Austro/Prussian War of 1866 and the distinct possibility of coming hostilities between Prussia and France. Whatever the reasons the Inverness volunteers were extremely keen and were accustomed to spend up to two hours drilling before their day's work. They were commanded by a Sergeant Major Pocock, a parade ground fanatic, whose emphasis on the importance of precision-drilling made a great impression on the young draper's assistant.

MacDonald's keenness for military life did not bring an enthusiastic response from his parents. At that particular time 'going for a soldier' meant, at best, long years overseas and almost certain loss of contact with one's family. This in no way deterred Hector, however, and in June 1870 he presented himself to a recruiting sergeant and enrolled in the 92nd regiment as a Gordon Highlander. In doing so he broke his indenture with William Mackay of the Royal Clan and Tartan Warehouse. In later years, after he had become an officer, MacDonald attempted to make amends and wrote to William Mackay courteously thanking him for the training he had provided. 'I may add that what you taught – punctuality, order, cleanliness, method and (here I fell with you and received a lesson) implicit faith and obedience – are the main attributes of a good soldier.'[30]

Whatever immediate regret MacDonald's enlistment brought to

his family he came from a martial region traditionally proud of its fighting men, whether over the years they supported their respective clan chiefs, the Stuart kings, Hanoverian monarchs, or their present queen. In this regard Hector was soon to give them much cause for pride in a way no draper's assistant, however successful he might prove in commerce, could possibly do. What was more, when he returned home on leave he not only looked a fine soldier with his broad shoulders and full chest, but they realised he was totally dedicated to his chosen calling. MacDonald was justly said to have enlisted with a drill book in his pocket, 'study, study, study was the keynote of his life, and promotion was the ambition ever in his head'.[31]

At the end of his initial training with the Gordons he was promoted lance corporal and after a few days leave with his family, he embarked for India where together with another fifty-one battalions, his regiment helped to garrison the vast and populous country segmented by its caste system and religious animosities that less than twenty years before had risen in bloody revolt against British rule. When Hector MacDonald joined, the Gordons had already been in the sub-continent for three years. Despite the heavy demands of the climate, life in India was pleasant enough and for an ambitious soldier there was always the prospect of some battlefield experience in the northern border regions. As with other regiments, the Gordons' officers tended to come from landed families with private incomes of their own, while in the main its soldiers were from humble backgrounds who had often enlisted to escape unemployment or semi-starvation at home. But things were beginning to change and when, in 1871, the purchase of commissions was abolished, new opportunities – admittedly still more theoretical than practical – were open to soldiers aspiring to become officers.

During his early years in India such prospects were hardly of interest to MacDonald. His sights were set on non-commissioned rank. Promoted to full corporal he became a master in precision drilling, and even in later years when his responsibilities were far beyond the drill square he was never to lose his belief in its value for disciplinary purposes and unit cohesion. In 1874 he was sent for by his colonel, A. W. Cameron (son of Cameron of Lochailort). When he arrived he was told, 'Corporal MacDonald, there is a vacancy for a sergeant, and although you are a young soldier, I intend to make you one but I would have you remember that a sergeant in the Gordon Highlanders is equal to a member of parliament and I expect you to behave accordingly.' It was rapid promotion by any standards. As an indication of the high regard in which he was held, in the following year he was selected to act as detachment commander over a sentry party guarding a tent used by the Prince of Wales, the future Edward VII, when he visited India. In later years when the Prince of Wales met MacDonald during a reception at Marlborough House, he apparently asked him why they had not met before. MacDonald replied, 'Pardon me, sir, I think we have.'

'Where can that have been?'

'When you were in India, sir. I did sentry-go outside your tent. . . .'

The conversation ended with the prince holding out his hand saying, 'General MacDonald, you were doing sentry-go in 1876 and now you are a general in the British army. I am proud to have met you.'[32]

MacDonald's first taste of action came in Afghanistan under a young and energetic general, Frederick Roberts, later Field Marshal Lord Roberts. When Roberts led his Kabul field force, including the Gordons, on a punitive expedition into Afghanistan they were ambushed by fierce tribesmen in a narrow wooded pass called Hazar Darakht (the pass of a thousand trees). MacDonald was with one of his regiment's forward platoons together with a party of Sikhs. Acting entirely on his own initiative, he took a detachment of eighteen Gordons with forty-five men from the 3rd Sikhs to a position above the attackers and, in spite of the tribesmen's superior numbers, forced them to withdraw. Roberts' dispatches of 15 October 1879 contained the following reference to the incident: 'The energy and skill with which this party was handled reflected the highest credit on Colour-Sergeant Hector MacDonald, 92nd Highlanders, and Jemadar Sher Mahommed, 3rd Sikhs. But for their excellent services on this occasion, it might probably have been impossible to carry out the programme of our march.'[33]

During the next phase of Roberts' operation a patrol under the command of a Lieutenant Grant and MacDonald was sent to dislodge an obstinate group of the enemy. To do this they had to 'climb a bare hill, so steep that they were sometimes on all fours and they had the enemy firing down on them. But when the Highlanders reached the top they soon cleared it of the enemy'. Roberts' dispatch again cited

MacDonald, 'A non-commissioned officer whose excellent and skilful management of a small detachment when opposed to immensely superior numbers in the Hazardarakht defile was mentioned in my despatch of the 16th instant, here again distinguished himself.' MacDonald's full reward came in the new year when, at the age of twenty-seven, he was commissioned into the Gordon Highlanders in the rank of sub-lieutenant, the promotion coming as a direct result of Roberts' recommendation. From this time a myth was to grow up that the General had given MacDonald the choice of a commission or the Victoria Cross for his actions. This was almost certainly false but the Gordons showed generous delight in the honour given their new officer. The whole battalion turned out and the men of C company carried MacDonald to the officers' quarters shoulder high, a piper at their head, with the other soldiers turning out to cheer. Each man then in turn marched up, stood to attention and saluted him. The officers afterwards presented him with a sword and the sergeants with a dirk.[34] MacDonald wore the sword when he took part in Roberts' famous march to Kandahar.

The Gordons' next taste of active service came in 1881, when they were sent to South Africa to deal with the Boer rebellion. This was in the Transvaal with its population of Boer farmers, who by religion were strict Dutch presbyterians determined to safeguard their way of life. In 1877 the Transvaal had been annexed by Britain but with the return of William Gladstone's Liberal government of 1880 it was widely expected in the province that they would regain their independence. When this did not happen the Boers first refused to pay taxes then proclaimed their independence with Kruger as their civil leader and Joubert as their Commandant General. The Boers proved to be marksmen who were masters of camouflage and mobility. Along with other British units the Gordons were over-confident and utterly ignorant of the Boers' capability. After the Boers started besieging isolated British garrisons a relief army was gathered under Major General Sir George Colley to relieve them. Although the British got the worst of some small engagements the first large action occurred at Majuba Hill, a steep, high feature. General Colley reasoned that if he took the hill he could completely dominate the Boer positions below it. On the night of 26 February the British successfully occupied the position with 600 men, including 180 from the Gordon Highlanders. At first light Hendrina Joubert, wife of the

Boer commandant general, saw the British above the Boer positions at which 100 Boers volunteered to climb Majuba and dislodge them. The British knew they were coming but General Colley decided to wait until they were very close then in traditional fashion fire a volley on them. This gave the Boers precious time to reach the summit where they started to sweep it with well-aimed rifle fire. General Colley was soon killed and his soldiers started to run, ignoring their officers' orders to stand.

One of the very few who distinguished themselves that day when British forces occupying a seemingly impregnable position were wiped out by Boer irregulars a sixth their strength was 'Fighting Mac', who refused to be cowed by the flying bullets and men falling around him. As the Gordons' regimental historian related, 'Lieutenants Wright and MacDonald, 92nd regiment, behaved with the greatest coolness and courage, and to the last made every effort to turn the course of events.'[35] Before being overpowered MacDonald and his lance corporal, the only two left unwounded in his units were reduced to hurling rocks at the enemy when their rifles were empty.[36] Defiant to the last he was finally overpowered by four men but acknowledging a brave opponent and finding his sword had been presented by officers on his promotion, the Boers generously returned it to him.[37] MacDonald was taken to the Boer leader, General Joubert, where arrangements were made for his release, but before that took place he organised a picquet of his fellow prisoners to guard their dead commander, Sir George Colley. When MacDonald and the Gordons left South Africa they were determined to avenge the humiliation of Majuba Hill, where forty-four of their men died and fifty-two were seriously injured. Eighteen years were to pass before they had the chance.

After South Africa the Gordons returned to Scotland and for the next two years did duty in the Scottish capital. MacDonald, in particular, found the obligatory round of social duties irksome and, more serious still, ruinously expensive. There is evidence he was forced to borrow from his brother William to meet his debts and, because of his financial problems, while he looked extremely well in uniform, it was observed that his civilian clothes were neither very stylish nor well cut. In the circumstances he chose to spend much of his time in solitary walks about the city where early in 1883 he made the acquaintance of a schoolgirl of fifteen, Christina Maclouchan Duncan, the daughter of a schoolmaster. Before the Gordons left Edinburgh in June 1884 he married her in the old Scots style, by a private exchange of their troth, but in 1894 she had the marriage declared legal by the Court of Session. In her evidence to the court she said MacDonald had made her promise not to reveal the marriage although there was a male child of six years from the match: she also told the court 'that MacDonald sent money to support both her and the child and that he had behaved very nicely'. While the legal authorities knew of his marriage, MacDonald gave no details of it to the War Office; to his colleagues and the world at large he remained a bachelor. He only saw his wife infrequently, usually after intervals of years: he is known to have met her briefly in 1892, during 1899 on his return from Omdurman and finally in 1903. In fact they were together on no more than four brief occasions throughout nineteen years of marriage. There were strong reasons for concealing the marriage, since like most other regiments, the Gordons strongly discouraged matrimony before an officer reached captain's rank. In later years there would be equal or better reasons for him to conceal it.

By 1884, no doubt to his considerable relief, MacDonald was bound once more for a foreign country – Egypt – after having transferred to his regiment's first battalion. In Egypt the Gordons joined Garnet Wolseley's forces in their attempt to relieve the eccentric but fearless General Charles Gordon. Gordon was sent out to supervise the evacuation of British nationals in face of a fanatical uprising by an Egyptian religious teacher who styled himself as the Mahdi, Islam's long-awaited apostle, and was beleaguered in Khartoum the capital of the Sudan. With the expedition's failure and Gordon's death the British began reorganising the Egyptian army for future use in the Sudan against the Mahdi and Hector MacDonald was among the British officers and non-commissioned officers appointed 'to stiffen its backbone'. For an officer obliged to live on his pay with a wife and son to support such service would have undeniable attractions, since on their secondment officers were raised to one rank above the one they held in the British Army and were granted a higher rate of pay. In the rank of captain, MacDonald was seconded to the Egyptian Gendarmerie under their colourful commander, Colonel Valentine Baker, an able soldier whose career in the British army had been wrecked when in August 1875 he was convicted of indecently assaulting a young girl in a railway carriage. The Middle Eastern theatre at this time seemed to breed a race of military eccentrics or, at the very least British officers who could be identified as 'characters'.

It was MacDonald's privilege to come under the eye of another notable and highly individual soldier, Horatio Herbert Kitchener, who became Egyptian Army commander in 1892. Kitchener required his officers to be single, believing that without feminine distractions he could command their undivided loyalty. MacDonald had therefore absolutely no reason to reveal his 'secret' marriage. Working on such principles Kitchener succeeded 'in surrounding himself with an impressive band of extraordinarily youthful colonels who were completely imbued with their chief's methods and ideals.'[38]

Although the youngest, MacDonald was to become one of those colonels. In 1888 he was already commanding Sudanese troops that Kitchener had raised for the army of Egypt and whom MacDonald had set about moulding by a combination of endless drill and thorough training. During 1889 MacDonald's 11th Sudanese battalion was involved in fighting that occurred between Egypt and the Sudan over disputed border regions. Here his opposing commander was Osman Digna, a capable soldier who during 1884 had already inflicted two major defeats on the Egyptian forces. MacDonald plainly did well, for he was mentioned in dispatches and awarded the handsome Egyptian decoration of the Khedive's Star. Queen Victoria subsequently gave him permission to wear the Star on his dress uniform. Equally important, he was himself becoming thought of as a character. During the Battle of Gemaizeh, for instance, G.W. Steevens, the war correspondent for the *Daily Mail*, reported him shouting at his men in broad Scots to prevent them from breaking ranks and throwing themselves at the enemy. 'Finally he rode up and down in front of their rifles and at last got them steady under a heavy fire from men who would far rather have killed themselves than him.'[39]

By his personal bravery, straightforwardness and constant emphasis on discipline, MacDonald succeeded in turning his Sudanese battalion into an impressive fighting unit. He himself delighted in the story that arose about him during one of the frontier battles when in order to be heard above the gunfire and other clamour of war he had to roar out his orders. His men, mistaking his shouting for anxiety or fear, crowded round him and began to stroke his legs, saying, 'Don't be afraid we are here and we shall protect you. Have no fear, it is all right.'[40] For his successes MacDonald was awarded the DSO and in 1891 he was gazetted major, but to his regret he had to transfer his commission to the Royal Fusiliers because, as a seconded officer, there were no vacancies for him in the Gordons. By now Hector MacDonald was clearly one of Kitchener's favoured men.

In Egypt under Kitchener officers could expect action and then more action. Engrossed by the prospect of reconquering the Sudan, Kitchener came to think of leave as a superfluous luxury – a not unwelcome attitude for MacDonald, as leave was bound to be expensive and unlike most of his contemporaries he did not enjoy the benefit of a private income. In 1896 MacDonald had a further chance of action when he was promoted to brevet lieutenant colonel and given command of the 2nd Sudanese Brigade, engaged in the invasion of the Dongola province. Kitchener saw this as the first step in the overthrow of Khalifa Abdullah, son of the Mahdi and the Sudanese leader. As a result of their leader's prowess on the battlefield the Sudanese brigade soon came to be known as MacDonald's Black brigade; it contained the four best Sudanese battalions, with extensive fighting experience along the frontier. In 1896 their first engagement at a place called Firket demonstrated that the whole of MacDonald's brigade could fight well. It succeeded in dislodging Dervishes from the hills surrounding the town and, by MacDonald's sound use of the quick-firing guns, its casualties were kept to a small fraction of those suffered by the enemy.

Moving down the Nile, Kitchener despatched a column, including the 2nd Brigade, to the town of Abu Hamed, where they easily brushed aside the opposing Dervishes. This was followed by a further success at Berber. In early 1898 an engagement occurred between the British forces and two of the Sudanese leader's lieutenants, the Emir Mahmud and MacDonald's earlier rival, Osman Digna. The British artillery inflicted many casualties before Kitchener ordered an unimaginative frontal attack with MacDonald's brigade taking the centre of the line. Despite considerable casualties the British prevailed. It was a mark of the esteem in which Kitchener held 'Mac' that, during the triumphant march into Berber following the battle, he had MacDonald ride beside him and gave the 2nd Brigade the honour of leading the military units into the town. After a much-earned period of recuperation and leave, which MacDonald spent close by in game shooting and fishing on the Nile, the offensive resumed. The troops used were the British 1st Brigade under General Andy Wauchope, a fellow Scot and friend of MacDonald, the Sudanese 1st Brigade under MacDonald himself, and three regiments of cavalry. In support were 44 field guns and 20 Maxims with 36 naval guns and an additional 24 Maxims in gun boats.[41] Amazingly the ratio of Kitchener's close fire support exceeded that given the early BEF battalions in France during 1914, where they were of course fighting a far more formidable enemy.

MacDonald's brigade habitually acted as point, or leading formation, and was in the forefront of every action. Its commander encouraged his men to adopt what he considered were the best traditions of Scottish regiments. After one of his battalions, the 9th, fought beside the Seaforths at the battle of Ginnis, they began to adopt the practice of wearing kilts and carrying their own colours into battle. By such devices he hoped to develop their fledgling military traditions, although it was, of course his own military qualities that were of most importance. About this time the war correspondent G.W. Steevens wrote in both affectionate and respectful terms about 'Mac' as a leader:

> He had seen more and more varied service than any man in the force . . . In person the "old Man" is of middle height, but very broad – so sturdily built that you might imagine him to be armour-plated under his clothes. He walks and rides with a resolute solidity bespeaking more strength than agility.[42]

Whereas Kitchener treated the press with contempt and in the process earned Winston Churchill's unyielding enmity, 'Mac' was shrewd enough to adopt a different approach, fully appreciating the influence of such men who wove their words so skilfully and whose reports returned quickly to the home country. As someone who also found himself outside the social circles of the typical regular officer, his relations with these gifted, if often eccentric, press representatives were comradely. He apparently offered them the use of his bath tub and took care to feed them well, and it is from them and other observers that accounts of MacDonald's masterly control during Omdurman, the crowning battle of the war on 2 September 1898, are forthcoming. In Kitchener's official dispatch of the battle his conduct received no more than carefully limited appreciation.

Omdurman was a triumph for superior British weaponry and organisation against an amazingly brave but naïve enemy. The 25,000 strong expeditionary force had formidable artillery support provided by the gunboats, together with eighty additional cannon armed with the new lyddite and shrapnel shells and forty-four quick-firing Maxim machine guns. Facing them was the Khalifa's army of between 50 to 60,000 armed only with primitive weapons. The Khalifa's chance of victory lay either in keeping his forces within the sheltering walls of Omdurman fort to the south or launching a night attack on Kitchener's forces, when their supporting fire would be largely negated. He failed to take either option and there was, therefore, only one possible outcome for the battle. Kitchener never expected the Dervishes would be foolish enough to attack him in broad daylight, but when he heard they were advancing he cancelled his orders for a general advance and positioned his forces in a semi-circle behind a thorn fence (or zariba) with their backs to the Nile. On the left were Brigadier General Lyttleton's 2nd British Brigade, followed by Major General Wauchope's 1st British Brigade. Colonel Maxwell with his 2nd Egyptian Brigade took the centre, while on the right flank stood MacDonald and Lieutenant Colonel Lewis with the 1st and 3rd Egyptian brigades. The Egyptian cavalry and the Camel Corps were stationed on the Kerreri ridge to the right of the position.

Under the Khalifa the Dervish army was grouped into three main divisions, one under Osman Azrak, a second under Sheikh El Din (with orders to make for the Kerreri Hills), and the third placed in a position of general reserve under the Khalifa and his brother, Yakub, ready to exploit battlefield successes as they appeared. These were supported by two considerably smaller groups to the north and south commanded by Ali Wad Helu and Ibrahim Khalil respectively.

At about 6 a.m. the Dervishes came in sight of the British forces. Their attempt to outflank the right flank was foiled by Lieutenant Colonel Broadwood and his Camel Corps supported by two river gunboats, while on the left and centre Osman Azrak's men were scythed down by a deadly combination of accurate rifle fire and the steady rat-a-tat of the Maxim guns. By 8 a.m. the Dervishes' casualties of 26,000 exceeded the total strength of the expeditionary force and Osman Azrak's division took no further part in the battle.

Kitchener now decided to seize Omdurman before the Khalifa could reorganise his forces. In this operation the 21st Lancers, including the youthful Winston Churchill, made a most gallant, if unnecessary, charge against superior numbers of the enemy under Ibrahim Khalil, losing almost a quarter of their 320 officers and men in the process. Their heroic action attracted enormous publicity, but meanwhile a far more serious situation was developing on the right flank, where General Hunter had instructed MacDonald, his most experienced commander, to change places with Lewis' brigade. As 'Mac' moved westwards he became separated from Lewis by nearly a mile. At that point he became aware of Yakub's army, some 20,000 strong, coming round Jebel Surgham to attack him. When his troops grew excited by the vast numbers of the approaching enemy and began to fire at random he rode in front of them and, with incomparable coolness, knocked up their rifles to make them cease fire. When he ordered them to recommence it was with well-aimed, disciplined volleys, fired company by company. By this means they succeeded in holding the enemy off but, just as the pressure eased slightly, MacDonald caught sight of a new Dervish army of 12,000 men under Sheikh El Din approaching him from the Kerreri Hills. Still under heavy fire from Yakub, MacDonald began moving individual battalions to face the new danger. Fortunately help was now coming with Wauchope's leading battalion of the Lincolnshires, whose rapid volleys tore great holes in the attackers' lines.

By 10.30 a.m. the tide had turned and MacDonald's men were able to commence advancing. 'The battle had been won and the march to Omdurman was resumed.'[43] Including his wounded and those made prisoner, the Khalifa lost about 31,000 men against Kitchener's 430, but MacDonald's brigade suffered 128 casualties, more than a quarter of the British total. Kitchener had gained a great victory, Mahdism was destroyed and the Sudan became part of the British overseas empire. To many of those on the battlefield, however, Omdurman was more of a massacre than anything else, and the more expert of them knew that Kitchener's tactics had been far from perfect. As Captain Douglas Haig of the Egyptian cavalry observed afterwards, 'Kitchener should have thrown his left flank forward and then drawn in his right . . . to cut the enemy off from Omduran. But he spread out his force and left one section of it dangerously exposed.'[44]

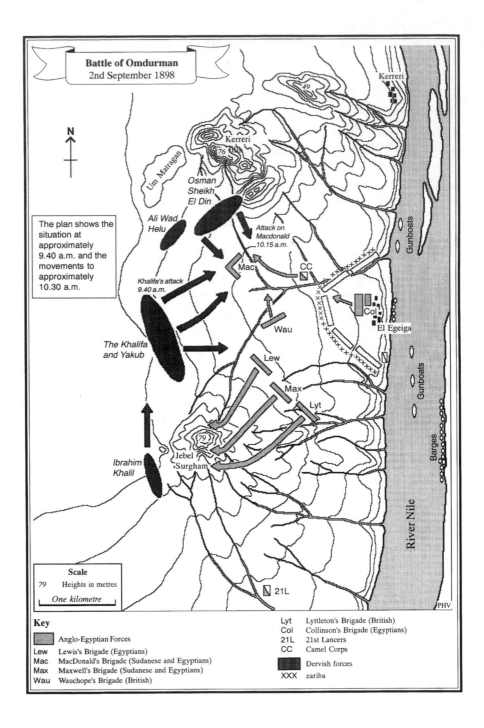

Battle of Omdurman
2nd September 1898

The plan shows the situation at approximately 9.40 a.m. and the movements to approximately 10.30 a.m.

Kerreri

Kerreri Hills

Osman Sheikh El Din

Um Matragan

Attack on Macdonald 10.15 a.m.

Mac

CC

Gunboats

Ali Wad Helu

Khalifa's attack 9.40 a.m.

Col

El Egeiga

The Khalifa and Yakub

Wau

Lew

Max

Gunboats

Lyt

Ibrahim Khalil

Jebel Surgham

River Nile

Barges

Scale
79   Heights in metres
One kilometre

21L

PHV

Key

Anglo-Egyptian Forces
Lew   Lewis's Brigade (Egyptians)
Mac   MacDonald's Brigade (Sudanese and Egyptians)
Max   Maxwell's Brigade (Sudanese and Egyptians)
Wau   Wauchope's Brigade (British)

Lyt   Lyttleton's Brigade (British)
Col   Collinson's Brigade (Egyptians)
21L   21st Lancers
CC   Camel Corps

Dervish forces
XXX   zariba

244

In the prevailing military climate it was only to be expected that the charge of the 21st Lancers would be given by far the greatest prominence in Kitchener's dispatch but to most battlefield observers 'Fighting Mac' was the true hero of the day. Bennet Burleigh, the *Daily Telegraph*'s war correspondent, wrote that, 'No force could have been in time to save [MacDonald's brigade] had they not fought and saved themselves.'[45] He said that MacDonald 'achieved the victory entirely off his own bat, so to speak, proving himself a tactician and a soldier as well as what he has long been known to be, the bravest of the brave'.[46] Burleigh concluded his report with the words 'The army has a hero and a thorough soldier in MacDonald and if the public want either they need seek no further . . . Had the brilliant, the splendid deeds of arms wrought by MacDonald been done under the eyes of a sovereign, or in some other armies, he had surely been created a General on the spot.'[47] Burleigh's regard for MacDonald was re-echoed by G.W. Steevens, who witnessed the battle within the lines of MacDonald's 1st Brigade: '. . . the cockpit of the fight was MacDonald's. The British might avenge his brigade; it was his to keep it and to kill off the attack. To meet it he turned his front through a complete half-circle, facing successively south, west and north. Every tactician in the army was delirious in his praise . . . He saw everything; knew what to do; knew how to do it; did it.'[48] Such regard was shared by two independent military observers, Lieutenants Alford and Sword, who wrote 'The whole force of the attack was concentrated against MacDonald's brigade, and but for the consummate generalship of their leader, the Sudanese must have been destroyed.'[49]

As befits the victors of a famous engagement, honours and promotions were lavished on those who took part. Kitchener was raised to the peerage, the major generals were created KCBs and Victoria Crosses were awarded to four cavalry officers. Hector MacDonald's reward was to be made an extra ADC to the Queen, which while an honour carried 'neither pay nor emolument', and Burleigh for one was in no doubt he was insufficiently rewarded. It was no surprise to him that the press, 'particularly in that of the far north there has been much adverse comment on the ungenerous treatment accorded to their countryman'.[50]

With the fighting over, Hector MacDonald began to realise the pressures he had been under for so long. He wrote 'I am tired, and

I have been over-working'.[51] It was hardly surprising: his whole career had been a struggle, and for the last fourteen years of it he had been training and fighting ceaselessly under the most demanding conditions. But however much he might have hoped for it, there was to be little relaxation at home, for he found himself lionised, especially in Scotland. Many dinners were given in his honour, the Clan MacDonald society of Glasgow gave him a sword valued at £250, and at Dingwall he was granted the freedom of the burgh. The 'bachelor' general was entertained in great houses across Scotland. At all such times MacDonald, the human epitome of 'service, discipline and duty' was invariably modest and unassuming. Before he returned to London he was granted the freedom of the Scottish capital.

In London he learned of his new command, which was to be in India in the local rank of brigadier general. He was no doubt also delighted to learn that the 2nd battalion of the Gordon Highlanders was one of the regiments under his command. But India was not the place for him at this time.

By now the Second Anglo-Boer War had commenced. Britain's justification was the Transvaal's continued refusal to give voting rights to the vast numbers of *uitlanders* (foreigners) who entered the country after the huge gold strike of 1886. Underlying everything, however, was the question of extending British influence throughout southern Africa but as far as the army was concerned there was the long-felt wish to revenge Majuba Hill where MacDonald himself had been taken prisoner by the Boers. Mac's friends were in no doubt he was bitterly disappointed at not being given the chance to take part in the fighting there. Marooned in his Indian station, reports abounded of him being 'far below form', both depressed and irritable, unapproachable to his juniors and uninterested in the social rounds required.

It was fortunate for him that his chance for renewed action came relatively quickly. In January 1900, at Magersfontein, the Highland Brigade, commanded by General Andy Wauchope, his firm friend of Sudan days, was defeated and their commander killed. 'Fighting Mac' was the obvious successor. With MacDonald's appointment as commander of the Highland Brigade other significant changes were also made in the hierarchy of the army as a whole. Lord Roberts assumed overall command and Kitchener went out as his assistant. In the light of his past record, much was expected of MacDonald and he was warmly welcomed, among others, by the war correspondents in South Africa, including (Sir) Arthur Conan Doyle. There was scarcely time for any radical changes but, like General Montgomery before the battle of El Alamein, MacDonald deliberately got out amongst his units to help them regain confidence.

The Brigade had its first encounter on 5 February 1900, when it was assigned to take a hill at Koodoesberg Drift, as part of a plan to persuade the Boer leader the British were about to attempt a relief of Kimberley from the west. The Highland Brigade accomplished its task but after the Boers had evacuated the hill it was ordered to withdraw. In the House of Commons this caused a mischievous Irish Nationalist MP to ask, 'Has fighting Mac been beaten?' The withdrawal was evidence that conditions in South Africa were far different from those in the Sudan. The Boers were both formidable and elusive enemies who when outfaced by the enemy would take evasive action by decamping on their hill ponies. In South Africa there were no easy battle honours and unlike his predecessor, Roberts was not prepared to risk defeat on the field. Instead he favoured the use of superior artillery to drench the Boers' defended positions and, copying the enemy, formed groups of mounted infantry who could deploy in massive sweeping movements. Under Roberts the infantry were to be given no opportunity for set place battles. However, at Paardeberg where the British forces trapped General Cronje with his 5000-strong army, a battle dominated by the infantry seemed certain. After Roberts had fallen ill the Highland Brigade came under Kitchener's command and following an exhausting forced march, they were required to make a frontal attack which resulted in the Brigade suffering considerable casualties. When Roberts returned he ended the assault and successfully brought the Boers to surrender through the use of his much superior firepower. Yet hardly surprisingly, MacDonald's divisional commander, General Colville, was full of praise for the Brigade's performance, calling it 'a very fine feat . . . of which they will always be proud'.[52] Colville also paid tribute to the spirit of the Highlanders, and their sound tactics with 'their Brigadier's preference for turning movements around an enemy's position rather than direct assaults'.[53] He concluded that even 'their determination to overcome all obstacles would have availed them little but for the energy and resourcefulness of their Brigadier'.[54]

Unfortunately MacDonald was wounded at Paardeberg, a chance

bullet hitting him in the ankle. It was not a particularly serious wound but the healing process was drawn out and MacDonald was a reluctant patient, nor was his temper improved when he found the Highland Brigade taken out of the front line to guard lines of communication. During his enforced idleness he initiated a stream of letters both to his superiors and to the press containing ideas that were not universally popular, in particular – together with Roberts – he expressed strong support for universal conscription. 'Mac' had come to be seen as a difficult subordinate, and when Kitchener replaced Roberts as commander-in-chief he disbanded the Highland Brigade and relieved MacDonald of his command. Kitchener sent a telegram to Roberts in London suggesting that 'Mac' be returned to India.

When MacDonald returned to London he was knighted by the king for his leadership in South Africa and Lord Roberts, now chief of the Imperial general staff, entertained him to dinner before he set off for India. There was little reason to believe this second stint of duty as a district commander would be any happier than the first. His lack of enthusiasm was such that on his arrival MacDonald (with three months leave owing him) immediately asked for leave of absence. Roberts consulted the King and they agreed that he should be allowed to visit Australia and New Zealand where 'Mac' proved an immediate success, so much so that *The Times* suggested he should be offered the post of commander-in-chief of the Australian army. Nothing however came of this and he returned to the Indian sub-continent where he was given a slightly more senior position as commander of the British troops in Ceylon, carrying with it a higher rate of pay.

Despite its marginal advantages, Ceylon was not a posting calculated to excite him, and there were indications that in Ceylon itself the prospect of his arrival was not universally popular. After MacDonald's death Roberts wrote to Kitchener mentioning earlier accounts of MacDonald's behaviour in India, and it is entirely possible that when he assumed his appointment in Ceylon during March 1902 the Governor there, Sir Joseph West Ridgeway, might already have held him under some suspicion. 'Mac' was certainly not a success with the 'tea planters' society, often spurning their invitations to social events and committing the unforgivable sin of appearing to favour the company of Burgher families of mixed blood. This did not help his popularity, but much more seriously, a report surfaced of an incident alleged to have taken place between him and some native boys in a railway carriage. Such offences were not punishable under Ceylon law, but the Governor ordered MacDonald home on extended leave in the likely expectation that his superiors would arrange another appointment for him.

On MacDonald's arrival in London he visited his wife and son, who were living in Dulwich, and in all probability explained how he intended facing the accusations. On 18 March 1903 MacDonald experienced a most distressful interview with his former chief, Lord Roberts, which was very probably followed by one with the king.[55] Roberts told him outright that he could not stay in the army unless he cleared his name.[56] This meant placing himself before a court martial.

Unfortunately no evidence exists as to the specific charges. When Trevor Royle, MacDonald's biographer, visited the Public Record Office he discovered the Judge Advocate's records for Ceylon and India during 1903 were listed as missing. We do know, however, that Roberts certainly wrote to Kitchener for assistance with officers to officiate over MacDonald's impending court martial and ended his communication on a distinctly sceptical tone. 'He protests his innocence, but, if he is innocent, why on earth did he not insist upon having the matter cleared?' The military establishment gave Hector MacDonald no choice; he had to return to Ceylon for his court martial.

On the first leg of his return journey MacDonald was alone in a Paris hotel when the story broke in the press. In his pride and despair he went to his room and shot himself through the right ear with an 8mm pistol which he had probably bought the previous day. On hearing the terrible news his brother, William, set off for Paris on 26 March together with his cousin the Reverend James MacDonald – 'preaching Mac' – to collect the body. On their arrival they were stunned to learn that a solicitor on behalf of MacDonald's wife had arrived earlier and made arrangements for the body to be returned to Britain. That was not all: apparently Lady MacDonald, after identifying herself to the adjutant general, Sir Kelly Kenny, had made arrangements for a dawn funeral to be held on Monday, 31st March in Edinburgh.

William and James travelled overnight from King's Cross to Scotland on the same train as Lady MacDonald, accompanied by her solicitor and son Hector. However, Lady MacDonald's attempt to bury her husband both quickly and secretly misfired badly. The body remained at King's Cross station all day, and when it was transferred to the overnight train for Scotland a large crowd of London Scots cast floral tributes into the goods van containing the coffin, while two pipers played the lament 'The Flowers of the Forest'. Next morning at five minutes to six, as the train steamed into Edinburgh's Waverley Station, about 100 people stood on the platform. They subsequently followed the funeral cortege in an assorted collection of cabs and carriages. Within Dean cemetery, Edinburgh, the proceedings lasted a bare twenty minutes, but the ordinary Scottish people who so admired their fighting soldier were not so easily denied. On the following Sunday 30,000 of them were waiting outside the cemetery gates 'to pay homage to a hero whom everyone there looked on as being second only in importance to William Wallace and Robert the Bruce'.[57]

The indecent haste of a funeral that in its brevity denied the dignity due to such a national figure – whatever the circumstances of his death – led to a spate of rumours and correspondence in both the *Scotsman* and the *Glasgow Herald*. The pride of all Scotland, not to say the relevant clan societies, was outraged by the treatment of their stalwart, brave son. The manner of his death was questioned, particularly the bullet wound behind his right ear which was unusual though by no means impossible, in suicide attempts. As well as theories about his possible murder came another, namely that Hector MacDonald was not dead, that the body had been someone else's and he had assumed another identity. In later years there were reports of him being seen in the uniform of a Japanese officer during the Russo-Japanese war and, strangest of all, that 'Mac' went across to the Germans and replaced a senior Prussian officer, Von Mackensen, who was dying of cancer. Today it seems incredible that this outlandish theory ever should have gained so much support, since Von Mackensen was four inches taller than MacDonald and considerably slimmer; he also had two wives and five sons and remained much in the public eye until his death in 1945.

The fact is that in Scotland people refused to believe their champion had fallen in such a way, which led to a spate of conspiracy theories based on the conviction that he had been badly treated, even framed by others who were jealous of his sterling qualities. Shortly after MacDonald's death an anonymous financier sponsored a committee of Scots to visit Ceylon and unsurprisingly their findings, published on 29 June 1903, found MacDonald totally innocent of the charges laid against him. But neither Kitchener nor Roberts, who certainly should have known the facts, showed any willingness to help MacDonald retire quietly or to 'disappear' in some other remote command far away from Ceylon. Whatever Roberts' high principles, he had been known to help others and apparently during the same year he had suppressed a serious homosexual incident in the brigade of Guards.

But MacDonald, that 'great simple, lion-hearted man with the spirit of a child', had few friends and no influence in the army's higher echelons nor with the king. Whatever his past triumphs on the battlefield he would be made to answer whatever charges were formulated. In Scotland, especially in the extreme north-west, there was outrage over the treatment of their outstanding son and his shabby, almost secret, interment.[58]

A fund was set up and in May 1907 the foundation stone was laid for a magnificent monument on the crest of Mitchell Hill cemetery, Dingwall, similar to the Wallace Memorial at Stirling. The cemetery overlooks the town and from almost every viewpoint in the little burgh the monument occupies the skyline. Although MacDonald's body might still rest in distant Edinburgh, in Dingwall no one, kinsman or visitor, can fail to be aware of the tall castellated memorial erected to commemorate him. While 'Mac' was an unsophisticated man, solitary and ill at ease in civilian society, he was a natural soldier with great military virtues who came alive on the battlefield, where he fully understood the importance of tradition combined with firm discipline in subduing his soldiers' natural fears. It was Hector MacDonald's fate that when his hour came in the Sudan he was acting as the hammer of an army commanded by a great logistician rather than a genuine battlefield commander, and when at Omdurman his skills saved Kitchener's reputation against a primitive, if more numerous enemy, his deeds tended to be overshadowed by the British army's obsession with cavalry actions. When he managed to get back to active service his time in South Africa was curtailed because of his wound. In any case his Highland Brigade had few opportunities to show its great strengths and he himself virtually no chance to demonstrate his evolving tactical skills.

Hector MacDonald appealed to his countrymen for the military ability that enabled him to rise above his humble beginnings, for his modesty, his immense bravery and coolness on the field of battle, and not least because of the final injustice done to a gallant Scottish outsider with no influence or friends in high places. Yet the man behind the stereotype was more complex than many imagined and, after almost a century since his death, there are still reports that evidence will surface to exonerate him. According to William, his eldest brother, while he was undoubtedly strong physically, Hector was more sensitive than most men, and any matter that troubled him affected him much more deeply than he would admit to the outside world. This might help to explain 'the haggard look in his face and the strange look in his eyes' when he met a fellow officer in Paris very shortly before his death[59] although he was, of course, under the severest pressure.

Like many others, and Scottish soldiers in particular, Hector MacDonald appeared to need the stimulus and comradeship of war. Without it he seemed to have little purpose and in the jungle of the civilian world, which since early manhood he had successfully avoided and whose rules he probably never fully acknowledged, he was undoubtedly vulnerable. Other men might excel in different areas, but it was in his preparations for battle and in the conduct of war that he flourished and showed his very considerable powers of leadership.

CHAPTER EIGHT

WORLD WAR ONE – DOUGLAS HAIG (1861–1928)

'He might be, he surely was, unequal to the prodigious scale of events, but no one else was discerned as his equal, or better.'

Winston Churchill

O F ALL THE SCOTTISH commanders considered in this book none has aroused more controversy than Douglas Haig. With Haig – as with John Moore in Spain – the impact of the horrific conditions and casualties associated with their operations has tended to detract from their achievements. In Haig's case the casualties were immeasurably higher and, coming as they did from his citizen armies, their effects were felt across the face of Britain. In Scotland, the casualty levels were proportionately higher than for the United Kingdom as a whole and the resultant effects on its young manpower, in particular those who might reasonably have been considered as the leaders of the future, were grave in the extreme.

On 11 September 1918, for instance, the Australian general Sir John Monash (whom it must be recognised had a chauvinistic regard for his Australian soldiers compared with British troops) wrote, 'The best troops of the United Kingdom have long ago been used up and we now have a class of man who is without initiative or individuality. They are brave enough, but are simply unskilful. They would be all right if properly led, but their officers, particularly the junior officers, are poor; young men from the professions and from office stools in the English cities, who have had no experience whatever of independent responsibility or leadership.'[1]

Haig's campaigns are still just within living memory and the innate sense of loss and waste from his war makes any balanced assessment of his performance on the battlefield all the more difficult. As the American historian Barbara Tuchman has expressed it: 'The Great War of 1914–18 lies like a band of scorched earth dividing the earlier period from ours. In wiping out so many lives which would have been operative on the years that followed, in destroying beliefs, changing ideas and leaving incurable wounds of disillusion, it created a physical as well as a psychological gulf between two epochs.'[2]

The effects of World War One not only shocked those who lived before or during it but after World War Two with its much lower death rates where British servicemen were concerned, a new generation of critics reopened the subject of military leadership during World War One.

Where there is anger, or deep emotion, cool analysis is generally the casualty. The biographies of Haig published after World War One probably came too soon to be truly analytic, but fifteen years or so after World War Two interest in the previous conflict burst out again. Inevitably the quality of Douglas Haig's leadership became the subject of renewed attention by commentators both favourably and critically disposed towards him. Given the continuing level of partisanship it is likely that Haig's definitive biography has yet to be written.[3] The approach here is necessarily far more limited than any full-length treatment, concerned as it is primarily with his place alongside other great Scottish commanders.

No other Scottish – or British – soldier has ever commanded more men than Haig when he was commander-in-chief in France from 17 December 1915 until the time of the armistice. At that time Haig's formations exceeded 1,750,000 men, compared with Montrose's 5000 at Kilsyth, Abercromby's 15,000 at Aboukir, Wellington's 24,000 at Waterloo or Campbell's 31,000 at Lucknow.

Responsibility for such massive numbers does not of itself create a great commander, although when faced by an enemy of almost equal strength it can increase his problems of control to a remarkable degree. So, too, may a protracted campaign, when the strain and loneliness of supreme command can diminish the strongest of men. Haig not only presided over a massive establishment but he commanded for a remarkably long time; as a commander-in-chief for three years, he was involved in the planning of countless battles, large and small. In comparison, Montrose's great campaign lasted less than a year, the campaign masterminded by Bruce that ended with

Bannockburn spread over a year at most (although in reality far less than that), while Colin Campbell's active service during the Crimean War lasted for 19 months. Haig's equivalent in World War Two, Bernard Montgomery, was 8th Army commander for seven months, and less than a year after the allies landed in France on D-day (June 1944) the war ended.

Together with the scale of his responsibilities and the length of his time in France, Haig had to operate in a most adverse military environment. During World War One all the leaders in France had to wrestle with a situation where defence was in the ascendant and once they had failed to turn their opponents' flanks, their forward movement was limited by a continuous chain of trench lines stretching across Europe. For the greater part of the war neither side had the means of breaking the deadlock. When the Germans moved to the offensive late in the war their use of so-called shock troops caused their best soldiers to suffer unacceptably high casualties. Prior to this, the option for offence lay with Britain and France, but it was not until almost at the end of 1917 that the British tank, for technological as much for tactical reasons, became a potent weapon.

In the fighting in France during 1916–18 the casualty levels were unparalleled and, to British minds, virtually unthinkable. But the loss levels were broadly similar for all the combatants – it was continental warfare at its costliest. Whereas in the past Britain had found other nations to bear the brunt of the land fighting, this time her allies were found wanting and British forces, expanded to unheard-of levels, were locked in a conflict in which the vastly improved killing power of weaponry made any offensive hideously costly. This was Haig's battlefield.

When events follow a prescribed path leadership is relatively easy; it is at moments of crisis and adversity that commanders show their worth. For the combatants on the Western Front things rarely went according to expectations and the penalties for errors were enormous. Yet during the whole conflict, in spite of his vast responsibilities, and even at times of grave disappointment and serious reverses, Haig never lost his nerve, never lost the confidence of either his army commanders or, for that matter, the vast majority of his troops. Unlike France, Germany and Russia, the British experienced no trouble on any scale among their land troops. This says much, of course, for the British soldiers but it says much for their commander, too. In the context of the time it can be seen as practical and moral leadership of a high order. Haig never lost sight of his goal – success in the war – even when reverses and losses were threatening to engulf him and his political opponents (including the Prime Minister) were doing their best to bring him down.

To have faith and tenacity was, of course, invaluable in the context of Haig's campaigns, but it would have been monstrous had it not been accompanied by his military professionalism in pressing for better weaponry, in instituting endless training programmes to help men better survive the terrible battlefield, accompanied by a constant search for initiatives that might help break the impasse. One of Haig's biographers, Duff Cooper, in his attempt to get to the heart of his subject, wrote, 'In his veins there ran the blood of the Covenanters and in his heart there remained the teachings of the Presbyterian religion which he had learnt at his mother's knee. And Oxford, which gave him a sense of his own importance, filled him also with the determination to do himself justice, and to succeed in the career that he had decided to adopt.'[4]

If by this Duff Cooper suggests that Haig's ambition and his Presbyterianism might lead him to accept casualties more stoically than commanders with less strong beliefs, or even infers that the situation required such a temperament, it is an assertion to be respected. Whether one has to agree with it is another matter. Such respect cannot be extended to the wave of commentators after World War Two who perpetuated the worst myths of World War One. A.J.P. Taylor, for instance, wrote: 'The opposing lines congealed, grew solid. The generals on both sides stared at these impotently and without understanding. They went on staring for nearly four years.'[5] In fact they devised great offensives, attempted to develop novel artillery support, used poison gas, and in the end (on the allied side at least) moving to an integrated form of all-arms attack.

The psychologist Norman Dixon – by his own admission no military expert – went even further and stated: 'Only the most blinkered could deny that the First World War exemplified every aspect of military incompetence.'[6] It is difficult to believe that all the commanders – German, French and British – could have been so stupid. British commanders, with the possible exception of Sir John French and Hubert Gough, proved at least the equal of their allied counterparts and, in spite of the magnificent German staff training, to those of their opponents as well. If the British commanders were the donkeys that Alan Clark suggested in his post World War Two book they deserve to be condemned, and Haig most of all.[7] The fact is they were not.

Some eighty years on, the myths are beginning to be stripped away. Contrary to the belief that all senior officers inhabited luxurious chateaux far from danger, a recent and meticulously researched book 'Bloody Red Tabs' has proved conclusively that the casualty levels among senior officers were in fact, surprisingly high, even in relation to other wars.

Whatever his immense difficulties it must be acknowledged that Haig's command structure was less than perfect. Apart from the adverse environment in which they found themselves, when the British began their series of offensives, Haig's army commanders were remarkably inexperienced in controlling large numbers of men. For example during Britain's last experience of war from 1899–1902 against militant Boer farmers, Henry Rawlinson, who commanded Haig's Fourth Army in France, was in charge of a mobile column. During fourteen months' mobile warfare he killed sixty-four Boers and lost just twelve of his own men. When commander-in-chief in France Haig, while excellent at drafting dispatches, could never be called a good verbal communicator. This was a serious weakness both when he was visiting troops and in his dealings with his own army commanders. With his attacks in 1916, for instance, it was Haig's practice to send out detailed instructions to each army commander and then to a large extent let him carry them out in his own way. Haig was not as tyrannical as Wellington, who allowed nothing contrary to his directives, nor did he possess Montgomery's ability to make absolutely sure his orders were fully understood. For a major operation Haig customarily moved his own headquarters adjacent to that of the particular army involved but in any verbal discussions with the army commander there was all too often the possibility of some misinterpretation. Compared with more eloquent commanders his subordinates had less opportunity to gain the benefit of Haig's own experience.

Both the virtues and limitations of Haig's system of command can be seen in the manner of his preparations for the first great offensive on the Somme in 1916 and for a smaller operation two years later, that presaged a new tactical doctrine and the use of advanced weaponry that would bring about Germany's final surrender. With

Douglas Haig, and any other senior officer for that matter, both his personal circumstances and the pattern of his previous military career help to provide some clues towards his performance at the climax of his career.

Like many other Scottish commanders the profession of arms marked a powerful strand in the Haig family history. It can be traced back as far as Petrus de Haga, a Norman knight who accompanied William the Conqueror at the time of his invasion. Haig's father, John Haig, was a whisky baron. He had eleven children, of whom Douglas was the youngest son, but it was his mother who was most influential during Douglas' early years. She not only devoted her whole life to her children but sowed the seeds of the deep religious belief that became so important to Haig in later life. His father died when Douglas was seventeen and his mother followed her husband a year later. Henceforth it was his elder sister, Henrietta, who exerted an important influence on him.

As a child, Haig, like Moore, was headstrong and wilful and gave little indication of intellectual ability. After attending day school in Edinburgh he went to Clifton College, a quintessentially English public school whose entrance examination was not considered too demanding. Haig did not distinguish himself at Clifton, although a contemporary remembered him as 'a quiet determined youngster' who was strong physically. While he was not a particularly skilled rugby footballer he was 'one of the keenest and hardest working forwards in the School House Team'.[8]

After Clifton Haig entered Brasnose College, Oxford, where he clearly took the advice of its legendary principal, Dr Cradock, to ride – 'I like to see the gentlemen of Brasenose in top boots.'[9] He went on to become an excellent horseman and played polo to a high standard. Haig enjoyed the college club life and worked well enough, if not with the greatest enthusiasm; due to sickness he did not take his finals but by now his sister's influence had persuaded him to choose the army as a career.

At twenty-three, his ambition stirred, he entered Sandhurst where he performed outstandingly, being older and more mature than most of his contemporaries, becoming Senior Under Officer and excelling in almost everything. Despite his riding skills he showed no interest in hunting with the renowned Sandhurst pack, nor in Camberley's hectic merry-go-round of social activities. With some justice his contemporaries considered him aloof and taciturn. He was just above medium height with broad shoulders and a strong physique, and undeniably handsome in a square-jawed way, but unlike most of his contemporaries he had no women friends; women did not appear to attract him.

In February 1885 Haig was commissioned into the cavalry – the 7th (Queen's Own) Hussars, in which he spent his first nine years on regimental duties. As a cavalry officer his outstanding skills on the polo field did him no harm and he was soon made adjutant. Sport by no means filled his life for in addition to his administrative duties he came to show an enthusiasm for study, in particular the accounts of past military campaigns. Haig's next objective was to enter the Army Staff college at Camberley. While staff training was not yet considered as important as it would be in later years Haig realised the letters p.s.c. (passed staff college) were immensely important to an officer with his ambitions. His first attempt was foiled by his shortcomings in arithmetic (a compulsory subject at the time) and because of his colour-blindness, a far more difficult hurdle to overcome. However after producing a quite excellent written report upon the contemporary German army the problem of his colour-blindness was waived. At Camberley, Haig performed well. It was the practice there for students to work in groups on selected tactical assignments. Haig excelled at perceiving the solutions although he was impatient with the staff college jargon which was required when he and his colleagues submitted their findings. Undoubtedly serious and an acute observer who could work fast, he was marked out by Colonel C.D.R. Henderson, the doyen of Sandhurst lecturers, as a future commander-in-chief.

Such eminence must have seemed far beyond the reach of a captain who was already thirty-six years of age, whatever his ambitions. During the next five years, however, events moved more in his favour: he served on Kitchener's staff in the Sudan in the final stages of his war against the Dervishes, followed by a period with General French in the Anglo-Boer War. Apart from displaying coolness at Omdurman – Haig handled his Egyptian cavalry with great confidence when falling back before a much more numerous enemy – he became known as an independently minded staff officer critical of sloppiness and incompetence at whatever level it occurred. After Omdurman when writing to his friend Sir Evelyn Wood (later Field Marshal Sir Evelyn Wood) Haig was tart in his criticisms of Kitchener's choice of a frontal attack and for good measure he put forward his alternative battle plan. As French's Brigade Major in South Africa, Haig drew up memoranda of training rules that would improve the army's fighting potential against the Boers, including regulations for cavalry to fight dismounted and infantry to use open formations. In the later stages of the Anglo-Boer War Haig was made commanding officer of the 17th Lancers. Under his leadership the regiment achieved a high standard of military efficiency and although he was much moved when one of his squadrons suffered serious casualties in a brush with a detachment of Boers commanded by Jan Smuts, at a social level Haig remained as remote as ever. On return from South Africa in 1902 Haig became a brevet colonel, and was appointed ADC to King Edward VII. He had been mentioned in dispatches four times. For the next year he was with the 17th Lancers in Edinburgh, a relatively relaxed time during which he took up golf. This sport involved considerable exercise particularly on Sundays when as a Scottish sabbatarian he would not use his car, but walk the four miles to and from the links.

In October 1903 Haig went to India where he joined Kitchener. There he founded a permanent cavalry school and wrote a series of tactical exercises that ensured the cavalry could shoot accurately. In 1904 Haig was made a major general and in the following year he returned to England on leave. Since being made ADC to the King they took to corresponding regularly and in the process became good friends. On Haig's arrival the King invited him to Windsor Castle for Ascot races. It was a visit that would change Haig's personal life forever. At the age of forty-three, the seemingly confirmed bachelor met and married a Miss Dorothy Vivian, one of Queen Alexandra's maids of honour. He met her on a Thursday, proposed on the golf course two days later, and they were married during the following month. Such a marriage could do no harm to his career and despite the speed of his courtship it was to prove a happy match. His wife was devoted and after her training at court, invariably discreet. Haig appeared equally loving and there was no doubting the new happiness that marriage brought to his life although, if anything, his public image remained more aloof than ever. Following their honeymoon in Warwickshire the bride and bridegroom returned to India.

From this point onwards Haig's career accelerated. In 1906, as

Director of Military Training, he was working with Richard Haldane, the new Secretary of State for War, to modernise the army for the European war that both saw as inevitable. This included forming the Territorial Army, creating an Expeditionary force and giving the army professional direction through one central committee instead of the old system where there was a division of powers between the commander-in-chief responsible for training and personnel and the services that supplied and supported the army. The General Staff committee was to be headed by the Chief of the General Staff and presided over by the Secretary of State for War. In 1909 Haig returned to India as Chief of Staff to reorganise the Indian army for a wartime role and then in 1912 he was appointed commander-in-chief at Aldershot, to command the army's only active corps. Through a seemingly endless series of tactical exercises he trained it for war. He also set out with his customary determination to know its members, both officers and senior soldiers. With the officers this was relatively easy and he accomplished it through holding small, informal dinner parties for twelve or so, four times a week. But, while the soldiers experienced a new professionalism and urgency in their training which they realised was the result of their commander's commitment and determination, as a man he remained more of a figurehead than a flesh-and-blood leader.

At this time Haig could, as Duff Cooper concludes, be justly associated more with the tradition of the Scottish Covenanting commanders than their more swashbuckling counterparts like Montrose or Dundee. His belief in himself and Britain's cause was unshakable, but his mind was deep rather than broad. While an avid student of military matters, he showed little interest in politics and read almost nothing outside military publications, certainly no light fiction – and he was never able to enjoy the cut and thrust of debate, partly because of his inarticulateness, partly because his own ideas were already well-thought out and because he was not disposed to play the devil's advocate in challenging them. From the way his career had advanced at the commencement of World War One Douglas Haig was certainly destined for the highest rank. In his work with Richard Haldane and later in India he had shown his ability as a senior staff officer and during his tour at Aldershot he had already commanded the largest British Army formation at that time. His prospects were enhanced when during the first eighteen months of the war on the Western

Front he was to gain invaluable experience of command in the field, first as a corps, then as an army commander.

In August 1914 as the British Expeditionary Force formed up just south of the Belgian town of Mons its leaders were unaware that they straddled the route of the projected German thrust through Belgium and Northern France. Once into Northern France it was to take a great sweep encompassing Paris to first encircle and then destroy the French armies. Placed across its axis the British four divisions (110,000 men) commanded by Field Marshal Sir John French together with the French Fifth Army of ten divisions under General Lanrezac were in grave danger of being enveloped by three German armies totalling thirty-four divisions.

At Mons on 23 August the German forward elements made contact with the advanced English battalions. It was somewhat of a surprise for both, especially the tightly packed German formations who suffered heavy losses from rapid and well-aimed rifle fire. Virtually all the German attacks were directed against II Corps, under Haig's fellow commander, General Smith-Dorrien, which sustained 1600 casualties to Haig's forty. While such casualties were by no means excessive the weight of the German attacks compelled both the French and British to give way. The BEF's retreat from Mons that continued for fourteen days in a south-westerly direction along 166 endless miles took on the epic quality of Moore's withdrawal to Corunna. Continued withdrawal taxes any army's morale and tests its commanders' qualities to the limit. Haig came out of the experience well. For the most part he proved a fine corps commander, always forward when needed, cheerful, observant and resourceful in keeping his tired men going. Beneath his impression of determined optimism he was of course forced to keep his doubts about the strategic use of the BEF to himself although nothing could hide the fact that he was usually far ahead of his commander-in-chief in his tactical reading of the battlefield situations. When roused from sleep he had the ability to grasp the situation quickly, give the necessary orders and fall asleep again. Haig's methods of command were far from the later stereotyped images of him snug in a safe headquarters. As his Intelligence officer John Charteris observed at the time, 'In many ways D.H. is his own Chief of Staff. He knows so much more about fighting than any of the staff, and he goes around the divisions and brigades so constantly that his Chief of Staff has little to do except to see that things go smoothly!'[10]

Nonetheless they did not come through the retreat unscathed. While normally robust, Haig suffered a serious gastric attack and he had not fully recovered when German units commenced a night attack on I Corps as it passed through the French town of Landrecies. His Corps Headquarters was with the forward troops and he barely escaped capture. In the confusion Haig ordered the whole town to be organised for defence; he also requested that II Corps, who were at Le Cateau some eight miles away, should be sent to help him. In fact II Corps were under much more serious attack but after an obstinate stand – which they made against Sir John French's wishes – Smith Dorrien successfully disengaged his men. Haig quickly recovered his health and with it his confidence, although after his experience at Landrecies he was sure that as a rule senior officers should not be too closely involved in frontline fighting. Three days after Landrecies Haig learned from the Royal Flying Corps that the Germans had altered their line of advance and in doing so had exposed their flank upon which he urged the French Fifth Army to counter-attack, offering them the full assistance of I Corps. Unknown to Haig, its commander General Lanrezac was already under firm orders from his commander-in-chief, General Joffre, to do just that. To Haig's disappointment and anger Sir John French then categorically forbade I Corps to assist the French.

On 6 September the French assumed the offensive against the over-extended and near-exhausted German armies who were in turn forced to give way and the BEF joined in the allied advance northwards. The British crossed the River Marne virtually unhindered as the Germans moved back to prepared positions behind the more northerly River Aisne. Unfortunately the relatively leisurely nature of the advance foiled any chance of exploiting a gap that Haig had been aware was developing between the German First and Second armies. A stalemate developed on the Aisne and there followed attempts by both sides to out-flank each other as they moved towards the coast. With the German seizure of Antwerp and their developing threat to the channel ports, the BEF was secretly withdrawn from the Aisne and sent to Flanders to help safeguard the seaborne links with Britain. This was strongly supported by Haig. Once there Sir John French ordered a general advance against an enemy he reckoned was no more than a Corps strong. On this occasion I Corps' Intelligence Section was far less sanguine about the Germans' strength which actually totalled five divisions (a minimum of ten Corps).

In the battle that followed a quarter of a million British soldiers fought for three weeks against much superior forces – the Germans had raised an entirely new army for the purpose. Haig's I Corps was heavily engaged and at one point after a German attack produced confused reports. Haig decided to see things for himself. Amid the continued gunfire and the backward streams of wounded men the imperturbable Haig moved up the Menin road at a slow trot with part of his staff behind him. He saw little more than the confusion of the moment but as the Official History said the way he went about it did much to restore confidence. The momentary panic at Landrecies was never repeated. The distinguished military writer Basil Liddell Hart was in no doubt who was responsible for the remarkable performance of the 'old British Regular Army' at Ypres. 'The failure of the higher commanders to grasp the situation left the real handling of the battle to Haig and his divisional commanders. And they for want of reserves could do little more than cement the crumbling parts of the front, by scraping reserves from other parts, and encourage the exhausted but indomitable troops to hold on.'[11]

On 20 November 1914 Haig was promoted to full general as a recognition of his work with I Corps and on Christmas Day the BEF was reorganised into two Armies, First Army under Haig, with Smith Dorrien in command of Second Army. During the stalemate that had developed Haig's immediate concern was the state of the trenches held by his men. It was not just the mud and the standing water; there was a serious lack of necessary equipment for such warfare. Haig pressed endlessly for better weapons, more heavy guns, standardised hand bombs, trench mortars and lighter machine guns. He also realised they needed better junior commanders to use them – younger and quick-thinking men.

In 1915, as Sir John French's outstanding Army commander Haig became involved in mounting the first two British offensives in support of the French at Neuve Chapelle in March and at Loos in September. He quickly absorbed the two chief lessons from their relative failure. In March, at Neuve Chapelle he tried to achieve surprise by using a concentrated bombardment followed by rapid forward movement; after gaining good initial successes further advances stalled, and Haig closed the offensive down. At Loos he adopted a more methodical form of barrage but the commitment of the reserves was delayed – for which Haig blamed French – and once more the attack ground to a halt.

By late 1915 it was clear to the soldiers in France and to the British political leaders that Sir John French was not up to his responsibilities as commander-in-chief. In reply to direct questions Haig felt compelled to acknowledge as much to the King. French tended to oscillate from optimism to despair and therefore was never fully in control; equally importantly he did not work well with his French counterparts. Prior to the battle of Loos, for instance, he had bitter disagreements with General Joffre who was unimpressed with French's military views. In fact French had lost the confidence both of his political masters and his army commanders. In December 1915 the inevitable happened and Haig took over. Here was a commander sure of his own and his troops' abilities, if only they could be given adequate weaponry and sufficient training. Haig needed no reminding about the justice of the British cause and because of this he was sure victory must come, however long and hard the process might be. He must have been particularly pleased to receive an unreserved endorsement from Richard Haldane. 'I have for months past wished that you had been in London from the beginning – with the supreme direction of the war and the opportunity of playing chess against the Great General Staff of Germany. You have a great strategical mind – a rare gift in this country.'[12] There was general satisfaction in both royal and high political circles that Haig was in command. Yet as Haig read Haldane's generous tribute he could have been forgiven for thinking the chess analogy was rather too neat, for if war could be likened to chess he had already lost some major pieces through the terrible losses suffered by the French and the ominous difficulties being experienced by the Russians. By the end of August 1914 – which now seemed so far away – the French had sustained a third of a million casualties and had lost a tenth of their regular officers. By the end of 1915 another million men had been lost. As for the Russians, apart from their serious shortages of munitions and other equipment by August 1915 they had a total of a million and a half soldiers in captivity. He must have been aware of other checks upon his actions, namely how unprepared his own armies were and the powerful role of public opinion in Britain. At this time, Colonel A. Court Repington,

The Times correspondent, doubted whether any commander would be sufficiently 'fearless of public opinion to incur the losses which must be suffered in any attempt to pierce the enemy's fortified front'.[13] Haig never regarded public opinion that highly but it was to be for the high number of casualties in his first giant offensive as commander-in-chief that Haig will never be forgotten, and probably never forgiven. It took place on the Somme, not his favoured location but one that was chosen because British military policy at this time was subject to French control. Virtually no criticisms have been made against the campaign from a strategic point of view, namely, that by means of a big push it aimed at defeating the German field army. But whereas in the planning stages it was agreed that the French were to take the major part, the German attack on the pivotal French fortress at Verdun so drained formations from elsewhere that instead of forty divisions the French contribution was reduced to sixteen of which only five attacked on the opening day.

The British therefore – who had to extend their front – did not enjoy the same numerical superiority considered vital in the original plan. This important consideration aside it was the tactical handling that has continued to arouse intense anger and near disbelief ever since.

Nothing can alter the fact that on 1 July 1916 eleven British divisions, with five French divisions to their right, rose out of their trenches to attack the German positions opposite them. It was a set piece operation that had been planned since 1 March 1916. When the day ended the British army had 57,470 casualties of whom 993 officers and 18,247 soldiers were dead. These totals were close to the combined manpower of Wellington's army at Waterloo together with Abercromby's at Aboukir. With such a battle, heavy casualties were fully to be expected but unbelievably the gains were trifling. As commander-in-chief it was Haig's battle and the final responsibility was, of course, his.

The offensive arrangements were the result of his particular command system. It has already been mentioned that after his initial and detailed briefing it was his practice to allow his army commanders to draw up their own battle plans, which they were required to forward to GHQ for comment. On the Somme the main burden of the attack was taken by General Sir Henry Rawlinson's Fourth Army, which had been formed for the purpose. A month after Rawlinson began making his preparations Haig was sent the battle plan. Rawlinson's aim was relatively modest, to take the enemy's first and second trenches and 'to kill Germans'. Haig read it and was not satisfied; he wanted the limit of the first advance extended in order to create an opportunity of getting across the Somme River and being able to fight the enemy in the open. For this purpose a Reserve army under Sir Hubert Gough, with its higher cavalry component, was made ready to push through the gap Haig intended Rawlinson to create.

It seems worth asking why Haig, a cavalryman and newly appointed commander-in-chief, demanded amendments to his infantry general's plans. There was, of course, Haig's main objective of attempting a damaging blow to the Germans' battle worthiness and not, as Rawlinson proposed, a grinding down process. This might legitimately have been thought over-ambitious at this stage of the war, but any supreme commander was likely to baulk at Rawlinson's vague objective to kill Germans. There were, too, Haig's own earlier experiences at Neuve Chapelle and Loos: at Neuve Chapelle after the initial success progress had foundered and at Loos after excellent early gains the reserves were not there to follow up. In both instances, following an appropriate preliminary barrage, the taking of the front line seemed relatively straightforward. Haig, the staff officer turned commander, had seen that the problem was to maintain momentum and this he wanted Rawlinson to do. Tragically on the Somme, the momentum hardly started.

This was due in part to Haig's gentlemanly form of delegation and the fact that at this stage Rawlinson held the same rank as his commander-in-chief. Haig had urged Rawlinson to shorten the bombardment so that 'the Germans would have less warning of the attack . . . and advised also that the German trenches should be rushed as soon as the barrage lifted on the day of the attack.'[14] Rawlinson would not agree and Haig held back from directly ordering him to make the changes. In the event this was to prove hideously costly, but neither Rawlinson nor Haig anticipated the increased difficulties in taking the first line.

Additionally there were serious shortcomings in information. British intelligence did not realise the extent of German resourcefulness and their advances in fortress building and multi-storied dugouts. As John Masefield wrote, 'From without, one saw nothing, *even close at hand*, but heaps of rubble and chalk. Underneath, linking cellar to cellar and foundation to foundation, were deep, strongly-panelled passages, in which, at intervals, were posts for machine guns, so arranged that the muzzle of the gun in its embrasure was only a few inches above the level of the ground outside.[15] Neither British patrols nor the crude aerial photography of the day had been able to discover the extent of the German preparations. Secondly, British artillery, although much increased over the sector to be attacked, was by no means sufficient. On his rounds Haig found the attacking staffs quite satisfied with the scale of the bombardment and the arrangements for wire cutting, but they were dangerously over optimistic. The British had only half the French artillery concentration and – as if this was not enough – British ammunition was defective with one in three shells failing to explode. Haig had proposed concentrating the barrage on certain key areas but this was not done. Adding to these problems for the British, Marshal Foch asked that the preparatory barrage be prolonged for a further two days.

The third factor contributing to the debacle was that, following Verdun, the Germans were confident that after the most concentrated barrage men could emerge unhurt from concrete emplacements or from out of shattered trenches, and still bring their machine guns into deadly operation.

Though Rawlinson was undoubtedly at fault GHQ had to shoulder the blame for much of the disaster. Following Neuve Chapelle and Loos Haig had come to valid conclusions about the use of artillery and the need for reserves to be close up but he had not realised sufficiently the extent of the improvements in defensive systems. More seriously still, he did not make sure his own tactical assessments were acted upon. The same criticism could be made for the actual tactics used on the ground. GHQ was responsible for its guideline directives emphasising the all-out nature of the offensive. Its memorandum of 8 May 1916 stated that the 'attack must be driven home until the endurance of the enemy is broken down' and 'all must be prepared for heavy casualties'. However, the actual tactics used were based on notes issued by the Fourth Army itself to its soldiers, most of whom were not regulars and were as yet unbloodied by a major battle. Because of their inexperience these took the form of deliberate drills based on precise and detailed orders, instructing men to move forward in waves close behind each other – an instruction directly contrary to Haig's own.

As planned, the French attacked first and, by using quick and flexible tactics, they secured their initial objectives with only light losses. In the British sector, though, there was a deadly interval between ending the barrage and sending the attackers forward and the Germans, who had been given vital time to emerge from their trenches and man their guns, professed themselves amazed to see soldiers walking steadily towards them in extended lines. 'I could see them everywhere; there were hundreds. The officers were in front. I noticed one of them walking calmly, carrying a walking stick. When we started firing we just had to load and reload. They went down in their hundreds. You didn't have to aim, we just fired into them. If only they had run, they would have overwhelmed us.'[16] The German artillery turned from the French and concentrated on the British lines. Fourth Army headquarters had not only laid down rigid and unrealistic tactics, but they refused to allow their inexperienced troops the freedom to adapt if things did not go according to plan. The slaughter continued.

Almost inconceivably Haig did not know the extent of the catastrophe during the first day. Land lines were broken, the officers he sent to gather information were killed, and the troops taking part in the costly shambles simply stuck it out. At the end of day two he still believed his losses had been about 40,000 rather than 60,000 on the first, followed by more on the second. Given the situation his ignorance was understandable, but nothing could absolve Haig from his initial over-optimistic estimation that led to such over-matching of his untried formations, or from subsequently allowing his committed army commander to ignore directives from GHQ that would surely have mitigated the disaster. The losses were compounded, for, owing to Haig's lack of information, the Fourth Army was denied his authority either to reinforce success where it occurred or close down fruitless attacks.

As Rawlinson reeled under his fearful losses he failed to exploit successes on the right wing gained by both the French and his own troops. The offensive continued for, despite British shock and outrage over the first day of the Somme, the protracted French crisis over Verdun forced Haig to continue. However, from now on the attacks were more skilfully conducted, enemy losses rose and, as a result of the Germans' stubborn counter-attack policy, sometimes exceeded those of the attackers. Both Haig and his armies were learning. With the British assault of 14 July that marked the ending of the battle's first phase, Haig still delegated the final planning to his respective army commanders, but he adopted a far tougher attitude with them over the tactical details. The gratifying result was a short creeping bombardment, followed by a surprise assault on the German front lines which proved completely successful. As before, the essential problem which faced the attackers was to keep up the momentum while moving through deep lines of defence. As yet this seemed insoluble.

The Battle of the Somme lasted until 14 November; when it came to an end the British had lost 400,000 men and German losses were almost as heavy. Yet, in spite of the offensive's first terrible day and Germany's continued fighting strength, many of Haig's aims were achieved. The Germans drew back from Verdun and, while they had not been defeated on the Somme, they had lost the core of their battle-hardened army in the fighting. Perversely the British, who often translate their defeats into victories, have treated the campaign as an unrelieved disaster. The short-term view of the death toll that included so many potential leaders from among Kitchener's volunteers probably rendered it inevitable. Haig's medium term justification of it on the grounds that he had the greater manpower resources also appears less than convincing. But it was not a battlefield defeat.

Haig's final communique at the end of the war went far to explain his military purpose in France and in particular on the Somme. Defeat there could conceivably have resulted in France being driven out of the war; it could also be seen in the context of Haig's strategic objective which was the defeat of the main German army. This was certain to be immensely difficult after Germany had established itself in Belgium and northern France, and while there was the strong possibility of the Russian and Italian fronts breaking down. Added to this were the inevitable delays before Britain's armies could intervene at anything like their full strength and the further time lag before troops from the Empire, and finally the Americans, could allow the allies to exert their superior manpower. As Haig rightly observed, Britain's general unpreparedness at the beginning of the war led directly to the loss of many thousands of brave men and no doubt the unpreparedness applied to Haig himself more than he realised. To Haig the war in France was seen as a single continuous campaign which the allies, possessing the moral advantage and potentially superior forces, would win. It meant suffering, sacrifices and inevitable reverses before such success could be achieved. But this was a world away from acknowledging that he condoned heavy casualties. The first day of the Somme aside, he knew them to be inevitable but he constantly sought to gain the tactical advantage and to find improved ways of waging war. At no time, however, could he ignore the need to work with France, Britain's senior partner in the land war, even though this was frequently at the expense of his own tactical considerations.

The next year, 1917, could be seen as the year of major setbacks for Haig. In December 1916 the French replaced General Joffre as commander-in-chief of the French Army by General Nivelle who offered a new plan for a rapid victory; in fact if his attack did not succeed in breaking through within forty-eight hours he undertook to stop it. Such words delighted both the French Government and Lloyd George, the new English Prime Minister who had replaced Asquith in December 1916. To complement the French attack Haig was required to mount an attack of his own at Arras to draw off German reserves from Nivelle's operation. This opened on 9 April 1917 but after encouraging early gains momentum was lost. On 16 April Nivelle's attack commenced. It was a disaster with only one of the three armies involved making any worthwhile gains; these were nearly all lost through a German counter attack. The resulting collapse in French morale and the mutinies in their armies made a further large British attack essential. The timing of the battle was not Haig's (he had favoured the end of May), and the anticipated support from the French was not forthcoming, but in his directives for Third Ypres Haig showed how much he had developed his command methods. While he still believed in giving his army commanders ultimate responsibility for their individual operations he now bombarded them with lists of Socratic questions to make sure their preparations met his own demanding standards. In Herbert Plumer, his Second Army Commander, and equally with Plumer's Chief-of-Staff, Charles Harrington, Haig had two men who would cheerfully meet such requirements. 'Trust, Training and Thoroughness' were their watchwords. Plumer made sure all his commanders knew the whole operation in which they were involved and their roles in it. It was regrettable that Plumer did not have control of the whole offensive at Third Ypres but Haig appointed

Hubert Gough to command the Northern sector who, according to John Terraine, never shared Haig's appreciation of a battlefield.

Haig's working relationship with his Army commanders also depended on the calibre of his own Headquarters staff to see his remit was carried out. Here he had the disadvantage of two less than outstanding players in the vital positions of his Chief-of-Staff and Head of Intelligence. Launcelot Kiggell held the former post until early 1918. Haig valued his advice and liked him personally for the gentlemanly Kiggell was utterly loyal and immensely hard-working, but he was seen as the man who minded the machine and to Haig's Army commanders, appeared hardly more than his master's mouthpiece. The contrast between Kiggell and Freddie de Guingand, Montgomery's Chief-of-Staff in World War Two, who had full responsibility for transmitting Montgomery's directives to his Army commanders, could hardly be greater. With John Charteris, his Head of Intelligence, Haig had a different problem. Charteris, Haig's former ADC, was certainly not afraid to make assessments but in the majority of cases his intelligence reports on German front-line casualties and weaknesses in their morale were constantly over-optimistic. In October 1917, at the height of the 3rd Ypres offensive, Charteris' conclusions about Germany's resources being so stretched that the country would soon have to accept peace were directly at variance with the more realistic findings of George MacDonagh, the Director of Military Intelligence in London.

Notwithstanding, at Third Ypres – despite the terrible conditions encountered – Haig did show greater flexibility of command. After the offensive opened and General Plumer achieved his outstanding success by capturing the German fortified salient on Messines Ridge, General Gough's impatience to get on with things brought disappointing results, and rain – no less than four times the rainfall of the equivalent period during 1915 and 1916 – bedevilled every effort. In the final stages Haig looked again to Plumer for a well conducted series of limited 'bites' on the German positions. When after three and a half months the Canadians finally took the ruined village of Passchendaele, Haig closed the offensive down. To understand the rationale behind such a prolonged conflict in a morass of mud it must never be forgotten that it was conducted against the background of the Russian Revolution and that country's exit from the war, the collapse of the Italian front at Caporetto and the inability of the French armies to mount anything but small set attacks.

Third Ypres was followed by the disastrous attempt to end the year on a successful note by using massed tanks, 381 of them, in a raid on the German Hindenburg Line at Cambrai. Due to Third Ypres there were insufficient reserves to exploit any success and this put a time limit on the offensive. General Byng's Third Army in whose sector it was to take place allowed the offensive to become rather more ambitious in scope. As a result, after a great initial success, all the gains were lost when the attackers were unable to hold the Bourlon Ridge that Haig had identified as crucial. What was more, Haig appeared to have wasted the element of surprise with this new secret weapon of war without exploiting it to the full.

Haig may have been compelled to mount Third Ypres, but his statement that it brought the destruction of the enemy's field forces nearer had a hollow ring when the exhaustion of the British army became apparent, together with the delays in supplying drafts to bring units back to strength. His logic would have been more convincing if American manpower had been ready to tip the balance but much equipping and training was needed before this could become possible. By the year's end, Lloyd George was mounting a determined campaign to replace Haig but, despite the disappointments in France, no credible replacement could be found.

If it were possible, 1918 started on an even worse note for the British commander. This came in the form of the terrible reverse caused by a ferocious German offensive supplemented by fresh divisions from Russia. Once more Haig's system of command showed its limitations. Hubert Gough, who had not been outstanding at Third Ypres, was now commander of the Fifth Army that faced the main fury of the assault. He did not apparently understand what Haig had required from him in the construction of rear defence lines. Yet Haig, by his calm and sound reaction to the crisis, proved brilliant in adversity, and at his request General Plumer sent units from Second Army to help fill gaps in the British defences. Haig urgently required assistance from the French but their pessimistic commander, Pétain, refused to respond asserting that he, too, was about to be attacked by overwhelming forces. This convinced Haig that a unity of command over both the French and British forces was essential; to achieve this he pledged himself willing to work under

Marshal Foch as Generalissimo and to accept his own downgrading. This brought about long-needed co-operation, but the scale of the difficulties facing a British commander in France at this time could still be seen in the casualty figures. These were a powerful response to the politicians who had so criticised Haig's offensive actions for, following the German offensive of spring 1918, the British lost 236,300 men, compared to the 244,897 during the 105 days of the Passchendaele campaign the preceding autumn.

It says much for Haig's character and heart that, at a time when his army was so much weakened, when another German attack was very probable and his own dismissal always possible, he began to plan the counterstrokes that would destroy the Germans within the same year. The first offensive would presage the tactics used in the later attacks and anticipate many of the methods used during World War Two.

Towards the end of June, General Rawlinson submitted a plan for his Australians 'to improve his army's position south of the Somme'. Haig approved on condition that some American troops should take part, that Rawlinson should have an adequate reserve of tanks and a cavalry division would be at hand 'if the enemy bolts'.[17] The latter seemed a futile hope.

The detailed planning for the Battle of Hamel was entrusted to the Australian, General Monash, a Jewish civil engineer and part-time soldier. The contrast between an Antipodean Jew and the Presbyterian commander-in-chief must have been marked, but Haig had already admired Monash's work and supported his appointment above that of other candidates. Punctilious like Haig, Monash worked out his battle plan as if it were an orchestral score, where the various arms and units became the instruments and the tasks they performed their respective musical phrases. Every individual unit was required to make its entry precisely at the proper moment and contribute its phrase to the general harmony. This involved the Plumer technique of operational orders being examined at conferences attended by every participating commander and head of department until all had exactly the same understanding of them. At Hamel, new aerial photographic techniques gave everyone an excellent idea of the actual German positions. Haig went over every detail with Monash and was undoubtedly won over by his approach. 'Monash is a most thorough and capable commander who thinks out every detail of any operation and leaves nothing to chance. I was greatly impressed with his arrangements.'[18]

Prior to the battle, Monash compelled his men to work with the tanks, which were far different from the early models. Just one man could drive the Mark V; it was equipped with a more powerful engine and its armour was much improved. In attendance were the light Whippet tanks equipped with an engine for each track, four Hotchkiss light machine guns and the capability of travelling at an unheard-of eight miles an hour. Despite their unfortunate earlier experiences, with the enthusiasm of their own general the Australians became converted.[19]

The extent of the planning could be seen when eight minutes before zero hour of 3.10 a.m. on 4 July 1918 the artillery began a bombardment with smoke and high explosive rounds. This they had done for the previous fortnight (although before 4 July they mixed in gas rounds as well) but now at the same time sixty tanks went at full speed over the half-mile from their forming-up point to the start line. To drown out the noise of their engines the Air Force kept up incessant patrols of low-flying aircraft, old models with particularly noisy engines. At 3.10 the guns changed to a creeping barrage 200 yards in front of the advancing infantry. Simultaneously machine guns swept the entire front with flanking fire. As the barrage lifted the lumbering tanks, with infantry directly behind, were up on the enemy positions. Most of their targets, nearly always machine-gun posts, were either quickly crushed under the tank tracks or neutralised with the case shot from their guns. The plan was for the attackers to pass the strong points in Vaire and Hamel woods lying on their right flank and make for the high point of the spur that ran from the main plateau to the river Somme some 2500 yards beyond their front line. This was immediately to the east of the ruined village of Hamel. If captured, it was expected not only to prove an important observation post up the Somme but act as a useful jumping off place for a subsequent attack.

Unlike previous attacks the battle was over in less than an hour and a half, with the high ground firmly in allied hands. At the consolidation stage four carrier tanks brought up barbed wire, corrugated iron, water and much needed small arms ammunition. Their load was equivalent to that carried by no less than 1250 infantrymen. During the battle itself, aircraft dropped additional

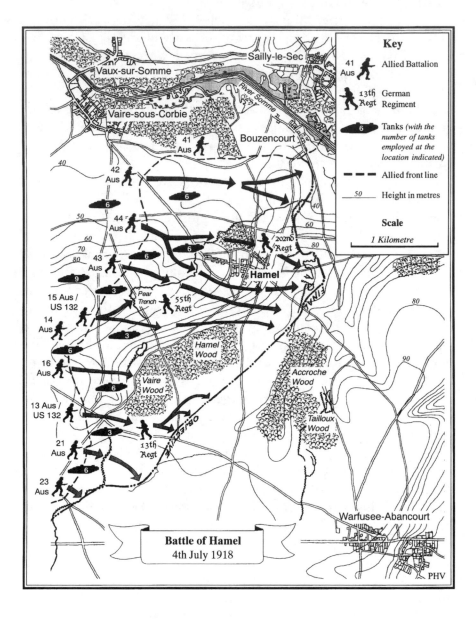

Battle of Hamel
4th July 1918

ammunition for the Vickers machine guns. Assessments of Hamel have varied although its success was unquestioned. A recent account concluded, 'The outstanding feature of the action was economy – for the infantry, economy in lives and labour, and for the guns, economy in shells and effort – and this saving was due to the tanks. But the success was due to the combination of all arms.'[20] It was undoubtedly economical and cost-effective with the Australian and American casualties amounting to just 1400, many of them lightly wounded, while apart from the considerable number of German casualties 1472 prisoners were taken, together with a large quantity of arms including heavy guns, machine guns and anti-tank weapons.

However, there was no stinting with the back-up as the ten battalions involved were supported by no less than 432 guns and more than 100 machine guns to provide cross fire. Above all it was a carefully synchronised operation, a triumph for Monash and for his champion, Haig, in both conserving manpower and using the latest technology, of which Haig thoroughly approved. As the 'cock a hoop' Monash wrote about his success in his war letters, 'The battle was the first definite offensive on a substantial scale which had been undertaken by any of the armies of the Allies on any front since the close of the autumn campaign of 1917 and the opening of the German offensive in the early spring of 1918. Its success converted the whole thoughts of the Allies from an attitude of the pure defensive to an attitude of offensive, and it begun to dawn upon the High Command that it was, after all, possible to do something else but sit down and take the cuffs and kicks of the enemy. The psychological effect of the battle of Hamel was electric and startling.'[21]

While understandably elated Monash seemed somewhat unfair to Haig, who had already been thinking about aggressive action. What Monash did was demonstrate how the offensive could best be resumed and how, through a unified combination of all arms, spearheaded by the much-improved tanks, a war of movement was again possible. Haig fully appreciated this as his subsequent diary entries reveal, and he was only too pleased to explain the new opportunities that were opening up. As Monash's letters revealed, 'People came from far and near to hear all about it and find out "how it was done" and GHQ published a special pamphlet describing the battle plan and the new tactical methods which I employed. There is no doubt at all that it was the success of this battle which induced

Marshal Foch to undertake a counterblow on 18 July, which had the effect of arresting the German rush on Paris, for as you know, on 15 July the enemy had pushed to within 40 miles of the French capital, and that was his very last success of the war.'[22]

Whether it was the outcome of this success alone that inspired Marshal Foch's counterblow is somewhat less certain. Even before the success of Hamel became fully apparent, Haig was considering other ways to use the new technology becoming available. He advocated the concentration of aircraft, for instance, on bombing a limited objective (diary of 5 July). But Monash was quite right to say that following Hamel Haig certainly began to consider larger attacks based on the principles so successfully used there. For instance Rawlinson's Fourth Army was allocated 534 tanks, with 800 supporting aircraft, for a new assault. Haig ruled that tanks should only be used if the accompanying troops were thoroughly practised in working with them. Deception was again to be used, this time to baffle the Germans about the formations opposite them. On 8 August in the Somme valley the combined British-Australian-Canadian attack went in and, where before, progress was accustomed to be measured in yards, the Canadians advanced an astonishing eight miles. Haig's appreciation of the new situation could be seen in his diary notes of 13 and 22 August, 'Reinforcements should be sent to where we are gaining ground' and '. . . All units should go straight for their objectives while reserves should be pushed on where we are gaining ground'.

From now on Haig's diary showed that when he had reports from his army commanders that opposition was stiffening and heavy casualties would probably result if they tried to go further, he immediately ordered such movements to be postponed in favour of more promising ones.

Immediately following the attack of 8 August another part of the front, at Bapaume, was being considered as the place for a major new attack. Unbeknown to the allies the offensive of 8 August had been the blackest day of the war so far for the German army. It had lost some 27,000 men, but more important than the actual figures was the fact that more than two-thirds of these had surrendered as prisoners. An indication of how far Haig's thinking had moved beyond that of the military planners in London was revealed at this time. Haig was sent a War Office paper outlining British future military policy.

It was an immensely detailed piece of work and outlined a final offensive during 1919 or even 1920, with the use of some 10,500 tanks! As Haig contemptuously remarked: 'Words, words, words, lots of words and little else . . . Great attention to figures without sufficiently careful analysis of what the human state of the various units is.'[23] His divergence from London became startlingly apparent a month later when Haig received a caution with regard to possible heavy losses when he attacked the Hindenburg Line.[24] In effect it said that if serious losses occurred the responsibility would be solely his. Haig wrote: 'What a wretched lot of weaklings we have in high places at the present time!'

Meanwhile Haig and Foch were skilfully co-ordinating their attacks and trying as best they could to conserve their forces' mechanical spearheads. Their belief in coming victory was seen to be justified when on 27 September the British, Australians and Americans made a break through the Hindenberg Line twelve miles wide and six miles deep. German resistance was finally breaking and, as Haig visited Foch on 6 October, the Marshal handed him a newspaper with the accompanying words, 'Here you have the immediate result of the British piercing the Hindenberg line. The enemy has asked for an armistice.'[25] Victory was now sure but during October 1918, when the armistice preliminaries were being discussed, large-scale fighting continued and British casualties alone amounted to a further 5438 officers and 115,608 soldiers. To the inexpressible relief of all on the allied side the armistice was at length concluded on 11 November.

Nothing was easy for the land commanders in France but under the guidance of a Lowland Scottish soldier, the British Empire, together with its allies, finally succeeded in defeating the world's premier military power. As John Terraine put it: 'Under his dogged leadership over a period of three years his troops had endured its highest casualties in any war, suffered one of its worst defeats and won one of its most decisive victories in the field.'[26] Whether there could have been a better way of winning than through the carnage of the war's main theatre on the Western Front is open to debate, but it must not be forgotten that in the war three and a half million men were used, under lesser generals, in 'side shows' that achieved comparatively little of strategic value.

In his first formal public address after the war Haig addressed the students of St Andrews University. By this time his final war dispatches had been circulated explaining his conduct of the war, including the reasons for continuing the battle of the Somme until summer had turned to winter, and for keeping Third Ypres going through to November. The subject he chose at St Andrews was morale, the superior confidence of the British forces. He was unapologetic. 'Our courage was heightened and our resolve made stronger by the conviction that we were fighting, not only for ourselves and for our empire, but for a world ideal in which God was with us.'[27]

It was a theme to stir the idealism of the young and inevitably alert his critics, but for such a firm believer it lay at the root of his determined optimism. Such post hoc justification through his dispatches or his address at St Andrews cannot, of course, satisfy Haig's determined critics. Any observer of his term as commander-in-chief is led to wonder whether a relatively unimaginative Haig, armed with such moral certainty, considered alternatives to the Western Front less strongly than he might have done, was led to retain commanders when they had shown serious limitations, was less eager to penetrate the minds of his opponents than some of his other great predecessors, and as a firm believer with a strong Calvinistic streak, was more eager than some to accept the terrible blood-letting before victory was achieved. Equally, one must acknowledge that like the American Federal general, Ulysses Grant, he had an indomitable offensive spirit and under this commander his men's morale never failed and it was the Germans, faced with such obstinacy, together with the skilful handling of new weapons against them and the prospect of fresh American manpower, that were forced to acknowledge defeat.

After the war Haig devoted his life to his ex-servicemen, including officers. His great influence was crucial towards the amalgamation of the different ex-servicemen's associations into the British Legion. Haig was the Legion's first President but despite his best efforts in the post-war years those who had served with him in France, particularly the disabled, faced a terrible struggle to gain employment. Haig worked as hard as ever; the night before his death he was answering personal letters from ex-servicemen.

Haig died in the year preceding the Wall Street crash. He missed the darkest hour of the modern capitalist system and the sharp recovery from 1933 onwards fuelled in part by preparations for a resumption of the war which, despite the immense sacrifices and achievements of Haig and his men, was yet unresolved.

≈

CHAPTER NINE

WORLD WAR TWO –
DAVID STIRLING (1915–1990)

'We are pilgrims, Master; we shall go
Always a little further'

J.E. Flecker, 'The Golden Journey to Samarkand'
(Inscription on the Clock, Bradbury Lines, Hereford)

T HE CONDITIONS OF WAR during World War Two and the
challenge its commanders faced were quite different from those
of the previous conflict in France where for much of the time two
sides occupied fixed trench lines or prepared for bloody set piece
offensives in which material gains were – until the final stages
at least – measured in yards. In comparison the main theatres of
World War Two saw movement and mobility: in North Africa the
two sides oscillated along the 1400 mile-long coastal strip while in
Russia, after the Germans penetrated to the gates of Moscow and
Leningrad, the Russians were to drive them back a full 1000 miles
to Berlin. It is therefore fitting that David Stirling, a champion of
mobility, should be different from the dour, endlessly determined
Douglas Haig and, indeed, different from the other earlier Scottish
commanders who fought on behalf of the British establishment. While
they were professional soldiers, Stirling's service was limited to the six
years of war and even then he was much too restless and unorthodox
to remain in an established regiment. Stirling was a brilliant eccentric
who fitted no mould. After having discarded his uniform he spent a
further forty-five eventful, if largely unfulfilled, years in a Britain that
was far less interested in his multi-racial and environmental objectives
than in shorter-term aims. His ideas were fifty years or more ahead of
their time.

Unlike the other commanders considered in this book Stirling never rose to high rank, never commanded more than a regiment and never took part in a great battle. The unit he created came to be known as L detachment of the SAS brigade; the SAS stood for the Special Air Service which, in fact, did not exist and, when asked, Stirling would reply that the L referred to learners! A senior officer from the 'later' SAS, General Sir Peter de la Billiere, has called Stirling a modern Robin Hood and this is a fair description of a man who placed such emphasis on secrecy and surprise together with the need to keep one step ahead of his opponents.[1] Stirling insisted on working with small numbers of men – in his case units of three- or four-man patrols, with the ability and firepower to penetrate silently behind formal defence lines and to inflict disproportionately large amounts of damage. The revolutionary part of Stirling's thinking lay in his firm belief that his handful of men constituted a powerful strategic weapon which, used properly, could provide an effective short cut to the terrible costs of orthodox warfare.

Despite his essential unorthodoxy, many other parallels can be drawn between David Stirling and the earlier Scottish commanders: he was unfailingly patriotic; like Sir John Moore and Sir Ralph Abercromby he was temperamentally unable to stop taking risks; like Montrose he was an idealist, unafraid to swim against the accepted precepts of contemporary wisdom; like Sir John Hepburn with his Scottish brigade he was an elitist (although Stirling's elitism depended as much on his companions' standards of performance as on their backgrounds); and finally, like the vast majority of his illustrious predecessors, he believed firmly in an all-seeing God – in Stirling's words 'le bon dieu of soldiers and civilians alike'.

David Stirling came from a Scottish family with a long and distinguished record of service to the Stuart cause. Their ancestral seat was at Kier in the geographic triangle bounded by Doune, Dunblane and the city of Stirling, just north of the traditional gateway to northern Scotland where so many important battles had been fought against southern invaders. David was one of six children, four boys and two girls. His father, General Archibald Stirling, had married somewhat late in life and, after meritorious service in World War One and while the children were still young, inclined towards a scholarly and somewhat reclusive life so that for the most part the children were brought up by their mother, a Lovat, who was far younger than her husband. She allowed her children a loose rein, although the practice of religion figured highly in a family that has remained proudly Catholic.

David Stirling was a difficult child, wilful and endlessly mischievous, whose early problems were compounded by a speech impediment that was only cured by an operation. When young, following a quarrel or setback, he tended to take himself off for long periods at a time. Like other male members of the family he was sent as a boarder to Ampleforth College, in his case before he was nine years of age. The school's maxim was 'a love of God and a responsibility to one's country and fellow man,'[2] but such moral convictions appeared to have no immediate effect upon the young David Stirling for he showed little inclination to work hard in any area of school life. On entry he was quite small compared with many of his friends, but he went through a remarkable burst of growth so that, by the time he was admitted to Cambridge University, he was six feet five inches tall. At Cambridge he succeeded in distinguishing himself, although not at his studies, since much of his enthusiasm and energy were given to nearby Newmarket, where he considered himself something of an expert at backing horses, and to the many and various parties that abounded. There were echoes of St Augustine when in later life he talked about Cambridge with his biographer Alan Hoe: 'Cambridge was fun in those days. If there was a serious side to life it totally escaped me. I knew that eventually I would have to face the realities of my future life but – not yet.'[3]

His industrious search after pleasure resulted in him being sent down. His senior tutor allowed him to select three from the twenty-three offences brought against him; the three he chose were those he thought would be least offensive to his mother.

There followed an attempt to become an artist but after an enjoyable year with the Bohemian group in Paris, his tutor gave him the sad news that, while he certainly possessed the creative talent, he lacked the necessary drawing skills to succeed. After a crisis meeting with his mother he decided on an architectural career. Lacking any ability at mathematics and with little skill in accurate drawing, this failed too.

During a subsequent discussion with his mother he told her he wanted to be the first man to climb Everest; nothing would deter him from what he saw as a five-year project, and permission was granted. His first year was spent with two German guides climbing in Switzerland, at the end of which he enlisted in the Scots Guards supplementary reserve (his father's regiment) whose methods of training by no means impressed him. In mid-1938 he broke his obligation to attend their camps and parades by journeying to Canada where he planned to work his way across the country climbing its peaks and travelling on horseback along the length of the continental divide. In British Columbia he became a cowboy finding that cold nights under the stars after full days in the saddle helped to give him the physical toughening-up he sought so keenly. The winter of 1938–9 was spent climbing in the Rocky mountains, from where he intended working his way down the Rio Grande to Mexico, but this project was abandoned when he learned of the outbreak of war. He telephoned his mother at Kier for advice; she replied succinctly, 'Return home by the cheapest possible means.'

He was soon back in uniform. At twenty-four, junior guardsman David Stirling was an easily recognisable figure. Even among tall men his six feet five inch frame made him stand out, as did his physical strength, and he was not less noticeable for personal attitude. Like many others who attended the dreaded Guards Depot at Pirbright he found the endless 'square bashing' irksome, but he was even more impatient with many of the lectures and training procedures based for the most part on the instructors' experiences during the previous war. His scepticism and critical observations were not always appreciated and characteristically he found relief in London nightlife, invariably returning later than was allowed and being confined to barracks for frequent and lengthy periods. On completion of his training his report described him as 'an irresponsible and unremarkable soldier'.

Pirbright was followed by a posting to the 5th Battalion the Scots Guards, the 'Snowballers', who were to be trained as part of a proposed Expeditionary Force to Finland. Here Stirling could excel and he was a revelation to the Senior staff: his days in the Swiss Alps had made him a proficient skier and he was rapidly promoted to sergeant and made an instructor. When Finland collapsed he returned to Pirbright where the routine was relieved by visits to White's Club in London.

It was there that he heard of plans to raise a unit of army commandos, highly trained men who would be used to destroy specific targets of importance. Stirling volunteered. By now his family background and the qualities he had shown with the 'Snowballers' caused him to be accepted as a newly commissioned lieutenant. As a Commando he revelled both in the company of fiercely dedicated companions and in the demanding training set them. He was caught up in the general air of expectancy that is inseparable from such units, although whilst they were training in Scotland he was highly critical of the noise created by the relatively large groups involved, which seemed to him contrary to the teaching he was being given about the art of silent killing. Stirling was maturing: he was less prone to moodiness and personal withdrawal and in the process of training emerged as a gently spoken, superbly fit man both liked and listened to by his Commando soldiers. Inevitably he could never resist challenging perceived wisdoms, but as Ernie Bond, his platoon sergeant, said: 'He never flapped and no matter how quickly things happened you always had the feeling that he'd already thought things out.'[4]

As part of 8 Commando due to take part with others in an attack on Rhodes, Stirling and his platoon sailed to the Middle East; on the journey out he played cards with Randolph Churchill, also a young officer with 8 Commando, who learning from Evelyn Waugh about Stirling's love of cards and backgammon had sought him out. It cost Churchill a good deal of money. Stirling summed up his opponent – as he would others – with clinical accuracy, concluding that Randolph so loved to talk he could never concentrate long enough on his cards to win.

After the Germans entered Cyrenaica it was proposed to disband the Commandos, who had taken part in three costly raids from the sea. Despite their continuing day and night exercises, however, Stirling entered enthusiastically into the Cairo night life, taking full advantage of the fact that his brother, Bill, was part of the British Embassy staff there and had a spacious flat which acted as David's base. Although David Stirling was never absent from exercises, a series of escapades in the British military hospital led to the ordering of a Board of Officers to decide if he were a malingerer, or even whether he should be court-martialled for cowardice.

Quite unaware of the proposed Board, Stirling met Captain Jock Lewes, also of 8 Commando, who had acquired fifty parachutes destined for India. Lewes had obtained permission for himself and 'half a dozen others' to conduct informal experiments with them. To Lewes, an ex-Oxford rowing blue, who was eager to see further action, they seemed to offer an alternative to the seaborne landings that had failed. Stirling agreed to take part in Lewes' experiment to deliver combat troops by means of parachute. On his initial jump Stirling's parachute caught on the aircraft's tailplane and ripped. After an alarmingly rapid descent, his body drove into the ground and his spine hit a boulder which, to all appearances, paralysed his legs. Stirling recovered consciousness to find himself in hospital and it was only after what he saw as agonisingly slow progress that he began to recover some movement; it took a week to move his toes after which progress was more rapid. The period of enforced inaction gave him the opportunity to consider the purpose of the Commandos and his own role in the war. Similar periods of inaction had led other men, notably Winston Churchill between the wars after being knocked down by an American cab and John F. Kennedy, forced to lie flat on his back after his boat had been sunk, to reconsider the direction their careers should take.

David Stirling's thoughts centred on the offensive potential in the use of small formations of like-minded men. He firmly rejected the feasibility of landing Commandos from the sea against strongly defended positions. But his mind kept returning to the great sea of sand, about the size of India, to the south of the narrow coastal strip in North Africa where fighting was being conducted between the British 8th Army and Erwin Rommel's German Afrika corps. To be effective, commando-like groups must at all costs preserve surprise, potency and mobility. How could this best be done? From his hospital bed Stirling tried his new ideas out on Jock Lewes, his fellow Commando and parachutist, and together they concluded that, if men were to be dropped to sabotage rear installations, such as aircraft and fuel, they would have to be able to get away in vehicles waiting for them at the edge of the desert. With his trained mind Jock Lewes forced Stirling to define his own ideas more carefully. Whatever the actual means of delivery, Stirling became quite clear that such patrols would not just be nuisance raiders but would constitute a strategic military option, and their personnel must be directly under the control of the theatre commander. If they were to fall into the hands of lower authorities his highly trained men were only too likely to be poached.

Stirling was aware that the deputy chief of general staff at the time was General Neil Ritchie: somehow he had to engineer an interview with Ritchie and persuade him not only about the feasibility of his plan but for him to recommend it to his senior commander as well. Still in his hospital bed but with the valuable assistance of Jock Lewes, Stirling wrote out a memorandum of action for a special service unit to coincide with the November 1941 offensive of 8th Army. The details were logically and clearly expressed but the memorandum was handwritten in pencil, and did not follow the style required for staff papers at that time.

As ever, Stirling's approach was unusual. One blistering hot morning in July 1941 a car drove up to the main entrance of Middle East headquarters and a young officer in battledress, sporting the single pip of the most junior commissioned rank, climbed out and, using crutches, swung his body up to the entrance. Joining a group of visitors he was halfway through the entrance gate when the guard checked him. 'Sir, your pass, please.' Stirling replied, 'Oh, yes of course,' and fumbled in his pockets. This was followed by an apology. 'I'm sorry, but I must have left it behind. I've got an important appointment and I'm late. You couldn't overlook it just this once, could you?'

Although the Stirling charm was working overtime, it was met with the reply: 'No pass, no entry, sir. You'll have to go back to the hospital for it.'

During this exchange Stirling had noticed a gap in the perimeter wire near the guardhouse. He withdrew and, leaning against a tree, waited. When a couple of staff cars drove up together and the passes of their occupants were being examined he stood his crutches against the tree and squeezed through the gap behind the sentries. With no crutches he lurched precariously as he hurried towards the path leading to the main building. Near the steps of the building a sentry noticed him, and then saw his crutches leaning against the tree. 'Sir!' the sentry shouted, and then bellowed, 'Stop that man!' By this time Stirling had disappeared through the front door.

Stirling not only lacked a pass, but he had no appointment, and he quickly became aware of the noise of pursuit from outside growing louder. He staggered down one corridor and then another, until he came to a door marked 'Adjutant-General'. This seemed important enough to begin with. He pushed it open and walked in, coming face to face with a major whom he had antagonised at Pirbright. Stirling explained himself and said he had plans which would severely disable the German air force on the ground. As he began to take his memorandum out of his pocket, the major stopped him with the words: 'Whatever lunatic idea you have, Stirling, forget it. I'll do everything in my considerable power to make sure that you go back (to your unit) and as soon as possible.'[5] As Stirling saluted and went towards the door the major's phone rang. It was a complaint from the sentry on the main gate about an officer breaking past his guard post.

Stirling hurried away unsteadily, diving down another corridor before he paused at a door marked D.C.G.S. (Deputy Chief of the General Staff). He knocked and walked in, where he found General Ritchie, deputy chief of staff, Middle East forces. Ritchie looked up in surprise. David Stirling apologised for his entry but insisted he had vital business for the general's attention. Stirling was given a seat and, incredibly, the general began to read the memorandum intently, despite it being handwritten and in pencil. He did so for ten minutes and then said brusquely: 'I think this may be the sort of plan we are looking for. I will discuss it with the commander-in-chief and let you know our decision in the next day or so.' Before he let Stirling go, he explained that a major from the adjutant general's branch would have to work with him on the organisational side if the commander-in-chief decided to go ahead.[6] He pressed his buzzer and Stirling's old foe from Pirbright appeared. The General explained how 'the Major' might have to support Stirling at short notice. When both had been dismissed into the corridor the major spat out his message: 'I will do my duty no matter how disagreeable, but I trust, Stirling, you will not be expecting any favours.' In the next few hours General Ritchie made himself familiar with David Stirling's credentials, namely that he came from an old Scots family with two brothers in the Scots Guards and another currently third secretary with the British Embassy in Cairo, while his cousin, Lord Lovat, was the commander of the Scottish Commandos. There were advantages in having such powerful connections, even if they had not been consulted. While the possibility of a court martial was almost bound to have come out, Stirling's parachuting venture was likely to have ended any suspicions about his nerve and General Auchinleck, a Scot who would have known of Stirling's pedigree, would have surely discounted them.

Providentially, David Stirling's proposal came at a favourable time as Churchill was vigorously pressing the commander-in-chief to attack Rommel. Three days after meeting Ritchie, Stirling was summoned to a meeting with Auchinleck attended by Ritchie and Smith, the Pirbright major. His plan was rigorously questioned, but at the end of the meeting Stirling was promoted to captain and given authority to recruit up to six officers and sixty soldiers, a high proportion of whom could be senior ranks. The naming of the unit came about vicariously. At that time a part of the deception operations organised by Brigadier Dudley Clarke to unsettle the Germans had been the creation of something called the First Special Air Service brigade. This in fact did not exist, but under its title dummy parachutists and mock gliders were positioned to suggest the build-up of a specialist glider and airborne unit. Brigadier Clarke proposed that Stirling adopt the name SAS and thus his embryonic force became L detachment, SAS brigade.

Stirling started recruiting his officers from 8 Commando, and to his delight he 'captured' Jock Lewes, together with four others. Last of these was Paddy Mayne, a renowned Irish international rugby player, who was at the time in close arrest for striking his commanding officer. The NCOs followed, including among them some from Jock Lewes' earlier period of service and also Ernie Bond, Stirling's former platoon sergeant. By the end of an afternoon he had all the soldiers he needed.

Because of the antipathy of the staff major responsible for their administrative support, the embryo unit was issued with ancient tents and virtually no furniture with which to equip them, so Stirling solved this problem by mounting a night raid on a New Zealand unit which was away on exercise. This produced a full set of furnishings, including a bar and a piano. The Egyptians, who were known to be expert thieves, were suspected of the theft and the culprits were never found.

Jock Lewes devised a ferocious training programme which Stirling decided that all ranks would undergo. Designed to build up physical stamina and confidence and to improve the speed of reactions it was followed by the experience of surviving on minimum water during the blazing heat of the Egyptian days and, crucially, the practice of desert navigation. Last of all came parachute training in which anyone not reaching the required standards had to leave immediately. There were no recognised training methods, and L detachment ended up jumping off a vehicle moving at 30 miles an hour. As regards explosives, after an expert supplied by Major Smith proved distinctly unhelpful, the remarkable Jock Lewes devised a bomb which was a mixture of plastic explosive, thermite and oil that on impact both ignited and exploded. Lewes' bomb was ideal for men to carry, being malleable and capable of being fashioned into blocks weighing rather less than a pound.

The new unit was now ready for action, but Stirling first set his teams a challenge which he hoped would help demonstrate their competence. He struck a bet with an RAF group captain that they could enter RAF Heliopolis airfield at any time and place bombs on the aircraft there (it was agreed that sticky labels would be used instead of the actual bombs). Despite guards being put on full alert and the mounting of regular air patrols, all the groups succeeded in moving across ninety miles of desert to approach the aerodrome without being seen; they then successfully penetrated the perimeter defences to leave labels on all the aircraft. Stirling won his bet and some senior officers at Middle East Land Forces were impressed; more importantly, the confidence of L detachment SAS increased immeasurably.

General Auchinleck's offensive was set for 18 November 1941 and L detachment took upon itself the task of being dropped by parachute with the objective of attacking five forward airfields. The detachment's strength at this time was a modest sixty-two men, making five patrols of twelve men each with an officer in command. Upon reaching their target the officer was free to split them into smaller groups if he thought it necessary. David Stirling himself commanded one of the patrols.

The results were disastrous. Windspeeds up to thirty knots were being recorded, twice the maximum for jumping, but nevertheless David Stirling went ahead, in spite of advice from the brigadier who was co-ordinating the operation that it should be cancelled. As a result the drop was wildly inaccurate. Of the five aircraft used, one was never heard of again. Another was downed and its members became casualties or were 'taken prisoner'. Three aircraft released their parachutists, a number of whom were injured in the heavy drop. Of the original sixty-two men just twenty-two returned and only Stirling's and Mayne's groups reached the enemy positions, but without the bombs and other equipment with which to inflict the proposed damage. Remnants of three groups successfully made their way back to the proposed desert rendezvous with the Long Range

Desert Group,[7] and during the 200-mile drive back to the Long Range Desert Group's main base, David Stirling was silent and absorbed: by its end he had decided that dropping the SAS by parachute was too hazardous, and that from now on he would have to persuade the LRDG both to carry them reasonably close to the target and pick them up afterwards.

With the failure of their first important mission Stirling feared they would be disbanded, but General Ritchie, now promoted to 8th Army commander, had known of the appalling weather conditions and remained sympathetic. What they could not afford was another débacle. Using his depleted numbers, on 22 December Stirling was ready for his second operation, also aimed against enemy airfields but with the start point at the oasis of Jalo along with the LRDG. The composite plan was simple enough, even if its implementation was far less easy. On 8 December Stirling and Mayne, with ten men, would set off in LRDG vehicles and be taken without striking distance of Sirte, the airfield considered most important at that time. The day after, Lewes would embark for Agheila airfield. Both patrols would attack on the night of 14–15 December. Later, on 18 December, Captain Bill Fraser would move to attack Agedabia airfield.

On their approach the LRDG vehicles were seen from the air and strafed, but Stirling was not to be diverted and, with just one other companion, went on to Sirte airfield. To their dismay, while they lay up close to the airfield waiting to synchronise their attack with Mayne's, all the aircraft took off. However, Mayne's party destroyed twenty-four aircraft at Tamit airfield without suffering a single casualty. Lewes too had found his airfield empty but Fraser's four man patrol destroyed no less than thirty-seven aircraft at Agedabia without losing a single man. L detachment had destroyed sixty-one aircraft, vehicles and a number of enemy soldiers: to equal such a total the RAF would have needed to mount a whole series of bombing raids, and even then the airfield might well have been alerted to the coming attacks. Working on the principle of reinforcing success David Stirling decided to set off the very next day and repeat the exercise. This time they destroyed another thirty aircraft, but they also lost Jock Lewes, and Fraser's party, having missed the rendezvous, had to march 200 miles in eight days to reach safety.

Because of their small numbers and the important part Jock Lewes had played in every stage of the group's development, his death was severely felt. On the last day of 1941, a member of his group, Jim Almonds, wrote: 'I thought of Jock, one of the bravest men I have ever met, an officer and a gentleman, lying out there in the desert barely covered with sand. No one will stop by his grave or pay homage to a brave heart that has ceased to beat – not even a stone marks the spot.'[8]

This time David Stirling did not mind reporting the outcome of his raids to General Auchinleck who, after congratulating him, asked Stirling about his future plans. Stirling emphasised the importance of security in their case: if their patrols could reach the target areas undetected then anything was possible. Stirling boldly told Auchinleck of his initial stipulation that they should work to the commander-in-chief and no one else, and that there must be no radio or written communications regarding L detachment's movements and targets. Auchinleck agreed to the conditions and asked how many more men were needed to build on their remarkable success so far; Stirling requested fifteen men and undertook to strike again in about three weeks' time, when there was no moon. To this Auchinleck replied that fifteen men were not enough and that Stirling could recruit up to six more officers and a further forty men, concluding the meeting with the words: 'Well done, Stirling, and from now you have the rank of major which may help a little.'

David Stirling had a week before he returned to the base oasis of Jalo for his final preparations. It was not just the Germans and Italians that he feared but also a double-pronged threat from his own side. Rigid and traditionalist staff officers at the headquarters were keenly jealous of the 'jollies' made by his special forces and the rapid promotion of their madcap leader (Stirling's description of these was 'fossilised layers of shit'). He was also afraid that the SOE (Special Operations Executive) functioning in the Middle East at that time would, before long, claim all secret operations as theirs and insist on bringing his tiny L detachment under their control, which Stirling knew would inevitably change, if not destroy, its function. To prevent any telephone conversations being overheard he deserted his tiny office at headquarters for his brother's spacious flat in Cairo. This not only appeared more secure but was far more convenient for social arrangements and even revolver shooting matches.

Threatened with so many doubters and predators, Stirling realised that activity was paramount: he needed to demonstrate further the remarkable capability of his small force, and to show that as a strategic weapon it could equally be moved to other theatres of war and used against other targets. Despite Cairo's social diversions Stirling successfully tackled many of his basic administrative problems. His recruitment needs were temporarily solved by absorbing a squadron of Free French parachutists, highly trained men eager to fight. And, although Middle East headquarters objected strongly, Stirling decided his force should have an identity of its own. He accepted the pattern submitted by his sergeant, Bob Tait, for a badge consisting of a flaming sword crossed at the base with the scrolled motto, 'Who Dares Wins': his men were to wear the wings on their shoulders after completing their parachute training and on their breasts after taking part in a successful operation. Visiting General Auchinleck wearing the new insignia, he found Auchinleck not only raised no objections but actually admired it.

Another move forward for L detachment SAS was the close relationship which David Stirling formed with Middle East Headquarters Air Reconnaissance unit, where aerial photographs were so vital for men who proposed approaching installations at night.

The detachment's projected new target was the port of Bouerat on the North African coast, where with help from two members of the Special Boat Squadron equipped with a collapsible canoe, Stirling hoped to mine fuel tankers. After a hazardous approach the raiders found the harbour empty of ships and had to content themselves with blowing up installations and fuel tanks, but the Bouerat operation was constructive in that it helped to demonstrate the flexibility of the SAS concept. Despite losing their radio vehicle after being bombed from the air (which meant a complete break in communications) they reached the target, their only casualties on this occasion being the three wireless operators in the vehicle. Stirling believed it was still possible they were captured rather than killed.

Stirling's next target was twofold: the major port of Benghazi together with its adjacent airfields. The raid developed into a series of breathtaking incidents involving Fitzroy MacLean and Randolph Churchill. MacLean had been persuaded into joining the SAS by Stirling who told him 'it was a good thing to be in', and he had been put in charge of their two inflatable boats. Randolph Churchill, while a previous member of 8 Commando, was included for the very good reason that if he witnessed their work it could only help their cause with his father. For thirty-six hours Stirling and his SAS moved around the harbour area of Benghazi, at one stage openly attempting to inflate their boats, but because of problems with these craft they destroyed no ships, although on their departure they torched a petrol dump outside the town. While they acquired priceless information for a future raid, the immediate results of the foray were somewhat disappointing.

During this period David Stirling was working under tremendous strain. He believed it essential he should lead his men into action, but while the others were able to enjoy short and much-needed periods of relaxation, he was forced to spend his time trying to obtain supplies and support for the next operation. It was, therefore, to his considerable surprise when Middle East Land Forces asked for his help and guidance over how the SAS could relieve the German air attacks on a vital convoy running the Mediterranean gauntlet to Malta. He asked for the French forces involved to be put fully under his command, and promised that during the next dark period of 13–14 June he would commit eight patrols to attack eight different targets, all of them airfields, including one at Heraklion in Crete. A maximum of five men would make up each patrol and six of the patrols would be French.

Stirling's own patrol (including corporals Seekings and Cooper) succeeded in their task of blowing up aircraft spares at Benina airport, the German's main repair base for fighters and bombers. They ignited a vast fuel dump but placed most of their bombs in hangars full of ME 110s and Stuka aircraft. Mayne's patrol had far greater difficulties. At Berka airfield their arrival coincided with an RAF raid, so the airfield was full of wide-awake German troops. After laying bombs on a fuel dump they had to fight their way off the aerodrome, and even then the Germans dispatched vehicles to capture them. They split up and after individual fire fights ran into each other on the way back to the agreed rendezvous. A day later they were back with Stirling and the Long Range Desert Group. The French patrols experienced mixed fortunes but the one under Colonel Bergé's command that raided Heraklion airfield succeeded in destroying twenty-one planes, four trucks and a petrol dump. In total thirty-seven aircraft were accounted for, together with thirty aircraft engines and various fuel and ammunition dumps. With good reason David Stirling could claim the raids had some effect on easing the path of the Malta convoy, but its losses were still very great: out of seventeen ships only two reached Malta, but their cargoes kept the island going for eight weeks, at the end of which five more ships got through and Malta was saved.

Since its inception the SAS had destroyed a total of 143 planes alone and by now it had more than 100 trained members. At this time the desert war was going very badly for 8th Army. Tobruk had fallen and the Germans had already crossed into Egypt. It was a great opportunity for the SAS to show its effectiveness and Stirling accordingly decided the best use for his men was to attack the German airfields that were providing support for their advancing troops. On 1 July he planned to raid six or seven airfields – but in a new and daring fashion. He planned to keep his men some three weeks in the desert, using new American jeeps which had been fitted with obsolete Vickers K aircraft guns. This was in itself a story. By chance Stirling had stopped at an RAF workshop to see what he could pick up. They had 12 Vickers K guns and told him he could have the lot. He piled them into the back of his staff car and drove to a Royal Engineers maintenance depot where they fitted out his own vehicle (the so-called 'Blitz Buggy') and most of the jeeps with fore and aft guns.[9]

As before, the operation was masterminded from his brother's flat in Cairo, the centre of so many other activities. 'On the sofa were sitting some girls and some other officers discussing the racing form at Gezira, whilst across all this we talked about bearings and petrol and ammunition, or sat sprawled on the floor over maps of the desert trying to think above the sound of the gramophone.'[10] Meanwhile the Germans were only forty miles from Alexandria. It was a long and dangerous drive from Cairo, initially through German positions and then in most difficult conditions. The intention was to strike at the airfields on 8 July at 1 a.m. in a raid timed to coincide with a planned counter-attack by 8th Army: one large group under Stirling and Mayne would harry a line of airfields from Fuka to Bagush, a second group would raid Sidi Barrani and a third the airfields in the areas of El Dhaba.

In the event Mayne experienced difficulties with wet fuses but still managed to destroy more than twenty aircraft, while Stirling decided to sweep across the airfield in his jeeps, firing machine guns into the undamaged aircraft and thus accounting for a further twelve planes. The other patrols inflicted damage on another twelve aircraft between them. The return journey was again punctuated by air attacks and pursuit by enemy vehicles but all reached the rendezvous uninjured except for one Frenchman who had a shell splinter in his thumb.

Stirling constantly strove to vary the pattern of his raids in order to keep the enemy guessing. Now he intended to increase operations from the moonless periods of each month to striking every few days, but to do this he needed regular replenishments of supplies along with daily (and accurate) intelligence reports.

By this time the Afrika corps was feeling the effects of the SAS operations. The very scale of their successes forced them to be taken seriously and the title 'The phantom major' was freely used by the Germans. Yet amazingly Stirling was still not being given due credit by many at Middle East headquarters, who insisted on labelling his patrols as saboteurs. 'I still had not succeeded in getting those morons to understand that this was a new form of warfare we were developing, not a young man's whim. *The SAS was a new weapon; this was an absolutely fundamental principle and, if it was allowed to develop and mature, it would be accepted as a permanent feature in the British Army Order of Battle.*'[11] The SAS was unquestionably based on maximum achievement for minimum cost and it seemed almost incomprehensible that many of the staff could not acknowledge its almost unlimited potential, though it was not warfare as they knew it. Most importantly, in David Stirling the SAS had a leader equal to the task. As Lieutenant Colonel Peniakoff (Popski) described him: 'With a light heart and cool courage he inspired in his men a passionate devotion and led them to thrilling adventures. Where we plodded he pranced.'[12]

The SAS's next target was a major airfield near Fuka which held a number of JU52s, the German passenger aircraft in such short supply. They attacked when the moon was full: twenty jeeps in double line formation burst onto the airfield, their sixty-eight machine guns firing at 1000 rounds per minute. Timing and direction-finding played a vital part in their success and their only casualty was one of the gunners. Back in the desert they buried him in the middle of nowhere and stood for two minutes round the pathetic heap of sand and stones, each with their own thoughts. While Stirling was planning to spend twelve days on another daring project, harrying soft-skinned targets near the line at El Alamein, he was given the signal to return. The orders became more pressing and back at headquarters, he heard of the new project with dismay. It was a repeat of Stirling's earlier plans to attack Rommel's supply depots at Tobruk, Benghazi and Barce, but this time the raids were to be large-scale, with the SAS plus other troops (250 men in all) and 80–100 vehicles, in an attack on Benghazi alone. Another force would attack and destroy Barce, whilst a third, with naval and Commando support, would take and hold Tobruk for a short time.

Stirling was given the bait of having much greater responsibility in the future but he knew the attacks went against all the principles he had followed so far: they would include men who had not undergone the rigorous SAS training; the chances of surprise in such a large operation were slim in the extreme: above all Stirling hated being tied so closely to a long-term, pre-arranged time schedule. The inspiration behind the plan was Colonel John Haselden, an Arab expert with no experience comparable with that of the SAS. Winston Churchill who was in Cairo at that time changing both the theatre commander and the leader of 8th Army met Stirling and listened to his own plan to attack Benghazi and also his fears for such a large undertaking. But the Benghazi raid went ahead and, in the event, it was a disaster. The Germans were expecting it and a quarter of the SAS force taking part was lost. Only at Barce was the attack successful, where it was carried out on SAS lines of action.

Amazingly, after such a setback Stirling found the SAS was now an accepted part of the order of battle and could be recruited up to regimental strength – something around 1000 men, although Stirling realised that now the SAS was an official regiment he could raise sister regiments both in the UK and other theatres of war. For instance by January 1943 Stirling was thinking of bringing the SAS in North Africa up to brigade strength (3000 men). But this was in the future: now more than anything else the failure of Haselden's plans had highlighted the SAS's virtues, its speed of planning and deployment, its versatility and competence in action, the courage of all its members and the leadership qualities of Stirling himself. Belatedly, the staff began to recognise the calibre of a man who, at twenty-five, had risen from second lieutenant to lieutenant colonel in little more than a year, and to acknowledge that not since the Anglo-Boer War had a new regiment been added to the army establishment. Many also began to admit that this man might be far more formidable than the playboy they had first thought him to be.

Stirling's was, of course, by no means the largest or, despite his successes, the most renowned of the private armies proposing to exploit the military possibilities of the vast sea of sand and it was obviously important that these various forces should be co-ordinated. Probably best known was the Long Range Desert Group, invaluable for providing transport for Stirling's SAS and other irregulars, but whose basic role was to operate deep in the desert gathering information about enemy movements, etc. Also legendary were the Commandos who provided the first SAS personnel and with whom Stirling linked up for the Tobruk raid. Much of the Commandos' most responsible work, like the 1942 Dieppe Raid designed to test Hitler's defences against invasion, was of course carried out in North-west Europe. Active in the Mediterranean was the Special Boat Section founded as early as 1940 and hived off from the Commandos. Finally there were the other national groups like the Libyan Arab Force (Senussi Arabs, mainly refugees from Italian Cyrenaica), the Greek Sacred Squadron, fanatical Turkish fighters called Kalpaks and a force under the command of Major Vladimir Peniakoff (Popski's Private Army). Colonel Sean Hackett was appointed to the task of avoiding any serious duplication in their efforts and to maximising the effectiveness of their initiatives. Despite Stirling's early qualms the two men immediately developed a mutual liking and Hackett responded to Stirling's enthusiasm, approving his plans to destroy the aircraft and fuel dumps that could lead to a crippling of Rommel's logistic support. Stirling told Hackett he needed more men, and quickly; together they visited the new 8th Army commander, Bernard Montgomery, and Stirling put forward his request for 150 men, both experienced officers and NCOs. After Auchinleck and Ritchie, Montgomery's reaction was quite unexpected. He looked long and silently at both Stirling and Hackett before replying: 'If my understanding is correct you wish to take some of my men. You want only my best men; my most experienced and dependable men. I am very proud indeed of my men and I expect them to do great things in the very near future. What, Colonel Stirling, makes you assume that you can handle these men to greater advantage than myself? If I give them to you they will miss the offensive.'

Hackett entered the conversation at this point. 'Perhaps they won't be ready for the next offensive – but they'll be ready for the one after.' This was met by Monty's utterly confident riposte: 'I don't intend another offensive. The next one will be the last one. What's the matter? Why are you smiling, Stirling?'

'Nothing really, sir, but we heard that from the last general and the one before him.'

Monty's anger was unconcealed. 'You failed in Benghazi and come here asking, no, demanding the best of my men. In all honesty, Colonel Stirling, I'm not of a mind to associate myself with failure.' Monty swept out but invited them to lunch in the Headquarters mess at his expense. Both took full advantage of the offer. When he had calmed down David Stirling realised that, given Montgomery's attitude, he had again to make the SAS presence felt if it was not to be allowed to fade away. Previously he had intended a series of concentrated and unceasing raids against about 100 miles of Rommel's communications. Now he planned to form his experienced men into a squadron, with Mayne leading them, with the object of raiding the coast road and railway line to Mersa Matruh. He himself would have to concentrate on recruiting and training men at Kabrit, along the Suez Canal, in readiness for use by the end of November.

He submitted a plan to use the SAS in conjunction with Montgomery's next offensive in December. This was accepted and Stirling proposed he should accompany them as they moved to their rendezvous, in order to continue their training until the last moment. He promised Sean Hackett he would return as soon as possible. By now Monty had been won over and had been heard to say at dinner: 'The boy Stirling is mad. Quite, quite mad. However in war there is often a place for mad people . . . Yet if it comes off I don't mind saying it could have a really decisive effect on my forthcoming offensive.' The offensive proved successful and the SAS, while taking casualties which in percentage terms equalled those of the first parachute operation, played a valuable role in keeping large numbers of German manpower occupied. While they were taking a brief respite over Christmas 1942 Montgomery sent 500 cigarettes and a bottle of whisky for each man. Stirling returned to Middle East Headquarters, as promised, eager to establish a regiment of SAS in both the eastern and central Mediterranean, another for the projected Italian front and a fourth against the second front in Europe.

He decided to seal his SAS case by a bold coup: not only would be provide support for Monty but he himself would conduct a detailed reconnaissance for 8th Army and then continue on his journey in order to be the first formation to link up with the Allied 1st Army in northern Tunisia. For this purpose David Stirling's patrol was divided into two sections. The leading one under Captain Augustin Jordan was captured by a large Italian force on 28 January. Stirling's own party, with five jeeps and fourteen men, was aiming for the Gabes 'Gap' where there were considerable concentrations of enemy troops who unfortunately had been put on alert by the taking of Captain Jordan the day before. After successfully negotiating the Gap, Stirling found a deep wadi that appeared to offer perfect cover and fell into an exhausted sleep. He and his immediate companion, Lieutenant McDermott, were woken by a command in German. A small man waving a pistol led them to a company of 500 Germans, who by a remarkable chance had happened to be carrying out a training exercise to track down the SAS. Their captor turned out to be the unit dentist.

The man who had taken so many risks and handled his three-man patrols with such brilliance now found himself in German hands. In the past fourteen months his men had destroyed more than 400 aircraft, innumerable fuel dumps and caused widespread disruption – figures that could only confirm Stirling's claim that a new strategic weapon had been created. The question was, what would happen now that its mentor and leader had seemingly been taken out of the action? David Stirling's determination was not to be underrated. On the first evening of their captivity both Stirling and McDermott let out deafening yells and ran into the darkness relying on their speed and fitness to avoid recapture. They never met up again and Stirling covered at least ten miles before stopping on the fringes of a built up area. He was given refuge – along with tea and dates – by an Arab but moved off again when it was dark. As he was making his way to his patrol's agreed rendezvous he could not resist investigating an airfield that lay roughly on his course. Such information would be invaluable for a future SAS raid! Having spent three precious hours there and being further delayed by unexpectedly hard going, he laid up all day in sparse shrubland. In the late afternoon a young Arab came upon him and offered to take him to food and water. He led Stirling straight into the hands of an Italian unit of experienced soldiers. They bound him tightly and he was eventually flown to GAVI, a fortress sitting on top of a rocky outcrop – the Italian version of Colditz.

Here David Stirling was compelled to exchange the endless vistas of the desert, with its blood red sunsets and great canopy of stars, for a cell and the confined space of an exercise area. One daring escape attempt failed, but with the possibility of Italy's surrender and the likely repatriation of prisoners of war, further attempts were postponed. When the Germans took over GAVI Stirling was one of the last prisoners to be found, hiding in a cavity beneath a lavatory seat. On the train journey to Germany, Stirling and his friend, Jack Pringle, escaped from their cattle truck, only to be recaptured two days later. A few days afterwards they escaped again from a camp at Markt Pongau in Austria by throwing a blanket over the camp's perimeter fence before diving into the river at its base while they were being fired on by machine guns placed on the watch towers. Pursued by tracker dogs they reached the Alps but were betrayed by an Austrian farmworker and sent to Berlin. From there they went to Nuremberg and then to Marisch Trubau, a prison camp in Czechoslovakia, where Stirling gained the support of all the inmates for a mass escape to coincide with an attack by the Czech resistance. The Germans however were alerted to his plans and he was moved to Brunswick and finally, in August 1944, to Colditz. There Stirling and Pringle shared a cell with the legendary Douglas Bader.

In Colditz, escape was so difficult that it was virtually impossible and Stirling spent his time working on plans for the SAS role in the Far East, as well as taking advantage of the books in the prison's excellent library. It was April 1945 before he was released. When he returned to England, 'impatient to see my family and get back to the SAS,' he found the SAS, now increased to five brigades, was variously scattered in France, Germany and Norway. It had distinguished itself under the command of Brigadier 'Mad' Mike Calvert, although it had undoubtedly been used on more purely tactical operations than Stirling would ever have envisaged. Stirling subsequently had three meetings with Churchill to discuss the SAS role in the Far East, in particular a plan for cutting the great Manchurian railway and operations on the trunk roads from the north that were used to supply the Japanese army in Malaya. All this was rendered unnecessary however by the dropping of two atomic bombs and the consequent rapid surrender of Japan.

The war was over but David Stirling still had most of his life before him, and his subsequent activities not only reveal an essential part of the man but also help to explain the continuing role of the SAS unit he created.

Throughout most of his remaining forty-five years his questioning mind soared far beyond the imagination of others. But unlike his wartime career when the military authorities gave the 'boy Stirling' his head – principally because they had almost nothing to lose from his modest demands on their resources – in peacetime he found himself marginalised for his controversial and disturbing insights into contemporary problems. One great difficulty lay in Stirling's breadth of activity: part businessman, part military adventurer and part political philosopher, his ceaseless initiatives overlapped and could at times work against each other.

It has to be acknowledged that Stirling was often his own worst enemy in his commercial ventures. Brilliant at devising new business opportunities, he was repeatedly slow to relinquish his personal control and appoint the necessary managers. The truth is that Stirling, who had never really known personal financial hardship, was never a natural businessman: he was more a prophet and merchant adventurer, but one who would always sacrifice commercial success for wider principles.

In 1945 Stirling moved to Salisbury, Rhodesia. In Africa the precepts he had learnt at Ampleforth came back to him and he saw, as never before, that colour, race and creed were unimportant in the eyes of God. It was in the spirit of such principles that he floated the idealistic 'Capricorn Africa Society' which, with the USA as its model, was to be a great new dominion for the lands of eastern and central Africa stretching between the Abyssinian border and the Limpopo river.

His imagination was fired with the idea of a partnership within it of all races, creeds and colours, which with its immense resources he anticipated in the following century would be capable of equalling the success of the United States.

Stirling's grand concept was killed by Prime Minister Harold McMillan's pragmatic 'winds of change' speech that signalled approval of independent and competitive nationalism among the emergent African states. The moderate road of development as envisaged by the Capricorn Society could never hope to survive the pressing nationalist interests of the individual colonial territories, spanning as they did the two extremes of apartheid on the one hand and Marxist ideology on the other. Stirling's vision was for an Africa in the year 2053 rather than at the end of World War Two.

There followed many more projects, all stemming from Stirling's own strong sense of patriotism, his belief in democratic traditions and his concern both for world society and the planet it inhabited. He embarked on a television campaign to help rural Africans have a wider understanding of the world outside. At its peak his Television International Enterprises (TIE) operated twelve independent stations and supplied Africa, India and the Middle East with a whole series of programmes. Then just when it was becoming established, and could have made him extremely wealthy, he moved in another direction.

Stirling was an ardent environmentalist thirty years before the movement gathered strength worldwide. He strongly believed that nations which were determined on confrontation with their rivals were out of date and misguided, and that they should enter into a new atmosphere of trust in which mankind would aim to share amicably the world's resources, technological advances and educational facilities for the betterment of all. Africa was uppermost in his mind when he formulated these ideas. Even so it would be quite wrong to see David Stirling as no more than a starry-eyed idealist. He well knew that before such environmental ideas could become reality it was essential to meet both communist and nationalist adventurers in the fighting terms they understood, and it was here that he believed the SAS still had an important role to play.

While at the end of the war 'the British General Staff could see no proper role for the SAS'[13] and disbanded it on 8 October 1945, Stirling witnessed its rebirth as 21 SAS Regiment, a squadron of reservists and territorials amalgamated with the Artists' Rifles' territorials in London. Stirling kept himself at arms' length from his brainchild but during the 1950s he was to see the formation of 22 SAS Regiment by 'Mad' Mike Calvert when it operated along with normal British units in the jungles of Malaya, followed by a highly successful operation in the Oman and during the 1960s with General Sir Walter Walker in Borneo.

During 1963 Stirling himself took part in discussions at White's Club regarding possible military assistance to the beleaguered rulers

in the Yemen. The British government's problem was that a belliger-
ent Nasser of Egypt had landed troops to assist a military coup in
Yemen to oust the royalist government, and the ruling Iman had been
driven into the mountains. The Secretary of State for Foreign Affairs,
Alec Douglas-Home, explained to Stirling that since the tribes were
rallying round the Iman and as Egypt controlled only a few roads,
it would therefore be immoral for HM government to recognise the
new revolutionary power.

Stirling acted as both host and cover in a series of meetings with
Jim Johnson, the retired commanding officer of 21 SAS(TA), at the
end of which it was decided to infiltrate a small team of mercenaries
into Yemen with the purpose of attacking Egyptian aircraft there.
Naturally this was an initiative which the British government could
not recognise officially and there could be no question of using 22
SAS. As a result Johnny Cooper of L detachment days was given
command of a team largely made up of retired SAS personnel,
augmented by members of the French SAS. As well as their direct
raids they also trained the royalists to become a fighting force, with
such success that at the time of a ceasefire in 1965, a minimum of
54,000 Egyptian troops had been sucked into the Yemen conflict
with only a little progress to show for it.

At the same time Stirling was contacting Lieutenant Colonel John
Woodhouse, the then commander of the SAS whom he held in high
regard, to consider the most appropriate role for the modern SAS.
Fully aware of the USSR's subversive activities and their calculated
fostering of international terrorism in both the Middle East and
Africa, he gave it as his opinion that nothing was 'being done to
combat the growing and sinister communist influence'.[14] In certain
instances the SAS could oppose such forces successfully although
the roles assigned to it by the government would always be limited
by their political sensitivity. Encouraged by the successes of the
semi-irregulars in Yemen he considered setting up a service to act
in countries that Her Majesty's government could not assist overtly
and others that would never ask formally for SAS aid. Together with
Woodhouse, Stirling formed a security company called 'Watchguard
International' with certain moral restrictions placed upon its man-
date: its assistance was limited to the offer of instructional training
as opposed to active support and it would not accept a commission
from any government composed of a racial minority nor with policies

hostile to the British government. Stirling initially saw opportunities for Watchguard in the Middle East, but he realised its use was relevant in Africa as well, and he even considered offering a service to the CIA against, for instance, the drug barons that were cause for concern in South America.

An organisation such as Watchguard had to preserve its impartiality and Stirling, who was politically to the right of the average Conservative would never consider placing it unreservedly at the disposal of the British government, whatever its political hue. In any case the international situation was changing and in practical terms the agency suffered a serious setback by failing to disassociate itself from the 'Hilton assignment' episode of March 1971, when plans to liberate 140 prisoners of Colonel Gadaffi confined in the Tripoli Hilton were foiled by the Italian authorities. In 1972 Stirling severed his connection with Watchguard, but there were others who saw the potentialities of the idea and went on to make substantial profits in offering mercenaries in a less restricted way.

As late as 1986 Stirling entered the field of security again with a firm called KAS, which was far more limited in purpose than Watchguard and concentrated on issues particularly close to his heart. An offshoot called Country Guard gained some successes in the fight against poaching and Project LOCK was directed against the African poachers of rhinos and elephants, but the cost of the latter was high and he finally closed down KAS a few months before his death.

In the 1970s as Stirling turned his attention to problems within his home country he took renewed care to distance himself from the contemporary SAS. At a time of considerable and damaging industrial unrest, rising to a peak just prior to the election of Margaret Thatcher in 1979, he grew concerned over the danger of a slide into totalitarianism, fearing that the militant tendency working within the great unions could subvert the legitimate powers of Parliament. He therefore formed the 'Greater Britain League' to encourage trade union moderates to stand their ground, which later evolved into the Better Britain Society. This operation was unashamedly visionary, although perhaps as much a reaction to the widespread pessimism and major industrial difficulties that were being experienced during much of the 1970s. The movement's objectives included a new Bill of Rights and the devolution of legislative, administrative and financial powers to Scottish, Welsh and English assemblies, all strictly subject to the 'supreme court' of the House of Commons. (Such proposals could have come directly from the Labour Party manifesto of 1997.) Another of his ideas was for an Educational Bill to restore competition and the search after excellence in schools, together with a modified curriculum. The society strongly supported the movement 'for true industrial democracy' and the restoration of the country's world status through economic reforms, which would allow it to re-exert its traditional influence worldwide.

As for his wartime brainchild, during the last decade of his life Stirling was delighted with the 'modern SAS', both for its efficiency at tackling instances of terrorism and for the expedition made by two of its members to the High Himalayas, a goal which he had never been able to achieve himself.

Finally, and belatedly, the honours list of 1990 included his award of knight bachelor, which came only as the result of determined lobbying by the SAS but which was an honour that gave him huge pleasure.

Stirling died in the London Clinic in October 1990, having earlier taken the last sacraments. His funeral was at St Cumins, a church on the shores of Loch Morar where lands had been in his family since the Middle Ages. At the graveside, according to tradition, the ropes that lowered the coffin into the grave were held by everyone present regardless of status.

As with the greatest of earlier commanders David Stirling had the ability to analyse the seemingly intractable problems cast by the iron threat of war and, with his unorthodox mind, he was able to discover a means to thwart the plodding routines of others. Like John Moore's light division that went on to achieve more than any equivalent formation in its day, Stirling's three to four man patrols were able to penetrate the very sinews of war, if led with the daring and disregard for danger that was Stirling's trademark. Like the values that Moore insisted on for his light division, values that are as relevant to the present day army as to Moore's, the standards Stirling set for the SAS enables it to continue his aims not only in support of regular forces but in the vital contemporary role of anti-terrorism.

As the ultimate tribute to Stirling, military commander and innovator Tony Geraghty places his creation of the SAS in the forefront of contemporary military development 'as the shape of armies to come: compact, sophisticated, selective in their targeting and capable in a limited war of controlling immense firepower. It is the military mainstream'.[15]

CONCLUSION

≈

THE SCOTTISH COMMANDERS

In the course of this book the Scottish commanders described have not only fought for different masters but on quite different battlefields. Bruce's premier battle was on the carseland of his native country while Douglas Haig had the problem of breaching unbroken trench lines across the north European plain. David Stirling's theatre was the arid desert of North Africa, while Colin Campbell's greatest task was to capture an Indian city the size of Paris with fortified temples and mean narrow streets. Their means of fighting have also changed over the years. Weaponry has evolved from the time of William Wallace and Robert Bruce when opposing forces used close combat weapons and offensive capability came largely from mounted horsemen to David Stirling's battlefield with its destructive, long-range, artillery, airpower capable of taking the offensive across continents, tanks and modern communications. If these contrasts are not enough the commanders' battlefield responsibilities seem to defy comparison. Montrose's army numbered no more than 5000 at its peak, Haig's establishment in France came to be measured in millions, while David Stirling's forces never exceeded a handful.

However, in spite of such immense differences the profiles of Scottish commanders reveal certain consistencies. As a body they displayed amazing courage, both moral and physical. In this, of course, the Scots have no monopoly. With any successful commander personal bravery is a 'sine qua non'. It would be difficult, for instance, for other commanders to outdo the bravery of Alexander the Great who in the course of his victories suffered twenty-one wounds, one from an arrow that pierced his ribs and entered a lung. He endured the arrow's removal without a murmur. In following the fortunes of commanders over the centuries one can only be amazed at their apparent sangfroid as they faced the likely prospect of ghastly wounds or death – especially when medical science was rudimentary and any treatment was equally or more painful than the original injuries. Despite the Scottish commanders' undoubted courage and the important part it plays in their profile no-one could claim they were special in this respect.

A more discernible characteristic appears to be the Scots' love for fighting, for getting themselves directly involved. This trait has made the Scottish soldier renowned and it is also evident among his commanders. Following Bannockburn the eagerness of Scottish commanders to close with the English undoubtedly caused them serious problems. Their impatience with the preliminary jockeying for advantage and their eagerness to exchange blows contributed, more than anything else, to their sequence of defeats, while on the Continent the Scottish mercenaries founded their reputations on a zest for fighting, where they proved themselves the bravest of the brave.

This was equally so with the Jacobite leaders. Montrose relished battle and always sought it, where his cool daring and inspired 'feel for ground' brought him almost unbroken success. It was the right strategy when his enemies were poised to unite against him, but there is little doubt fighting and risk-taking suited Montrose's temperament. His successor, Dundee, was killed when he was yards ahead of his men, waving his hat for them to follow. Like Montrose, it was not pure rashness on Dundee's part: he knew his Highlanders expected such leadership from him. It was an attitude he heartily endorsed and refused to abandon when the chief Lochiel warned him of the dangers. Lord George Murray was equally eager, fighting in the vanguard at both Prestonpans and Falkirk and emerging from his amazing charge at Culloden unhorsed and bloody.

As for the Covenanter generals, in their early days both Leven and Leslie rode with the thick of the action, while MacKay, with the unshakeable confidence that arose from a literal interpretation of the Bible, with its rewards for God's champions, relished battle and was killed fighting.

Even when Abercromby was an old man he tended to be uneasy and impatient until he reached the point where the struggle raged most fiercely. John Moore seemed to know only one method of leadership, inspiring his men from the front and falling upon the enemy, an eagerness that brought him many wounds and to his death in battle. Hector MacDonald was a natural battlefield animal, both fearless and energetic, and it was for this he was awarded his initial commission. Although Colin Campbell looked to gain his victories with a minimum of casualties, he was far less careful with his own life and relished being involved in the action throughout his long career. As a junior officer in the Boer War, Douglas Haig was a brave and confident cavalry commander and as a Corps commander was always well up with things. He never lost the belief that a strong enemy could only be beaten by offensive actions.

Finally with David Stirling, his wish to close with his opponents verged on the outrageous and his companions were always amazed when this large, somewhat ungainly, man took on the feline grace of the hunter in the pleasure he felt at approaching an enemy position.

Even so, the urge to 'get stuck in' personally has hardly been confined to Scottish commanders. King Gustavus Adolphus, the great Swedish commander of the 17th century felt compelled to be at the forefront of his attacking forces. He would not take care and, after a succession of wounds, was killed in battle. The same desire was shown by the pugnacious American tank commander of World War Two, George S. Patton, and taken to extremes by General George Armstrong Custer, who knew no other way.

Yet Custer's mindless – if in some ways magnificent – aggression does not match up to the Scottish brand of command. While no-one would deny their love of fighting, the most senior of the Scottish commanders were thoughtful enough to stay back to control their battles. Wallace used his sword to good effect in hand-to-hand fighting during his early, relatively small engagements against the English, and Bruce was also noted for the skilled use of his personal weapons, but at the crucial battles of Stirling Bridge and Falkirk Wallace took up a position where he could orchestrate things as indeed did Bruce at Bannockburn. The same thinking applied with Haig who, after he became commander-in-chief, was accustomed to move his tactical headquarters adjacent to or slightly behind that of the Army Commander involved in a particular offensive.

Another characteristic that can be attributed to Scottish commanders has been their confident non-conformity, their rugged independence of mind, and at times, their non-observance of commonly adopted courses of action, probably best summed up as 'maverick qualities'.

Such independence of mind can be seen in Wallace, the outlaw and modest squire, who was never fully accepted even by his own nobility. War for him was to the death, an interpretation that did not always find favour with his more calculating feudal superiors. And Bruce, the anointed king and legendary commander, began his long uphill journey to free Scotland in the most unorthodox way possible by committing blasphemy when he murdered his great Scottish rival, the Red Comyn, before the high altar of Dumfries church. Similarly, it is not difficult to view the Jacobite generals as mavericks. Montrose turned against the Covenanter cause and opted for the king's service. Once committed he led the feared Highlanders against their fellow Scots and then compounded this by enlisting the support of Alasdair MacDonald, 'Colkitto', the Scoto/Irish chief. Dundee was an attainted traitor who, like Montrose, rode roughshod against the tide of contemporary Scottish opinion by supporting the unpopular Stuart king, James II and, like Montrose, looked for support among the turbulent Highlanders. Lord George Murray had taken part in the 1715 uprising, and although he signed an oath of allegiance to the Hanoverian monarchy, he turned his coat when Prince Charles Edward appealed to him for his help. Of the later commanders, Abercromby was amazingly independent. He was ready to sacrifice his military career by his sympathy for the American revolutionaries and was quite unruffled by disapproval from London. Like the Roman Cincinnatus he was happy to stay in retirement until his abilities compelled the authorities to recall him.

John Moore was never fully accepted by the establishment: he was blazingly honest and as a result could be surprisingly undiplomatic, although, in spite of his idiosyncrasies his ability made it unthinkable he could be ignored for long. Colin Campbell twice resigned his military appointments in protest at what he considered was unjust treatment. It was only after his active career had ended that he was created Lord Clyde. Hector MacDonald was never fully accepted by his military superiors, who viewed him essentially as a source of fighting strength when they needed it. He died the tragic death of a maverick, alone and condemned out of hand.

On the other hand Douglas Haig, the inscrutable and remote, rose to the rank of field marshal. This did not mean he was universally popular and less determined men ensured that he would never be short of enemies while his lack of verbal fluency was almost certainly bound to cause disfavour among politicians. Despite his logical mind and unshakeable determination Haig's career would never have prospered as it did without the invaluable support of the king and Richard Haldane, the Secretary of State for Defence. If not a maverick in the strictest sense, Haig was by nature an outsider who was generally unimpressed by much of contemporary wisdom.

David Stirling was an arch maverick; as a young man he was utterly unorthodox; in his more mature years his maverick qualities were indelibly stamped on all he thought and did. As a result he found the greatest difficulty convincing the authorities to take his ideas seriously.

Maverick commanders have by no means been confined to Scotland. Among the leading British field commanders of World War Two, Bernard Montgomery, uniformly challenged contemporary ideas and only got the chance to command 8th Army when the selected candidate, General 'Strafer' Gott, was killed in an air crash. The supreme maverick was probably General Douglas MacArthur, brilliant self-apologist and wartime soldier who took the unprecedented step of publically challenging his ultimate superior, President Harry Truman, over using atomic bombs to resolve the Korean War in 1951. Such instances of maverick commanders, however notable, do not alter the fact that as a group Scottish commanders are distinguishable for their outsider qualities and their fierce sense of independence.

Outsiders, whether real or perceived, tend to approach problems from a different perspective and the Scottish commanders, influenced by their country's distinctive educational tradition, have tended to bring a rigour and logic to military problems that others might accept as insoluable, something akin to a scientific approach to warfare.

It is likely that William Wallace was trained to question accepted wisdom by his uncle who tutored him at Dunipace abbey, and he showed himself a battlefield innovator by using a thicket of spearmen to meet what appeared to be an overwhelming threat posed by English cavalry. He recruited archers in a further attempt to protect his new formation against that other formidable English weapon, the long bow.

Robert Bruce also proved himself a true student of war, being not content to use Wallace's schiltron formation in defence but training it for offensive action. At Bannockburn he calculatingly prepared the anticipated site of battle as a killing ground for the English army by strengthening its natural features with man-made pits and then subsequently trapped and compressed the English between two tidal watercourses.

All three Jacobite commanders were able strategists and tacticians who considered carefully how to make maximum use of the fighting traditions within their forces. Montrose and Dundee, in particular, were acutely aware of the interaction between military success and political benefit.

Abercromby used his legal mind to decide how best to reform a British army that had fallen to an abysmal level during the latter part of the 18th century. To this end he stressed the need for a high standard of professionalism on the part of its officers and even more revolutionary he proposed a much more caring approach towards the men with, for instance, everyone sharing in the privations that occurred during campaigns. Contrary to the customs of his age he advocated greater self – rather than imposed – restraint, and far less use of corporal punishment. John Moore was to carry Abercromby's reforms through and become one of the British army's most distinguished trainers of men with his creation of the famed Light division, a body which became so valuable to Wellington in the Peninsula. Moore's own rigorous, intellectual approach to any operation of war was demonstrated by his ultra detailed planning followed by painstaking rehearsals for the sea-landing at Aboukir.

Colin Campbell (Lord Clyde) followed the Scottish tradition in taking great care of his men but his particular contribution to the science of war was the application of firepower; accurate small arms fire whilst men were on the move and, above all, the overwhelming use of artillery. Hector MacDonald had undoubted limitations and his approach cannot be described as scientific but he raised natural drill to a level that enabled his colonial troops to keep their cohesion and execute difficult and complex movements during the heat of battle. Douglas Haig can be seen as a genuinely scientific soldier. In his discussions with Richard Haldane, his ideas about how best to fashion Britain's armed forces in readiness for the anticipated European War, were undoubtedly influential. By 1918, after earlier disappointments he had thought out the necessity for all military arms to work closely together and for the importance of mobility to be maintained at all costs. David Stirling was a theorist as much as an active soldier with his innovative thinking about the way special forces could be used strategically.

Able commanders have as a rule been expected to make a study of war and strategy. Napoleon, one of the most successful, advised his Marshals to read and re-read the Great Captains. Like Marshal Ney they were not all keen on reading. In any case the maxims of war should never be applied uncritically and a good proportion of the Scottish commanders were not only students of war but quite prepared to consider how they could improve contemporary military practices.

Such initiatives require self-confidence and the Scottish commanders were helped in this by their strong belief patterns and the emphasis they placed on high personal integrity.

Such qualities might have been specified with one man in mind – William Wallace. His uncle's teaching gave him a strong if simple faith which helped, for instance, to carry him through the terrible sufferings of his execution. His integrity was unquestionable for without it he would not have proved such an exceptional national leader in the face of so many who doubted his powers, and his unyielding patriotism, at a relatively early stage of Scottish history. He has remained a beacon to future generations.

Bruce was certainly a believer in the power of religion who used pious ceremonies as a means of helping and inspiring his troops at times of great danger. And once Bruce, the king, had set himself upon his path to Scottish independence his personal integrity and loyalty towards his followers was unimpeachable.

The Jacobites were strong believers who trusted implicitly in the mercy of their maker, even if they did not parade their religion as openly as some of their contemporaries and their sense of loyalty to a Scotland ruled by the Stuarts went almost beyond belief. After Montrose had been condemned to death, he was combing his long hair when he was visited by the fanatic Wariston, who chided him for his vanity. His response was noteworthy for its confidence: 'While my head is my own, I dress and arrange it. Tomorrow when it is yours you may treat it as you please.' On the scaffold his faith was unshakeable: 'I shall pray for you all. I leave my soul to God, my service to my prince, my goodwill to my friends, my love and charity to you all.'

The importance of religion to the Covenanters was obvious and all-pervasive, although MacKay was the most extreme among them. Both Leven and Leslie, while paying their due tributes to their God sensibly kept their temporal interests in sight.

In the case of the Victorians, Abercromby was both a believer and a man of integrity. Although he unsurprisingly had doubts about some of the unreal assignments given him he nevertheless remained entirely loyal to the British establishment. This said, his practical and spiritual home remained north of the border. Almost the same remarks could be made for John Moore. It was the fate of both men to die far away from their native land. Colin Campbell was certainly a believer. While irascible and frightening at times, his integrity was never in doubt, nor was his concern for his troops.

Of the two 20th-century commanders, Douglas Haig's strong personal beliefs gave him the necessary conviction to keep his head in the most adverse circumstances. Priding himself on being a man of his word he scorned politicians, especially his opponent Lloyd George, whose ideas he decried as being far more flexible. Haig's enthusiasm for the British Empire and its ethical values was total.

David Stirling certainly had strong religious values instilled into him by his mother. Indeed her teaching was so effective that on various occasions during his later life, his principles prevented him from taking full advantage of the many commercial opportunities he had created. He, too, was fiercely and unwaveringly patriotic.

Scottish commanders were, of course, not alone in being strong believers nor in valuing their integrity so highly. There could hardly have been a more fervent Christian soldier than the Confederate General Thomas (Stonewall) Jackson. He was said to stand head and shoulders above his fellows in moral ascendancy and scarcely less so in military ability. The same religious intensity could be seen in the British commander, Henry Havelock, whose name will always be linked with the relief of Lucknow during the Indian Mutiny. In spite of such strong believers, unlike the Scottish commanders, both the 19th century British and American military establishments had their share of non-believers or doubters. Wellington gave relatively little attention to religion although he seemed to believe that God had been with him at Waterloo. The majority of Wellington's generals in the Peninsular War, like Robert Crauford, Robert Hill and Thomas Picton were not great believers. Theirs was a materialistic age. All three senior Federal Generals, Ulysses Grant, William Sherman and Philip Sheridan similarly appeared to lack strong religious beliefs.

*   *   *

The particular skills and characteristics of senior military commanders down the centuries give virtually endless scope for both comparison and conjecture. How for instance would Alexander the Great have performed with huge impersonal armies using modern weaponry? How would the famous British commander of World War Two, 'Bill' Slim, have coped in an age before air supply? One has the distinct feeling they would both have proved successful in any age for both well understood the principles of war fighting. So too did the leading Scottish commanders and it was their understanding of this together with their love for fighting, their sense of being outsiders, their analytic approach to the problems of their profession, their very seriousness demonstrated through their religious beliefs, their fierce pride and integrity which made them both distinctive and formidable soldiers.

Arguably they appear to have been given less recognition by past and present historians than they deserve. In September 1997 the American military historian, Lieutenant Colonel Michael Lanning, drew up a list of the one hundred top military leaders of all time. While some bias towards his home country could reasonably be expected (which arguably came with the placing of George Washington in first place), he featured nineteen Britons in his top selections and among these identified just two Scots, Ralph Abercromby at 47th and Colin Campbell (Lord Clyde) in 56th place. There was no mention of Robert Bruce, William Wallace, Montrose or Haig, although General Pershing featured at number forty-one, notwithstanding the fact that his experience was limited to operations in France from July to November 1918, for which the British and the French organised the training and supplied the equipment.

Military historians are unlikely ever to agree on ratings for the world's greatest commanders and their attempts to do so are made infinitely more difficult by factors like timing and luck beyond the commanders' control. Despite his ability and sequence of successes, Montrose ended a glorious loser. On the other hand Wellington took command in the Peninsula at a time when he could build on the work already laid down by Abercromby and Moore – and no one could deny he seized the opportunity in brilliant fashion.

Along with timing and luck the extent of one's acceptability by the Establishment will always tend to play a massive part towards success, and some Scottish commanders have not enjoyed the best of luck nor projected the most favourable images. Moore and Dundee were both commanders with image problems at some time in their careers: Moore was also a remarkably unlucky commander when, like Dundee, he was killed at the moment of a victory that without him could not be exploited. On the other hand Wellington's luck was proverbial; at Waterloo almost every member of his staff was wounded or killed when close beside him, while he escaped unscathed.

With Haig the question of image can be seen to be vitally important. He had many of the qualities needed to succeed in France during 1916–18 but both the skills he showed in timing his counter-offensives during 1918 and his final successes were overshadowed by his armies' casualties. He will probably never escape the charge of condoning them (although equivalent casualties were suffered by his opponents).

The achievements of William Wallace and Robert Bruce are unlikely to receive their due credit not for any fault of the commanders themselves but because of the remote theatre where they occurred and for their limited effect in global terms.

For such reasons it is probable that as a group Scotland's warrior sons will never be given the full acknowledgement their skills deserve and they will not feature as highly as they might on the roll call of the world's greatest soldiers. They are more likely to be remembered for their doughty fighting hearts than for their other outstanding qualities. This seems particularly unjust when the intellectual approach to warfare adopted by some of the later commanders placed such emphasis on strong motivation, self-discipline and qualities of force cohesion that are as important to success on contemporary battlefields as then. The tactical and human principles that animated John Moore's Light Division and the stress on self-reliance, fitness and high professionalism in David Stirling's SAS have had profound and lasting effects on the British military establishment and, by extension, on Western military establishments as a whole. Other British commanders may have enjoyed more glory but it is not too late for commanders during the early War of Independence or even Haig, to enjoy a degree of re-appraisal.

However, the Scottish commanders featured in this book would probably not worry overmuch about whether or not they have received their due acknowledgement. What mattered most to such men was that they enjoyed their fighting and, above all, believed in what they fought for.

SELECT BIBLIOGRAPHY

Contemporary Accounts

Baillie, The Rev Robert. The Letters and Journals, 3 vols. The Bannatyne Club.
A Discourse on the Death of Marshal Keith, Edinburgh, 1764.
Elcho, David, Lord. A Short Account of the Affairs of Scotland in the Years 1744, '45 and '46, Edinburgh, 1907.
Forbes, The Rev. Robert. The Lyon in Mourning, a collection of speeches, 1746–1775.
Haig Papers, Diary 29 June 1918, 1 July 1918, 31 July 1918, 1 September 1918.
Haig Papers, Rectoral Address at St Andrews, 14 May 1919.
Chevalier *Johnstone's* Account of the Rebellion of 1745.
Lindsay, Robert of Pinscottie, Histoire.

Select Bibliography Miscellaneous

Alford, Henry S.L. and *Sword*, Lt. W. Dennistoun. The Egyptian Soudan, its Loss and Recovery, 1898.
Balcarres, Colin Lindsay, third earl of. Memoirs touching the revolution in Scotland 1688–90, 1714.
Balhaldie, Drummond of. Memoirs of Sir Ewan Cameron of Lochiel, Edinburgh, 1841.
Barbour, The Bruce, edited and translated by G. Eyre Todd, Edinburgh, 1907.
Barrington, Michael. Grahame of Claverhouse, Viscount Dundee, 1911.
Baynes, John. Soldiers of Scotland, 1988.

Browning, Beatrice. The Life and Letters of Sir John Moore, Oxford, 1823.

Buchan, John. Montrose, 1949.

Buchan, John. Montrose and Leadership, Lecture at the University of St Andrews, OUP 1930.

Burleigh, Bennet. Khartoum Campaign 1898, 1899.

Burnet, Gilbert, Bishop of. History of his own Time, Oxford 1833.

Burton, History of Scotland, Edinburgh, 1873.

Buxhoeveden, Baroness Sophie. A Cavalier in Muscovy, 1932.

Campbell, David. General Sir Hector MacDonald, 1900.

Cannon, Richard. Historical Record of the First Royal Regiment of Foot to 1847, 1847.

Cassar, George. Kitchener, Architect of Victory, 1977.

Charteris, Brigadier General John. Field Marshal Earl Haig, 1929.

Clarendon, Edward Hyde, 1st Earl of. The History of the Rebellion and the Civil Wars in England, Oxford 1866.

Clark, Alan. The Donkeys, 1981.

Colville, Major General, Sir H.E. The Work of the Ninth Division, 1901.

Cooper, Duff. Haig, 1935.

Cowan, Edward J. Montrose, 1977.

Cowles, Virginia. The Phantom Major, 1988.

Cromb, David L. Hector MacDonald, The Story of his Life, Stirling 1903.

Cust, Lady Elizabeth. Some Account of the Stuarts of Aubigny in France (1442–1672), 1891.

Cutlack, F.M. War Letters of General Monash, 1935.

Dingwall Museum, MacDonald Papers: The Northern Chronicle of 16 November 1904; Evening News of 30 March 1903.

Dixon, Norman F. On the Psychology of Military Incompetence, 1976.

Dodds, Glen Lyndon. Battles in Britain 1066–1746, 1996.

Duke, Winifred. Lord George Murray and the Forty-Five, London 1926.

Dunfermline, Lord James. Sir Ralph Abercromby, a Memoir by his Son, Edinburgh 1861.

Fergusson, J. William Wallace, Guardian of Scotland, Stirling 1938.

Fletcher, David (Editor). Tanks and Trenches, First Hand Accounts of Tank Warfare in the First World War, 1996.

Forbes, Archibald. Colin Campbell, Lord Clyde, 1895.

Fortesque, The Hon. Sir John. Six British Soldiers, 1928.

Fraser, Sir William. The Melvilles, Earls of Melville and the Leslies, Earls of Leven, Edinburgh 1890.

Fuller, Major General J.F.C. Sir John Moore's Light Infantry Instruction of 1798–9, JAS for Historical Research, Vol xxx no. 122.

Fuller, Major General J.F.C. Sir John Moore's System of Training, 1924.

Gardiner, Samuel R. History of the Great Civil War, 1987.

Gardyne, Lt. Colonel C. Greenhill. The Life of a Regiment, the History of the Gordon Highlanders from 1816 to 1898, Edinburgh 1903.

Geraghty, Tony. Who Dares Wins, The Story of the SAS 1950–1997, 1980.

Gleig, The Revd. G.R. Lives of the most eminent British Military Commanders, 1832.

Grant, James. British Heroes in Foreign Wars, 1858.

Grant, James. Sir John Hepburn, Edinburgh 1851.

Hall, Edward. The Union of the Two Noble and Illustre Famelies of Lancastre and York, 1809 Edition.

Hamilton, Nigel. Monty, the making of a General, 1981.

Henderson, Andrew. Memoirs of the Life and Actions of James Keith, Field Marshal in the Prussian Armies, 1759.

Hoe, Alan. David Stirling, 1992.

Jackson, General Sir William and Field Marshal Lord Bramall. The Chiefs, 1992.

Kinglake, Alexander William. The Invasion of the Crimea, 1863.

Ladd, James D. SAS Operations, 1986.

Laffin, John. Scotland the Brave, 1963.

Lanning, Lt. Colonel Michael Lee. The 100 most Influential Military Leaders, 1997.

Linklater, Magnus and *Hesketh*, Christian. Bonnie Dundee, Edinburgh 1992.

Low, Charles Rathbone. Soldiers of the Victorian Age, 1880.

McNair Scott, Ronald. Robert the Bruce, King of Scots, Edinburgh 1996.

Mack, John of Rockfield. The Life of Lt. General Hugh MacKay.

Mackay, John. An Old Scots Brigade, Pallas Armata 1991.

Mackay, Major General Hugh. Memoirs of the war carried on in

Scotland and Ireland 1682–1691, Edinburgh 1833 (Bannatyne Club).

Mackenzie, Agnes Muir. Robert Bruce, King of Scots, Edinburgh 1934.

Mackenzie, W.M. The Battle of Bannockburn, Strong Oak Press, 1989.

Mackenzie, W.M. The Secret of Flodden, Edinburgh 1931.

Magnus, Philip. Kitchener, Portrait of an Imperialist, 1958.

Masefield, John. The Battle of the Somme, 1968.

Maurice, Major General Sir J.F. The Diary of Sir John Moore, 1904.

Middlebrook, Martin. The First Day of the Somme, 1971.

Montgomery, John. Toll for the Brave, 1963.

Moore, James Carrick. The Life of Sir John Moore, Edinburgh 1834.

Napier, Major General Sir W.F.P. History of the War in the Peninsula, 1851.

Nicholson, Ranald. Scotland, The Later Middle Ages, Edinburgh 1989.

Parkinson, Roger. Moore of Corunna, 1976.

Prebble, John. The Lion in the North, 1974.

Reese, Peter. Wallace, Edinburgh 1996.

Reid, Stuart. The Campaigns of Montrose, Edinburgh 1990.

Reid, Stuart. Like Hungry Wolves, 1994.

Robertson, Field Marshal Sir William. From Private to Field Marshal, 1921.

Roy, James McLiver. Old Take Care, The Story of Field Marshal Sir Colin Campbell, Lord Clyde, Glasgow 1985.

Royale, Trevor. Death before Dishonour, Edinburgh 1982.

Sadler, John. Scottish Battles, Edinburgh 1996.

Seymour, William. Battles in Britain 1066–1547, 1975.

Shadwell, Lt General. The Life of Colin Campbell, Lord Clyde, 1881.

Simpson, Grant G. (Editor). The Scottish Soldier Abroad 1247–1967, Edinburgh 1992.

Small, John (Editor). The Poems of William Dunbar, Edinburgh 1843.

Smithers, A.J. Sir John Monash, 1973.

Steevens, G.W. With Kitchener to Khartum, Edinburgh 1898.

Taylor, A.J.P. The First World War, 1966.

Terraine, John. Douglas Haig, The Educated Soldier, 1963.

Terry, Charles Sandford. The Life and Campaigns of Alexander Leslie, 1899.

Tomasson, Katherine. The Jacobite General, Edinburgh 1958.

Tuckman, Barbara W. The Proud Tower, 1966.

Watson, Bruce. The Great Indian Mutiny, 1991.

Wilkinson, Spenser. From Cromwell to Wellington, 12 Soldiers, 1899.

Williams, Ronald. The Heather and the Gale, 1997.

Williams, Ronald. Montrose, Cavalier in Mourning, 1975.

Ziegler, Philip. Omdurman, 1973.

NOTES

CHAPTER ONE

1 Reese, Peter. *Wallace*, Edinburgh 1996, 39.
2 Fergusson, J. *William Wallace: Guardian of Scotland*, Stirling 1938, 84.
3 MacNair Scott, Ronald. *Robert the Bruce, King of Scots*, 1996, 104.
4 Barbour, J. *The Bruce,* edited and translated by G. Eyre Todd, Edinburgh 1907, 184.
5 McNair Scott, *op. cit.*, 149.
6 Barbour, J. *The Bruce*, STS, 1894, 195.
7 Mackenzie, W. M. *The Battle of Bannockburn, A Study in Medieval Warfare*, Strong Oak Press 1989, 40.
8 Barbour, *op. cit.*, 189.
9 Barbour, *ibid.*, 192.
10 MacKenzie, *op. cit.*, 62.
11 *Scalacronica*, 141.
12 Barbour, *op. cit.*, 205–6.
13 Barbour, *ibid.*, 210–12.
14 Barron, E. W. M. *The Scottish War of Independence*, Edinburgh 1914, 475.
15 Mackenzie, Agnes Muir. *Robert Bruce King of Scots*, Edinburgh 1934, 283.
16 Paterson, Raymond Campbell. *For the Lion. A History of the Scottish Wars of Independence 1296–1357*, Edinburgh 1996, 69.

CHAPTER TWO

1 Nicholson, Ranald. *Scotland. The Later Middle Ages.* Edinburgh 1989, 126.
2 Prebble, John. *The Lion in the North*, 1974, 122.
3 Sadler, John. *Scottish Battles*, Edinburgh 1996, 59.
4 Paterson, Raymond Campbell. *For the Lion, A History of the Scottish Wars of Independence 1296–1357*, Edinburgh 1996, 181.
5 Prebble, *op. cit.*, 155.
6 Nicholson, *op. cit.*, 574.
7 Lindsay, Robert of Pinscottie. *Historie*, I, 98.
8 Since 1507 the Scots had manufactured large guns in Stirling and

Edinburgh and in 1511 they had been assisted at Edinburgh by French craftsmen.

9 Mackenzie, W.M. *The Secret of Flodden*, Edinburgh 1931, 38–9.
10 Hall, Edward. *The Union of the Two Noble and Illustre Famelies of Lancastre and York*, 1809 Edition, 558.
11 Seymour, William. *Battles in Britain 1066–1547*, 1975, Vol. I, 203.
12 Mackenzie, *op. cit.*, 21.
13 Mackenzie, *op. cit.*, 81.
14 Nicholson, *op. cit.*, 604–5.
15 Mackenize, *op. cit.*, 84.
16 One commentator, Dodds, described the reserve being used in close support of the king's division. It helped to drive Surrey back somewhat before being halted.
17 Nicholson, *op. cit.*, 605.
18 Dodds, Glen Lyndon. *Battles in Britain 1066–1746*, 1996, 113–4.
19 Seymour, *op. cit.*, Vol I, 217.
20 Paterson, Raymond Campbell. *My Wound is Deep, A History of the later Anglo-Scots Wars, 1380–1560*, Edinburgh 1997, 198. (Account of William Patten, *The Expedition into Scotland of Edward, Duke of Somerset.*)

CHAPTER THREE

1 *The Scottish Soldier Abroad 1247–1967*, edited by Grant G. Simpson, Edinburgh 1992, vii.
2 Grant, James. *The Scottish Soldiers of Fortune*, 182–3.
3 Wood, Stephen. *The Auld Alliance, Scotland and France; The Military Connection*, Edinburgh 1989, 31–4.
4 Grant, *op. cit.*, 182.
5 Wood, *op. cit.*, pp. 39, 40.
6 Cust, Lady Elizabeth. *Some Account of the Stuarts of Aubigny in France* (1442–1672), 1891, 26.
7 Bennet, Michael. *The Battle of Bosworth*, 1985, 110.
8 Rouse, A. L. *Bosworth Field and the Wars of the Roses*, 1967, 220.
9 Taylor, F. L. *The Art of War in Italy 1494–1529*, 1993, 28.
10 A copy of this exists in Lord Bute's collection of mss.
11 The Scottish Text Society: *The Poems of William Dunbar*, edited by the late John Small, Edinburgh 1843, 64.
12 Grant, James. *Sir John Hepburn, Memoirs and Adventures*, Edinburgh 1851, 5.
13 Dupuy, Trevor Nevitt. *Gustavus Adolphus Father of Modern War*, New York 1969, pp. 54–66; Men at Arms Series 235. *The Army of Gustavus Adolphus Infantry*, 1991. Men at Arms Series 262. *The Army of Gustavus Adolphus, Cavalry*, 1993.

14 Cannon, Richard. *Historical Record of the First Royal Regiment of Foot to 1846*, 1847, 9.

15 Grant, James. *The Scottish Soldiers of Fortune*, 182–3.

16 Grant, *ibid.*, 182.

17 Cannon, *op. cit.*, 11.

18 Grant, James. *Sir John Hepburn, op. cit.*, 185.

19 Cannon, *op. cit.*, 20.

20 Grant, James. *Sir John Hepburn, op. cit.*, 191.

21 Grant, *ibid.*, 201.

22 Gazette de France, 6 October 1633, *Dictionary of National Biography*, Vol ix, 1908, 610.

23 Mackay, John. *An Old Scots Brigade*, Pallas Amata 1991, Vol. III, 193.

24 Parker, Geoffrey. *The Military Revolution*, Cambridge University Press 1996, 38.

25 Buxhoeveden, Baroness Sophie. *A Cavalier in Muscovy*, 1932, 314.

26 This diary, which occupies six large quarto volumes, is preserved in the archives of St Petersburg and a few extracts were published by the Spalding Club of Aberdeen under 'Passages from the Diary of General Patrick Gordon' (Eugene Schuyler, *Peter the Great*, 1884, Vol. 1, 257).

27 Buxhoeveden, *op. cit.*, 279.

28 Buxhoeveden, *ibid.*, 288.

29 Buxhoeveden, *ibid.*, 289.

30 Buxhoeveden, *ibid.*, 317.

31 Henderson, Andrew. *Memoirs of the Life and Actions of James Keith. Field Marshal in the Prussian Armies*, 1759, 7.

32 A Discourse on the Death of Marshal Keith read before the Royal Academy of Sciences at Berlin (Edinburgh 1764), 19.

33 *Ibid.*, 24.

34 *Ibid.*, 29.

35 Henderson, *op. cit.*, 37.

36 Duffy, Christopher. *Frederick the Great, a Military Life*, 1985, 82.

37 Duffy, *op. cit.*, 175.

CHAPTER FOUR

1 Williams, Ronald. *The Heather and the Gale*, 1997, 48.

2 Buchan, John. *Montrose*, 1949, 63.

3 Buchan, *op. cit.*, 101. Montrose was by no means alone here. The Revd Robert Baillie, a Presbyterian minister whose letters and diaries gave much information about this period believed initially that the covenant contained nothing against the King's authority. Baillie, *Letters and Journals* I, 67, 8.

4 Buchan, John. 'Montrose and Leadership'. Lecture at the University of St Andrews. OUP 1930, 13.

5 Cowan, Edward J. *Montrose for Covenant and King*, 1977, 101.
6 Buchan, John. *Montrose, op. cit.*, 137.
7 Williams, Ronald. *Montrose, Cavalier in Mourning*, 1975, 141. Grant, I. F, *In the Tracks of Montrose*, Edinburgh 1931, 168.
8 Buchan, John. *Montrose*, 273 (Wishart, Dedication).
9 While no commentator disputes that Montrose was outnumbered. Buchan talks of about 7000 enemy infantry while the more sceptical Reid, along with Sadler, puts them at only some 3000.
10 Williams, Ronald. *Montrose, op. cit.*, 193.
11 Sadler, John. *Scottish Battles*, Edinburgh 1996, 112.
12 Williams, Ronald. *Montrose, op. cit.*, 234 (letter published in Mercurius Aulicus on 10 May 1645).
13 Seymour, William. *Battles in Britain 1642–1746*, 1975, 131.
14 Reid, Stuart. *The Campaigns of Montrose*. Edinburgh 1990, 105.
15 Williams, Ronald. *Montrose, op. cit.*, 244.
16 Stuart Reid and Edward Cowan both differ from John Buchan about the place of the river crossing, favouring the ford at Mountgarrie to the north-east of Alford.
17 Sadler, *op. cit.*, 125.
18 Cowan, *op. cit.*, 211.
19 Buchan, John. *Montrose, op. cit.*, 223.
20 Seymour, *op. cit.*, 136.
21 Reid, *op. cit.*, 141, 2.
22 Cowan, *op. cit.*, 218.
23 William, Ronald. *Montrose, op. cit.*, 271.
24 Seymour, *op. cit.*, 137.
25 Reid, *op. cit.*, 157.
26 Williams, Ronald. *Montrose, op. cit.*, 290.
27 Buchan, John. *Montrose, op. cit.*, 338–9.
28 Reid, *op. cit.*, 174–8.
29 Cowan, *op. cit.*, 236.
30 Williams, Ronald. *Montrose, op. cit.*, 287.
31 Williams, Ronald. *Montrose, op. cit.*, xiii.
32 Williams, Ronald. *Montrose, ibid.*, 53.
33 Fraser, Sir William. *The Melvilles, Earls of Melville and the Leslies, Earls of Leven*. Edinburgh 1890, Vol. 3, 385.
34 Williams, Ronald. *Montrose, op. cit.*, 69.
35 The Letters and Journals of Robert Baillie, Principal of the University of Glasgow, in three volumes (Bannatyne Club 73, vol. I, 11).
36 Fraser, *op. cit.*, 395, 407.
37 Clarendon, Edward, Earl of. *The History of the Rebellion and Civil Wars in England*, Oxford 1866, iv, 23.
38 Terry, Charles Sandford. *The Life and Campaigns of Alexander Leslie*, London 1899, 155.

39 Terry, *ibid.*, 158.
40 Baillie, *Letters, op. cit.*, Vol. II, 100.
41 Clarendon, *op. cit.*, VII 275.
42 Gardiner, Samuel R. *History of the Great Civil War*, 1987, Vol. I, 226.
43 Seymour, *op. cit.*, Vol. 2, 1975, 92.
44 Gardiner, *op. cit.*, Vol. I, 380.
45 Seymour, *op. cit.*, Vol. 2, 98–9.
46 Terry, *op. cit.*, 354.
47 *Dictionary of National Biography*, 1909, Vol. xi, 952.
48 Clarendon, *op. cit.*, X, 68.
49 Acts of Parliaments of Scotland, Vol. vi, part ii, pp. 68, 88.
50 Seymour, *op. cit.*, Vol. 2, 102.
51 Gardiner, *op. cit.*, Vol. ii, 1, 2.
52 Baillie, *Letters, op. cit.*, 209.
53 Williams, Ronald. *Montrose, op. cit.*, 287.
54 Gardiner, *op. cit.*, Vol. II, 356.
55 Gardiner, *ibid.*, Vol. ii, 356.
56 Gardiner, *ibid.*, Vol. iii, 251.
57 Cowan, *op. cit.*, 292 (account taken from the Wardlaw Manuscript).
58 Clarendon, *op. cit.*, Vol. xii, 135.
59 Burton. *History of Scotland*, Edinburgh 1873, Vol. vii, 26.
60 Clarendon, *op. cit.*, Vol. xiii, 51.
61 Clarendon, *ibid.*, Vol. xiii, 5.
62 Clarendon, *ibid.*, Vol. xiii, 73.
63 Clarendon, *ibid.*, 79.
64 State Papers, Dom Ser, 1651, 437.

CHAPTER FIVE

1 Barrington, Michael. *Grahame of Claverhouse, Viscount Dundee*, 1911, 66 (Quoted from Captain John Crichton's Memoirs).
2 Hamilton, Nigel. *Monty, the Making of a General*, 1981, 158.
3 Hamilton, *op. cit.*, 156.
4 Barrington, *op. cit.*, 81, 82.
5 Linklater, Magnus and Hesketh, Christian. *Bonnie Dundee*, Edinburgh 1992, 109.
6 Balcarres, Colin Lindsay, third earl of. *Memoirs touching the revolution in Scotland 1688–90*, 1714, pp 22–28.
7 Letters of John Grahame of Claverhouse, Viscount of Dundee, Edinburgh 1826 (Bannatyne Club 15), 34.
8 Barrington, *op. cit.*, 228.
9 Linklater, and Hesketh, *op. cit.*, 179.
10 Balhaldie, Drummond of. *Memoirs of Sir Ewan Cameron of Lochiel, Chief of Clan Cameron*. Abbotsford Club, Edinburgh, 1841, 240.

11 MacKay, Major General Hugh. *Memoirs of the war carried on in Scotland and Ireland 1682–1691*, Edinburgh 1833, 17 (Bannatyne Club).

12 Balhaldie, *op. cit.*, 237.

13 Linklater, and Hesketh, *op. cit.*, 172.

14 Barrington, *op. cit.*, 275.

15 Philip, James of Almerieclose. *Grameid*, 164.

16 Balhaldie, *op. cit.*, 243.

17 Barrington, *op. cit.*, 339.

18 Linklater, and Hesketh, *op. cit.*, 204.

19 Barrington, *op. cit.*, 349 (Constable – Maxwell MSS and Nairne Papers).

20 Barrington is convinced the style is inimitably that of Dundee. Unfortunately many of King James' private papers were destroyed by fire at St Germains but doubts about the letter's authenticity were not raised until 1826.

21 Letters of John Graham of Claverhouse, *op. cit.*, 84, 85.

22 Linklater and Hesketh, *op. cit.*, 220.

23 In the works of C. Sandford Terry, Michael Barrington and latterly of Magnus Linklater and Christian Hesketh, Dundee has finally been released from the splenetic and biased approach of Lord Macauley.

24 Burnet, Gilbert Bishop. *History of his own time*, Oxford 1833, Vol. iv, 47.

25 MacKay, John. *The Life of General Hugh MacKay*, Edinburgh 1836 (Bannatyne Club no. 53).

26 MacKay, *ibid.*, 18.

27 MacKay, *ibid.*, 22.

28 Mack, John of Rockfield. *The Life of Lt. Gen. Hugh MacKay*, Edinburgh 1836, 44.

29 Sadler, John. *Scottish Battles*, Edinburgh 1996, 158.

30 Linklater, and Hesketh, *op. cit.*, 1996, 210.

31 MacKay, Major General Hugh. *Memoirs, op. cit.*, 53.

32 Mack, John of Rockfield. *op. cit.*, 49.

33 MacKay, John. *op. cit.*, 50.

34 MacKay, Major General Hugh. *op. cit.*, 77.

35 MacKay, John. *op. cit.*, 131.

36 *Dictionary of National Biography*, 1909, Vol. xii, 570.

37 Sadler, *op. cit.*, 196.

38 Elcho, Lord David. *A Short Account of the Affairs of Scotland in the Years 1744, 1745, 1746.* Edinburgh 1907, 406.

39 Tomasson, Katherine. *The Jacobite General*, Edinburgh 1958, 17.

40 Tomasson, *ibid.*, (Atholl Chronicles), 20.

41 Duke, Winifred. *Lord George Murray and the Forty-Five*, 1927, 66.

42 Tomasson, *op. cit.*, (Chevalier Johnstone's account), 32.

43 Elcho, *op. cit.*, 250, 251.

44 Sadler, *op. cit.*, 201.
45 Tomasson, *op. cit.*, 47.
46 Tomasson, *ibid.*, (Kirkconnel), 57.
47 Elcho, *op. cit.*, 277.
48 Elcho, *ibid.*, 289.
49 Elcho, *ibid.*, 340.
50 Tomasson, *op. cit.*, 147.
51 Tomasson, *ibid.*, 159.
52 Elcho, *op. cit.*, 430.
53 Reid, Stuart. *Like Hungry Wolves, (Culloden Moor, 16 April 1746)* 1994, 56.
54 Tomasson, *op. cit.*, 200.
55 Forbes, Revd. Robert. *The Lyon in Mourning, a collection of speeches, 1746–1775*, 257.
56 Tomasson, *op. cit.*, 203.
57 Tomasson, *ibid.*, 206.
58 Forbes, *op. cit.*, 266.
59 Forbes, *op. cit.*, 261.
60 Duke, *op. cit.*, 189.
61 Tomasson, *op. cit.*, 238–9.
62 Tomasson, *ibid.*, 248–9.
63 Chevalier Johnstone's Account of the Rebellion of 1745, 1821 (Second Edition), Iii.
64 Chevalier Johnstone, *ibid.*, Iii.

CHAPTER SIX

1 James, Lord Dunfermline. *Sir Ralph Abercromby KB, A Memoir by his Son*, Edinburgh 1861, 3, 4.
2 In Michael Lee Lanning's latest attempt to gauge the 100 most influential military leaders Abercromby is included, while there is no place for Moore. (Lanning, Lt Colonel Michael Lee, *The 100 Most Influential Military Leaders*, 1997).
3 Fortesque, The Hon. Sir John. *Six British Soldiers*, 1928, 153.
4 Gleig, The Revd. G. R. *Lives of the Most Eminent British Military Commanders*, 1832, Three vols. Vol. II, 248.
5 *From Cromwell to Wellington: 12 Soldiers*, edited by Spenser Wilkinson, 1899, 323, 324.
6 James, Lord Dunfermline. *op. cit.*, (Conclusions of a distinguished general officer), 304.
7 Fortesque, *op. cit.*, 152.
8 James, Lord Dunfermline. *op. cit.*, 42–3.
9 James, Lord Dunfermline. *ibid.*, 44.
10 Gleig, *op. cit.*, 203–4.

11 Fortesque, *op. cit.*, 128.
12 Fortesque, *ibid.*, 129.
13 James, Lord Dunfermline. *op. cit.*, 214.
14 Fortesque, *op. cit.*, 140.
15 Fortesque, *ibid.*, 144.
16 Gleig, *op. cit.*, 231.
17 James, Lord Dunfermline. *op. cit.*, 291.
18 Fortesque, *op. cit.*, 151.
19 Mackesy, Piers. *The Strategy of Overthrow 1798–99*, 1974, 137–8.
20 Mackesy, Piers. *War Without Victory, The Downfall of Pitt, 1799–1802*, Oxford 1984, 58.
21 Mackesy, Piers. *The Strategy of Overthrow, op. cit.*, 185.
22 Bunbury, General Sir H. E. *Memoir and Literary Remains of Lieutenant-General Sir Henry Edward Bunbury*, 1868, 29.
23 Parkinson, Roger. *Moore of Corunna*, 1976, 3.
24 Browning, Beatrice. *The Life and Letters of Sir John Moore*, Oxford 1823, 8.
25 Moore, James Carrick. *The Life of Sir John Moore*, 1834 2 Vols. Vol. I, 35.
26 Parkinson, *op. cit.*, 78.
27 *London Gazette* of 26 June 1798.
28 Browning, *op. cit.*, 1923, 102.
29 Moore, *op. cit.*, Vol. I, 250.
30 *Journal of the Society for Army Historial Research Vol. XXX no 122*, Summer 1952. Sir John Moore's Light Infantry Instruction of 1798–9 edited by Major General J. F. C. Fuller.
31 Fuller, Colonel J. C. *Sir John Moore's System of Training*, 1924, 118–119.
32 Fuller, *ibid.*, 155.
33 Fuller, *ibid.*, 163.
34 Parkinson, *op. cit.*, 205.
35 Browning, *op. cit.*, 206.
36 Maurice, Major General, Sir J. F. *The Diary of Sir John Moore*, 1904, 2 Vols., Vol. II, 272.
37 Parkinson, *op. cit.*, 181.
38 Parkinson, *ibid.*, 194–5.
39 Parkinson, *ibid.*, 195.
40 Parkinson, *ibid.*, 201–2 (Moore's Diary of 24 December 1808).
41 Browning, *op. cit.*, 251 General Order of 6 January 1809.
42 Brownrig, *ibid.*, 258.
43 Parkinson, *op. cit.*, 235.
44 Fuller, *op. cit.*, 217.
45 Fortesque, *op. cit.*, 228.

CHAPTER SEVEN

1 Shadwell, Lt. General. *The Life of Colin Campbell, Lord Clyde,* 1881, Vol. I, 7–8.
2 Napier, Major General Sir W. F. P. *History of the War in the Peninsular,* 1880, Vol. V, 193.
3 Napier, *ibid.,* 35.
4 Shadwell, *op. cit.,* 78–9.
5 Forbes, Archibald. *Colin Campbell, Lord Clyde,* 1895, 32.
6 Shadwell, *op. cit.,* 91–2.
7 Shadwell, *ibid.,* 93.
8 Shadwell, *ibid.,* 205–6.
9 Forbes, *op. cit.,* 80–1.
10 Shadwell, *op. cit.,* 302–3.
11 Low, Charles Rathbone. *Soldiers of the Victorian Age,* 1880, 407.
12 This manoeuvre was unauthorised, but Campbell had earlier practised his regiments in it and he made it a standard drill for those under his command.
13 Shadwell, *op. cit.,* Vol. I, 325.
14 Shadwell, *ibid.,* Vol. I, 325.
15 Roy, James Mcliver. *Old Take Care, The Story of Field Marshal Sir Colin Campbell, Lord Clyde,* Glasgow 1885, 51.
16 Roy, *op. cit.,* 56.
17 Roy, *ibid.,* 62.
18 Shadwell, *op. cit.,* Vol. I, 418.
19 Forbes, *op. cit.,* 123.
20 Watson, Bruce. *The Great Indian Mutiny,* 1991, 85.
21 Watson, *ibid.,* 88.
22 Watson, *ibid.,* 90.
23 Watson, *ibid.,* 220.
24 Harris, John, *The Indian Mutiny,* 1973, 172.
25 Forbes, *op. cit.,* 107.
26 Cook, H. C. B. *The Sikh Wars 1845–6, 1848–9,* 1975, 200.
27 Kinglake, Alexander William. *The Invasion of the Crimea,* 1863, Vol. II, 349.
28 Robertson, Field Marshal Sir William. *From Private to Field Marshal,* 1921, 31.
29 Cromb, David, L. *Hector MacDonald. The Story of his Life.* Stirling 1903, 16.
30 Campbell, David. *General Sir Hector MacDonald,* 1900, 45.
31 Dingwall Town Hall, Foulis. Scrap book 3.
32 Montgomery, John. *Toll for the Brave, The Tragedy of Major General Sir Hector Macdonald,* 1963, 84

33 Royle, Trevor. *Death before Dishonour, The True Story of Fighting Mac*, Edinburgh 1982, 44.
34 Gardyne, Lt. Colonel C. Greenhill. *The Life of a Regiment, the History of the Gordon Highlanders from 1816 to 1898*, Edinburgh 1903, Vol. II, 165.
35 Gardyne, *ibid.*, 202.
36 Gardyne, *ibid.*, 207.
37 Gardyne, *ibid.*, 209.
38 Magnus Philip Kitchener. *Portrait of an Imperialist*, 1958, 81.
39 Royle, *op. cit.*, 79.
40 Royle, *ibid.*, 81.
41 Royle, *ibid.*, 89.
42 Steevens, G. W. *With Kitchener to Khartum*, Edinburgh 1898, 57, 58.
43 By far the clearest account of the battle is to be found in George H. Cassar's book *Kitchener, Architect of Victory*, 1977, 85–92.
44 Ziegler, Philip. *Omdurman*, 1973, 163.
45 Burleigh, Bennet. *Khartoun Campaign, 1898*, 1899, 185.
46 Burleigh, *ibid.*, 193.
47 Burleigh, *ibid.*, 209.
48 Steevens, *op. cit.*, 280, 281.
49 Alford, Lt. Henry, S. L. and Sword, Lt. W. Dennistoun. *The Egyptian Soudan, its Loss and Recovery*, 1898, 263.
50 Burleigh, *op. cit.*, 289, 290.
51 Montgomery, *op. cit.*, 72.
52 Colville, Major General Sir H. E. *The Work of the Ninth Division*, 1901, 37.
53 Colville, *ibid.*, 124.
54 Colville, *ibid.*, 211.
55 John Montgomery in *Toll for the Brave* is in no doubt that Hector MacDonald had an audience with the king although Trevor Royle is not convinced.
56 Royle, *op. cit.*, 128.
57 Dingwall Museum, MacDonald Papers, *The Northern Chronicle*, Wed, Nov. 16, 1904.
58 Royle, *op. cit.*, 140.
59 Dingwall Museum MacDonald Papers, Account of British Officer, *Evening News* of 30 March 1903.

CHAPTER EIGHT

1 *War Letters of General Monash*, edited by F. M. Cutlack, 1935, 268.
2 Tuchman, Barbara W. *The Proud Tower*, 1966, xiii.
3 The most thorough and authoritative study of Douglas Haig so far is that of John Terraine (*Douglas Haig, The Educated Soldier*, 1963) but in the author's words this is not a biography, as such, but a study of him as a soldier.
4 Duff Cooper. *Haig*, 1935, 20.
5 Taylor, A. J. P. *The First World War*, 1966, 34.
6 Dixon, Norman F. *On the Psychology of Military Incompetence*, 1976, 80.
7 Clark, Alan. *The Donkeys*, 1961.
8 Charteris, Brigadier General John. *Field Marshal Earl Haig*, 1929, 5.
9 Duff Cooper, *op. cit.*, 19.
10 Terraine, John. *Douglas Haig, The Educated Soldier*, *op. cit.*, 141.
11 Liddell Hart, Basil. *A History of the World War*, 1930, 94.
12 Terraine, *op. cit.*, 170.
13 Terraine, *ibid.*, 135.
14 Middlebrook, Martin. *The First Day of the Somme*, 1971, 76, 77.
15 Masefield, John. *The Battle of the Somme*, 1968, 30.
16 Middlebrook, *op. cit.*, Account by Musketier Karl Blenk, 169th Regiment, 157.
17 Haig Papers, H 125 [Vol. 27] Diary, 29 June 1918.
18 Haig, Diary, 1 July 1918.
19 Smithers, A. J. *Sir John Monash*, 1973, 213.
20 Fletcher, David (editor). *Tanks and Trenches, First Hand Accounts of Tank Warfare in the First World War*, 1994, 131.
21 *War Letters of General Monash*, *op. cit.*, 275.
22 *Ibid.*, 275.
23 Diary, 31 July 1918.
24 Diary, 1 September 1918.
25 Terraine, *op. cit.*, 471.
26 Terraine, *ibid.*, Preface xvii.
27 National Library of Scotland, Haig Papers, Rectorial Address at St Andrews of 14 May 1919.

CHAPTER NINE

1 Hoe, Alan. *David Stirling*, 1992, Foreword, ix.
2 Hoe, *ibid.*, 19.
3 Hoe, *ibid.*, 24.
4 Hoe, *ibid.*, 49.
5 Hoe, *ibid.*, 67.

6 Cowles, Virginia. *The Phantom Major*, 1988, 15–16.
7 The Long Range Desert Group was a wheeled unit operating deep in the desert in an intelligence capacity. It listened in, for instance, to enemy troop movements.
8 Hoe, *op. cit.*, 114.
9 Cowles, *op. cit.*, 168.
10 Cowles, *ibid.*, 170.
11 Hoe, *op. cit.*, 182–3.
12 Cowles, *op. cit.*, 189 (Popski's Private Army).
13 Ladd, James D. *SAS Operations*, 1986.
14 Hoe, *op. cit.*, 369.
15 Geraghty, Tony. *Who Dares Wins. The Story of the SAS 1950–1992*, 1980, xiv.

INDEX